International Trade Policies in the Era of Globalization

Ahu Coşkun Özer
Marmara University, Turkey

A volume in the Advances in Finance, Accounting, and Economics (AFAE) Book Series

IGI Global
DISSEMINATOR OF KNOWLEDGE

Published in the United States of America by
IGI Global
Business Science Reference (an imprint of IGI Global)
701 E. Chocolate Avenue
Hershey PA, USA 17033
Tel: 717-533-8845
Fax: 717-533-8661
E-mail: cust@igi-global.com
Web site: http://www.igi-global.com

Library of Congress Cataloging-in-Publication Data

Names: Ozer, Ahu Coskun, 1981- editor.
Title: International trade policies in the era of globalization / Ahu Coskun Ozer, editor.
Description: Hershey, PA : Business Science Reference, [2019]
Identifiers: LCCN 2019003638| ISBN 9781522595663 (hardcover) | ISBN 9781522595687 (ebook) | ISBN 9781522595670 (softcover)
Subjects: LCSH: Commercial policy. | International trade.
Classification: LCC HF1411 .I5678 2019 | DDC 382/.3--dc23 LC record available at https://lccn.loc.gov/2019003638

This book is published in the IGI Global book series Advances in Finance, Accounting, and Economics (AFAE) (ISSN: 2327-5677; eISSN: 2327-5685)

British Cataloguing in Publication Data
A Cataloguing in Publication record for this book is available from the British Library.

All work contributed to this book is new, previously-unpublished material.
The views expressed in this book are those of the authors, but not necessarily of the publisher.

For electronic access to this publication, please contact: eresources@igi-global.com.

Advances in Finance, Accounting, and Economics (AFAE) Book Series

ISSN:2327-5677
EISSN:2327-5685

Editor-in-Chief: Ahmed Driouchi, Al Akhawayn University, Morocco

MISSION

In our changing economic and business environment, it is important to consider the financial changes occurring internationally as well as within individual organizations and business environments. Understanding these changes as well as the factors that influence them is crucial in preparing for our financial future and ensuring economic sustainability and growth.

The **Advances in Finance, Accounting, and Economics (AFAE)** book series aims to publish comprehensive and informative titles in all areas of economics and economic theory, finance, and accounting to assist in advancing the available knowledge and providing for further research development in these dynamic fields.

COVERAGE

- Ethics in Accounting and Finance
- Economics Geography
- Fiscal Policy
- Health economics
- Microfinance
- Microeconomics
- Risk Analysis and Management
- Public Finance
- Macroeconomics
- Corporate Finance

IGI Global is currently accepting manuscripts for publication within this series. To submit a proposal for a volume in this series, please contact our Acquisition Editors at Acquisitions@igi-global.com or visit: http://www.igi-global.com/publish/.

The Advances in Finance, Accounting, and Economics (AFAE) Book Series (ISSN 2327-5677) is published by IGI Global, 701 E. Chocolate Avenue, Hershey, PA 17033-1240, USA, www.igi-global.com. This series is composed of titles available for purchase individually; each title is edited to be contextually exclusive from any other title within the series. For pricing and ordering information please visit http://www.igi-global.com/book-series/advances-finance-accounting-economics/73685. Postmaster: Send all address changes to above address.

Titles in this Series

For a list of additional titles in this series, please visit:
https://www.igi-global.com/book-series/advances-finance-accounting-economics/73685

Behavioral Finance and Decision-Making Models
Tripti Tripathi (Jiwaji University, India) Manoj Kumar Dash (Khallikote University, India) and Gaurav Agrawal (Indian Institute of Information Technology and Management Gwalior, India)
Business Science Reference • ©2019 • 333pp • H/C (ISBN: 9781522573999) • US $215.00

Global Challenges in Public Finance and International Relations
Deniz Şahin Duran (Tokat Gaziosmanpaşa University, Turkey) Yusuf Temür (Tokat Gaziosmanpaşa University, Turkey) and Doğan Bozdoğan (Tokat Gaziosmanpaşa University, Turkey)
Business Science Reference • ©2019 • 304pp • H/C (ISBN: 9781522575641) • US $225.00

International Financial Reporting Standards and New Directions in Earnings Management
Jonas da Silva Oliveira (Instituto Universitário de Lisboa (ISCTE-IUL), Portugal) Graça Maria do Carmo Azevedo (University of Aveiro, Portugal) and Augusta da Conceição Santos Ferreira (University of Aveiro, Portugal)
Business Science Reference • ©2019 • 342pp • H/C (ISBN: 9781522578178) • US $225.00

Throughput Accounting in a Hyperconnected World
Ionica Oncioiu (European Academy of the Regions, Belgium)
Business Science Reference • ©2019 • 362pp • H/C (ISBN: 9781522577126) • US $195.00

Organizational Auditing and Assurance in the Digital Age
Rui Pedro Marques (University of Aveiro, Portugal) Carlos Santos (University of Aveiro, Portugal) and Helena Inácio (University of Aveiro, Portugal)
Business Science Reference • ©2019 • 404pp • H/C (ISBN: 9781522573562) • US $225.00

International Firms' Economic Nationalism and Trade Policies in the Globalization Era
Harish C. Chandan (Argosy University, USA) and Bryan Christiansen (Global Research Society, LLC, USA)
Business Science Reference • ©2019 • 299pp • H/C (ISBN: 9781522575610) • US $215.00

For an entire list of titles in this series, please visit:
https://www.igi-global.com/book-series/advances-finance-accounting-economics/73685

IGI Global
DISSEMINATOR OF KNOWLEDGE

701 East Chocolate Avenue, Hershey, PA 17033, USA
Tel: 717-533-8845 x100 • Fax: 717-533-8661
E-Mail: cust@igi-global.com • www.igi-global.com

Editorial Advisory Board

Table of Contents

Detailed Table of Contents

Union (EAEU) has made only the first steps on the way towards its development. The EAEU has already managed to create a free trade zone with Vietnam, some agreements have been signed with Iran and China. Each of these agreements has its own specifics. The purpose of this chapter is to identify the economic feasibility and political significance of these preferential trade agreements for the countries of the EAEU and their external partners, as well as to determine the potential expansion of the network of preferential trade agreements of the EAEU.

If one country attacks another country's trade with taxes and quotas, it is defined as a trade war. It is aimed to protect the domestic market from competition. The U.S.-China trade war begun on March 1, 2018, and was centered on the customs duty of 25% for the imported steel and 10% for the imported aluminum. The protectionist measures against each other in both countries have increased day by day. However, the impact of these protectionist measures on global trade is not yet known. In this chapter, the effect of the U.S.-China trade war on global trade is analyzed. For this reason, the export data of the U.S. to China and the global export data yearly is compared. According to the results of the linear regression analysis, if the value of the goods export of the U.S. to China increase 1 unit, the value of global export of the goods increases to 58 units. While the trade wars decreased the goods export from the U.S. to China, it has decreased global goods exports too. In 2018, developments in global commodity exports and the U.S. goods exports to China were observed in the same direction.

This chapter analyzes the trade war between the United States of America and China. The United States of America and China are the two biggest trade leaders in the world. The United States supported China for its integration to world trade. The United States accused China of pursuing unfair trade policies. The United States increased tariffs against Chinese imports and China undertook retaliation measures against the United States' tariff increases. The two countries entered a period of a trade war and they started to implement protectionist policies on each other. These protectionist policies between the United States and China are seen as trade wars and could affect the world trade liberalization adversely. As they are trade partners too, it is better for both countries to end this war and to reach an agreement, because trade liberalization efforts could fail.

The increased commercial protection of countries as a result of the Great Depression caused the effects of the global crisis to deepen and last longer. Many countries took short-term steps to minimize the negative social impacts of the crisis by implementing protectionism. However, the crisis was gradually deepened and exerted long-term impacts on macroeconomic variables. The international platform made several attempts to reduce protectionism. However, following the global economic crisis in 2007-2009, the barriers to international trade have increased in many countries, especially in the USA. In many countries, inward-looking protectionist economic policies have been increasingly preferred. Thus, the global impact of countries' adoption of protectionism in their international trade policies has begun to be discussed in terms of the pros and cons for partners. This study analyzes the pros and cons of international trade protectionism on the basis of the impact of trade on macroeconomic variables. The results show that not only protectionism but also free trade produces both winners and losers.

On December 8, 2019, the Union State will celebrate its twentieth anniversary. During this time, a fairly long way has been covered - the main institutions were built, the tools for deepening and intensifying integration were defined, the people of Russia and Belarus acquired new opportunities. The Union State of Belarus and Russia is an actual research topic, since regional integration is now the trend of global development. And it is the Union State that is viewed by experts as the basis of the integration processes in the post-Soviet space. The Union State acts as a tool for enhancing integration processes in general in the post-Soviet space and explains to the citizens of the countries the advantages of these processes. The purpose of this study is to analyze the dynamics of the integration process within the framework of the Union State, to determine its factor in the intensification of regional integration in the post-Soviet space.

This chapter aims to analyze the US's foreign policy priorities toward Jordan in the communications of Obama, through the period from 2009 to 2017. It answers the

the chapter first finds the risk is distributed unevenly between the exporter and the importer. Then findings are evaluated to open a new avenue of future research, constructed on the inquiry whether emerging economies like Turkey can establish trust in their trade with developed economies by using blockchain technology.

The study aims at evaluating and comparing trade effects of tariff liberalization on bilateral trade between Russian and its Asian trade partners: China, India, Thailand and Vietnam. The partial equilibrium model - the Software for Market Analysis and Restrictions on Trade (SMART) model - underlies the research methodology. The authors calculate the trade effects of 1% linear cut of customs duties imposed on key commodity groups of mutual import flows and identify elasticities of bilateral import of different commodity groups on customs duties. On the basis of a comparative analysis of the results obtained, the authors formulated a set of conclusions regarding the efficiency of tariff regulation of imports in different countries and industrial sectors, tracking the changes of the influence of tariff liberalization on the dynamics of import of various categories of goods (depending on the value added and technological effectiveness).

During the last quarter century, a remarkable global growth was experienced in Foreign Direct Investment (FDI), especially the developing countries, considered FDIs as an important factor in overall economic development strategies. The developing countries aim to attract foreign capital to strengthen their local economy, increase market opportunities, and provide better services to the society. For this purpose, these nations implement various types of tax incentives. Although there are several studies on the effectiveness of tax incentives in FDI, the issue has not been tackled with respect to developing countries. The present study scrutinized the effectiveness of corporate tax incentives in developing countries based on FDI. In conclusion, it could be suggested that tax incentives may be effective in increasing FDI; however, in this group of countries with low level of investments and complex laws in taxation and other fields and could not cope with innovations, red tape and poor governance, it is also important to develop the organizational infrastructure for investments.

Preface

Globalization has caused implementing new international trade policies. Commercial walls between countries have removed with the globalization. The world trade has increased with the abolition of commercial barriers between the countries. However, there are still the trade barriers among the countries, so the future of the world trade has become uncertain. In the fields of international trade studies, trade policies and trade barriers among the countries, etc., there exists a need for an edited collection of original research in this area. This book aims to provide relevant theoretical frameworks and the latest empirical research findings in the international trade. The subjects included are globalization and implementation of foreign trade policies, the effects of foreign trade policy instruments on foreign trade, the impact of the implementation of tariff and non-tariff instruments on countries, globalization and international trade liberalization, trade protectionism in the globalizing world, the economic effect of trade protectionism, arguments against protectionist policy, advantages and disadvantages of trade protectionism, trade wars, the effects of trade wars on global trade.

Associate Professor Vasilii Erokhin analyses the transformation and food security status of China's agricultural trade in the chapter of "Transformation of China's Agricultural Trade in Response to Emerging Tensions on the Global Market." He states that 'despite being the most populous country in the world, China has succeeded to ensure self-sufficiency on major kinds of food and agricultural products. However, the country still depends on food imports of soybeans, meat, and many other agricultural products. The analysis of China's foreign trade in food and agricultural products and food security status of the country on major kinds of agricultural commodities demonstrates that import volumes grow as domestic demand is restructured in favor of qualitative food products of high nutrient value amid the progressive degradation of agricultural lands and shrinking possibilities for agricultural production in China. Currently, the majority of such value-added food products is imported from the USA. In the situation of trade tensions and tariff escalations between the USA and China, the agricultural sector is one of the most vulnerable. By raising import tariffs on food and agricultural products in response to the recent US protectionist policies, China may face a situation of food insecurity. The possible solution to the improvement of food security is the intensification of domestic agricultural production and, primarily, diversification of imports.'

Associate Professor Maria Lagutina analyzes the economic feasibility and political significance of preferential trade agreements for the countries of the EAEU and their external partners, in the chapter "Preferential Trade Agreements of the Eurasian Economic Union: Economic Feasibility and Political Significance." According to the Lagutina, EAEU is clearly increasing its international prestige by intensifying its international relations, especially negotiations on the establishment of free trade areas with the third countries, nevertheless, it is hard to say that the potential in this area has already been realized, the existing agreements with Vietnam, Iran and China are the first steps to the EAEU integration into the system of world trade. In this chapter it was showed that at this stage, the development of the network of free trade agreement with the third countries has not so much economic as political reasons in the case of the EAEU, the EAEU has pretty small economic value and therefore most of the current agreements with the third countries are rather declarative and have more political significance, therefore, it is essential that the ongoing negotiations on the establishment of FTAs would bring the benefits not only political and image, but practical and purely economic.

Also, Associate Professor Elena Maslova and Dr. Ekaterina Arapova evaluate and compare trade effects of tariff liberalization on bilateral trade between Russian and its Asian trade partners: China, India, Thailand, and Vietnam, in the chapter "Influence of Tariff Liberalization on Bilateral Trade: Implications for Russia and Its Asian Trade Partners." According to the Maslova and Arapova, elasticities of import flows on customs duties are very different. They state that 'The sample average import demand elasticities vary from -0,04 to -0,37 for the 1%-linear cut scenario and the variation of coefficients is very high dependently on the commodity group. The price elasticity of Russian imports turns out to be on average relatively lower than that of Chinese or Indian imports from Russia. In the case of Thailand, the situation is reversed - Russian imports are relatively more sensitive to changes in Thai import value.'

According to the Assistant Professor Ahu Coşkun Özer, in the chapter "The Effect of the U.S.-China Trade War on Global Trade," trade war between the U.S. and China effected the global trade. In the first two months of 2018, the year of the trade wars, the U.S. exports to China decreased by 28 percent, while global commodity trade decreased by only 7 percent. The. U.S. exports to China were $ 12 billion 382 million in March 2018, when the trade war began, while global exports of goods amounted to 1 trillion 540 million dollars in the same month. With the effect of trade wars, in April 2015, the U.S. exports to China decreased by 17 percent and global exports of goods decreased by 5 percent in the same period. While trade wars decrease the goods export of the U.S. to China, it decreases in global goods exports. In 2018, developments in global commodity exports and the U.S. goods exports to China has been in the same direction. These are shows that protectionist policies causes the negative results to global trade.

Also, Assistant Professor Birgül Cambazoğlu explored the pros and cons in trade protectionism in the chapter "Trade Protectionism: Pros and Cons." It is stated that if a country resorts to protectionism in foreign trade for understandable and justifiable reasons and benefits from it, it might have a negative impact on other countries. She states that it is still uncertain which counter-attacks will be made by countries that are negatively affected, therefore, the potential global effects of this domino effect are very hard to clearly estimate so preferring protectionism to reverse the negative effects of free trade might not produce the expected effect.

Assistant Professor Büşra Karataşer evaluates the globalization from historical aspect in the chapter "Globalization in the Ottoman Empire: An Evaluation With Regard to the Naval Institutions and International Trade Policies." She states that 'In the 19th century, both wars and reforms left the Ottoman economy in a difficult position. With the aim of increasing the commercial activities of the state, the Ottoman Empire entered into a trade agreement with European states to increase the volume of external trade. However, concessions granted to foreigners prevented Ottoman citizens from trading profitably. After the Ottoman-Russian War, the Ottoman Empire signed a trade treaty with Russia, but this treaty caused the Ottoman State to lose its independence in external trade. However, despite all the negative effects, the international trade of the Ottoman Empire increased between 1830 and 1910.'

Also, Dr. Natalia Eremina evaluates the economic cooperation between Russia, Belarus, and the Union States, in the chapter "Forms and Mechanisms of Economic Cooperation Between Russia and Belarus Within the Union States: Tasks, Problems, Achievements." It is stated that 'the Union State created special opportunities for trade interactions between Russia and Belarus, which had previously developed within the framework of the USSR. It is important that mutual trade has a particularly beneficial effect on the development of border regions of the two countries. In addition, Russia and Belarus have formed a single transport corridor, important for the development of trade in Eurasia. Note that the volume of mutual trade, as well as the variety of imports and exports, is gradually increasing. This proves that the Union State really promotes the growth of trade interaction. The Union State suits everyone, from the political establishment, to the citizens of the two states.'

Associate Professor Aslı Taşbaşı, Associate Professor Yeşim Pınar Sarıca, and Assistant Professor Ahmet Hakan Yüksel, analyse the risk allocation and trust in Turkey's trade, in the chapter "An Analysis of Risk Transfer and Trust Nexus in International Trade With Reference to Turkish Data." It is stated that 'Turkish trade data shows that the country's trade partners have invariably chosen to bear minimum risk in their trade with Turkey, with preferences towards the most guaranteed methods of payment. Risk transfer patterns –in long tradition and in their extremely solid form- are at loss of Turkey, whether the country is in an exporter or an importer status. Data proves that the most commonly preferred type of payment in Turkey's exports is cash on delivery, which is the method preferred when the exporter aims to gain the trust of the importer. Leading type of payment in Turkey's imports on the other hand is cash in advance, which shows that the exporter is in absolute risk avoidance. Normally, it can be expected that the exporters, which insist trading with this payment method, may not compete with alternative markets offering more attractive payment terms to the importer, which seemingly is not the case for Turkish imports.'

Also, Assistant Professor Simla Güzel explores the effect of the tax incentives on foreign direct investments in the chapter "The Efficiency of Corporate Tax Incentives in Developing Countries Based on Foreign Direct Investments." She states that it is not possible to suggest that tax incentives, which are important in increasing FDIs in developing countries, are sufficient alone, goal-oriented tax incentives should be enforced by a strong administrative capacity and it is also necessary to highlight the effectiveness of tax policies and policies on sufficient infrastructure, macroeconomic stability, rule of law, etc.

Assistant Professor Özlem Toplu Yılmaz evaluates the trade war between the United States of America and China in the chapter "USA-China Trade Wars: Back to Protectionism in World Trade." According to the Yılmaz 'Establishment of GATT was a milestone for world trade liberalization which was initiated by the United States. Protectionist policies lessen in time but China had stayed out of the system. The United States supported China's WTO membership to achieve a fair and more market-oriented trade in the world, as China was one of the largest traders. After China's WTO membership, trade disputes between China and the USA began. According to the United States Representatives, China was not a responsible member of the WTO by pursuing unfair trade policies. The United States increased tariffs against Chinese imports and the trade war between the countries started. For every tariff increase by the United States, China undertook retaliation measures. United States of America has always been the pioneer for the liberalization of world trade. Without reaching the desired level of liberalization in trade yet as expected in the WTO Doha Tour, these protectionist measures of the United States of America and also of China are disappointing since all the efforts to liberalize trade from the 1995 Uruguay Round onwards, could fail. Protectionist policies between the United States and China are seen as trade wars in the world and could affect the world trade liberalization adversely so it is better for both countries to end this war and to reach an agreement, cause trade liberalization efforts could fail. Both countries have to reach an agreement, and have to change their trade policies. The USA and

China had better end the trade war. Otherwise, the United States' efforts for trade liberalization would be wasted. The two countries are the world trade leaders. It will be their benefit to end the trade war.'

Suadiq Mehammed Hailu and Abdela Yasin Saliya aim to investigate the short- and long-run impact of devaluation on the trade balance of Ethiopia in the chapter "The Impact of Devaluation on Balance of Trade: The Case of Ethiopia." Their empirical finding show that 'the long run Real Effective Exchange Rate (REER) significantly and negatively correlated with trade balance. The error correction coefficient which shows the adjustment of disequilibrium in the subsequent year is also significant. The empirical result indicated that devaluation of birr can improve the trade balance of Ethiopia. However, in reality the trade balance of Ethiopia is not improved through a consecutive birr devaluation. This may be resulted from the non-responsiveness of import to devaluation of birr, shortage of import substitute domestic products and dependency of exports on primary agriculture products.'

Ayman Al Sharafat evaluates the US's foreign policy priorities toward Jordan in the communications of Obama, in the chapter "The United States Interest in the Middle East During the Obama Administration: Jordan – A Case Study." According to the Al Sharafat, Obama's foreign strategy and approach had been driven by the maxim of 'multilateral retrenchment', which designed to achieve the United States foreign commitments, reshape its standing among the world powers, and transfer burdens onto foreign partners, The United States of America under the Obama administration substantially depended on Jordan to solve many regional complex issues and crisis. It is stated in the chapter that 'The United States of America under Obama administration substantially depended on Hashemite Kingdom of Jordan to solve many regional complex issues and crisis. Particularly, regarding Arab-Israeli peace negotiations, and counterterrorism, the Obama administration put a large-scale of military commitment in the Middle East after terrorist groups started appearing in Iraq and Syria, and it stepped up a lot of efforts to work with its allies in the region. Jordan was a main player in the campaign against terrorism; it contributed along with the US in many airstrikes around the region. The United States during the Arab Spring recognized that Jordan's stability was crucial to its interests in the Middle East. Therefore, the US intensified its support to the Kingdom. Also, during Syrian refugees' waves to Jordan, the United States prevented Jordan from being overwhelmed by refugees.'

Acknowledgment

This book is a product of research and support of many individuals to whom I would like to express my gratitude. I thank all the chapter contributors representing 4 countries, respected universities, research institutes, and organizations. I wish to express my sincere thanks to Professor Nalan Gürel (Marmara University) who always supported me in my academic career. Also, I thank to my husband, Teoman Özer, who always supported me in the book project, and I thank to my girls Çağla Su and Ece, who patiently waited to me throughout the book project.

Chapter 1
Transformation of China's Agricultural Trade in Response to Emerging Tensions on the Global Market

Vasilii Erokhin
https://orcid.org/0000-0002-3745-5469
Harbin Engineering University, China

ABSTRACT

China has worked to ensure future food self-sufficiency, but still depends on the imports of many kinds of agricultural products. Imports grow as domestic demand is restructured in favor of qualitative food products of high nutrient value amid the progressive degradation of agricultural lands, and shrinking possibilities for agricultural production. Currently, the majority of such value-added food products is imported from the USA. By raising import tariffs in response to the recent US protectionist policies, China may face a situation of food insecurity. This chapter reviews the recent tendencies in China's foreign trade in food and agricultural products, analyses food security status of China on major kinds of agricultural commodities, discusses current US-China trade relations and reorientation of China's foreign trade in food and agricultural products, and provides possible solutions to the improvement of food security by means of intensification of domestic agricultural production and diversification of imports.

DOI: 10.4018/978-1-5225-9566-3.ch001

INTRODUCTION

International trade is a commonly accepted tool to increase the utilization of competitive advantages of a country by the involvement into the global exchange. In the open international market, competition spurs domestic producers to increase efficiency and cut production costs, while, in turn, producing competitive internationally-traded products have a significant impact on trade volumes and patterns of a country (Levchenko & Zhang, 2016) and determines relative positions of domestic producers in external markets (Maitah, Kuzmenko, & Smutka, 2016).

Commonly, there is a positive relationship between openness, export to GDP ratio, and economic growth (Afonso, 2001; Sun & Heshmati, 2010; Frankel & Romer, 1999). Theoretical models demonstrate that trade openness improves the efficiency of the allocation of world resources, and the comparative advantage gained will improve production and trade. As a result, national income will increase above the production frontier curve. Omoju and Adensaya (2012) registered a significant impact of trade openness on national income and ability of a country to enhance growth through higher total factor productivity.

It is also widely accepted that openness to trade increases the level of competition, improves firms' productivity, and brings more business opportunities to local enterprises, thus leading to improved economic development. Wagner (2007) found that promoting exports led to more intense competition and improvement in terms of productivity, while Lee (1995) discovered that increased imports of those products which were not available in the domestic market resulted in the increased productivity of manufacturing. Lamaj (2015) reports that the continuing reduction and removal of trade barriers has enabled more than 500 million people to lift themselves out of poverty in the past three decades, including 400 million in China. Yanikkaya (2003) argues that trade liberalization does not necessarily lead to growth but finds that trade barriers are positively associated with growth, especially for developing countries.

Despite significant efforts aimed at promoting international competition, there are sectors in which foreign trade policies are yet only partially adapted to the challenges associated with today's globalized economy (Perez Motta, 2016). Agricultural trade is one of such specific cases due to the vital importance of agricultural production and trade for ensuring food security. Both global and national dimensions of food security of a particular country are developed under the influence of two major types of economic policy, which are often countered with one another. On the one side, there is a global trend towards liberalization of economic and trade relations, which is facilitated in the framework of international organizations and various alliances of countries. Reduction and removal of administrative barriers to agricultural trade are mandated by the World Trade Organization (WTO). On the other side, countries tend to protect domestic producers, support the purchasing power of consumers, and promote domestic products abroad. Competition has led to a situation in which many countries have become food dependent, while others managed to benefit from easier access to foreign markets and unified framework of global trade in food (Lawrence & McMichael, 2012).

In agriculture, where production is affected by many variables, including natural factors, changes in trade policy do not go smooth. Trade liberalization can affect the availability of certain foods by removal of barriers to imports, but also to foreign investments in the development of domestic production. Thow and Hawkes (2009) found that availability of processed food has risen in developing countries after foreign direct investment by multinational food companies. Thus, changes in trade policies have facilitated the rising availability and consumption of foods. Dorosh (2004) found the positive contribution of trade liberalization to food security and stabilization of supply and food market. Protection policies, including administrative restrictions of food imports with a view to increasing food self-sufficiency of the country, on the contrary, may cause unnecessary social costs and place food self-sufficiency into conflict with the goals of food security and poverty reduction. Warr (2011) studied the effects of an import ban on rice introduced in Indonesia and concluded that it let to achieve the required level of food self-sufficiency, but at the expense of reducing food security.

Target markets are continually evolving, while the expansion of export trading involves food security issues. Ghosh and Ghoshal (2017) state that despite the increased access to a wide range of affordable and nutritious food, structural changes in global food market have put in place concerns and challenges related to food prices, stability of food supply, and trade-economic aspects of food accessibility and affordability. That is why it is crucial to track changes in trade policies and interpret them in terms of food production and trade in agricultural commodities, so both agricultural producers and exporters may fit well with the changing requirements of domestic resources and global market. Two-thirds of the world's one billion hungry reside in Asia, many of them in China (Asian Development Bank, n.d.). In previous decades, China has demonstrated unprecedented success in reducing poverty by lifting over 850 million of people above the $1.9 poverty line with the percentage of people living in extreme poverty falling from 88% in the 1980s to only 2% in the 2010s (Tan, 2018). However, as China's agriculture is an integral element of globalized food market, food and trade policies of China and other market actors affect food prices bringing about price volatility and food security concerns since many people still spend a substantial part of their income on food and related goods. This chapter overviews China's foreign trade in agricultural commodities and food, assesses possible effects of rising protectionism in global trade in food, and puts forward a set of recommendations aiming to ensure food security of China amid the progressing shares reallocation in the global food market.

BACKGROUND

International trade in agricultural products has been on the top of the global agenda throughout the last decades. Governments lay emphasis on implementation of a wide range of tools that affect the competitiveness of domestic farmers and influence the structure of exports. The countries with a competitive advantage in the processed agricultural markets capture the majority of the trade (Liapis, 2011), while those countries which specialize in primary agricultural commodities decrease their share of the global market and lose their ground in international competition. It is true not only for the least developed countries, which have very limited abilities to expand exports of their processed products but even for such big agricultural producers and exporters as China.

Before the economic reforms of 1980s, China's foreign trade had been restricted down to exporting surplus raw materials and simple manufactured goods to cover payments for imported goods (Sun & Heshmati, 2010). Since the start of trade liberalization, the country has been deeply integrated into the global trade system, experienced unprecedented economic growth, and skyrocketed to become one of the major exporters and importers worldwide. Dohmen (1976), Lu (1997), Mariani (2013), Hamrin and Zhao (1995), Wu (2006), and Liberthal (2004) provided in-depth analysis of foreign trade policy of China in general. Cass, Williams, and Barker (2003), Lardy (2002), Panitchpakdi and Clifford (2002), and Anderson, Martin, and van der Mensbrugghe (2010) studied the implications of China's membership in the World Trade Organization (WTO) on both China's internal policies and foreign trade.

Economic transformations have caused the substantial increase in productivity in agricultural sector and thus resulted in the improvement of food security of Chinese people. By now China has achieved self-sufficiency on major kinds of food and agricultural products on the level of about 91-97% of domestic consumption. However, taking into account scarce land resources coupled with the world's biggest population, China remains heavily dependent on agricultural imports. With the integration of China's agriculture into the global economy and accession to the WTO, agricultural production and trade are now facing competition from home and abroad (Cheng, 2007). The growth of import is conditioned by the restructuring of domestic demand in favor of qualitative food products of high nutrient value amid the progressive degradation of agricultural lands and shrinking possibilities for agricultural production in China. Zhou (2010) records growth of consumption of food products of higher quality, nutrient value and price in China (meat and meat products, milk and dairy products, and seafood) – to the prejudice of cheaper and fewer nutrient crops. Consequently, Chinese meat and dairy producers demand more crops as fodder for agricultural animals, which increases the load on agricultural lands and accelerates their degradation (Liu & Diamond, 2005). According to Nath et al. (2015), by 2030, China will need to increase agricultural lands under crops by 21% to be able to meet the growing internal demand for food. According to Gao (2017), China's demand for cereals will rise up to 700 million tons in 2020, including imports of 100 million tons. By 2022, China will double import of feed grain, beef, and pork, as well as increase purchases of soybeans by 40%. Huang, Wei, Cui, & Xie (2017) predict China's overall food self-sufficiency to reduce to 91% by 2025.

Economic development along with progressing urbanization and transformation of food consumption patterns are likely to bring increased demand for major crops, including corn, rice, soybeans, and wheat (Gro Intelligence, 2018). Particularly, by the 2030s, the demand for corn is projected to rise up to 300 million tons per year (currently, it is about 250 million tons), for soybeans – up to 180-190 million tons (about 100 million, respectively) (Figure 1).

In view of expected rise in consumption of food, Zhu (2016); Yu, Elleby, and Zobbe (2015), Yu, Feng, Hubacek, and Sun (2016), and Zhou (2010) consider high dependence of China on imports as a potential threat to food security. Zhang and Cheng (2016) show that China's grain imports have continued to grow in spite of increased domestic grain production in the 2010s. In 2004-2014, grain imports nearly tripled, and imports of rice, wheat, and corn increased eightfold. Zhang (2016) points out that large-scale agricultural imports, particularly, soybeans from the USA, has almost destroyed domestic soybean production sector causing China

Figure 1. Projections of China's demand for major crops by 2035, million tons per year
Source: Author's development based on Gro Intelligence (2018)

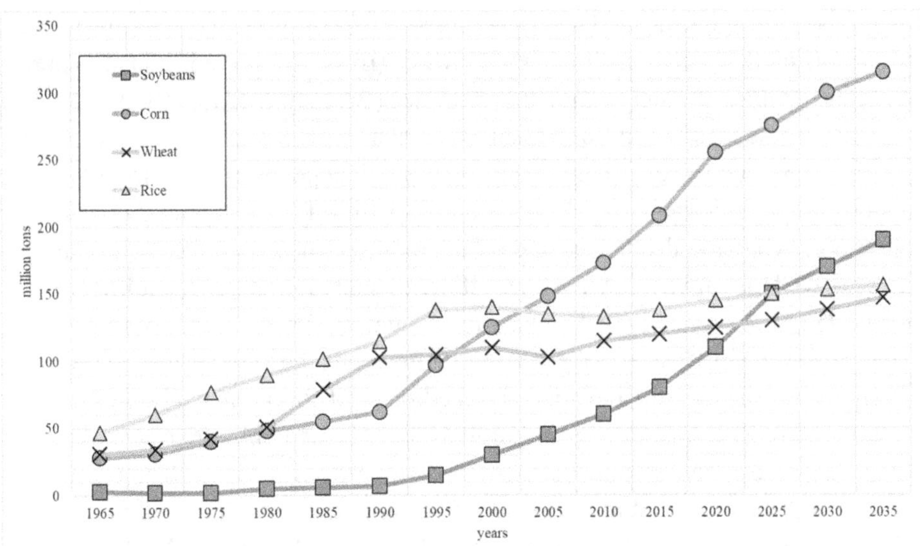

to lose control of its supply chain to foreign producers and suppliers. In a situation of expanding trade tensions between the USA and China and, potentially, between China and other countries, such over-reliance on foreign food supply equips China's counterparts with a power to influence on China's trade policies by pressing its food market and threatening food security of its population.

MAIN FOCUS OF THE CHAPTER

China's Foreign Trade in Agricultural Commodities and Food

Institutional changes, technological development, and increase in investment attractiveness in agricultural production in China could not have happened without market transformations. They started with a restricted number of agricultural products and expanded to the entire agricultural sector. Since 1978, China has pursued trade liberalization (Sun & Heshmati, 2010), which, in turn, has facilitated smooth transformation of the country from a planned economy to a market-oriented one and contributed to the overall agricultural production growth and the change in commodity structure since the early 1990s (Huang et al., 2017; Park, Jin, Rozelle, & Huang, 2002; Huang & Rozelle, 2006). Since joining the WTO in 2001, China has undertaken a series of tariff reductions policy towards agricultural products (mostly, rice and wheat) and changed its position in the global market from net exporter to net importer (Erokhin & Gao, 2018). Over the past decade, the total agricultural trade deficit has increased significantly to $40 billion (Figure 2).

Today, China is one of the major global producers of agricultural products. Its major export agricultural products are vegetables (fresh, prepared, and preserved), fish (fresh, chilled, frozen, dried, etc.), fruits (fresh, preserved, and prepared), crustaceans, mollusks, and aquatic invertebrates (Erokhin & Gao, 2018) (Table 1).

China has succeeded to ensure self-sufficiency on major kinds of food and agricultural products. Nevertheless, the country still depends on food imports being the world's top importer of soybeans, cotton, palm oil, and sugar. About 80% of consumed soybean and other agricultural products, such as milk and sugar, are imported to China. Soybean imports significantly increased from 0.3 million tons in 1995 to 95 million tons in 2017, presently accounting for two-thirds of the world's soybean market (Cui & Shoemaker, 2018). China is one the world's biggest importer of palm oil, sugar, meat, fish, fruits, and feeding stuff for animals (Table 2).

China's largest supplier of agricultural products is the USA which accounted for about 20% of the value of China's agricultural imports during 2015-2017 (Figure 3).

In 1995-2017, the combination of top five suppliers of agricultural products to China is rather stable. In 2017, however, Brazil has overtaken the USA to become the

Figure 2. China's agricultural trade in 1995-2017, $ billion
Source: Author's development based on United Nations Conference on Trade and Development [UNCTAD] (2019)

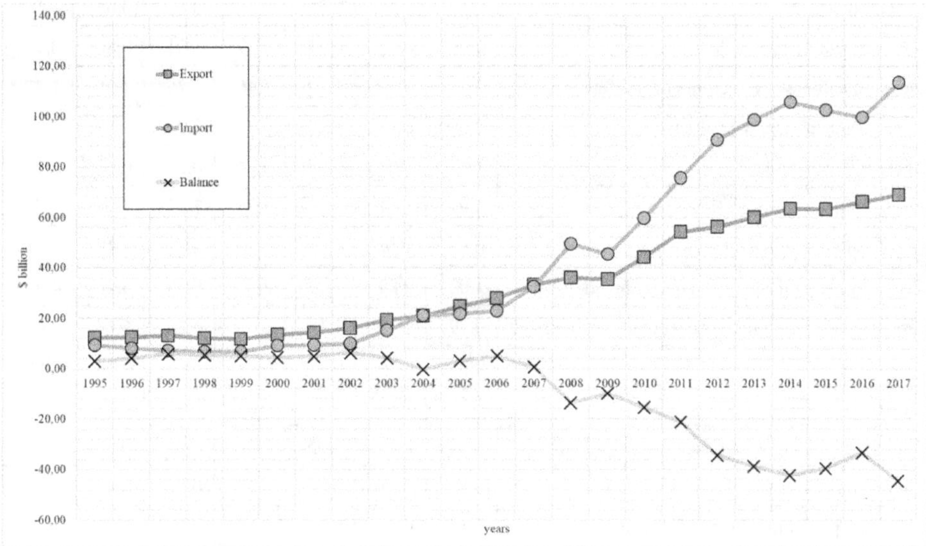

leading partner of China in agricultural trade (21.05% of China's total agricultural import in 2017, or $28.88 billion). The share of the USA in China's agricultural import declined from 21.66% in 2016 ($21.58 billion) to 19.09% ($21.66 billion) in 2017 (Figure 4).

Effects of Tariff Escalations on China's Agricultural Trade

Dependence of China on imports of agricultural commodities and food is expected to increase in the future. The growth is projected due to the restructuring of domestic consumption in favor of high-nutrient food products (Chang, DeFries, Liu, & Davis, 2018) amid the deterioration of opportunities of agricultural production in China (Jash, 2015). By 2022, China's import of feeding stuff for animals, beef, and pork will double, while the import of soybeans will increase by 40%. By 2020, China's demand for cereals will reach 700 million tons, 100 million tons of which will be imported.

China's import of such value-added food products as soybeans and meat is focused on the USA (over $26 billion in total). In the situation of trade tensions and tariff escalations between the USA and China, the agricultural sector is one of the most vulnerable. The U.S. economy is external-oriented, but to a lesser degree compared to that of China. In the USA, export-GDP ratio is 11.9%, while that in China is 19.2%.

Table 1. China's agricultural export in 1995-2017, $ billion

Product	1995	2000	2005	2010	2015	2016	2017
Live animals	0.50	0.38	0.33	0.45	0.60	0.65	0.56
Meat and edible meat offal	0.99	0.72	0.71	0.89	1.01	0.86	0.90
Prepared and preserved edible meat offal	0.33	0.49	1.19	1.46	1.76	1.65	1.87
Milk, cream, and milk products	0.03	0.05	0.10	0.06	0.06	0.08	0.09
Eggs and eggs' yolks	0.03	0.03	0.08	0.14	0.20	0.19	0.19
Fresh, chilled, or frozen fish	0.91	1.31	3.02	5.74	7.53	7.74	7.75
Dried, salted, or smoked fish	0.13	0.11	0.21	0.35	0.47	0.49	0.51
Crustaceans, mollusks, and aquatic invertebrates	1.02	0.84	1.12	2.70	5.32	5.48	4.47
Fish, prepared and preserved aquatic invertebrates	0.79	1.39	3.18	4.40	6.25	6.29	7.68
Rice	0.02	0.56	0.22	0.42	0.27	0.38	0.60
Maize	0.01	1.05	1.10	0.03	0.01	0.01	0.02
Cereals, excluding wheat, rice, barley, and maize	0.04	0.03	0.05	0.09	0.05	0.04	0.05
Meal and flour of wheat and flour of meslin	0.06	0.05	0.09	0.12	0.07	0.06	0.08
Cereal preparations, flour of fruits or vegetables	0.15	0.12	0.32	0.67	0.89	0.90	0.90
Vegetables	1.32	1.27	2.56	6.03	6.81	7.80	7.61
Prepared and preserved vegetables, roots, tubers	1.20	1.02	2.18	4.48	6.65	7.10	7.87
Fruits and nuts	0.44	0.35	0.91	2.41	4.88	5.21	5.06
Preserved fruits and fruit preparations	0.34	0.53	1.15	2.21	2.93	2.87	4.05
Sugar, molasses, and honey	0.29	0.18	0.28	0.73	1.01	1.14	1.16
Confectionery sugar	0.09	0.14	0.34	0.68	1.08	1.09	1.13
Coffee and coffee substitutes	0.01	0.02	0.05	0.14	0.45	0.95	0.43
Cocoa	0.03	0.02	0.06	0.10	0.11	0.09	0.06
Chocolate and food preparations with cocoa	0.01	0.01	0.05	0.11	0.33	0.34	0.32
Tea and mate	0.28	0.36	0.50	0.83	1.49	1.60	1.73
Spices	0.19	0.15	0.42	0.77	0.93	0.97	1.08
Feeding stuff for animals	0.35	0.30	0.50	1.98	2.68	2.77	2.66

Source: UNCTAD, 2019

Such trade position of China in relation to the USA limits the response resources in trade tensions. By raising import tariffs on food and agricultural products in response to recent U.S. protectionist policies, China may face a situation of food insecurity.

According to Zhang (2016), the USA supplied 36% of total China's oilseeds imports, 42% of cereals imports, 30% of cotton imports, and 25% of meat imports. Gale, Hansen, and Jewison (2015) report that the USA is also one of China's top three destinations for agricultural exports. Bilateral agricultural trade has experienced

Table 2. China's agricultural import in 1995-2017, $ billion

Product	1995	2000	2005	2010	2015	2016	2017
Live animals	0.04	0.05	0.11	0.27	0.55	0.39	0.36
Meat of bovine animals, fresh, chilled or frozen	0.01	0.01	0.01	0.08	2.32	2.52	3.07
Meat and edible meat offal	0.09	0.64	0.61	2.18	4.45	7.60	6.38
Milk, cream, and milk products	0.06	0.21	0.41	1.80	2.63	2.71	3.89
Butter and other fats and oils derived from milk	0.00	0.01	0.03	0.09	0.27	0.30	0.50
Cheese and curd	0.00	0.00	0.03	0.11	0.35	0.42	0.50
Fresh, chilled, or frozen fish	0.39	0.77	2.29	3.32	3.61	3.84	4.43
Dried, salted, or smoked fish	0.02	0.04	0.03	0.02	0.02	0.03	0.06
Crustaceans, mollusks, and aquatic invertebrates	0.18	0.39	0.52	0.98	2.70	3.06	1.80
Fish, prepared and preserved aquatic invertebrates	0.01	0.01	0.02	0.09	0.23	0.17	2.00
Wheat and meslin	2.03	0.15	0.76	0.31	0.89	0.80	1.03
Rice	0.43	0.11	0.20	0.25	1.47	1.59	1.83
Barley	0.24	0.31	0.43	0.54	2.86	1.14	1.82
Maize	0.82	0.00	0.00	0.37	1.11	0.64	0.60
Cereals, excluding wheat, rice, barley, and maize	0.06	0.00	0.00	0.04	3.02	1.49	1.12
Meal and flour of wheat and flour of meslin	0.01	0.01	0.01	0.01	0.02	0.01	0.05
Cereal preparations, flour of fruits or vegetables	0.02	0.02	0.06	0.22	0.86	0.98	1.03
Vegetables	0.08	0.09	0.53	1.56	2.72	1.95	2.12
Prepared and preserved vegetables, roots, tubers	0.01	0.04	0.06	0.12	0.28	0.27	0.25
Fruits and nuts	0.08	0.37	0.63	2.06	5.87	5.72	6.24
Preserved fruits and fruit preparations	0.00	0.01	0.07	0.27	0.58	0.66	0.84
Sugar, molasses, and honey	0.91	0.15	0.42	0.99	1.98	1.35	1.31
Confectionery sugar	0.03	0.03	0.03	0.06	0.20	0.20	0.21
Coffee and coffee substitutes	0.01	0.01	0.03	0.10	0.46	0.90	0.45
Cocoa	0.05	0.04	0.11	0.28	0.36	0.35	0.31
Chocolate and food preparations with cocoa	0.01	0.03	0.06	0.16	0.52	0.34	0.35
Tea and mate	0.00	0.00	0.01	0.06	0.12	0.12	0.17
Spices	0.01	0.01	0.01	0.03	0.06	0.06	0.06
Feeding stuff for animals	0.42	0.91	1.31	3.30	4.97	3.61	3.93
Margarine and shortening	0.01	0.11	0.02	0.07	0.29	0.31	0.42

Source: UNCTAD, 2019

Figure 3. Major suppliers of agricultural commodities to China in 2015-2017, percentage in total agricultural import
Source: Author's development based on UNCTAD (2019)

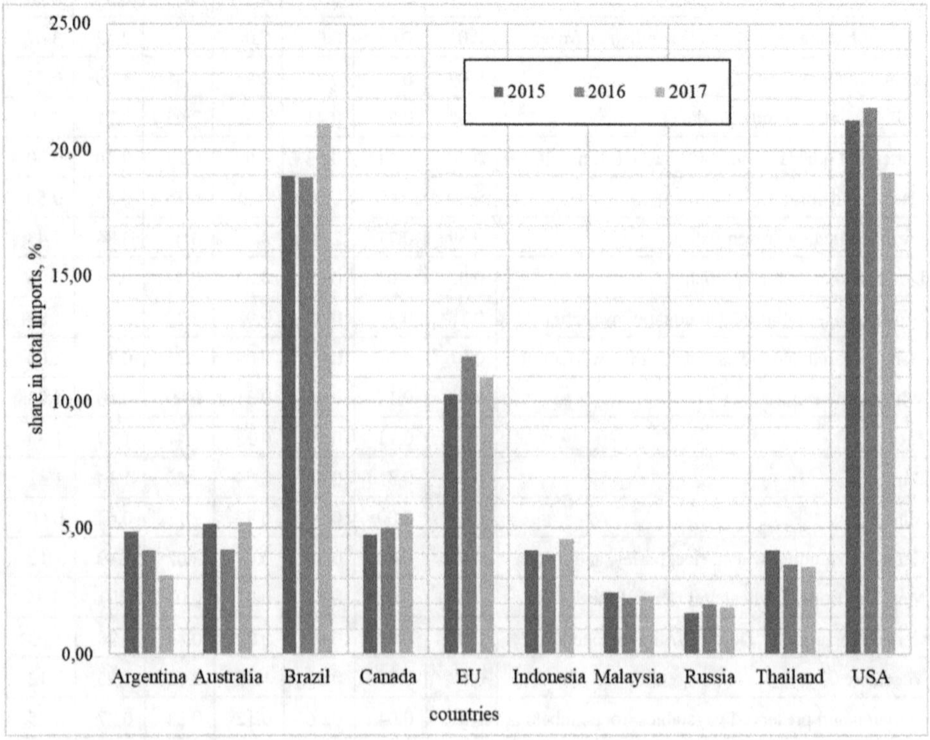

phenomenal growth from 2001, the year of China's accession to the WTO. U.S. imports of agricultural products from China increased from $1 billion in 2001 to almost $7 billion in 2017; whereas its agricultural exports to China skyrocketed from about $2.2 billion in 2001 to over $21.6 billion in 2017 (Figure 5).

In 2017, China was the USA's fourth-largest supplier of agricultural imports. Particularly, China is one of the major suppliers of canned fruits, farmed fish and shellfish, apple juice, garlic, mushroom, pet food, noodles, tea and spices to the USA (Table 3).

China is a major agricultural export market for the USA that has grown tremendously over the past two decades. In fact, China was the second-largest export market for the USA in 2017m behind Canada, accounting for 14% of the U.S. agricultural exports (Bakst, 2018). In terms of value, the largest China's agricultural import from the USA is soybeans totaling over $12.3 billion in 2017 (United States Department of Agriculture, 2018). The USA is also one of the major

Figure 4. Top five suppliers of agricultural commodities to China in 1995-2017, $ billion
Source: Author's development based on UNCTAD (2019)

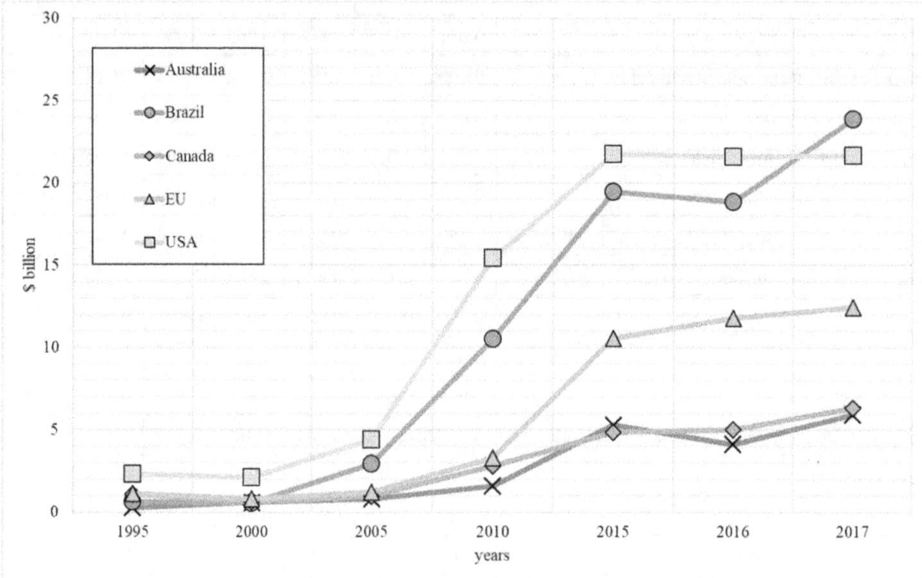

Figure 5. China-USA agricultural trade in 1995-2017, $ billion
Source: Author's development based on UNCTAD (2019)

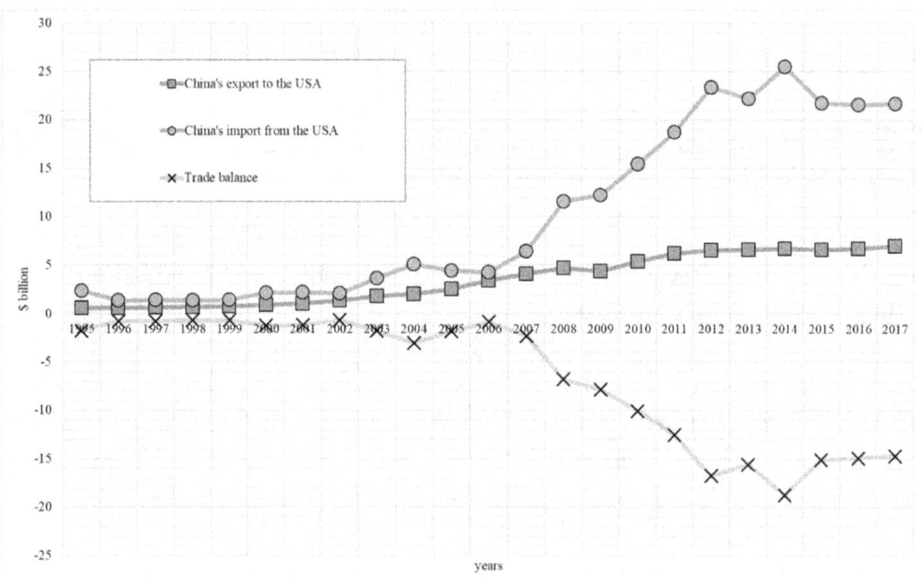

Table 3. China's agricultural export to the USA in 1995-2017, $ billion

Product	1995	2000	2005	2010	2015	2016	2017
Live animals	0.002	0.002	0.015	0.020	0.022	0.036	0.027
Meat and edible meat offal	0.001	0.002	0.008	0.005	0.002	0.002	0.004
Prepared and preserved edible meat offal	0.000	0.003	0.027	0.024	0.014	0.015	0.007
Eggs and eggs' yolks	0.002	0.003	0.002	0.004	0.007	0.007	0.007
Fresh, chilled, or frozen fish	0.092	0.216	0.689	1.260	1.243	1.155	1.191
Dried, salted, or smoked fish	0.001	0.004	0.030	0.051	0.069	0.057	0.054
Crustaceans, mollusks, and aquatic invertebrates	0.159	0.129	0.151	0.407	0.514	0.533	0.423
Fish, prepared and preserved aquatic invertebrates	0.021	0.170	0.408	0.835	1.292	1.226	1.452
Rice	0.000	0.000	0.000	0.000	0.001	0.001	0.003
Cereal preparations, flour of fruits or vegetables	0.008	0.005	0.013	0.037	0.059	0.065	0.065
Vegetables	0.027	0.030	0.135	0.314	0.379	0.396	0.364
Prepared and preserved vegetables, roots, tubers	0.095	0.061	0.184	0.385	0.432	0.616	0.687
Fruits and nuts	0.011	0.014	0.049	0.101	0.146	0.148	0.130
Preserved fruits and fruit preparations	0.017	0.057	0.178	0.413	0.591	0.547	0.591
Fruit and vegetable juices	0.004	0.038	0.182	0.412	0.330	0.316	0.324
Sugar, molasses, and honey	0.016	0.021	0.027	0.021	0.026	0.045	0.047
Confectionery sugar	0.004	0.017	0.072	0.142	0.151	0.140	0.142
Coffee and coffee substitutes	0.000	0.000	0.002	0.023	0.025	0.026	0.030
Cocoa	0.023	0.018	0.036	0.002	0.016	0.017	0.024
Chocolate and food preparations with cocoa	0.000	0.000	0.004	0.006	0.010	0.010	0.010
Tea and mate	0.018	0.015	0.032	0.063	0.105	0.111	0.099
Spices	0.009	0.015	0.049	0.095	0.106	0.104	0.120
Feeding stuff for animals	0.006	0.016	0.047	0.427	0.439	0.421	0.434

Source: UNCTAD, 2019

China's suppliers of meat and edible meat offal, cereals, fish, fruits and nuts, and feeding stuff for animals (Table 4).

Trade conflicts between the USA and China have escalated recently. China has threatened to impose a 25% tariff on 128 products, including agricultural commodities and food products, in response to a U.S. proposal to impose a 25% tariff on imported products from China (Taheripour & Tyner, 2018a). In April 2018, China began imposing tariffs on U.S. goods including soybeans, dairy, and pork, and more tariffs were added in July 2018 (Filloon, 2018).

Zhang (2016) finds that Chinese policymakers are convinced that over-reliance on the USA for agricultural imports could pose a threat to not only the country's

Table 4. China's agricultural import from the USA in 1995-2017, $ billion

Product	1995	2000	2005	2010	2015	2016	2017
Live animals	0.012	0.011	0.017	0.034	0.011	0.005	0.016
Meat of bovine animals, fresh, chilled or frozen	0.001	0.003	0.000	0.000	0.000	0.000	0.025
Meat and edible meat offal	0.069	0.417	0.247	0.405	0.519	1.347	1.160
Milk, cream, and milk products	0.015	0.021	0.059	0.165	0.250	0.232	0.368
Cheese and curd	0.000	0.000	0.001	0.013	0.054	0.041	0.060
Fresh, chilled, or frozen fish	0.037	0.046	0.307	0.563	0.757	0.674	0.902
Dried, salted, or smoked fish	0.002	0.001	0.000	0.000	0.001	0.002	0.000
Crustaceans, mollusks, and aquatic invertebrates	0.030	0.033	0.035	0.157	0.325	0.351	0.122
Fish, prepared and preserved aquatic invertebrates	0.000	0.000	0.001	0.001	0.003	0.005	0.295
Wheat and meslin	0.679	0.028	0.104	0.031	0.185	0.208	0.391
Maize	0.786	0.000	0.000	0.348	0.121	0.056	0.160
Cereals, excluding wheat, rice, barley, and maize	0.000	0.000	0.000	0.000	2.472	1.262	0.959
Meal and flour of wheat and flour of meslin	0.002	0.003	0.001	0.001	0.000	0.000	0.000
Cereal preparations, flour of fruits or vegetables	0.002	0.003	0.007	0.014	0.052	0.046	0.040
Vegetables	0.004	0.018	0.024	0.047	0.052	0.049	0.048
Prepared and preserved vegetables, roots, tubers	0.002	0.032	0.030	0.069	0.150	0.149	0.125
Fruits and nuts	0.007	0.049	0.106	0.382	0.523	0.573	0.760
Preserved fruits and fruit preparations	0.001	0.002	0.019	0.090	0.094	0.117	0.162
Fruit and vegetable juices	0.001	0.003	0.004	0.018	0.015	0.020	0.019
Sugar, molasses, and honey	0.001	0.005	0.015	0.037	0.063	0.049	0.068
Confectionery sugar	0.001	0.005	0.002	0.004	0.014	0.016	0.015
Coffee and coffee substitutes	0.001	0.001	0.005	0.010	0.013	0.017	0.022
Cocoa	0.000	0.003	0.005	0.024	0.012	0.009	0.001
Chocolate and food preparations with cocoa	0.003	0.014	0.006	0.009	0.028	0.026	0.028
Tea and mate	0.000	0.000	0.001	0.002	0.001	0.001	0.004
Feeding stuff for animals	0.041	0.120	0.097	1.004	2.745	1.500	0.921
Margarine and shortening	0.000	0.003	0.002	0.001	0.015	0.017	0.016
Edible products and preparations	0.006	0.048	0.095	0.151	0.421	0.443	0.515
Oil seeds and oleaginous fruits	0.039	1.185	3.164	11.359	12.437	13.923	14.004

Source: UNCTAD, 2019

food security but also national security. Consequently, China is diversifying away from the USA food imports by importing more from other countries, particularly, Brazil. China's agricultural import from Brazil increased rapidly in 2001-2013. After some decline in 2013-2016, the volume of import peaked up to $23.9 billion, whereas Brazil's surplus in agricultural trade with China reached a record high of $23.4 billion (Figure 6).

China's agricultural export to Brazil is very small. It has not increased substantially over the past decades. The structure has not changed too with vegetables being the leading commodity in China's export to Brazil (Table 5).

Brazilian exports to China, on the contrary, increased substantially. Particularly, export of soybeans soared after China slapped a 25% tariff on U.S. soy in response to U.S. tariffs on Chinese goods. In 2018, Brazil sent roughly 80% of its soybean exports to China. Total export of oil seeds and oleaginous nuts increased from $0.47 billion in 2000 up to $20.92 billion in 2017 (Table 6). Brazil's total soy area is expected to expand to a record 36.28 million hectares due to robust Chinese demand (Spring & Polansek, 2018). Brazil is also aiming to expand meat shipments to China, which is currently its top export destination for beef and chicken (Spring, 2018).

Similar to Brazil, the EU is increasingly becoming an important source of agricultural imports for China. Since 2001, agricultural imports from the EU increased from $0.63 billion to $12.45 billion in 2017. China-EU trade balance was positive for China till 2012, but since that year has declined down to $5.29 (Figure 7).

Figure 6. China-Brazil agricultural trade in 1995-2017, $ billion
Source: Author's development based on UNCTAD (2019)

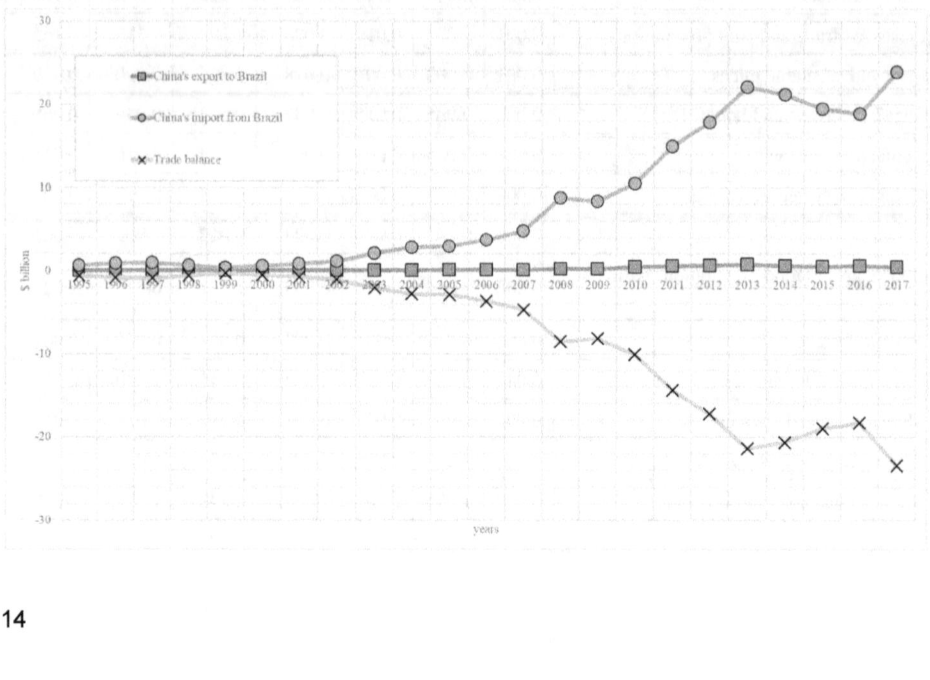

Table 5. China's agricultural export to Brazil in 1995-2017, $ billion

Product	1995	2000	2005	2010	2015	2016	2017
Fresh, chilled, or frozen fish	0.000	0.000	0.000	0.104	0.111	0.077	0.090
Dried, salted, or smoked fish	0.000	0.000	0.000	0.029	0.048	0.044	0.063
Crustaceans, mollusks, and aquatic invertebrates	0.000	0.000	0.000	0.002	0.008	0.013	0.020
Fish, prepared and preserved aquatic invertebrates	0.000	0.000	0.000	0.001	0.003	0.004	0.004
Cereals, excluding wheat, rice, barley, and maize	0.000	0.000	0.000	0.001	0.001	0.001	0.001
Cereal preparations, flour of fruits or vegetables	0.000	0.000	0.000	0.002	0.001	0.002	0.003
Vegetables	0.019	0.006	0.041	0.205	0.145	0.258	0.123
Prepared and preserved vegetables, roots, tubers	0.002	0.002	0.012	0.053	0.079	0.071	0.058
Preserved fruits and fruit preparations	0.000	0.000	0.000	0.009	0.016	0.016	0.024
Sugar, molasses, and honey	0.000	0.000	0.001	0.002	0.003	0.003	0.004
Confectionery sugar	0.000	0.000	0.000	0.002	0.003	0.003	0.006
Cocoa	0.000	0.000	0.000	0.006	0.000	0.001	0.001
Tea and mate	0.000	0.000	0.000	0.001	0.001	0.001	0.001
Spices	0.000	0.000	0.001	0.001	0.001	0.002	0.003
Feeding stuff for animals	0.000	0.002	0.005	0.028	0.029	0.029	0.033

Source: UNCTAD, 2019

Table 6. China's agricultural import from Brazil in 1995-2017, $ billion

Product	1995	2000	2005	2010	2015	2016	2017
Meat of bovine animals, fresh, chilled or frozen	0.000	0.000	0.000	0.025	0.287	0.765	0.872
Meat and edible meat offal	0.000	0.000	0.133	0.536	0.705	1.239	0.989
Fresh, chilled, or frozen fish	0.000	0.000	0.000	0.000	0.003	0.005	0.004
Dried, salted, or smoked fish	0.000	0.000	0.000	0.000	0.000	0.000	0.001
Fish, prepared and preserved aquatic invertebrates	0.000	0.000	0.000	0.000	0.000	0.000	0.003
Preserved fruits and fruit preparations	0.000	0.000	0.003	0.029	0.025	0.031	0.026
Fruit and vegetable juices	0.001	0.005	0.047	0.082	0.068	0.070	0.079
Sugar, molasses, and honey	0.076	0.000	0.000	0.504	0.944	0.705	0.370
Confectionery sugar	0.000	0.001	0.000	0.000	0.001	0.001	0.000
Coffee and coffee substitutes	0.000	0.000	0.003	0.004	0.014	0.011	0.014
Spices	0.000	0.000	0.000	0.000	0.001	0.001	0.002
Feeding stuff for animals	0.000	0.019	0.005	0.012	0.008	0.014	0.015
Oil seeds and oleaginous fruits	0.002	0.466	2.381	8.148	16.887	15.552	20.916

Source: UNCTAD, 2019

Figure 7. China-EU agricultural trade in 1995-2017, $ billion
Source: Author's development based on UNCTAD (2019)

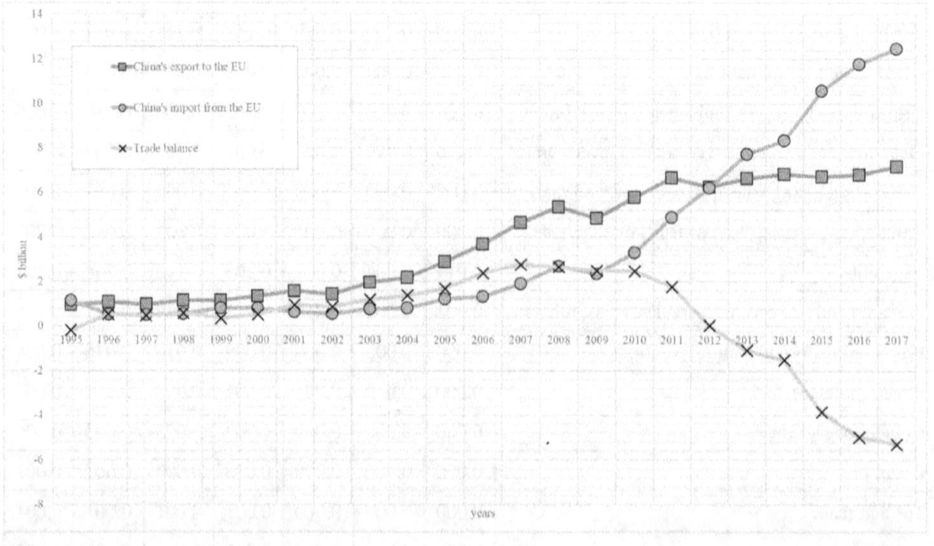

Major export commodities are fresh, chilled, and frozen fish; prepared and preserved vegetables, roots, and tubers; feeding stuff for animals; crustaceans, mollusks, and aquatic invertebrates; preserved fruit and fruit preparations (Table 7).

Import from the EU has been diversifying in the past years. Major import commodities are edible products and preparations (increase from $0.04 billion in 2000 to $3.55 billion in 2017); meat and edible meat offal (increase from $0.10 billion in 2000 to $2.50 billion in 2017); milk, cream, and milk products (increase from $0.07 billion in 2000 to $1.10 billion in 2017); cereal preparations, flour of fruits and vegetables (increase from $0.01 billion in 2000 to $0.22 billion in 2017) (Table 8).

Tariff escalations between such large actors as China and the USA will initiate trade diversion and change the global agricultural market substantially. Taheripour and Tyner (2018b) evaluated the global economic impacts of Chinese tariffs on their imports of U.S. soybeans, corn, wheat, sorghum, and beef. In the case of soybean, it is demonstrated that the total decline in U.S. soybean exports is not as large as the decline in Chinese imports, as exports to some other regions increase. Chinese imports from the USA will fall by 48%, but U.S. global exports will fall 24%. Exports to other countries make up about half of the loss in Chinese exports. Brazil and other exporters capture more of the Chinese market, and the USA takes some of the markets that other exporters give up (Taheripour & Tyner, 2018b). In general, the 25% Chinese tariff could reduce exports of U.S. soybeans to China by about 17

Table 7. China's agricultural export to the EU in 1995-2017, $ billion

Product	1995	2000	2005	2010	2015	2016	2017
Live animals	0.001	0.002	0.001	0.004	0.002	0.001	0.002
Meat and edible meat offal	0.129	0.052	0.013	0.029	0.022	0.017	0.022
Prepared and preserved edible meat offal	0.007	0.001	0.001	0.075	0.112	0.090	0.099
Eggs and eggs' yolks	0.000	0.000	0.000	0.000	0.001	0.001	0.001
Fresh, chilled, or frozen fish	0.041	0.206	0.674	1.316	1.375	1.356	1.372
Dried, salted, or smoked fish	0.001	0.002	0.018	0.068	0.056	0.072	0.067
Crustaceans, mollusks, and aquatic invertebrates	0.059	0.102	0.083	0.445	0.407	0.518	0.527
Fish, prepared and preserved aquatic invertebrates	0.005	0.068	0.273	0.242	0.328	0.324	0.346
Rice	0.000	0.012	0.000	0.001	0.000	0.001	0.001
Cereals, excluding wheat, rice, barley, and maize	0.004	0.005	0.007	0.011	0.006	0.005	0.003
Cereal preparations, flour of fruits or vegetables	0.006	0.006	0.017	0.038	0.037	0.034	0.034
Vegetables	0.144	0.155	0.330	0.702	0.693	0.615	0.501
Prepared and preserved vegetables, roots, tubers	0.171	0.223	0.427	0.729	0.671	0.713	0.658
Fruits and nuts	0.025	0.021	0.097	0.215	0.318	0.310	0.313
Preserved fruits and fruit preparations	0.037	0.061	0.201	0.416	0.376	0.370	0.486
Fruit and vegetable juices	0.003	0.039	0.135	0.131	0.048	0.034	0.091
Sugar, molasses, and honey	0.040	0.026	0.012	0.097	0.194	0.151	0.175
Confectionery sugar	0.009	0.024	0.052	0.089	0.103	0.095	0.094
Coffee and coffee substitutes	0.001	0.004	0.012	0.065	0.130	0.165	0.122
Cocoa	0.008	0.000	0.017	0.050	0.080	0.051	0.019
Chocolate and food preparations with cocoa	0.001	0.001	0.002	0.005	0.011	0.007	0.007
Tea and mate	0.050	0.054	0.035	0.075	0.123	0.117	0.142
Spices	0.007	0.008	0.031	0.090	0.189	0.223	0.249
Feeding stuff for animals	0.031	0.037	0.010	0.224	0.463	0.534	0.632

Source: UNCTAD, 2019

MMT in the long run. In an attempt to compensate the losses on China's market, the USA would export more to the EU and the rest of the world. Taheripour and Tyner (2018b) predict total U.S. soybean exports to the world to drop by 14 MMT and China's soybean imports from the USA to drop by 32.6 MMT. In this case, U.S. soybean exports go up by 1.9 MMT to the EU and by 10.7 MMT to the rest of the world. The proposed Chinese tariffs will not significantly affect the global markets for corn, wheat, and sorghum or cause significant changes in the total U.S. exports of these products. However, the tariffs decrease U.S. exports of corn, wheat, and

Table 8. China's agricultural import from the EU in 1995-2017, $ billion

Product	1995	2000	2005	2010	2015	2016	2017
Live animals	0.008	0.007	0.010	0.016	0.068	0.057	0.045
Meat and edible meat offal	0.008	0.099	0.065	0.536	1.981	3.492	2.504
Milk, cream, and milk products	0.020	0.070	0.100	0.299	0.745	0.800	1.099
Butter and other fats and oils derived from milk	0.000	0.000	0.010	0.008	0.038	0.044	0.069
Cheese and curd	0.000	0.000	0.004	0.016	0.057	0.072	0.090
Fresh, chilled, or frozen fish	0.032	0.045	0.191	0.201	0.175	0.127	0.170
Dried, salted, or smoked fish	0.002	0.010	0.001	0.001	0.002	0.002	0.002
Crustaceans, mollusks, and aquatic invertebrates	0.007	0.014	0.016	0.037	0.066	0.084	0.062
Fish, prepared and preserved aquatic invertebrates	0.000	0.000	0.002	0.001	0.004	0.005	0.066
Wheat and meslin	0.360	n.d.	0.119	0.000	0.001	0.000	0.000
Barley	0.097	0.091	0.060	0.121	1.108	0.148	0.053
Maize	0.000	0.000	0.000	0.004	0.042	0.003	0.002
Cereals, excluding wheat, rice, barley, and maize	0.061	n.d.	0.000	0.000	0.002	0.002	0.000
Meal and flour of wheat and flour of meslin	0.000	0.001	0.000	0.000	0.000	0.000	0.001
Cereal preparations, flour of fruits or vegetables	0.004	0.005	0.023	0.056	0.182	0.220	0.217
Vegetables	0.001	0.007	0.004	0.009	0.028	0.040	0.038
Prepared and preserved vegetables, roots, tubers	0.003	0.005	0.007	0.020	0.061	0.049	0.060
Fruits and nuts	0.000	0.001	0.002	0.004	0.048	0.066	0.089
Preserved fruits and fruit preparations	0.001	0.000	0.016	0.052	0.074	0.086	0.084
Fruit and vegetable juices	0.000	0.001	0.006	0.025	0.039	0.035	0.046
Sugar, molasses, and honey	0.002	0.007	0.014	0.019	0.032	0.036	0.042
Confectionery sugar	0.003	0.004	0.004	0.009	0.044	0.039	0.043
Coffee and coffee substitutes	0.000	0.000	0.002	0.011	0.034	0.035	0.049
Cocoa	0.000	0.002	0.005	0.009	0.020	0.021	0.019
Chocolate and food preparations with cocoa	0.001	0.012	0.034	0.114	0.362	0.213	0.210
Tea and mate	0.000	0.000	0.001	0.003	0.006	0.007	0.007
Spices	0.000	0.000	0.001	0.001	0.003	0.004	0.004
Feeding stuff for animals	0.015	0.060	0.044	0.065	0.187	0.159	0.194
Margarine and shortening	0.000	0.000	0.002	0.003	0.022	0.023	0.026
Edible products and preparations	0.004	0.044	0.100	0.338	2.266	2.670	3.552

Source: UNCTAD, 2019

sorghum to China by 42% (0.11 MMT), 82% (0.74 MMT), and 13% (0.68 MMT), respectively (Taheripour & Tyner, 2018b).

SOLUTIONS AND RECOMMENDATIONS

Despite the ongoing reorientation of China's agricultural imports from the USA to alternative sources, food security of the country remains threatened, particularly, for soybeans. In the situation of escalation of trade tension between China and the USA, China has a narrow set of options to react. For China, it is not possible to increase domestic agricultural production, particularly, of cash crops, due to a critical deficit of agricultural lands and deterioration of their productive qualities. Increase in soybean production is only possible by means of decrease in acreages of other crops.

Global market of soybeans is a duopoly with domination of the USA and Brazil. When tariffs on U.S. imports are increased, China will have to continue increasing purchasing in Brazil, which, in turn, drive up the prices. Potential price surge will initiate the rise in costs along the production chains globally. Soybeans are used not only in food industry but also as feeding stuff for animals, particularly, in swine production. China is the largest pork consumer in the world and the third-largest market for U.S. pork. In 2017, China succeeded to increase domestic production of pork and thus reduced imports. However, pork prices are very volatile due to the specifics of production cycle and sporadic epidemics. Consequently, stability of supply on the domestic market and prevention of price hikes are not only economic issues of food security, but also a political goal.

As in the case of soybeans, operative switching of China's agricultural import from the USA to alternative suppliers of pork is challenging. The prospective trade partners are Vietnam and the countries of Southeast Asia. China is also experiencing deficit of fruits, particularly, dates, which are imported from the USA. To diversify fruit imports, China should increase purchases from Vietnam and the countries of Latin America (Peru and Argentina).

To some extent, China's food security cooperation is leaning towards Russia and the countries of Central Asia. In contrast to China, these countries are abundant with fertile land. As China-Russia relations have improved significantly over the past years, China's growing investment in agricultural sector in Russia and the countries of Central Asia and Eurasian Economic Union creates an opportunity to improve China's food security.

FUTURE RESEARCH DIRECTIONS

Although the current China-USA trade dispute continues to evolve, it is valuable to understand the potential negative impact on global agricultural trade and to be informed of possible consequences of tariff escalation and trade distortions on global market share reallocations. Threats of trade tensions on agricultural trade shook the agricultural production globally, that is why a deeper analysis is required in the sphere of the trade policy impact on not only agricultural trade, but also changes in agricultural production, producer prices, and welfare. It is important to determine the actual level of security of domestic food market with an account of the internationally recognized reference nutrient intakes. There should be monitoring of the level of security of certain market over the certain period of time, which allows comparing it with both the official statistics reports and levels of food self-sufficiency and assessing influences of various foreign trade policies on food security.

CONCLUSION

International trade has an important role to play in increasing food self-sufficiency, which is a proportion of imported food in domestic consumption, but also in improving food security. Transforming paradigm of international economic relations causes rising influence of integration and trade liberalization on domestic food markets of developing and emerging countries. In the conditions of globalizing agricultural trade, adaptation of domestic food markets should go in the two directions: promotion of external opportunities and overcoming of internal bottlenecks.

Despite being the most populous country in the world, China has succeeded to ensure self-sufficiency on major kinds of food and agricultural products. However, the country still depends on food imports of soybeans, meat, and many other agricultural products. The analysis of China's foreign trade in food and agricultural products and food security status of the country on major kinds of agricultural commodities demonstrates that import volumes grow as domestic demand is restructured in favor of qualitative food products of high nutrient value amid the progressive degradation of agricultural lands and shrinking possibilities for agricultural production in China. Currently, the majority of such value-added food products is imported from the USA. In the situation of trade tensions and tariff escalations between the USA and China, the agricultural sector is one of the most vulnerable. By raising import tariffs on food and agricultural products in response to the recent US protectionist policies, China may face a situation of food insecurity. The possible solution to the improvement of food security is the intensification of domestic agricultural production and, primarily, diversification of imports.

ACKNOWLEDGMENT

This chapter is a part of the project supported by the project HEUCFJ170901 (Harbin Engineering University, China).

REFERENCES

Afonso, O. (2001). *The Impact of International Trade on Economic Growth*. Porto: University of Porto.

Anderson, K., Martin, W., & van der Mensbrugghe, D. (2010). China, the WTO and the Doha Agenda. In D. Greenaway, C. Milner, & S. Yao (Eds.), *China and the World Economy* (pp. 1–20). London: Palgrave Macmillan. doi:10.1057/9781137059864_1

Asian Development Bank. (n.d.). *Agriculture and Food Security Issues in Asia and the Pacific*. Retrieved from https://www.adb.org/sectors/agriculture/issues

Bakst, D. (2018). *Agricultural Trade with China: What's at Stake for American Farmers, Ranchers, and Families*. Retrieved from https://www.heritage.org/agriculture/report/agricultural-trade-china-whats-stake-american-farmers-ranchers-and-families

Cass, D. Z., Williams, B. G., & Barker, G. R. (2003). *China and the World Trading System: Entering the Millennium*. New York, NY: Cambridge University Press. doi:10.1017/CBO9780511494482

Chang, X., DeFries, R. S., Liu, L., & Davis, K. (2018). Understanding Dietary and Staple Food Transitions in China from Multiple Scales. *PLoS One*, *13*(4), e0195775. doi:10.1371/journal.pone.0195775 PMID:29689066

Cheng, G. (2007). China's Agriculture within the World Trading System. In I. Sheldon (Ed.), *China's Agricultural Trade: Issues and Prospects* (pp. 81–104). Beijing: International Agricultural Trade Research Consortium.

Cui, K., & Shoemaker, S. (2018). A Look at Food Security in China. *NPJ Science of Food, 2*. doi:. doi:10.103841538-018-0012-x

Dohmen, H. (1976). China's Foreign Trade Policy. *Inter Economics*, *11*(7), 197–201. doi:10.1007/BF02929005

Dorosh, P. A. (2004). Trade, Food Aid and Food Security: Evolving Rice and Wheat Markets. *Economic and Political Weekly*, *36*(39), 4033–4042.

Erokhin, V., & Gao, T. (2018). Competitive Advantages of China's Agricultural Exports in the Outward-Looking Belt and Road Initiative. In W. Zhang, I. Alon, & C. Lattemann (Eds.), *China's Belt and Road Initiative: Changing the Rules of Globalization* (pp. 265–285). London: Palgrave Macmillan. doi:10.1007/978-3-319-75435-2_14

Filloon, W. (2018). These Are All the Foods Being Affected by Trump's Trade War. *Eater*. Retrieved from https://www.eater.com/2018/7/18/17527968/food-tariffs-trump-canada-china-mexico-eu

Frankel, J. A., & Romer, D. H. (1999). Does Trade Cause Growth? *The American Economic Review*, *89*(3), 379–399. doi:10.1257/aer.89.3.379

Gale, F., Hansen, J., & Jewison, M. (2015). *China's Growing Demand for Agricultural Imports*. Washington, DC: U.S. Department of Agriculture, Economic Research Service.

Gao, T. (2017). Food Security and Rural Development on Emerging Markets of Northeast Asia: Cases of Chinese North and Russian Far East. In V. Erokhin (Ed.), *Establishing Food Security and Alternatives to International Trade in Emerging Economies* (pp. 155–176). Hershey, PA: IGI Global.

Ghosh, I., & Ghoshal, I. (2017). Implications of Trade Liberalization for Food Security under the ASEAN-India Strategic Partnership: A Gravity Model Approach. In V. Erokhin (Ed.), *Establishing Food Security and Alternatives to International Trade in Emerging Economies* (pp. 98–118). Hershey, PA: IGI Global.

Gro Intelligence. (2018). *China's Road Map to Food Security*. Retrieved from https://gro-intelligence.com/insights/chinas-roadmap-to-food-security

Hamrin, C. L., & Zhao, S. (1995). *Decision-Making in Deng's China: Perspectives from Insiders*. Armonk, NY: M.E. Sharpe.

Huang, J., & Rozelle, S. (2006). The Emergence of Agricultural Commodity Markets in China. *China Economic Review*, *17*(3), 266–280. doi:10.1016/j.chieco.2006.04.008

Huang, J., Wei, W., Cui, Q., & Xie, W. (2017). The Prospects for China's Food Security and Imports: Will China Starve the World via Imports? *Journal of Integrative Agriculture*, *16*(12), 2933–2944. doi:10.1016/S2095-3119(17)61756-8

Jash, A. (2015). *China's Quest for Food Security: Challenges & Policies*. Retrieved from https://papers.ssrn.com/sol3/papers.cfm?abstract_id=2773903

Lamaj, J. (2015). The Impact of International Trade and Competition Market on Developing Countries. In *Proceedings of the International Conference "Managing Intellectual Capital and Innovation for Sustainable and Inclusive Society*. Bari: Management, Knowledge and Learning; Technology, Innovation and Industrial Management.

Lardy, N. R. (2002). *Integrating China into the World Economy*. Washington, DC: Brookings Institution Press.

Lawrence, G., & McMichael, P. (2012). The Question of Food Security. *International Journal of Sociology of Agriculture and Food*, *2*(19), 135–142.

Lee, J. W. (1995). Capital Goods Import and Long-Run Growth. *The Developing Economies*, *48*(1), 91–110. doi:10.1016/0304-3878(95)00015-1

Levchenko, A., & Zhang, J. (2016). The Evolution of Comparative Advantage: Measurement and Welfare Implications. *Journal of Monetary Economics*, *78*, 96–111. doi:10.1016/j.jmoneco.2016.01.005

Liapis, P. (2011). *Changing Patterns of Trade in Processed Agricultural Products*. Paris: OECD Publishing.

Liberthal, K. (2004). *Governing China: From Revolution Through Reform*. New York, NY: W. W. Norton.

Liu, J., & Diamond, J. (2005). China's Environment in a Globalizing World. *Nature*, *435*(7046), 1179–1186. doi:10.1038/4351179a PMID:15988514

Lu, N. (1997). *The Dynamics of Foreign-Policy Decisionmaking in China*. Boulder, CO: Westview Press.

Maitah, M., Kuzmenko, E., & Smutka, L. (2016). Real Effective Exchange Rate of Rouble and Competitiveness of Russian Agrarian Producers. *Economies*, *4*(3), 12. doi:10.3390/economies4030012

Mariani, B. (2013). *China's Role and Interests in Central Asia*. London: Saferworld.

Nath, R., Luan, Y., Yang, W., Yang, C., Chen, W., Li, Q., & Cui, X. (2015). Changes in Arable Land Demand for Food in India and China: A Potential Threat to Food Security. *Sustainability*, *7*(5), 5371–5397. doi:10.3390u7055371

Omoju, O., & Adesanya, O. (2012). Does Trade Promote Growth in Developing Countries? Empirical Evidence from Nigeria. *International Journal of Development and Sustainability*, *1*(2), 743–753.

Panitchpakdi, S., & Clifford, M. L. (2002). *China and the WTO: Changing China, Changing World Trade*. Singapore: J. Wiley & Sons.

Park, A., Jin, H., Rozelle, S., & Huang, J. (2002). Market Emergence and Transition: Arbitrage, Transaction Costs, and Autarky in China's Grain Markets. *American Journal of Agricultural Economics*, *84*(1), 67–82. doi:10.1111/1467-8276.00243

Perez Motta, E. (2016). *Competition Policy and Trade in the Global Economy: Towards an Integrated Approach*. Geneva: International Center for Trade and Sustainable Development; World Economic Forum.

Spring, J. (2018). Brazil Record Soy Exports to China Could Expand Further – Official. *Reuters*. Retrieved from https://www.reuters.com/article/brazil-agriculture-trade/brazil-record-soy-exports-to-china-could-expand-further-official-idUSL4N1XP5YI

Spring, J., & Polansek, T. (2018). Trump Trade War Delivers Farm Boom in Brazil, Gloom in Iowa. *Reuters*. Retrieved from https://www.reuters.com/article/us-usa-trade-china-brazil-insight/trump-trade-war-delivers-farm-boom-in-brazil-gloom-in-iowa-idUSKCN1ML0E7

Sun, P., & Heshmati, A. (2010). *International Trade and Its Effects on Economic Growth in China*. Bonn: Institute for the Study of Labor.

Taheripour, F., & Tyner, W. E. (2018a). Impacts of Possible Chinese 25% Tariff on U.S. Soybeans and Other Agricultural Commodities. *Choices*, *33*(2).

Taheripour, F., & Tyner, W. E. (2018b). *Impacts of Possible Chinese Protection on US Soybeans*. West Lafayette, IN: Purdue University.

Tan, W. (2018). China's Approach to Reduce Poverty: Taking Targeted Measures to Lift People out of Poverty. *United Nations*. Retrieved from https://www.un.org/development/desa/dspd/wp-content/uploads/sites/22/2018/05/31.pdf

Thow, A. M., & Hawkes, C. (2009). The Implications of Trade Liberalization for Diet and Health: A Case Study from Central America. *Globalization and Health*, *28*(1), 5. doi:10.1186/1744-8603-5-5 PMID:19638196

United Nations Conference on Trade and Development. (2019). *Statistics Database* [Data file]. Retrieved from http://unctad.org/en/Pages/Statistics.aspx

United States Department of Agriculture. (2018). *Top U.S. Agricultural Exports in 2017*. Retrieved from https://www.fas.usda.gov/data/top-us-agricultural-exports-2017

Wagner, J. (2007). Exports and Productivity: A Survey of the Evidence from Firm Level Data. *World Economy*, *30*(1), 60–82. doi:10.1111/j.1467-9701.2007.00872.x

Warr, P. (2011). *Food Security vs. Food Self-Sufficiency: The Indonesian Case*. Canberra, Australia: The Australian National University.

Wu, Y. (2006). *Economic Growth, Transition and Globalization in China*. Cheltenham, UK: Edward Elgar Publishing Limited.

Yanikkaya, H. (2003). Trade Openness and Economic Growth: A Cross-Country Empirical Investigation. *Journal of Development Economics*, *72*(1), 57–89. doi:10.1016/S0304-3878(03)00068-3

Yu, W., Elleby, C., & Zobbe, H. (2015). Food Security Policies in India and China: Implications for National and Global Food Security. *Food Security*, *7*(2), 405–414. doi:10.100712571-015-0432-2

Yu, Y., Feng, K., Hubacek, K., & Sun, L. (2016). Global Implications of China's Future Food Consumption. *Journal of Industrial Ecology*, *20*(3), 593–602. doi:10.1111/jiec.12392

Zhang, H. (2016). Food in Sino-U.S. Relations. From Blessing to Curse? In F. Wu & H. Zhang (Eds.), *China's Global Quest for Resources. Energy, Food and Water* (pp. 100–118). London: Routledge.

Zhang, H., & Chen, G. (2016). China's Food Security Strategy Reform: An Emerging Global Agricultural Policy. In F. Wu & H. Zhang (Eds.), *China's Global Quest for Resources. Energy, Food and Water* (pp. 23–41). London: Routledge.

Zhou, Z. (2010). Achieving Food Security in China: Past Three Decades and Beyond. *China Agricultural Economic Review*, *2*(3), 251–275. doi:10.1108/17561371011078417

Zhu, Y. (2016). International Trade and Food Security: Conceptual Discussion, WTO and the Case of China. *China Agricultural Economic Review*, *8*(3), 399–411. doi:10.1108/CAER-09-2015-0127

ADDITIONAL READING

Anderson, K., Jha, S., Nelgen, S., & Strutt, A. (2013). Re-examining Policies for Food Security in Asia. *Food Security, 5*(2), 195–215. doi:10.100712571-012-0237-5

Beloglazov, G. (2007). Food Security of the People's Republic of China and its Russian Vector. *Russia and Pacific RIM, 3*, 75–83.

Erokhin, V. (2017). Factors Influencing Food Markets in Developing Countries: An Approach to Assess Sustainability of the Food Supply in Russia. *Sustainability, 9*(8), 1313. doi:10.3390u9081313

Erokhin, V. (2018). Contemporary Foreign Trade Policy of China in the Region of Central and Northeast Asia. In A. C. Ozer (Ed.), *Globalization and Trade Integration in Developing Countries* (pp. 27–54). Hershey, PA: IGI Global. doi:10.4018/978-1-5225-4032-8.ch002

Erokhin, V., & Gao, T. (2018). Competitive Advantages of China's Agricultural Exports in the Outward-Looking Belt and Road Initiative. In W. Zhang, I. Alon, & C. Lattemann (Eds.), *China's Belt and Road Initiative: Changing the Rules of Globalization* (pp. 265–285). London: Palgrave Macmillan. doi:10.1007/978-3-319-75435-2_14

Erokhin, V., & Ivolga, A. (2012). How to Ensure Sustainable Development of Agribusiness in the Conditions of Trade Integration: Russian Approach. *International Journal of Sustainable Economies Management, 2*(1), 12–23. doi:10.4018/ijsem.2012040102

Erokhin, V., Ivolga, A., & Heijman, W. (2014). Trade Liberalization and State Support of Agriculture: Effects for Developing Countries. *Agricultural Economics – Czech, 60*(11), 524-537.

Estevadeordal, A., Freund, C., & Ornelas, E. (2008). Does Regionalism Affect Trade Liberalization Toward Nonmembers? *The Quarterly Journal of Economics, 124*(4), 1531–1575. doi:10.1162/qjec.2008.123.4.1531

Ghose, B. (2014). Food Security and Food Self-Sufficiency in China: From Past to 2050. *Food and Energy Security, 3*(2), 86–95. doi:10.1002/fes3.48

Henneberry, S. R., & Diaz, C. C. (2015). Food Security Issues: Concepts and the Role of Emerging Markets. In A. Schmitz, P. L. Kennedy, & T. G. Schmitz (Eds.), *Food Security in an Uncertain World* (pp. 63–79). Bingley, England: Emerald Group Publishing Limited. doi:10.1108/S1574-871520150000015005

Kneller, R., Morgan, C. W., & Kanchanahatakij, S. (2008). Trade Liberalization and Economic Growth. *World Economy*, *31*(6), 701–719. doi:10.1111/j.1467-9701.2008.01101.x

Raynolds, L., Murray, D., & Wilkinson, J. (2007). *Fair Trade: The Challenges of Transforming Globalization*. London: Routledge. doi:10.4324/9780203933534

Schmitz, A., & Meyers, W. H. (Eds.). (2015). *Transition to Agricultural Market Economies. The Future of Kazakhstan, Russia and Ukraine*. Boston, Oxfordshire: CABI. doi:10.1079/9781780645353.0000

Spoor, M., & Robbins, M. J. (Eds.). (2012). *Agriculture, Food Security, and Inclusive Growth*. The Hague: Institute of Social Sciences.

Windfuhr, M., & Jonsen, J. (2005). *Food Sovereignty: Towards Democracy in Localized Food Systems*. Heidelberg, Germany: FIAN ITDG Publishing. doi:10.3362/9781780441160

Wittman, H., Desmarais, A., & Wiebe, N. (2010). *Food Sovereignty: Reconnecting Food, Nature and Community*. Oakland, CA: Food First Books.

Zhou, Z., Liu, H., Cao, L., Tian, W., & Wang, J. (2014). *Food Consumption in China: The Revolution Continues*. Cheltenham, UK: Edward Elgar Publishing. doi:10.4337/9781782549208

KEY TERMS AND DEFINITIONS

Food Security: A condition when people have access to sufficient amounts of safe and nutritious food and are therefore consuming the food required for normal growth and development, and for an active and healthy life.

Food Self-Sufficiency: An extent to which a country can satisfy its food needs from its own domestic production.

Foreign Trade: The system of international commodity-money relations composed of foreign trade activities of all countries worldwide.

Tariff Escalation: A situation where the import duties on components or raw materials are lowest and move progressively higher on semi-finished goods upwards to the finished goods.

Trade Liberalization: A process of reduction or elimination of constraints in the sphere of international trade, including reduction or removal of customs tariffs, import quotas, abolishment of multiple exchange rates, and simplification of administrative requirements to import and export operations.

Trade Protectionism: A set of measures to limit imports or promote exports by putting up barriers to trade that countries use to limit unfair competition from foreign industries.

Trade War: A practice to counterbalance tariff rates in retaliation for the tariff rates of another country in an effort to gain trade advantages.

Chapter 2
Preferential Trade Agreements of the Eurasian Economic Union:
Economic Feasibility and Political Significance

Maria Lagutina
Saint Petersburg State University, Russia

ABSTRACT

One of the trends in the development of modern trade relations is the increase in the number of concluded preferential trade agreements (PTA), which are considered to be a tool for reducing tariffs and, as a consequence, reducing the costs of entering the domestic market of the partner country. Although the Eurasian Economic Union (EAEU) has made only the first steps on the way towards its development. The EAEU has already managed to create a free trade zone with Vietnam, some agreements have been signed with Iran and China. Each of these agreements has its own specifics. The purpose of this chapter is to identify the economic feasibility and political significance of these preferential trade agreements for the countries of the EAEU and their external partners, as well as to determine the potential expansion of the network of preferential trade agreements of the EAEU.

DOI: 10.4018/978-1-5225-9566-3.ch002

INTRODUCTION

The Eurasian Economic Union (EAEU), whose members are Armenia, Belarus, Kazakhstan, Kyrgyzstan and Russia, is an international regional organization that develops economic integration through the free movement of goods, services and people within this Union and has a status of international subject. Having completed of the institutional formation of the EAEU and having reached a certain level of integration between its member-states, the EAEU faced the question of integration into the global trading system. In the context of the crisis of the WTO system, many countries and groups of countries seek to gain the most comfortable conditions for themselves in foreign markets, primarily through the conclusion of various preferential and non-preferential agreements. The EAEU is no exception and today actively develops cooperation with the third countries that is conceptually fits into the Russian initiative of the "Greater Eurasian partnership", which is a current foreign economic strategy of the EAEU.

The purpose of this chapter is to identify the economic feasibility and political significance of the conclusion of the preferential trade agreements of the EAEU for the EAEU member-states and external partners of the EAEU under the preferential agreements.

The analysis is based mainly on analytical materials of Eurasian Economic Commission, Eurasian Economic Union, Eurasian Development Bank and Russian International Affairs Council, etc.

This chapter consists of three parts. The first part is devoted to analyzing of the mechanisms and priorities of international activity of the EAEU. The second part evaluates the current integration agenda of the 'external contour' of the EAEU. Here the author estimates the strong and weak sides of the existing agreements of the EAEU with the third countries (Vietnam, Iran and China). In the third part, the author focuses on the prospects of expanding the network of preferential trade agreements of the EAEU.

BACKGROUND

The general dynamics of the EAEU foreign trade in recent years is positive: according to the Chairman of the EAEC Board T. Sargsyan, "the foreign trade turnover of the EAEU member-states with the third countries in 2017 amounted to $ 633.8 billion, or 124.4% compared to the level of 2016. At the same time, the volume of exports from the EEU to the third countries increased by 25.4% compared to 2016, amounting to $ 386.6 billion in 2017. The volume of imports to the EAEU from the third countries increased by 22.9% in 2017 compared to 2016, reaching $ 247.2 billion." (Interview of the Chairman of the EAEC Board T. Sargsyan to The Economic Times, 2018). At this stage, the main trading partners of the EAEU are the EU and APEC countries. The main buyer of goods exported by the EAEU member-states is the European Union (53.9% of total exports), while import purchases come mostly from the APEC countries (43.7% of total imports of goods), with China occupying the first place. (Ob itogakh vneshney torgovli tovarami Evraziyskogo ekonomicheskogo soyuza, 2018). The presented figures show that the foreign trade policy of the EAEU has a multi-vector character at this stage.

The first experience of creating a free trade zone between the EAEU and Vietnam in 2015 is pretty positive. In addition, an Interim Agreement with Iran and an Agreement on cooperation between the EAEU and China were signed in 2018. About 50 countries from different regions expressed their desire to conclude trade agreements with the EAEU. However, if in some cases it is a question of signing a preferential trade agreement, in others, as, for example, in the case of China: "it is non-preferential, it is not an agreement on a free trade zone, that is, it does not concern the reduction of customs duties, but it is a trade and economic agreement that creates a legal framework for an alliance with China." (Ministr torgovli EAES Verinika Nikishina, 2018). In this regard, it is important to understand the reasons for the choice of different forms of international cooperation of the EAEU with different groups of the third countries.

In the case of the preferential agreements, countries offer more favorable conditions to each other than they do to the third countries. In a sense, this is a departure from the most-favored-nation principle, which is sanctioned by the GATT/WTO under the so-called temporary agreements leading to the formation of a Customs Union. Preferential agreements that provide for the maintenance of the national customs tariffs of each of the signatory countries should not even be considered as an initial stage, but as a preparatory stage of the integration process. No inter-state bodies are set up in the case of the preferential agreements. Preferential rules of origin are described in the free trade agreements which form certain conditions to control the possible deviations of trade flows and prevent the possibility of contact with products from countries that do not fall under preferences and transported through the territory of countries-partners in the free trade zone at lower rates. The non-preferential rules, however, are used primarily to determine the goods to which the MFNP (Most-Favored-Nation Principle) should apply (all WTO members) and subsequently to separate domestic goods from imported goods to which other trade policy instruments (anti-dumping measures, quantitative restrictions, quotas, etc.) may apply.

MAIN FOCUS OF THE CHAPTER

Issues, Controversies, Problems

Today the EAEU has already managed to create a free trade zone with Vietnam; some agreements have been signed with Iran and China. Each of these agreements has its own specifics. In this chapter the factors that determine the interest in the conclusion of such agreements with the EAEU as well as the factors that constrain the EAEU countries from concluding such agreements with individual partners are identified. It also deals the reasons for limiting the depth of such preferential agreements in different cases. Thus, in one case we are talking about the creation of an FTA with individual external partners, and in the other – only a framework agreement. It is important to identify the economic factors and political motives of the choice of different forms of agreements for different countries.

INTERNATIONAL ACTIVITY OF THE EAEU: STRATEGY, MECHANISMS AND PRIORITIES

After the entry into force of the EAEU Treaty on January 1, 2015, the EAEU received the status of international subject, which in practice means the right to carry out international cooperation and the ability to conclude international treaties with states, international organizations and international integration associations in coordination with member states (Podgotovka predlozheniy po razvitiyu mezhdunarodnogo sotrudnichestva s tret'imi stranami). At this stage, one of the most active activities of the EAEU is the development of the "external contour" of integration and external trade relations of the Union, which is conceptually reflected in the concept of "Greater Eurasian partnership" proposed by Russia in 2016. According to the President Putin's speech during the Saint Petersburg International Economic Forum in 2016, the project of "Greater Eurasian partnership" envisages (Vistuplenie Vladimira Putina na PMEF-2016):

- The exit of Eurasian integration forms the borders of the Post-Soviet Eurasian Space, which envisages the EAEU cooperation with other states and integration unions (first of all CIS partners, but also partners outside Post-Soviet space, among them China, India, Pakistan, Iran;
- The EAEU is perceived as one of the centers of broader integration, which will allow to solve technological problems, motivate and involve new participants in the process of technological development;

- The creation of a network of bilateral and multilateral trade agreements with different depth, speed and level of interaction, market openness, depending on the readiness of a national economy to such joint work (the possibility of creating free trade zones of the EAEU-SCO, EAEU-ASEAN, FTA with the third countries);
- The multi-vector feature of the project: it is open not only for Eastern, but also for Western partners, including the EU.
- "Eurasian partnership" is a foreign economic concept of the Union aimed at the formation of a complex, multi-level system of multilateral cooperation with the participation of the EAEU, ASEAN, APEC and SCO countries. The negotiating agenda for the formation of Partnership may include both traditional issues affecting trade and investment, and the development of markets for the next technological generations.
- The procedure for the implementation of the EAEU international cooperation is determined by the Treaty on the Eurasian Economic Union, according to which the Union "has the right to carry out international cooperation with states, international organizations and international integration associations and independently or jointly with member-states to conclude international treaties with them on issues within its competence." (Dogovor o Evraziyskom ekonomicheskom soyuze, 2014). The Supreme Eurasian Economic Council, the Eurasian Intergovernmental Council, the Eurasian Economic Commission and the Court of Justice of the Union carry out the planning and procedure of the EAEU international activities.
- Since 2015, the Supreme Eurasian Economic Council annually approves the document entitled "On the main directions of the international activities of the EAEU". Three key activities are planned for 2019: (O proekte resheniya Vysshego Evraziyskogo ekonomicheskogo soveta).
- Development of already established cooperation mechanisms within the framework of memorandums of cooperation, negotiations on preferential and non-preferential trade agreements;
- Interaction with interested parties in cooperation with the EAEU to create legal and institutional instruments of cooperation;
- Promotion of reliable and relevant information on the Eurasian economic integration and formation of a positive view of the Union as an effective and competitive international organization of regional economic integration.

As far as the country and regional priorities are concerned, the countries of the Commonwealth of Independent States (CIS), the European Union (EU), China, the countries with which the Memorandum of cooperation is concluded or is being negotiated will remain partners in 2019 – Singapore, Cambodia, Thailand, Cuba, Chile, Peru, Jordan, Morocco, the Faroe Islands, Moldova, the countries with which the free trade zone is concluded or is being negotiated-Vietnam, Singapore, Israel, Egypt, India, Serbia, as well as international organizations and regional economic associations – The United Nations (UN) and its regional economic commissions, the Organization for Security and Cooperation in Europe (OSCE), the Shanghai Cooperation Organization (SCO), the forum "Asia-Pacific Economic Cooperation" (APEC) and the Association of South-East Asian Nations (ASEAN), the Andean community, MERCOSUR, etc.

Despite the general rules and principles for the implementation of international activities of the EAEU, the EAEU member-states have different approaches to the formats and speed with which the Union should build its international relations. (Devyatkov, 2017). According to the Russian expert E. Alekseenkova, this is due to "the tasks of internal economic development and solving urgent problems that vary from country to country." (Alekseenkova, 2018). First and foremost, member-countries of the EAEU in different degree ready to take on the agreed commitments on trade in services and investment (for example, such obligations in the framework of the FTA with Vietnam took only Russia). In addition, there are differences in geographical priorities between the member-states: in particular, partnership with China and the European Union is a priority for Kazakhstan; for Armenia—with Iran and the European Union; Belarus is interested in the development of trade relations with the EU and other countries, including the countries of the "far arc" (Asia and Oceania, Africa and the Middle East, Latin America), while Kyrgyzstan does not show much interest in the development of the "external" integration contour.

THE CURRENT INTEGRATION AGENDA OF THE "EXTERNAL CONTOUR" OF THE EAEU

Today, the EAEU has three main mechanisms for building relationships with external partners:

1. free trade area agreement (FTA): for example, Free Trade Area Agreement with Vietnam; Interim Agreement leading to the formation of a Free Trade Area with Iran;

2. non-preferential trade agreements: Agreement on trade and economic cooperation with China;
3. memorandum of cooperation with the third countries and international organizations: the EAEU has signed more than 25 Memorandums of cooperation and interaction with international organizations (CIS, UN Economic Commission for Europe, UNCTAD, etc.) and the governments of the third states, including Mongolia, Chile, Peru, Singapore and Cambodia, etc.

The FTA Agreement between the EAEU member-states and Vietnam was signed in 2015 and became the first international treaty of the EAEU FTA with a third country, which actually legitimized the status of international subject of the EAEU in the eyes of the world community. Moreover, the FTA with Vietnam is currently the only institutionalized element of the "Greater Eurasian partnership."

According to the Russian expert N. Fedorov the choice of Vietnam can be explained by "the special character of Russian-Vietnamese relations and foreign strategy of Vietnam" since the USSR times, as well as the fact that in 2012 "the level of Russian-Vietnamese relations was raised to the level of 'comprehensive strategic partnership'" (Fedorov, 2016). It is also important that Vietnam has a rich experience of participating in such trade agreements, which can be useful for the EAEU countries that are just entering this path. At the same time, as the Russian expert A. Tsvetov notes, "the absence of competition of imported goods with analogues produced in the EAEU countries and Vietnam, as well as small volumes of bilateral trade allowed to sign an agreement that would have almost no negative consequences for the producers of the EAEU and in this sense would be safe." (Tsvetov, 2017). Indeed, the share of Vietnam in the total Russian trade turnover in 2013 was 0.43%; Russia's share in Vietnamese exports was 1.44%, in Vietnamese imports — 0.65% (in 2012 — 0.73%) (Orlov, 2014). As for the other members of the EAEU, for example, trade of the Republic of Armenia and the Kyrgyz Republic with Vietnam began to develop only after the signing of the Agreement from scratch. However, after New Zealand's refusal to negotiate a free trade zone with the EAEU in connection with the Ukrainian crisis of 2014, Vietnam has become the only country that provides access to the EAEU markets in the Asia-Pacific region.

It is no secret that Russia has been the most interested party in the conclusion of this Agreement, for which, despite the economic nature of the agreement, its signing was largely due to political motives. In particular, Russia's intentions to establish relations between the EAEU and the Asia-Pacific countries within the so-called "Turn to the East". In its turn, for Vietnam the incentive for the intensification of the dialogue on inclusion in the Eurasian integration processes was, on the one hand, "the slow progress in the negotiations on the establishment of the Trans-Pacific partnership (TPP)" (Fedorov, 2018, p. 79) by which Vietnam made it clear that there are alternatives to the American – centric system of economic integration, and, on the other hand, the desire to diversify its trade relations against the background of the dominance of the Chinese economy in the region. For this reason, experts often assess the EAEU FTA with Vietnam more as a political step than an economic one. But at the same time, undoubtedly, Vietnam is interested in obtaining preferential access to a new wide Eurasian market.

The text of the FTA Agreement between the EAEU and Vietnam deals primarily with the mutual abolition of trade duties and the establishment of a free trade regime. The Agreement regulates tariffs for various imported goods (textile and light industry, computer equipment, products), approves the system of exchange of customs office information and rules of trade in the market of services and investments. The Agreement provides not only for trade in goods but also services, mutual investment, movement of labor, exchange of technology and information. Initially, it was assumed that the relations of participants in these forms will be codified. (ZST EAES-Vietnam – chert kroetsya v melochakh, 2015). However, the signed document only coordinates trade in goods.

After the signing of the Agreement, the priority practical task was the need to increase the level of trade between the EAEU member-states and the Republic of Vietnam. (Lapenko, 2017, 213). In general, at this stage, the results of the Agreement are estimated positively: according to Vietnamese statistics, in 2016 the trade turnover between the EAEU and Vietnam increased by 23% compared to the previous year and amounted to about $ 3 billion. In 2017, this figure reached $ 4 billion, with Russia accounted for more than 90% of the trade turnover of the EAEU countries and Vietnam. (Soglashenie o zone svobodnoy torgovli mezhdu EAES i Vyetnamom, 2018). According to the EAEC, in 2018 the trade turnover increased by 36%: from $ 4.3 billion in 2016 to $ 5.9 billion in 2017. Both imports from Vietnam to the EAEU grew by 34.7% and exports to Vietnam by 39.5%. ("Liberalizatsiya torgovogo rezhima mezhdu EAES i Vietnamom pozvolila…," 2018).

However, it should be noted a number of constraints on the potential of free trade between the EAEU and Vietnam:

- Firstly, the Agreement on the free trade zone between the EAEU and Vietnam contains a number of restrictions: for example, the document establishes annual import limits for Vietnamese goods, within which imports to the EAEU are duty-free; if these volumes are exceeded, the EAEU has the right to apply import customs duties at the level of the single customs tariff rate by the EAEC Board (in practice, from March to December 2018, the EAEC applied a duty on some types of underwear from Vietnam); (Pototsky, 2018) in its turn, Vietnam until recently has been the key importer of Russian chrysotile, which occupies an important place in the structure of exports of Russian goods to Vietnam; however, the roadmap currently being developed by the Ministry of Construction of Vietnam to stop the use of chrysotile asbestos in the country by 2023 has already led to a significant reduction of exports of chrysotile from the EAEU (Pototsky, 2018)

- Secondly, the labor migration from Vietnam to the EAEU countries is limited to Russia, and as a potential labor market Russia is unlikely to replace Japan, Australia or the United States for Vietnam
- Thirdly, the lack of information: Vietnam lacks comprehensive research on Russia; Vietnamese businessmen suffer from a lack of information about the EAEU market. (Nemtsev, 2017)

The second country that signed an Agreement on the establishment of a free trade zone (FTA) with the EAEU is Iran. In May 2018, the parties signed an Agreement on the establishment of the FTA at the Astana Economic Forum. However, for a while the document is going to remain temporary and does not apply to all products. It is planned that in 3 years' time the parties will have resolved all disputes and then conclude a long-term agreement.

According to the text of the Interim Agreement, grain, certain types of meat, confectionery, pharmaceutical and metallurgical products will receive preferential access to the Iranian market. On the part of the EEU, preferences will be provided to certain types of Iranian vegetables and fruits, nuts, finished food products, as well as oil products, construction materials, textile products. The Agreement emphasizes the idea of establishing a business dialogue.

According to experts, the Iranian market is "interested in anything", and therefore the creation of the FTA gives "exceptional opportunities" for the business of the EEU countries (Bovdunov, 2018). However, in Iran there is a legal restriction on the minimum customs tariff - 4% and the Iranian partners immediately made it clear that they are not ready to discuss the full zeroing of the tariff within the framework of negotiations on the Interim Agreement, since this is a very sensitive issue.

As for as the interests of the EAEU are concerned, political reasons in addition to economic reasons are clearly seen. In particular, according to the Chairman of the EAEC Board T. Sargsyan: "This is an important document for us, because, on the one hand, we see that the US position towards Iran has changed, which is a challenge for many companies. On the other hand, the European Union is developing a new mechanism for working with Iran, so that the new measures applied by the United States would not affect European companies that work in Iran." ("EAES i Iran v 2019 godu…," 2018). It was probably the sanctions factor that favored the temporary nature of the Agreement. At the same time, it becomes important for both sides to diversify foreign trade relations in the context of the tense geopolitical situation in the region and the world.

The cooperation of the EAEU with Iran has geopolitical importance for countries of the EAEU:

- Firstly, through cooperation with Iran, the EAEU will gain access to the markets of the Middle East and to the most important transit routes, which directly contributes to the goals and objectives of the "Greater Eurasian partnership"
- Secondly, the free trade area with Iran will entail the accession of Pakistan and India, which is also actively negotiating the creation of the FTA, quite naturally, due to the realities of economic development
- Thirdly, Iran's cooperation with the EAEU will increase the attractiveness of the EAEU for the rest of Central Asia, as they will open up new economic and new transit opportunities
- Fourthly, after the establishment of such a free trade area the domestic Eurasian market may become more stable in relation to the expansion of Turkish and Chinese goods, which will have real competition

It is also important to note that Armenia, which has a common border with Iran, is showing a great interest in the FTA with Iran. Thus, Armenia gets great opportunities for the transit of Iranian goods across its borders to the markets of the other members of the EAEU, with the development of tourism and the creation of joint ventures are also looking very promising.

As for the existing challenges to cooperation between the EAEU and Iran, the following points can be noted:

- The sanctions can create difficulties during the establishment of a business dialogue
- The difference in Iran's relations with the EAEU member-states, which complicates cooperation within the EAEU
- The competition of the Chinese business structures, which are quite active both in the Iranian market and in the markets of the EAEU countries
- The lack of information of the parties about the national peculiarities of doing business, as well as the language barrier

The Agreement on trade and economic cooperation between the EAEU and the People's Republic of China was also signed at the Astana Economic Forum on May 17, 2018.

This step was one of the stages of conjugation of the EAEU and the Chinese Silk Road Economic Belt (SREB), which the parties agreed on in 2015. In the summer of 2016, a Joint Statement was signed on the transition to the negotiation phase of creating the Agreement on trade and economic cooperation between the EAEU and China. Negotiations with China lasted two years and were very difficult. According to a Russian expert Yevgeny Vinokourov: "there are two fundamental difficulties. First, the EAEU countries are not yet ready for the full-scale opening of their markets for Chinese imports. Too many industries, especially consumer goods, would fall victim to such a decision. Secondly, the interests of the EAEU countries in terms of cooperation with China are quite different." (Vinokurov, 2018). For this reason, the EAEU countries are objectively not ready for creating a free trade area with China, and the Agreement signed in 2018 between the EAEU and China is non-preferential and does not automatically reduce trade barriers.

The Agreement on trade and economic cooperation between the EAEU and China makes it possible to reduce barriers on entering into the Chinese market for the interested businesses of the EAEU countries and increases the transparency of regulating. It means reducing the level of non-tariff barriers, improving customs administration and simplifying trade procedures between China and the EAEU. In addition, Eurasian businesses will be able to resolve disputes with the Chinese side through the Eurasian Economic Commission. The Agreement is aimed at the formation of a legal framework between the EAEU and China on issues within the competence of the Union. The text of the Agreement sets out the legal framework for the further development of cooperation in such areas as trade protection measures, sanitary and phytosanitary measures, technical barriers to trade, customs office cooperation, e-commerce, intellectual property, sectoral cooperation, public procurement, competition. Its content forms trade rules based on WTO rules.

As already noted, China is the second key foreign economic partner of the EAEU (13.6% of the total turnover ("Analiz perspektivnikh napravleniy razvitiya evraziyskoy integratsii…," 2018, p. 24) after the EU countries. However, according to the Russian expert M. Shibutov, "in reality, there are no special relations between the EAEU with China, and no conjugation of the development or any other real, not 'lip service' cooperation is expected, and there is no economic basis for this." (Shibutov, 2018). At this stage, the EAEU has very small economic value and therefore most of the agreements with such economic giant as China are rather declarative. Thus, "in Kazakhstan, trade with China, as well as its investments in the Kazakh economy, falls every year, in Kyrgyzstan, China's investments are in fact quite small, China's economic cooperation with Belarus is tiny, Russia and China do not want and are not ready for long-term economic relations, so they do not invest in each other." (Shibutov, 2018). For the Chinese side, the signing of the agreements and treaties is more formal and often there are no practical steps behind these agreements.

In addition, the development of cooperation between the EAEU countries and China is seen as a political motivation, primarily coming from Russia. It should be recalled that until 2014, the Chinese initiative of the SREB was considered to be more competitive with the EAEU project. Some fears were expressed about the fact that Russia in case of realization of the Chinese plans could lose its position in Central Asia, and eventually in the post-Soviet space. Indeed, as China had taking on a substantial share of resources and financial costs for the infrastructure of the SREB, should be entitled to rely on controlling and distributing profits. For its part, the Chinese leadership initially tried to reassure its Russian partners about its new Eurasian strategy and launched an active campaign to explain its goals and mechanisms for the implementation of the "One Belt, One Road" initiative. Geopolitical changes in Eurasia also contributed to the convergence of the two countries ' positions: as it has already noted, as a result of the crisis of 2014, Russia's foreign policy was redirected towards Asia – "Russia's turn to the East", in connection with which interaction with China intensified; on the other hand, the US policy in the Asia - Pacific region prevented Russia and China from entering a new project of the Trans-Pacific partnership and actually pushed China and Russia to economic cooperation. As a result, in 2015, Russia and China officially agreed on the conjugation of the EAEU and the SBER and started negotiations on the mechanisms of this conjugation. However, the economic indicators reflect a somewhat different picture: the trade volume between China and the member states of the EAEU stood at $12 billion in 2017, while, as with the United States – more than $ 275 billion, the Netherlands – $ 55 billion, India – $ 51 billion, etc. (China exports, imports and trade balance By Country 2017).

There are other difficulties in the development of trade relations between the EAEU and China:

- Before the signing of the Agreement, a number of imbalances remained in the relations between China and the EAEU countries, the main of which is the dominance of the growth of trade cooperation in comparison with the investment cooperation; (Kitay – EAES, 2017) the beginning of negotiations on the Agreement was initiated to overcome this imbalance and increase investment cooperation between China and the EAEU
- The 2018 Agreement has a formal nature, which may limit the potential for closer trade and economic cooperation between the parties
- There are fears that in the conditions of Western sanctions being in force, the unilateral cooperation of the EAEU with China could potentially lead to an imbalance in the form of excessive economic dependence of the EAEU member states on China

PROSPECTS FOR THE DEVELOPMENT OF THE EAEU TRADE POLICY IN THE CONTEXT OF THE "GREATER EURASIAN PARTNERSHIP"

Today the prospects for the development of foreign trade relations of the EAEU countries are associated with the implementation of the "Greater Eurasian partnership" or "Greater Eurasia" initiative, which can give the opportunity to reduce trade and economic and, perhaps, political tension between the Russia, as a key member of the EAEU, and the EU, as well as to strengthen ties with the APR countries. The formation of "Greater Eurasia", as it was noted above, means the creation of a continental economic partnership from South-East Asia to Europe, based on a network of bilateral and multilateral trade agreements with different depth, speed and level of interaction - both in the format of free trade areas of the EAEU with the third countries, and in the format of inter-regional, inter-block trade and economic partnerships (for example, the EAEU-ASEAN, the EAEU-MERCOSUR, etc.).

According to the Russian expert A. Devyatkov (Devyatkov, 2017) the states with which the EAEU is negotiating the creation of the FTA can be divided into several groups:

1. Egypt and Serbia are the countries with which the EAEU maintains good political relations and has complementary trade flows, but there is a possibility to increase trade turnover and protect the most sensitive sectors at the same time
2. India is a great interest to Russian exporters, especially in terms of non-oil and high-tech exports, but the Indian market is well protected by various tariff and non-tariff barriers (for example, India applies a large number of different restrictive measures to products from the EAEU countries)
3. Singapore, Israel, and South Korea are the countries with which the EAEU would be interested in interacting in terms of investment cooperation and trade in services, but the main difficulty in the negotiations with these countries is to find the optimal balance between the benefits of all parties

It is obvious that the country preferences for the development of external relations of the EAEU are mainly oriented to the East at this stage. The only exception is Serbia, with which the FTA will open the Balkan market for the EAEU countries, and can also contribute to "establishing a dialogue with Europe". (Maksakova, 2018, 41).

Indeed, the “Greater Eurasia” project involves establishing close ties with the EU countries. The first proposals on the EAEU-EU conjugation were sent to the Chairman of the European Commission Jean-Claude Junker in 2015 and the European Commission was instructed to work out proposals on potential areas of cooperation with the EAEU (Umakhanov, 2018). Indeed, despite the crisis in modern Russian-European relations, there is an objective foundation for the mutual interest of the EU and the EAEU in integration cooperation: “the foundation for mutual interest is objectively there: it is based on territorial proximity, significant trade flows, the potential of investment relations, economic security issues, the interest of the EAEU countries in the transfer of European technologies, unresolved issues of development of cross-border infrastructure, the presence of common neighboring states.” (Vinokurov, 2014). The establishment of contacts between the two integration associations – the EU and the EAEU objectively corresponds to the economic and political interests of the member states and business communities of both Unions.

However, there is no understanding and clear vision of the conditions and mechanisms of possible economic cooperation between the EAEU and the EU in the political community, although there are active discussions on this topic at the expert level. For example, according to the experts of the Centre for Integration Studies of Eurasian Development Bank (EDB) and International Institute for Applied Systems Analysis (IIASA) in the middle of the 2020-s between the EU and the EAEU may be signed a Comprehensive Integration Agreement. (Evropeyskiy soyuz i Evraziyskiy ekonomicheskiy soyuz, 2016). As a motivation for the signing of such an Agreement, the experts identified the desire of the countries of both Unions to obtain economic benefits in the implementation of the Agreement on the establishment of a free trade area between the two blocks and the growing political and economic demand for the withdrawal of Russian-European relations from the sanctions logic. Paradoxically, in spite of the crisis in the Russian-European relations the EU remains the key trading partner of Russia and the EAEU countries as a whole.

However, we believe that serious obstacles remain on the way to elaborate concrete action plan or “road map” to conjugate two Unions, among them:

- Stagnation of the Minsk Agreement implementation, and the remaining tensions in the EU-Russia relations over the Ukraine
- The negotiations on possible EAEU – EU cooperation are conducted within the framework of Russia – EU dialogue, due to which relations between two Unions are defined by the crisis in Russian – European relations
- The absence of EU common approach on the issue of relations with Russia, the biggest economy of EAEU, and sharp disagreements between different EU member states over that issue

- The skepticism regarding the EAEU as an immature structure without clear perspectives (negative image of the EAEU and often absence of information on its activities), and therefore perception of EAEU as a non-equal partner for such a powerful union as EU, and as a result, unpreparedness of the EU to accept EAEU as an equal partner

Thus, in short-term perspective (up to 5 years) the situation will remain unclear, but the establishment of direct inter-regional connections between EU and EAEU within mentioned time frame is less likely. For in the coming 5 years the EAEU will deal with fostering integration connections within the Union, and development of external relations with the third states outside of Eurasian space (in the format of free trade areas or joint declarations of cooperation), while the EU will seek to solve its internal problems, such as implications of Brexit and migration crisis, and most probably, will strive to develop ties with states in the post – Soviet space.

As for as the interaction between the EAEU and ASEAN is concerned, in 2016 at the Russia – ASEAN Summit in Sochi (Russia), the heads of states agreed to create a joint research group for the implementation of the initiative to create an FTA between the EAEU and ASEAN. A Memorandum of Understanding between the EAEC and ASEAN was signed in Singapore in 2018. According to T. Sargsyan, "the conclusion of the Memorandum will contribute to the comprehensive expansion of trade, economic and investment cooperation between the EAEU member states and ASEAN member states." (EAES i ASEAN uglublyaut torgovo-ekonomicheskoe i investitsionnoe sotrudnichestvo, 2018). As a result, the parties will cooperate in such areas as customs office regulation and trade facilitation, sanitary and phytosanitary measures, technical regulation, e-commerce, trade in services and investment, as well as business development. However, while the trade relations of the EAEU with ASEAN countries are insignificant: ASEAN in 2017 accounted for less than 1.3% of exports and about 1.8% of imports of the EAEU countries. (Kheyfets, 2018, p. 108).

It is expected that the dialogue with ASEAN will lead to the project of a large inter-bloc free trade agreement, but step-by-step. Today in practice this idea is implemented yet through the FTA with Vietnam, the Memorandum of Cooperation between the EAEU and Thailand and the forthcoming Agreement on the establishment of the FTA with Singapore.

Russian experts are very ambiguous about the prospects of cooperation between the EAEU and ASEAN. So, A. Tsvetov believes that ASEAN is important for Russia as "a beautiful and appropriate addition to the reviving Asian policy of Russia." (Tsvetov, 2017). In other words, the expert notes to a greater extent the geopolitical motivation of the interaction between the EAEU and ASEAN countries. In his turn,

Ya. Lisovolik believes that "the EAEU-ASEAN partnership can be considered as a project of a hybrid continental-oceanic coalition, in which the basis of integration is formed not only by trade and investment effects, but also transport and logistics complementarity." (Lisovolik, 2017, p. 51). In this context, the expert offers a very interesting idea of a possible format for cooperation between the EAEU and ASEAN - through the Chinese BRICS+ initiative. Taking into account the fact that each BRICS member is also the leading economy in the sub-region that actively developing regional integration: Russia in the Eurasian Economic Union (EAEU), Brazil in Southern Common Market (MERCOSUR), South Africa in South African Development Community (SADC), India in South Asian Association for Regional Cooperation (SAARC) and China in Shanghai Cooperation Organization (SCO), within the framework of the China-ASEAN free trade agreement and, as well as in the perspective Regional Comprehensive Economic Partnership (RCEP). All BRICS countries in these regional integration structures can form the so-called 'internal regional partner circle of BRICS countries' (Lisovolik, 2017) that will be opened to numerous and flexible formats of cooperation on a bilateral or multilateral basis and not only through trade liberalization ('hybrid form of interregional ties').

Thus, it seems that the prospect of creating the EAEU-ASEAN FTA is quite real and the preparation of the Agreement is already underway in different directions: both bilaterally and multilaterally.

Finally, on November 25, 2014 the delegations of the Eurasian Economic Commission and the leading integration association of the states of South America – MERCOSUR held consultations on the draft of Memorandum on the cooperation in trade and economic issues. The key interest for the Latin America countries is the development of trade ties with new blocks that could to lead MERCOSUR to the global trade arena. In August 2015 MERCOSUR and the Customs Union of the EAEU signed a Memorandum of Understanding. However, the development of negotiations stopped in 2016 due to the political crisis in the countries of South America and the suspension of the membership of Venezuela in MERCOSUR. Finally, in April 2017 MERCOSUR agreed to expedite the signing of a treaty, which will include the possibility of negotiations on a comprehensive trade agreement. As an Argentinean expert Ariel S. Gonzalez Levaggi notes: "The process will not be easy, but it can become a platform for redirection of global trade flows from North to South". (Mamedov, 2017). In 2016, the officials of Argentina announced their ambition to become "the driving force in the promotion of relations between the EAEU and MERCOSUR" (Botta, 2017). Finally in 2018 Memorandum on the cooperation between the EAEU and MERCOSUR was signed. It is the framework for future relations, on the basis of which the areas of cooperation and the future dialogue will be determined.

Among the areas of cooperation along with the trade the development of technology has to prevail (for example, research in the field of agricultural technology or academic exchange, including study of languages). Cooperation between the EAEU and MERCOSUR has a great potential and can provide the creation of the new center of international integration: "the two Unions have territories in the 33 million square kilometers, a population of 450 million people and a combined GDP exceeds $ 8.5 billion (11.6% of world GDP in nominal terms)" (Rodríguez, 2015).

Meanwhile, there are a number of difficulties:

- The narrow range of trade between two regions
- The narrow range of Eurasian business circles which are involved in the Latin American region, (EAES i MERKOSUR nachinaut sotrudnichestvo v ekonomike, 2014)
- The lack of information about the EAEU and its activity in the Latin American countries, etc.

SOLUTIONS AND RECOMMENDATIONS

Today the main task of the EAEU is the creation of a network of bilateral and multilateral trade agreements with different depth, speed and level of interaction in the framework of "Greater Eurasian partnership". In this regards the following recommendations could be presented:

- To agree on countries' positions, approaches and views on the future development of integration
- To align the level of trade between the EAEU member-states and the third countries with which the EAEU has an agreement
- To involve Eurasian business companies in the development of international ties between the EAEU and the third countries
- To develop a specific action plan or "road map" for the practical implementation of the "Greater Eurasian partnership" initiative (with time constraints, terms, concrete mechanisms and instruments, etc.)
- To use the tools of public diplomacy in order to create a positive image of the EAEU and promote and explain its integration plans, both within the EAEU member states and among the prospective partners

FUTURE RESEARCH DIRECTIONS

Taking into account the latter trends in the development of the international cooperation of the EAEU with the third countries and international blocs, it is interesting to research the experience of conclusion the trade agreements between these countries (Vietnam, China, Iran, South Korea, etc.) and blocs (ASEAN and MERCOSUR) with other their partners (besides the EAEU), to compare them with the agreements with the EAEU and to determine their difference from the agreement with the EAEU.

CONCLUSION

Today, the EAEU is engaged in approving its status of an international subject and determining its place in the world trade system. The result of its quite active international activities is that the EAEU is clearly increasing its international prestige by intensifying its international relations, especially negotiations on the establishment of free trade areas with the third countries. Nevertheless, it is hard to say that the potential in this area has already been realized. The existing Agreements with Vietnam, Iran and China are the first steps to the EAEU integration into the system of world trade. In this chapter it was showed that at this stage, the development of the network of FTA with the third countries has not so much economic as political reasons in the case of the EAEU. At this stage, the EAEU has pretty small economic value and therefore most of the current agreements with the third countries are rather declarative and have more political significance. Therefore, it is essential that the ongoing negotiations on the establishment of FTAs would bring the benefits not only political and image, but practical and purely economic.

Today the prospects for the development of foreign trade relations of the EAEU countries are associated with the implementation of the 'Greater Eurasian partnership,' but the EAEU member-states have different approaches to the formats and speed with which the Union should build its international relations. Nevertheless, the expansion of opportunities for increasing the volume of foreign trade with the third countries and integration associations is one of the stable common expectations for all member-states of the EAEU, in which there is a request for coordination of foreign policy and foreign economic decisions. In addition, there is an expectation of expanding the list of countries and blocs with which preferential and non-preferential trade agreements will be concluded in the future. It is important to note that the current foreign trade policy of the EAEU has a multi-vector character at this stage.

It is obvious that today the country preferences for the development of external relations of the EAEU are mainly oriented to the East (Egypt, Singapore and India), but the 'Greater Eurasian partnership' project means establishing close ties with the EU countries. However, in short-term perspective (up to 5 years) the establishment of direct inter-regional connections between EU and EAEU is less likely. While it seems that the prospect of creating the EAEU-ASEAN FTA is quite real and the preparation of the Agreement is already underway in different directions: both bilaterally and multilaterally. As far as the prospects of the EAEU-MERCOSUR are concerned, the difficult current political situation, political changes and changes in political priorities in some MERCOSUR countries hinder the process of negotiations between two blocs as well.

REFERENCES

Alekseenkova, E. (2017). EAES k 2025 godu: prioriteti I ozhidaniya gosudarstv-chlenov [The EAEU by 2025: priorities and expectations of member-states]. In *Prospects of the development of the EAEU project by 2025* (pp. 6-37). Russian International Affairs Council.

Analiz perspektivnikh napravleniy razvitiya evraziyskoy integratsii s uchetom strategicheskikh zadach sotsial'no-ekonomicheskogo razvitiya Rossiyskoy federatsii I zadach rossiyskogo predsedatel'stva v EAES v 2018 godu. [The analysis of the perspective directions of development of the Eurasian integration with the strategic objectives of socio-economic development of the Russian Federation and objectives of the Russian chairmanship in the Eurasian Economic Union in 2018]. (2018). *Eurasian panorama, 3*, 24.

Botta, P. (2017, May 24). *Evraziyskiy soyuz pozvolit Yujnoy Amerike snizit zavisimost ot SSHA – argentinskiy expert [The Eurasian Union will allow South America to reduce its dependence on the US – an Argentine expert].* Eurasia Expert. Retrieved from http://eurasia.expert/evraziyskiy-soyuz-pozvolit-yuzhnoy-amerike-snizit-zavisimost-ot-ssha

Bovdunov, A. (2018, May 17). "Nashi tovari v Irane zhdut": chto dast stranam EAES zona svobodnoy torgovli s Tegeranom ["Our goods are waiting for in Iran": what will the EAEU countries get from the free trade area with Tehran]. *Russia Today*. Retrieved from https://russian.rt.com/world/article/514307-ira-eaes-zona-svobodnoy-torgovli

China exports, imports and trade balance By Country 2017 (2017). World Integrated Trade Solution. Retrieved from https://wits.worldbank.org/CountryProfile/en/Country/CHN/Year/LTST/TradeFlow/EXPIMP/Partner/by-country

Devyatkov, A. (2017). *Mezhdunarodnie svyazi EAES k 2025 godu [International ties of the EAEY by 2025].* Russian International Affairs Council. June 27. Retrieved from http://russiancouncil.ru/analytics-and-comments/analytics/mezhdunarodnye-svyazi-eaes-k-2025-g/

Dogovor o Evraziyskom ekonomicheskom soyuze [The Treaty on the Eurasian Economic Union]. (2014, May 29). Signed in Astana on May 29. Retrieved from http://www.eaeunion.org/files/history/2014/2014_2.pdf

EAES i ASEAN uglublyaut torgovo-ekonomicheskoe i investitsionnoe sotrudnichestvo [The EAEU and ASEAN deepen their trade-economic and investment cooperation]. (2018, November 14). Eurasian Economic Commission. Retrieved from http://www.eurasiancommission.org/ru/nae/news/Pages/14-11-2018-1.aspx

EAES i Iran v 2019 godu nachnut rabotat v rezhime zoni svobodnoy torgovli [The EAEU and Iran will start working in the free trade zone regime in 2019]. (2018, December 12).. Vesti. Ekonomika. Retrieved from https://www.vestifinance.ru/articles/111681

EAES i MERKOSUR nachinaut sotrudnichestvo v ekonomike (2014). [EEU and MERCOSUR begin cooperation in economy], November 26. Retrieved from https://news2.ru/story/432460/

Eurasian Economic Union. (2015, May 21). Agreement on trade and economic cooperation between the Eurasian Economic Union and its member States, of the one part, and the People's Republic of China, of the other part. Retrieved from https://docs.eaeunion.org/docs/ru-ru/01417817/iatc_21052018

Evropeyskiy soyuz i Evraziyskiy ekonomicheskiy soyuz: dolgosrochniy dialog i perspektivi soglasheniya [European Union and Eurasian Economic Union: longterm dialog and prospects of agreement]. (2016). St. Petersburg: CII EDB. Retrieved from https://eabr.org/upload/iblock/f28/edb_centre_2016_report_38_eu_eaeu_rus.pdf

Fedorov, N. (2016). *The free trade agreement between the Eurasian Economic Union and Vietnam in the context of Russian-Vietnamese relations.* ISA. Retrieved from http://web.isanet.org/Web/Conferences/AP%20Hong%20Kong%202016/Archive/07294803-8c93-4929-9d9d-6e843873e8ce.pdf

Fedorov, N. V. (2018). Soglashenie o zone svobodnoi torgovli mezhdu EAES i V'etnamom kak faktor rossiisko-v'etnamskikh otnoshenii [The Free Trade Agreement between the EAEU and Vietnam as a Factor of Russian-Vietnamese Relations]. *Comparative Politics*, (1), 74–90. doi:10.18611/2221-3279-2018-9-1-74-90

Free Trade Agreement between the Eurasian Economic Union and its member States, of the one part, and the Socialist Republic of Vietnam, of the other part. (n.d.). Eurasian Economic Commission. Retrieved from http://www.eurasiancommission.org/ru/act/trade/dotp/sogl_torg/Documents/EAEU-VN_FTA.pdf

Interim Agreement leading to formation of a free trade area between the Eurasian Economic Union and its Member States, of the one part, and the Islamic Republic of Iran, of the other part. (n.d.). Eurasian Economic Commission. Retrieved from http://www.eurasiancommission.org/ru/act/trade/dotp/sogl_torg/Documents/Interim%20Agreement%20EAEU-Iran_final.pdf

Interim Agreement on a free trade area between the EAEU and Iran. (2018, May 17). *Eurasian panorama*, *3*, 17-18.

Interview of the Chairman of the EAEC Board T. Sargsyan to The Economic Times. (2018, September 7). Retrieved from https://www.alta.ru/ts_news/62670/

Kheyfets, B.A. (2018). Perspektivi sozdaniya zoni svobodnoy torgovli mezhdu EAES i ASEAN [Prospects of a free trade area between the EAEU and ASEAN]. *Bulletin of Institute of Economics RAS*, *5*, 107-120.

Kitay – EAES: korrektsiya disbalansov [China – the EAEU: correction of imbalances]. (2017, July 10). Eurasian Development Bank. Retrieved from https://eabr.org/press/comments/kitay-eaes-korrektsiya-disbalansov/

Liberalizatsiya torgovogo rezhima mezhdu EAES i Vietnamom pozvolila za posledniy god narastit tovarooborot mezhdu storonami na 36% [The liberalization of the trade regime between the EAEU and Vietnam allowed to increase the trade turnover between the parties by 36%]. (2018, June 19). Eurasian Economic Commission. Retrieved from http://www.eurasiancommission.org/ru/nae/news/Pages/19-06-2018-2.aspx

Lisovolik, Y. (2017). Evraziyskiy ekonomicheskiy soyuz i ASEAN: otsenka vzaimodopolnyaemosti [The Eurasian Economic Union and ASEAN: assessment of complementarity] *International trends*, 15(3), 46-54. doi:10.17994/IT.2017.15.3.50.4

Lisovolik, Y. (2017, July 2). *Pereosmyslenie BRIKS: BRIKS+ i BRIKS++ [Rethinking of BRICS: BRICS+ and BRICS++]*. National Committee on BRICS research, Russia. Retrieved from http://www.nkibrics.ru/posts/show/589af8e76272695986020000

Maksakova, M. A. (2018). Problemi vneshney tiorgovli Serbii s ES i EAES [Problems of foreign trade of Serbia with the EU and the EAEU], Russian *Foreign. Economic Bulletin*, (1): 37–45.

Mamedov, S. (2017, August 07). *Soglashenie mejdu EAES i MERKOSUR razvernet globalnie torgovie potoki s Severa na Yug [The agreement between the EEU and MERCOSUR will redirect global trade flows from North to South].* Retrieved from http://mirperemen.net/2017/08/soglashenie-mezhdu-eaes-i-merkosur-razvernet-globalnye-torgovye-potoki-s-severa-na-yug/

Memorandum of understanding between Eurasian Economic Commission and Association of Southeast Asian Nations in the sphere of economic cooperation. (2018). Eurasian Economic Union. Retrieved from https://docs.eaeunion.org/docs/ru-ru/01319988/ms_22112018

Memorandum on the cooperation on trade and economic issues between the Eurasian Economic Union and Southern Common Market (MERCOSUR). (2018). Eurasian Economic Union. Retrieved from https://docs.eaeunion.org/docs/ru-ru/01320292/ms_21122018

Ministr torgovli EAES Verinika Nikishina: my idem k polnotsennoy zone svobodnoy torgovli s Iranom [Minister of trade of the EAEU Veronika Nikishina: we are going to a full-fledged free trade area with Iran]. (2018, November 10). BFM.RU. Retrieved from https://news.rambler.ru/other/41249616/?utm_content=rnews&utm_medium=read_more&utm_source=copylink

Nemtsev, Yu. (2017). Rossiya i Vietnam: Razvitie i protsvetanie [Russia and Vietnam: development and prosperity]. *International Affairs*, *4*(June). Retrieved from https://interaffairs.ru/news/show/17673

O proekte resheniya Vysshego Evraziyskogo ekonomicheskogo soveta "Ob Osnovnikh napravleniyakh mezhdunarodnoy deyatel'nosti Evraziyskogo ekonomicheskogo soyuza na 2019 god" [On the draft of the decision of the Supreme Eurasian Economic Council "On the main directions of international activities of the Eurasian Economic Union in 2019"]. (2018). Alta Soft. Retrieved from https://www.alta.ru/tamdoc/18r00164/

Ob itogakh vneshney torgovli tovarami Evraziyskogo ekonomicheskogo soyuza [On the results of foreign trade in goods of the Eurasian Economic Union]. (2018, April 24). *Analytical review*. Retrieved from http://www.eurasiancommission.org/ru/act/integr_i_makroec/dep_stat/tradestat/analytics/Documents/2018/Analytics_E_201802.pdf

Orlov, A. (2014, April 19). *Dorogoy vietnamskiy drug [The dearest Vietnamese friend].* Gazeta RU. Retrieved from https://www.gazeta.ru/business/2014/04/18/5998025.shtml

Podgotovka predlozheniy po razvitiyu mezhdunarodnogo sotrudnichestva s tret'imi stranami i mezhdunarodnimi organizatsiyami [Preparation of proposals for the development of international cooperation with the third countries and international organizations]. (n.d.). Eurasian Economic Commission. Retrieved from http://www.eurasiancommission.org/ru/act/integr_i_makroec/dep_razv_integr/Pages/Международное%20сотрудничество%20(old).aspx

Pototsky, A. (2018, August 8). Asbest protiv trusov. Rossiya postavit 'shlagbaum' dlya nizhnego belay iz Vietnama [Asbestos versus pants. Russia will put a 'barrier' for underwear from Vietnam]. *LIFE#Business*. Retrieved from https://life.ru/t/бизнес/1141663/asbiest_protiv_trusov_rossiia_postavit_shlaghbaum_dlia_nizhniegho_bielia_iz_vietnama

Rodríguez, A. N. (2015, March 20). Kak MERKOSUR i Evraziyskiy soyuz brosayut vizov Soedinennim Shtatam i gegemonii dollara [How MERCOSUR and the Eurasian Union challenge to the United States and the dollar hegemony]. *INOSMI*. Retrieved from http://inosmi.ru/world/20150320/226991984.html

Shibutov, M. (2018, July 12). *Sopryazhenie EAES i Kitaya: vozmozhno li? [The Conjugation of the EAEU and China: is it possible?].* Regnum. Retrieved from https://regnum.ru/news/2446781.html

Soglashenie o zone svobodnoy torgovli mezhdu EAES i Vyetnamom: pervie rezultati realizatsii. (2018). [Agreement on free trade area between the EAEU and Vietnam: first results of its realization]. October 19. ASEAN Centre in MGIMO-University, the MFA of Russia. Retrieved 7 February, 2019, from http://asean.mgimo.ru/ru/790-soglashenie-o-zone-svobodnoj-torgovli-mezhdu-eaes-i-vetnamom-pervye-rezultaty-realizatsii

Tsvetov, A. (2017, October 17). *Vmesto povorota: ASEAN i evraziyskiy proekt Rossii [Instead of turn: ASEAN and Eurasian project of Russia].* Carnegie Moscow Center. Retrieved from https://carnegie.ru/2017/10/17/ru-pub-73368

Umakhanov, I. (2018). Rossiya zainteresovana v podkluchenii evropeyskikh partnerov k proektu Bol'shogo evraziyskogo partnerstva [Russia is interested in joining the European partners to Greater Eurasian partnership]. Federative Council. Retrieved from http://council.gov.ru/events/news/91810/

Vinokurov, E. (2014, October 14). Evropeyskiy i Evraziyskiy soyuzi: povod dlya integratsii [European and Eurasian Unions: the reason for integration]. TASS. Retrieved from http://tass.ru/opinions/1597482

Vinokurov: soglasheniya EAES s Iranom i Kitaem nosyat kompromissniy kharakter [Vinokurov: the EAEU agreements with Iran and China have a compromise nature]. (2018, May 17). Sputnik Kazakhstan. Retrieved from https://ru.sputniknews.kz/economy/20180517/5654270/eaeu-soglashenie-iran-china.html

Vistuplenie Vladimira Putina na PMEF-2016 [Speech of Vladimir Putin in SPIEF-2016]. (2016, June 17). Vesti FM. Retrieved from https://radiovesti.ru/brand/60963/episode/1374750/

ZST EAES-Vietnam – chert kroetsya v melochakh [FTA EAEU-Vietnam: devil is in the details]. (2015, June 4). Russian International Affairs Council. Retrieved from http://russiancouncil.ru/analytics-and-comments/analytics/zst-eaes-vetnam-chert-kroetsya-v-melochakh/

ADDITIONAL READING

Lagutina M. (2018). Perspectives of Co-Existence of the EU and EAEU Integration Processes. The Case of Armenia. In *Perspectives of Co-Existence of EU and EAEU Integration Processes: The Case of Armenia* (pp. 48-93). Yerevan.

Lagutina, M., & Lapenko, M. (2017). Eurasian Economic Union and the Latin America: Framework of the Cooperation. In Eurasia-Latin America Strategic Engagement and Comparative Perspectives in Politics and Economics (pp. 161-177). Kultegin.

Lagutina, M., & Vasilyeva, N. (2016). *The Russian Project of Eurasian Integration. Geopolitical Prospects*. Lexington Books, Rowman and Littlefield.

Lapenko, M. V. (2017). Sozdanie zony svobodnoy torgovli mezhdu EAES i respublikoy Vietnam: itogi peregovornogo protsessa [Creation of free trade area between the EAEU and Vietnam: results of negotiating process]. *Bulletin of Saratov University. History International Relations*, *17*(2), 212–215. doi:10.18500/1819-4907-2017-17-2-212-215

Özer, A. C. (Ed.). (2018). Globalization and Trade Integration in Developing Countries. Hershey, PA: IGI Global. doi:10.4018/978-1-5225-4032-8

KEY TERMS AND DEFINITIONS

Eurasian Development Bank (EDB): An international financial organization established to promote economic growth in its member states, extend trade and economic ties among them, and to support integration in Eurasia.

Eurasian Economic Commission (EAEC): The permanent regulatory body of the Eurasian Economic Union (EAEU), which aimed to ensure the functioning and development of the EAEU, and developing proposals for the further development of integration.

Eurasian Economic Union (EAEU): An international organization for regional economic integration that has international legal personality and is established by the Treaty on the Eurasian Economic Union.

Free-Trade Area: Trade within the group is duty free but members set their own tariffs on imports from non-members (WTO's definition).

Greater Eurasian Partnership: The current Eurasian strategy of Russia, aimed at the formation of a complex, multi-level system of multilateral cooperation with the participation of the EAEU, ASEAN, APEC and SCO countries.

Preferential Trade Agreements (PTA): A trading bloc that gives preferential access to certain products from the participating countries. This is done by reducing tariffs but not by abolishing them completely.

World Trade Organization (WTO): The only global international organization dealing with the rules of trade between nations based on the WTO agreements; the goal is to help producers of goods and services, exporters, and importers conduct their business.

Chapter 3
The Effect of the U.S.-China Trade War on Global Trade

Ahu Coşkun Özer
Marmara University, Turkey

ABSTRACT

If one country attacks another country's trade with taxes and quotas, it is defined as a trade war. It is aimed to protect the domestic market from competition. The U.S.-China trade war begun on March 1, 2018, and was centered on the customs duty of 25% for the imported steel and 10% for the imported aluminum. The protectionist measures against each other in both countries have increased day by day. However, the impact of these protectionist measures on global trade is not yet known. In this chapter, the effect of the U.S.-China trade war on global trade is analyzed. For this reason, the export data of the U.S. to China and the global export data yearly is compared. According to the results of the linear regression analysis, if the value of the goods export of the U.S. to China increase 1 unit, the value of global export of the goods increases to 58 units. While the trade wars decreased the goods export from the U.S. to China, it has decreased global goods exports too. In 2018, developments in global commodity exports and the U.S. goods exports to China were observed in the same direction.

DOI: 10.4018/978-1-5225-9566-3.ch003

INTRODUCTION

Trade war is defined as an attack to a country's trade using protectionist policies, quotas and taxes. It is aimed to protect the domestic market from competition. China-the U.S. the trade war has begun on March 1, 2018, depended on custom duty 25% on imported steel and 10% imported aluminum. The protectionist measures against each other in both countries have increased day by day. However, the impact of these protectionist measures on global trade has not known yet.

There are samples of the trade war from the historical aspect. In the 1980's there was a trade war between the U.S. and Asian countries. In 1986, there was a trade war between the U.S and Japan. And the last trade war has been between the U.S. and China in 2018. The effect of the trade wars on global trade and the economies of the countries have not known yet.

In this research, the effect of the U.S.-China trade war on global trade is analyzed. For this reason, the export data of the U.S. to China and the global export data is compared by yearly. It is aimed to determine whether the U.S.-China trade war has an impact on global trade or not.

BACKGROUND

A trade war is defined as an attack on a country trade with protectionist policies implemented with taxes and quotas. When a country raises tariffs, the other country will respond with escalation and raise its tariffs ("Trade wars, Trump tariffs and protectionism explained," 2018). The conservationist policies of the two countries are applied mutually.

A trade war is a result of the protectionist policies, it occurs when the country raises its imports tariffs on another country's goods and that protectionist measures are applied using by tariffs. Tariff is tax on imported goods and services. Trade wars can start if a country perceive another country's unfair practices on trade or if domestic industries want to be protected by making expensive and less attractive imported goods. Trade war eliminates the advantages of free trade ("Trade War," n.d.).

As a result of trade wars, the protectionist policies applied by raising tariffs lead to an increase in prices. However, it is stated that the countries implementing these policies have gained competitiveness in certain sectors. With these policies, it is aimed that domestic enterprises are protected from competition. The impact of the protectionist policies in economies is the research topics. According to some studies in the literature, increasing the tariff causes welfare loss in countries. In addition, it is stated that both countries suffered from losses in tariff increase. For instance, according to Ossa (2014), if the optimal tariffs are 62% and when this rate to be 63%

of the countries losses from welfare because of the breakdown of the international trade policy and government welfare losses are average 2.9%. However, if the governments negotiate, the possibility of the country welfare gains are average 0.5%.

Yan Dong and John Whalley (2012) states that increasing the protection in the U.S. and China yield substantial gains to the U.S. but losses to China and Japan. Protectionist policies causes much more welfare losses to China rather than the U.S. According to the Dong and Whalley (2012) if the U.S. increases it tariffs on China to 25%, the U.S. has a welfare gain of 67.215 billion dollars but China has welfare loss 39.021 billion dollars, if China retaliates and increase its tariffs to 25% for the imported the U.S goods, the U.S. welfare gain falls to 59.753 billion dollars.

MAIN FOCUS OF THE CHAPTER

Issues, Controversies, Problems

In this study, the effect of the U.S.-China trade war on global trade is analyzed. For this reason, the export data of the U.S. to China and the global export data was compared by yearly. In this study, the growth charts were compared and the changes in the U.S. goods exports and global goods exports were compared also regression analyze was conducted to determine the effect of the trade war on global trade. Analyzes were conducted with the data from the first month of 2007 until December 2018. For this reason, the U.S. Census Bureau data on Trade in Goods with China and WTO's data on monthly merchandise export 70 countries were used. In the first stage, unit root test was performed for variables and in the second step, regression analysis was performed.

EXAMPLES OF TRADE WARS IN THE WORLD

There are samples of the trade war from the historical aspect. In 1980's there was a trade war between the U.S. and Asian countries. In 1986, there was a trade war between the U.S and Japan. Also, the last trade war has been between the U.S. and China in 2018.

In the 1980s, the U.S faced with Asia economic power by manipulating U.S. currency and putting non-tariff barriers into imports. On the other hand, the U.S. started to restrictions on areas such as electronics, automobiles and steel. In addition to that, there had been trade wars between the United States and Japan in the history due to unfair trade practices of Japan. The trade war was due to Japan's failure to comply with the agreement, signed in 1986, which prevented Japanese companies from selling their computer chip at a price lower than production costs to third countries.

The U.S. administration claimed that government of Japan had failed to permit on U.S. firms to win more than a 10% share of chip market in Japan To respond the Japan, the U.S. administration set a 100% tariff on imported goods from Japan to keep Japan goods out of the U.S. markets, worth 300 million dollars.(Edward, 1987).

The United States has begun to implement 25% additional custom duty for the imported steel and 10% additional custom duty for imported aluminum from the European Union, Canada and Mexico on 1 June 2018. That caused concern of the possibility on trade war between the E.U and the U.S. The E.U responded the U.S by imposing additional customs duties on some goods of the U.S and the E.U decided to move the issue to the WTO. The E.U used some retaliatory measures which were put into effect after 20 June 2018. Some products exported by the U.S., for example, bourbon whiskeys, rice, jeans, blueberries, motorcycles, orange juice, tobacco, steel containers and iron were imposed imposing additional customs duties. Financial dimension of the measures to be implemented by the E.U would be in the framework of the reciprocity principle. This means a level of € 2.8 billion in the first phase ("Dünya ticaret savaşı başladı," Haziran, 2018).

The history of the U.S.- China and the E.U trade war extended in March 2018. After the President Trump had announced that they did not accept the European duties on American automobiles there was a tension between the E.U and U.S. and Trump said that if the European duties on American automobiles were not removed, the U.S. would respond twice as hard. Europe and the U.S. have been in a trade conflict in March 2018, after the U.S. intended to impose tariffs on steel and aluminum on the E.U and the other U.S. allies. When the auto import tariffs have been compared between the U.S. and the E.U., the tariff rate is higher in the E.U. The tariff rate on auto imports from the U.S. had been 10% but the U.S. charged much less for European auto imports. Also, Trump's new metal tariffs has begun to be applied (Serhan, 2018).

HISTORY OF THE U.S.-CHINA TRADE WAR

The root of the U.S. and Chinese trade war was laid with the decision of the U.S. President Donald Trump on March 1, 2018, with the implementation of a 25% customs duty for imported steel and 10% customs duty for imported aluminum. Innovation was one of the most important topics of the trade war.

The next level of the trade war was the Washington's decision of 25% additional customs duty on more than 800 products imported from China on July 6, worth $ 34 billion. One of the most important topics of the trade war was innovation. The U.S. has been concerned about the beginning of losing its superiority in the field of innovation. China underlines the fact that the U.S. has implemented additional tax lists in lanes such as aviation, telecommunications and artificial intelligence. In fact, China was also retaliating for the U.S. by bringing 25% customs duty to the U.S. the products, worth $ 34 billion. China also informed the WTO that it would continue to work with other countries on free trade("ABD-Çin Ticaret Savaşı," 2018). While these additional customs duty applications continue between the two countries, both countries are expected to be conciliatory in the mobile phones and aircraft because China is an important market in these sectors for the U.S.

The fastest growing markets for China's mobile phones and laptops are developing countries like India, Latin America and Africa. In addition, the U.S. cannot disregard China as a market because by the end of 2015, 131 million iPhone were sold in China, while the number of the iphone sold in the U.S. was 110 million. Iphone is a very small part of the U.S. exports to China. It is estimated that China will buy more than 6810 aircraft from Boeing over the next two decades, it's worth will be around 1 trillion dollars. China has over 3 trillion dollars in foreign exchange reserves, while the US foreign exchange reserves are around 120 billion dollars. Trump's tariffs could even lead to the World Trade Organization (WTO) collapse, which would automatically trigger penalties against the United States and even lead to a higher tariff against the U.S. exports (Winter, 2017).

It is expected that the trade will be affected by roughly $250bn because of tariffs applied with 10% for the Chinese import goods worth of 200 billion dollars. It is said that White House is delaying the implementation of the tariff 25% in imports to shift manufacturing firms from China to the U.S. The real strategy is to shape the industry in the U.S rather than to make the world trade fairer.

American consumers will be the first loser in the U.S-China trade war because prices of the products will be high. The U.S. administration exempts consumer electronics, including smartphones, which include Apple's iPhone. China has to respond to Trump tariffs. Chinese bicycle helmets and baby chairs are also exempt. Tariffs are likely to increase domestic prices before the U.S. congressional elections (Chue, 2018).

DEVELOPMENTS IN CHINA TRADE

When China's foreign trade policy is generally evaluated, protectionist policies are implemented in some sectors. According to the Lee (2018) China put some non-tariff barriers to trade so that some critical sectors are not affected by international competition. Chinese imports have been controlled by different standards from state-owned companies for private and foreign companies (as cited in '2018 China–United States trade war,' n.d.) These non-tariff barriers are as follows (Lee, 2018):

- Authorized companies that can perform international transactions are limited.
- Applying security license to imported goods
- Using technical standards to protect domestic companies
- Foreign direct investment is not allowed in some sectors like telecommunications, distribution and financial services

In addition to these protectionist policies, additional tariffs have been introduced by China in the US-China trade battle. In the first nine months of 2018, the U.S. exports to China amounted to 93 billion, 363 million dollars. The U.S. exports to China, which was over 100 billion dollars from 2011 to 2017, began to decline in 2018, when the trade war began. This figure amounted to 129 billion, 893 million dollars in 2017, 115 billion, 545 million dollars in 2016, 115 billion, 873 million dollars in 2015, 123 billion, 657 million dollars in 2014, 121 billion, 746 million dollars in 2013, 110 billion, 516 million dollars in 2012, In 2011, it was 104 billion, 121 million dollars.

Figure 1. Export Value of the U.S. to China by Monthly

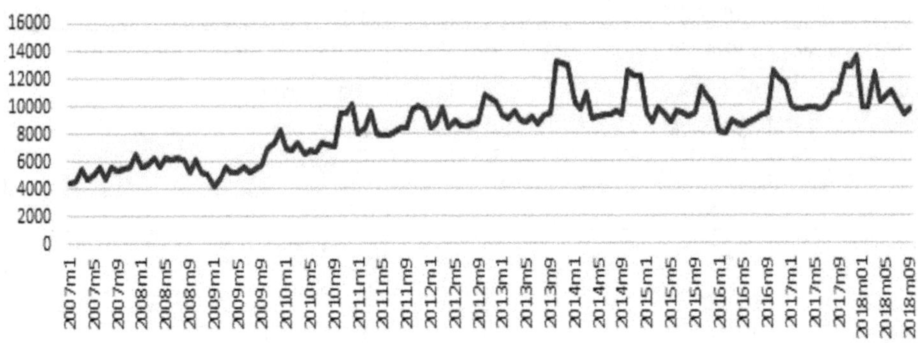

When the U.S. exports to China were examined in the last 12 years, the average annual exports amounted to 102 billion, 876 million dollars. On a monthly, this figure was 8 billion 573 million dollars. In the 12th month of 2017, just before the start of the Chinese trade war, exports amounted to 13 billion 644 million USD. After this month, the U.S. exports to China started to decline. In the first month of 2018, there was a 27% decrease in the monthly when it is compared to the last month of 2017. In that month, Trump implemented a 30% tariff on solar panels abroad.

The U.S. has begun to apply 30% customs duty on imported solar equipment on 22 January 2018. This implies a loss of 28 billion dollars for an industry that is based on components made abroad by 80% of its supplies. The Solar Energy Industries Association employs 260,000 employees and can cause tens of thousands of job losses in this sector (Eckhouse, Natter & Christopher, 2018). Also, China, the leader on manufacturing solar panel in the world, refused the tariffs. On the same day, new tariffs were applied for the imported washing machines. 20% tariff was imposed to 1.2 million washing machines. In data, the worth of the exported washers was 425 million dollars in 2016 from China to the U.S. (Wikipedia, n.d.).

After the March 1, 2018, the U.S. imposed the 25% custom duty of steel imports and 10% customs duty on aluminum imports, and the U.S. exports to China have started to decrease. China responded to the U.S. with imposing the 25% custom duties on products imported from the U.S. The U.S. exports to China decreased by 17% in April 2018 compared to the previous month with the effect of the custom duties.

Table 1. The U.S. export to China monthly

Months	The. U. S. Export to China Monthly (Million Dollars)	Monthly Change in the U.S. Exports to China Compared to the Previous Month (Percentage)
2017 November	12765,02115	-1,530561353
2017 December	13644,75017	6,891716127
2018 January	9835,25935	-27,91909541
2018 February	9806,09267	-0,296552221
2018 March	12382,08633	26,26931792
2018 April	10268,03546	-17,07346254
2018 May	10610,81755	3,338341481
2018 June	11115,62343	4,757464567
2018 July	10261,68804	-7,682298671
2018 August	9294,3443	-9,426750602

The Trump administration announced, in May 2018, that the U.S. would impose customs duties on Chinese goods of $ 50 billion, impose to restrictions on Chinese investments in the U.S. and China said it would retaliate (Petroff, Iyengar & Mullen, 2018).

The U.S. imposed customs duties on Chinese goods worth $ 34 billion. Beijing, on the other hand, is expected to retaliate against American products. The U.S. customs officers started imposing duties on $34 billion in Chinese goods after that the Chinese Ministry of Commerce issued a statement calling the U.S. move "typical trade bullying." (Tan, 2018). As a result of these events, the export of US to China also decreased by %7 in the months following these events.

In August 2018, the U.S. has applied new taxes on goods, the worth of the goods was 16bn$. China immediately responded by applying taxes on the same value of US products (US-China trade war: New tariffs come into force, 2018). In this month, compared to the previous month, exports of the U.S. to China decreased by 9%. Export declines in July and August of 2018 ranged from 7% to 9%.

In 2017, the U.S. imported goods worth was 505 billion dollars from China. This figure was approximately 447 billion dollars in the first ten months of 2018. In the first months of 2018, when the US trade war began, the US imports began to decline in China. Imports from China decreased by 14% in the following month after January 2018, when the 30% tariff on solar panels imports has been imposed. In February, March and April 2018, the U.S.'s imports from China decreased, but there was not a decline in the following months.

Table 2. The. U.S. imports from China monthly

Months	The U.S. Imports From China (Million Dollars)	Monthly Change in the U.S. Imports From China Compared to the Previous Month (Percentage)
January 2018	45,788.0	
February 2018	39,067.6	-14,68
March 2018	38,256.7	-2,1
April 2018	38,230.0	-0,1
May.18	43,797.4	14,5
June 2018	44,599.5	1,01
July 2018	47,096.0	5
August 2018	47,863.9	?
September 2018	50,032.1	
October 2018	52,233.0	
TOTAL 2018	446,964.2	

THE EFFECT OF THE U.S.-CHINA TRADE WAR ON GLOBAL TRADE

While the U.S. exports of goods to China did not show a big change in the first seven months of 2017, world exports of goods displayed large fluctuations in the same period and increased of 16.5%. The U.S. exports to China are approximately 10 billion dollars per month. In 2017, global exports of goods amounted to 1 trillion, 270 billion dollars per month.

In the first two months of 2018, the year of the trade wars, the U.S. exports to China decreased by 28%, while global commodity trade decreased by only 7%. The. U.S. exports to China were $12 billion, 382 million in March 2018, when the trade war began, while global exports of goods amounted to 1 trillion, 540 million dollars in the same month. With the effect of trade wars, in April 2015, the U.S. exports to China decreased by 17% and global exports of goods decreased by 5% in the same period.

The. U.S. exports to China began to fluctuate just before the trade wars. It follows a stable and straight forward direction.

Although, there are many numbers of variables affecting global trade, in this research, it is aimed to measure the impact of the good export value of the U.S. to China on global good export value. Augmented Dickey-Fuller Test was applied to determine if variables are stationary or have unit root. Since p-values are less than 1, the serial is determined as stationary, it does not contain unit root. Therefore, data can be used at their own level.

Figure 2. World commodity export

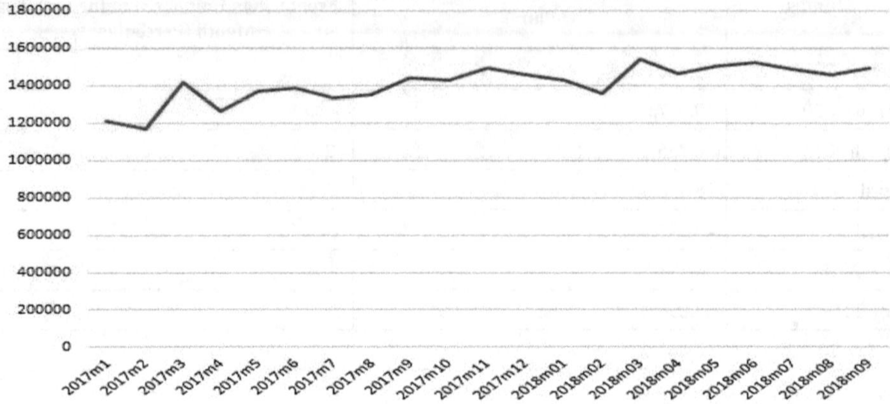

Figure 3. The U.S. export to China

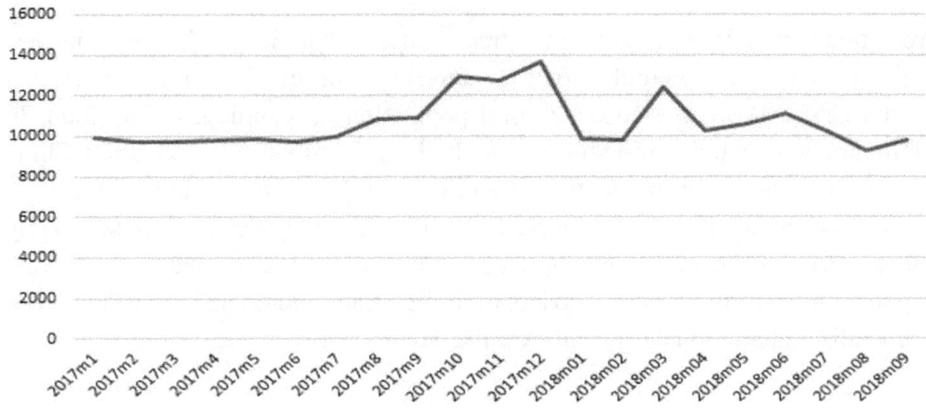

According to the results of the regression analysis conducted with data from the first month of 2007 to the last month of 2018, there is a linear relationship between the export of the U.S. to China and global exports of goods. The. U.S. exports of goods to China is determined as the independent variable, global exports of goods determined as a dependent variable. Descriptive power of the model is 59%. The U.S. exports of goods to China positively affects the world trade. According to analyze results, if the value of the goods export of the U.S. to China increase 1 unit, value of global export of the goods increase 58 unit. While trade wars decreased the goods export of the U.S. to China, it decreased in global goods exports. In 2018, developments in global commodity exports and the U.S. goods exports to China were observed in the same direction.

Table 3. The Linear Regression Results

Linear regression		Number of obs =		141		
		F(1, 139) =		165.49		
		Prob > F =		0.0000		
		R-squared =		0.5877		
		Root MSE =		1.1e+05		
	Coef.	**Robust Std. Err.**	**t**	**P>|t|**	**[95% Conf. Interval]**	
EXPORT	58.83569	4.573513	12.86	0.000	49.79304	67.87833
USCHINAEXPORT_ cons	765927.3	42341.95	18.09	0.000	682209.7	849644.8

SOLUTIONS AND RECOMMENDATIONS

Protectionist policies in international trade cause welfare losses for the countries. Liberalization of foreign trade provides gains for countries. China is a great market for the U.S. and other countries with a population of 1 billion, 417 million. In addition, China is the world's factory with cheap labor and in this respect China has a cost advantage in production. Therefore, the US-China trade war will have negative outcomes for both countries. The U.S.-China trade war has negatively affected the global export of goods. This war led to a decrease in the world exports of goods. As a result of these, barriers to foreign trade should be removed in order to liberalize international trade all over the world.

FUTURE RESEARCH DIRECTIONS

The impact of trade wars on countries can be evaluated in many different ways. In addition, the impact on the economic growth of the U.S.-China trade war can be analyzed. The effects of trade wars on the economic growth of countries can be analyzed. Research on the impact of protectionist policies in foreign trade will lead to current studies.

CONCLUSION

A trade war is defined as an attack on trade between the countries using the trade restrictive policies based on taxes and quotas. A country can raise its tariff to another country, that can hurt the economies of the other country and can lead to political tensions between two countries. There are samples of the trade war from the historical aspect. In 1980's there was a trade war between the U.S. and Asian countries. In the 1986, there was a trade war between the U.S. and Japan. And the last trade war has been between the U.S. and China in 2018. However, the impact of the trade wars is still not known.

The trade war between the U.S. and China depend on the 25% customs duty for imported steel and % 10 customs duty on imported aluminum in the U.S. It began in the beginning of the 2018. In the first nine months of 2018, the U.S. exports to China amounted to 93 billion 363 million dollars. The U.S. exports to China, which was over $ 100 billion from 2011 to 2017, began to decline in 2018, when the trade war began. In the first month of 2018, there was a 27% decrease in the monthly when it is compared to the last month of 2017. In that month, Trump implemented a 30% tariff on solar panels abroad. After March 1, 2018, the imposed the 25% custom duty of steel imports and 10% customs duty on aluminum imports, the U.S. exports to China have started to decrease. China response to the U.S. with imposing the 25% custom duties on products imported from the U.S. The US exports to China decreased by 17% in April 2018 compared to the previous month with the effect of the custom duties.

In the first two months of 2018, the year of the trade wars, the U.S. exports to China decreased by 28%, while global commodity trade decreased by only 7%. The. U.S. exports to China were $ 12 billion 382 million in March 2018, when the trade war began, while global exports of goods amounted to 1 trillion 540 million dollars in the same month. With the effect of trade wars, in April 2015, the U.S. exports to China decreased by 17% and global exports of goods decreased by 5% in the same period.

Also, according to the analyses results, there is a linear positive relation between the goods exports of the U.S. to China and global goods export. If the value of the goods export of the U.S. to China increase 1 unit, value of global export of the goods increase 58 unit. While trade wars decrease the goods export of the U.S. to China, it decreases in global goods exports. In 2018, developments in global commodity exports and the U.S. goods exports to China has been in the same direction.

REFERENCES

ABD-Çin Ticaret Savaşı. (2018). Sputnik News. Retrieved from https://tr.sputniknews.com/trend/abd-cin-ticaret-savasi-gumruk-vergisi-ithalat-ihracat/

China blasts Trump's new trade tariffs. (2018). CNN. Retrieved from https://money.cnn.com/2018/01/22/news/economy/trump-trade-tariffs-china-reaction/

Chue, B. (2018). Trump's trade war with China will affect all of us – this is how. *Independent*. Retrieved from https://www.independent.co.uk/voices/trump-china-trade-war-tariffs-us-metal-europe-uk-effect-a8543136.html

Dünya Ticaret Savaşı Başladı. (2018). Hürriyet Gazetesi. Retrieved from http://www.hurriyet.com.tr/ekonomi/dunya-ticaret-savasi-basladi-40863621

Eckhouse, B., Natter, A., & Christopher, M. (2018). President Trump Slaps Tariffs on Solar Panels in Major Blow to Renewable Energy. *Time*. Retrieved from http://time.com/5113472/donald-trump-solar-panel-tariff/

Edward, L. (1987). U.S.-Japan Trade War: The Opening Battle.Thomas A. Roe Institute for Economic Policy Studies. Retrieved from:http://s3.amazonaws.com/thf_media/1987/pdf/bg577.pdf

Lee, G. B. (2018). China's Forced Technology Transfer Problem— And What to Do About It. Retrieved from https://piie.com/system/files/documents/pb18-13.pdf

Monthly Merchandise Trade Value. (2018). WTO. Retrieved from https://www.wto.org/english/res_e/statis_e/daily_update_e/monthly_trade_e.xls

Office of the United States Trade Representative. (2018). President Trump Approves Relief for U.S. Washing Machine and Solar Cell Manufacturers. Retrieved from https://ustr.gov/about-us/policy-offices/press-office/press-releases/2018/january/president-trump-approves-relief-us

Petroff, A., Iyengar, R., & Mullen, J. (2018). The odds of a messy trade war between the US and China are rising again. *CNN*. Retrieved from https://money.cnn.com/2018/05/30/news/economy/trump-china-us-tariffs-trade-timeline/index.html

Ralph, O. (2014). Trade Wars and Trade Talks with Data. *The American Economic Review*, *104*(12), 4104–4146. doi:10.1257/aer.104.12.4104

Serhan, Y. (2018). How Do You Know When It's Officially a Trade War? *The Atlantic*. Retrieved from https://www.theatlantic.com/international/archive/2018/06/trade-war-us-europe/563504/

Tan, R. (2018). The U.S.-China trade war has begun. Here's how things got to this point. *Washington Post*. Retrieved from https://www.washingtonpost.com/news/worldviews/wp/2018/07/05/a-timeline-of-how-the-u-s-china-trade-war-led-us-to-this-code-red-situation/?utm_term=.cdb09dbf96f5

Trade war. (n.d.). Investopedia. Retrieved from https://www.investopedia.com/terms/t/trade-war.asp#ixzz5XwqZIP5z

Trade wars, Trump tariffs and protectionism explained. (2018, July 26). BBC. Retrieved from https://www.bbc.com/news/world-43512098

US-China trade war: New tariffs come into force. (2018). BBC News. Retrieved from https://www.bbc.com/news/business-45255623

U.S. International Trade Commission. (2018). Large Residential Washers: Investigation No. TA-201-076. Retrieved from https://www.usitc.gov/publications/safeguards/pub4745.pdf

Wikipedia. (2018). China–United States trade war. Retrieved from https://en.wikipedia.org/wiki/2018_China–United_States_trade_war#cite_note-:10-15

Wikipedia. (n.d.). 2018 China–United States trade war. Retrieved from https://en.wikipedia.org/wiki/2018_China%E2%80%93United_States_trade_war#cite_note-143

Winter, N. (2017). Why America would lose a trade war with China. *IMD*. Retrieved from https://www.imd.org/research-knowledge/articles/why-america-would-lose-a-trade-war-with-china/

Yan, D., & John, W. (2012). Gains and Losses from potential bilateral US-China Trade Retaliation. *Economic Modelling*. Retrieved from https://ac.els-cdn.com/S0264999312002222/1-s2.0-S0264999312002222-main.pdf?_tid=5dc7258f-bde3-40b3-a0d0-f13d5f5e71c5&acdnat=1543220182_c1b9f972f64c60cd733ecc67f4faaa0a)

ADDITIONAL READING

Findlay, R. & O Rourke, K.H. (2007). Power and Plenty: Trade, War, and the World Economy in the Second Millennium. Princeton University Press.

John, A., & Conybeare, C. (1987). *Trade Wars: The Theory and Practice of International Commercial Rivalry*. Columbia University Press.

Schlossstein, S. (1984). *Trade war: greed, power, and industrial policy on opposite sides of the Pacific*. Condon &Weed.

Zeng, K. (2004). *Trade Threats, Trade Wars*. University of Michigan Press.

Chapter 4
USA-China Trade Wars:
Back to Protectionism in World Trade

Özlem Toplu Yılmaz
TC İstanbul Yeniyüzyıl University, Turkey

ABSTRACT

This chapter analyzes the trade war between the United States of America and China. The United States of America and China are the two biggest trade leaders in the world. The United States supported China for its integration to world trade. The United States accused China of pursuing unfair trade policies. The United States increased tariffs against Chinese imports and China undertook retaliation measures against the United States' tariff increases. The two countries entered a period of a trade war and they started to implement protectionist policies on each other. These protectionist policies between the United States and China are seen as trade wars and could affect the world trade liberalization adversely. As they are trade partners too, it is better for both countries to end this war and to reach an agreement, because trade liberalization efforts could fail.

DOI: 10.4018/978-1-5225-9566-3.ch004

INTRODUCTION

China has become one of the largest economies in the world in recent years. China has been a member of the World Trade Organization on December 11, 2001, and the United States of America (USA) supported China to become a member of the organization. However, due to the tensions between China and the USA, the President of the United States asserted that their support for China's membership in the organization was a mistake. The USA accused China of stealing American technology and trade secrets and of causing unfair competition. Finally, the USA began to impose sanctions on China because the President of the USA argued that China's trade policy was harming American high-tech industries.

The efforts to liberalize the international trade, which began under the leadership of the United States, have changed direction recently, and the protectionist policies against China have been brought to the forefront by the American leadership. The increase in the tariffs that America and China pursued to each other has been called trade wars and they are considered to be negative for the world trade liberalization.

In this research, the role of China in the world trade after its membership of the World Trade Organization and also the trade relations between the United States and China will be examined. The source of the trade wars between China and the United States, and the sanctions imposed by the USA and China's retaliation measures will be analyzed. In addition, the trade disputes between America and China, which are carried to the World Trade Organization, will be mentioned. Finally, the possible impact of these protectionist measures on the liberalization of the world trade will be examined.

BACKGROUND

There are limited studies about the USA and China trade war, and they are published online. These studies and the approaches of the authors are summarized below.

Chunding Li,Chuantian He and Chuangwei Lin analyzed the effects of possible China–USA trade wars by using a multi-country global general equilibrium (GE) model in their article "Economic Impacts of the Possible China-USA Trade War". According to their simulation results, China will be hurt by the trade tensions with the United States. The United States can benefit from its trade policies against China, but may lose if China applies retaliation measures. America has a stronger bargaining power than China. According to the author, trade wars between China and America may hit most of the countries, distort the world trade, and reduce the world GDP.

Tao Liu and Wing Thye Woo examined the USA-China trade war in their article "Understanding the U.S.-China Trade War." According to the authors, the best solution of the trade tensions will be the policy changes in United States and China. About the industrial policy dispute, the authors concluded that the technology transfer of China is a crucial dispute, as China uses its market power and gains at the costs of its trade partners.

Myeong Hwan Kim examined the trade imbalance between the United States and China in his article "The U.S.-China Trade Deficit". The author expected to find a relationship between the United States' trade deficit and the imports from China. However, he concluded the United States' imports from China don't have any effect on the United States' trade deficit.

Amy Skonieczny analyzed the United States' trade liberalization campaigns with China and Russia to find out how the negative domestic perception of the two potential partner countries impacted pro-trade narratives and shaped 'outside' lobbying strategies in her article "Trading with the enemy: narrative, identity and U.S. trade politics". This article demonstrated how the domestic actors rely on existing country images – even when negative – to emotionally empower trade policy arguments and ironically glean legislative success.

Edward I-hsin Chen examined the U.S.-trade relations in his article "U.S.-China Trade Relations and Economic Distrust." He suggested that the areas of cooperation include clean energy, climate change, and China's huge holdings of U.S. treasury bonds; areas of competition include intellectual property rights, intellectual property theft, currency exchange rates, and investment access to one another's markets.

Saiful Alim Rosyadi and Tri Widodo analyzed the impact of the United States' tariff increases against Chinese imports in their article "Impact of Donald Trump's tariff increase against Chinese imports on global economy". They implemented a Global Trade Analysis Project (GTAP) model. According to the simulations, the policy might lead to a fall in the GDP and terms-of-trade. Welfare can decline in the United States and China. Another result would be an increase in the trade balance for United States.

Generally, the authors conclude that the trade wars between the United States of America and China will have negative effects on both sides. Especially, China will be affected more negatively. According to some authors, these trade wars will have a negative impact on the world trade, too. The solution relies on policy changes in both countries.

MAIN FOCUS OF THE CHAPTER

Trade Liberalization in China and China's WTO Membership

In the first years of the 1950s, private enterprises were able to carry on export and import corporations in China. Between 1956 and 1979, monopolistic structure prevailed in foreign trade. After 1979, China undertook some reforms to liberalize its foreign trade. In1984, besides, liberalizing the trade, China decided also to strengthen its foreign trade system by making use of exchange rates, customs duties, taxes, and credits (GATT, 1987, p. 11). In 1985, the export value of China accounted for 1,42% of the world total and most of the export commodities were primary products and textiles (GATT, 1987, p. 8). Before 1984, the customs regime played an important role to protect domestic production in China, but after 1984 customs policy changed. Foreign trade policy comprised of encouraging exports, promoting the necessities and improving the economy.

After trade liberalization efforts, China applied to achieve a status as a GATT contracting party in 1986. Previously, China signed the General Agreement on Tariffs and Trade (GATT) agreement in 1948 when it was established. However, China left the GATT system in 1949 after the revolution in the country. On July 10, 1986, China achieved its status as a contracting party to GATT. In the GATT Council, the Representative of the United States said that they would examine the China's foreign trade policy with great interest, and hoped to discuss the reforms that China was undertaking in its economy (GATT, March 04, 1987, p. 12).

WTO membership negotiations with China were conducted by the Working Party which was established under GATT in 1987. The scope of the negotiations in earlier times was China's trade regime for goods. Later the scope extended and included trade in services, new rules on non-tariff measures and rules relating to intellectual property rights. Several high-level officials from the Office of the United States Trade Representative traveled to China in the early 1999s to make bilateral talks on membership, which have been stalled for months (Lardy, 1999).

China reduced the tariff rates substantially and removed nontariff barriers on many products in time. China had attracted foreign direct investments and many firms shifted their production to China. Chinese cheap-priced goods were demanded from all over the world. The exports were rising but this favorable economic atmosphere changed as the Asian financial crisis broke out. The Asian financial crisis broke out in Thailand in 1997 and spread to the countries. China was also hit by the crisis. The devaluation of the currencies of Asian countries meant increased competition for China (Wang, 1999, p.539). So, the demand for Chinese products in international markets slowed down. China adopted restrictive trade measures to overcome Asian crisis like introducing non-tariff barriers which were inconsistent with the WTO principles. Despite this lesson of the Asian financial crisis, the United States demanded China's entry into the WTO (Lardy, 1999).

WTO concluded the accession negotiations of China on September 17, 2001, and China became the 143rd member of the WTO on December 11, 2001. China made commitments to liberalize its trade regime in order to enter the WTO. These commitments included (WTO, September 17, 2001):

- China will not provide any discriminatory measures to any WTO members.
- China will eliminate different treatments in pricing between the domestic goods sold in China and the goods produced for export.
- Price controls will not be applied to protect domestic industries and services producers.
- China will implement the WTO agreement. China's domestic laws and new legislation will be compatible with the WTO agreement.
- In three years after accession, the producers can trade all goods throughout the customs territory with limited exceptions.
- Export subsidies on agricultural products will not be used and no export subsidies will be introduced.

China removed the trade barriers gradually and has bound all tariffs for imported goods. Average bound tariff level in China decreased to 15% for agricultural products. For industrial goods, the average bound tariff level decreased to 8.9%. The highest tariff rates were applied to some industrial goods like photographic film, automobiles and related products (WTO, September 17, 2001). After the liberalization of trade, China's export grew rapidly and export as % of GDP recorded its highest level of 37,2% in 2006. That was 130,5% higher than in 1992 and 78% higher than in 2001 when China joined the WTO (Figure 1).

China's Accession to the WTO and Its Relationships With the Chinese Taipei, Hong Kong and Macau

Taiwan requested observer status in GATT in 1965, but UN General Assembly notified China as the only legitimate government. In 1992, GATT's Council of Representatives established a working party for accession request of Separate Customs Territory of Taiwan, Penghu, Kinmen and Matsu ("Chinese Taipei"). Chinese Tapei should not enter the GATT before China itself (WTO, 2001).

Figure 1. China, Exports of Goods and Services (% of GDP)
Source: World Bank, World Integrated Trade Solution, 2018

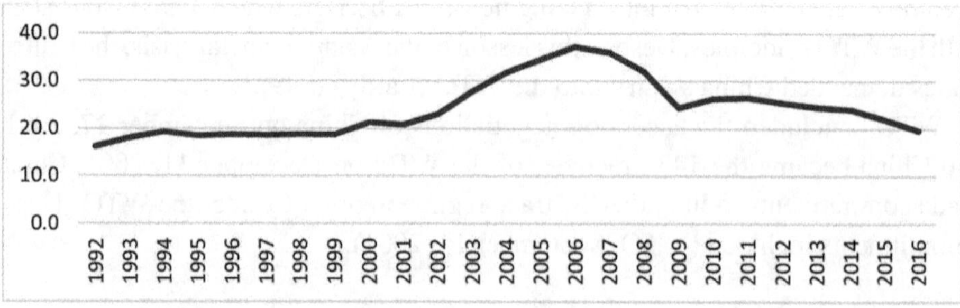

Hong Kong became also a contracting party of GATT on 23 April 1986. On 1 July 1997 China, resumed the exercise of sovereignty over Hong Kong and Hong Kong became a Special Administrative Region of China (WTO, 2001). Hong Kong would pursue its own economic and trade policies, using the name "Hong Kong, China". After WTO established, Hong Kong continued to be a member of World Trade Organization using the name of "Hong Kong, China."

In 1999, China resumed the exercise of sovereignty over Macau, and Macau became a Special Administrative Region of China, but has pursued its own economic and trade policies, using the name of "Macau, China". Macau became a contracting party of the General Agreement on Trade and Tariffs on January 11, 1991, and on December 20, 1999, Macau became a member of the WTO using the name of "Macau, China" (WTO, 2001).

USA-China Trade Relations and Trade Disputes Between USA and China in WTO

Chinese goods are demanded almost all over the world, also from the United States. China-United States trade relations deepened especially after 2001. The American imports from China increased and reached its highest level of $ 505.470 million in 2017.

American Demand for Chinese Goods

China's exchange rate regime has a crucial impact in the increase of China's exports. China has pegged yuan to the dollar. In January 1994, China devalued the yuan against the dollar by 33 percent and yuan/dollar rate stood at 8.7 (Figure 2) as part

Figure 2. Yuan/Dollar average rate
Source: Macrotrends, 2018.

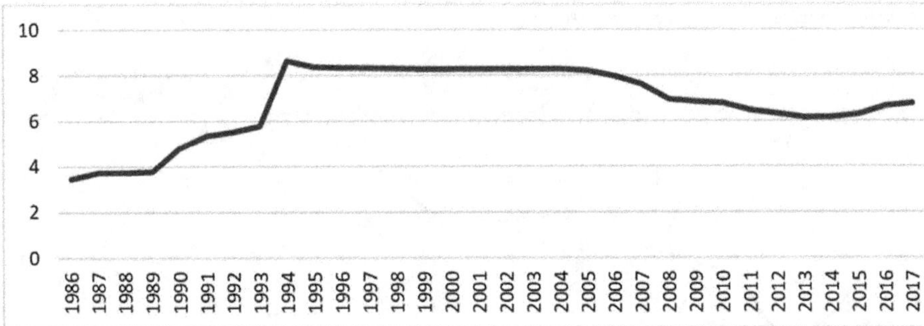

of the reforms to be a "socialist market economy" (Koh Gui Qing, 2012). After 1994, China's export to the United States also started to rise.

In April 1994, the yuan/dollar rate was around 8.28 and the central bank could intervene to make the value of the yuan stable. From 1999 to 2005, the U.S. dollar/renminbi[1] rate stayed at 8.28. In 2001, China joined the World Trade Organization and began to adjust its currency regime gradually. China's trade surplus with the United States let to the rise in yuan in 2003. In 2005, China revalued its currency against the dollar, amounting an appreciation of 2,1% of the renminbi and changed its exchange rate currency by introducing reference basket. The basket would comprise of the currencies of the countries to which China has a significant deficit in terms of foreign trade, external debt, and foreign direct investment. In 2009, China decided to internationalize its currency and allowed all firms in the country to use yuan in imports and exports contracts. In May 2017, China introduced a 'countercyclical' factor in setting the yuan central parity rate. Yuan central parity rate is determined by three factors: the bilateral exchange rate of the renminbi against the dollar, the theoretical yuan exchange rate and the countercyclical factor (Yu, 2018, p. 325). The Yuan/Dollar rate started to decrease after 2004 but the trade deficit of America with China had increased from year to year and recorded its highest level of 375,576 million dollars in 2017.

Besides the yuan/dollar exchange rate, Chinese goods are cheaper in the world because of the lower production costs, especially because of the labor costs which make up the high percentage of the production costs. China's labor costs, when compared with the labor costs in the United States, have a decreasing trend as shown in Figure 3.

Figure 3. Labor Costs in China and in the United States of America
Source: National Bureau of Statistics China, 2018

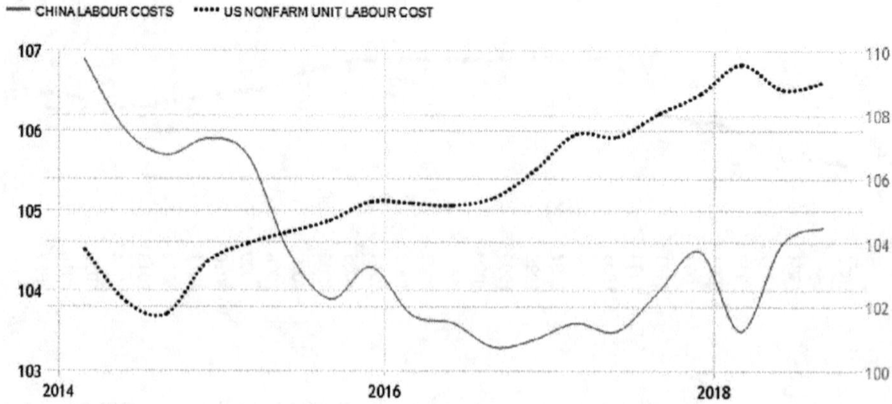

Labor Costs in China were about 105.80 Index Points from 2012 to 2018 and recorded as 104 Index Points in 2018. Labor costs in the United States increased from 105 Index Points in 2016 to its highest level of 109.60 Index Points in 2018 in the last ten years. The high labor costs in the United States can reduce the competitiveness of American firms in the world market.

The other advantage China offers is the ability to make things cheaper than can be made in other western manufacturing areas: Using cheaper materials, lead paint, lead solder, etc. can all be done in China (Diliberto, 2015).

China-United States of America Trade Relations

China ranks first in the world exports, while the United States ranks second. China is the second biggest importer in the world after the United States (WTO, 2018). In world imports, the United States ranks first. China is the second biggest export market of the United States alongside Canada with a share of 7,3%. The United States is the second biggest export market with a share of 15% and the second biggest import market in China with a share of 19,3% after Hong Kong (WTO, 2018).

Trade between the two countries is developing in favor of China's trade balance. American imports from China has an increasing trend, especially after China's membership in 2001, the imports grew rapidly (Figure 4). China's trade surplus was \$ 421.4 billion in 2017, while the United States reported a trade deficit of \$ 862.8 billion in the same year.

Figure 4. United States trade balance with China
Source: United States Census Bureau, 2018

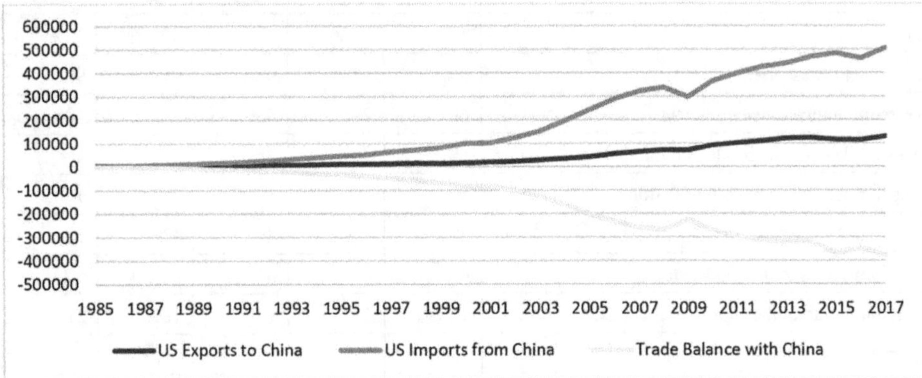

America exports many products from China. Soybeans, wheat, barley, steelmaking materials, petroleum products, natural gas liquid, industrial machines, medicinal equipment, chemicals, semiconductors, aircraft engines, equipment, passenger cars are the main export products. Table 1 shows the export products which have the biggest shares in the United States' export value. 23% of the total exports to China comprise of aircraft, engines, equipment and the export of soybeans accounts for 18% of total exports to China.

United States import many products from China. Table 2 shows the main products which have great shares in the import value of America. Cell phones, other household goods account for 21% of the total import value. Computers rank second and telecommunications equipment ranks third in total American imports, accounting for 13% and 10%, respectively.

Table 1. United States' exports to China

Commodity Description	2013	2014	2015	2016	2017
Soybeans	19%	21%	15%	20%	18%
Semiconductors	7%	8%	9%	9%	9%
Civilian aircraft, engines, equipment, and parts	18%	20%	22%	21%	23%
Passenger cars, new and used	12%	16%	13%	13%	15%

Source: United States Census Bureau, 2018.

Table 2. United States' imports from China

Commodity Description	2013	2014	2015	2016	2017
Computers	14%	14%	13%	12%	13%
Computer accessories	9%	9%	9%	8%	9%
Telecommunications equipment	6%	7%	8%	9%	10%
Apparel, household goods - cotton	5%	4%	4%	4%	4%
Apparel, textiles, nonwool or cotton	6%	7%	8%	7%	7%
Footwear	4%	4%	4%	4%	3%
Furniture, household goods, etc.	4%	5%	5%	6%	6%
Cell phones and other household goods, n.e.c.	17%	19%	19%	18%	21%
Toys, games, and sporting goods	7%	7%	8%	7%	8%
Televisions and video equipment	3%	3%	3%	3%	3%

Source: United States Census Bureau, 2018.

USA-China Trade Disputes

Since China joined the WTO in December 2001, the United States and China have established dialogues including trade and investment (Office of the United States Representative: China, Mongolia and Taiwan). The United States has supported China to pursue more market-oriented policies and to become a responsible WTO member. However, according to the United States, these efforts were not effective because China did not make sufficient attempts for moving toward a market economy (Office of the United States Representative: China, Mongolia and Taiwan). After China became the WTO member, China's trade policies were started to be complained in the Organization. The disputes between the WTO member states are dealt by Dispute Settlement Body (DSB). Then the DSB establishes dispute settlement panels and make consultations.

China's Complaints About the United States' Trade Measures

There are totally 15 disputes cases brought to the WTO, with China as complainant and with the United States as respondent. China's complaints to the World Trade Organization were about the United States' measures against Chinese imports. These measures include tariffs, anti-dumping duties, countervailing duties and safeguard measures that the United States imposed against some Chinese products like poultry, passenger vehicle and light truck tires, steel and aluminum products, renewable energy, crystalline silicon photovoltaic products, and steel products. The disputes broke down by subjects. From fifteen cases, six of the disputes were about the anti-dumping and countervailing duties of the United States against Chinese companies. Anti-dumping and countervailing duties are imposed when a firm dumps a product; i.e. when the firm exports a product abroad cheaper than it sells in the home market. The United States imposed these duties on the imports of coated free sheet paper, renewable energy, shrimp and diamond sawblades, and some certain products.

Three disputes are found about the safeguard measures that the United States imposed against Chinese firms. China's complaints to the WTO were about the safeguard measures on imports on certain steel products, aluminum products and imports of crystalline silicon photovoltaic products.

There are two cases about the rules and procedures governing the settlement of disputes with China that include tariff measures on certain goods from China in 2018. The dispute citing agreement on trade-related investment measures with China was about the measures related to renewable energy in 2018. There is one case in which China complained to the World Trade Organization about Sanitary and Phytosanitary Measures that the United States imposed against imports of poultry from China.

The United States' Complaints About Chinese Trade Measures

On the other side, the United States' complaints about China include 23 dispute cases. There are 23 disputes cases brought by the United States to the WTO. Three disputes comprised of anti-dumping and countervailing duties on grain oriented flat-rolled electrical steel, broiler products and on certain automobiles from the United States. There are two disputes citing *Agreement on Trade-Related Aspects of Intellectual Property Rights* with China as respondent and with the United States as the complainant.

Most of the disputes (12 cases) include the disputes citing *Protocol of Accession*[2] with China as respondent and with United States as a complainant. There were four disputes citing *General Agreement on Trade in Services* with China as the respondent and with the United States as the complainant. The disputes comprise Value-Added Tax on Integrated Circuits, Measures Affecting Trading Rights and Distribution Services for Certain Publications and Audiovisual Entertainment Products, Measures Affecting Financial Information Services and Foreign Financial Information Suppliers and Certain Measures Affecting Electronic Payment Services (WTO, Dispute Settlement Body).

There are 10 disputes which are about *the Agreement on Subsidies and Countervailing Measures that the United States complained about* China. Two of the total disputes contain the Trade-Related Investment Measures.

China and the United States agreed to pursue the DSB recommendations in the disputes in previous years. But the disputes in the last years are not concluded yet and the panels continue.

Trade Wars Between the USA and China

The United States supported China's WTO membership and expected that China would make efforts to be a market economy, but the United States was disappointed by China's trade policy. The United States accused China of implementing unfair trade measures and so conducted investigation about China's acts, policies, and practices related to technology transfer, intellectual property, and innovation under section of the Trade Act of 1974. The United States investigated China's laws, policies, practices, and actions that may distort trade and harm American intellectual property rights, innovation, or technology development (USTR, 2018, p. 4). According to the findings of the investigation (USTR, 22.03.2018: 4):

- China uses joint venture requirements, foreign investment restrictions to require or pressure technology transfer from U.S. companies.
- China deprives American companies of the ability to set market-based terms in licensing and other technology-related negotiations.
- China facilitates investment unfairly and transfers large-scale technology.
- China conducts and supports cyber intrusions into American commercial computer networks to gain unauthorized access to commercially valuable business information.

After the investigation, the trade war between the United States and China started. On March 8, 2018, the U.S. President Trump decided to impose an additional 25 percent tariff on steel imports and a 10 percent tariff on aluminum imports. His decision was based on the Article 232 of the Trade Expansion Act of 1962, in order to protect national security of the United States (U.S. Department of Commerce, 2018). Additional tariffs began to be implemented on March 23, 2018.

On April 2, China took retaliation measures and issued tariffs on $2.4 billion in American exports. After China's reaction, on April 3, USTR introduced a list of 1,333 products that would be subject to an additional duty of 25 percent (Office of the United States Trade Representative, 2018). The list amounting about $50 billion, included goods such as semiconductors, medical devices and flat-screen televisions (Tan, 2018).

On April 4, China took retaliation measures against the tariffs applied by the United States, by producing a list of 106 American goods, including soybeans, cars and airplanes, that could be subject to tariffs of 25 percent (Tan, 2018).

On May 29, 2018, the United States introduced a list of $50 billion of goods that are imported from China including industrially significant technologies would be subject to an additional 25 percent tariff on June 15, 2018 (Office of the United States Trade Representative, 2018).

On June 15, President Trump announced 25 percent tariff on $50 billion of Chinese goods. The list of 1,100 Chinese imports contain industrially significant technologies, including those related to China's "Made in China 2025" industrial policy (Office of the United States Trade Representative, 2018).

In September 2018, United States Trade Representative (USTR) announced a list of $200 billion worth of Chinese imports which are subject to additional tariffs. These tariffs would be effective on September 24, 2018 (Office of the United States Trade Representative, 2018). From January 1, 2019 onwards, the additional tariffs would increase to 25 percent.

The United States has applied two rounds of tariffs on Chinese goods, totaling 250 bn $; the first round amounted 50 bn $, and the second round amounted 200 bn $. These additional tariffs comprise of mainly intermediate goods (Table 3).

China imposed tariffs on $110bn of American goods, totally, comprised of mainly intermediate goods (Table 4).

President Trump has announced to threaten another $267bn worth of goods – which mean that the tariffs for almost all Chinese imports could rise (BBC News, 2019). 44% of this planned list comprised of capital goods. U.S. President also specified that "Tariffs have put the U.S. in a very strong bargaining position, if countries will not make fair deals with us, they will be 'Tariffed!' (FXStreet, 2018).

SOLUTIONS AND RECOMMENDATIONS

Tariff increases by the United States against Chinese goods and China's retaliation measures show that protectionism in trade came up again between the countries. In fact, the first step to liberalize international trade was taken by the United States Government and the United Kingdom in December 1945. The biggest trading countries in the world trade were invited to the reduce barriers at that time. On October 30, 1947, the GATT was signed by 23 countries. The United States demand for the new multilateral system to be based on the "most favored nation" (MFN) principle (Santana, 2017, p. 7).

GATT (WTO) contributed to the international trade liberalization with its rounds. The United States made efforts to liberalize trade in the world and in the first years of GATT, the United States requested the European Community[3] to reduce its subsidies but European Community did not take any steps, and there has not been any improvement. GATT's first rounds aimed to reduce tariffs. However. in the field of agriculture there was no liberalization until Uruguay Round. Uruguay Round (1986-1995) launched by America to liberalize agricultural trade, to reduce protectionist trade policies. At the end of the Uruguay Round, the GATT was transformed into World Trade Organization. In order to continue the liberalization

Table 3. The United States' tariffs on Chinese imports: product composition shifts between lists

Phase 1:	**$ 50 billion list**	53% Intermediate goods	42% Capital goods	4% Transport equipment	1% Consumer goods	<1% Other
Phase 2:	**$ 200 billion list**	50% Intermediate goods	25% Capital goods	24% Consumer goods	1% Other	
Potential Phase 3:	**$ 267 billion list**	15% Intermediate goods	44% Capital goods	40% Consumer goods	1% Other	

Source: Chad P. Bown, Euijin Jung and Zhiyao (Lucy) Lu, September 20, 2018.

of trade, further trade negotiations were decided at the end of the Uruguay Round, and in 2001 the Doha Tour started. Doha Tour did not come to an end because of the tensions between the United States and China in the Doha Round. United States and the European Union as the developed countries, and China and India on the developing side could not make any compromise about the safeguard measures. United States and the EU were criticized not to take sufficient steps to conclude Doha Tour and Doha Tour collapsed in 2008, but the United States claimed that they made enough concessions.

Table 4. Chinese Tariffs on the United States' imports: product composition shifts between lists

Response to Phase 1:	**$ 50 billion list**			
	63%	7%	2%	28%
	Intermediate goods	Consumer goods	Capital goods	Other
Response to Phase 2:	**$ 60 billion list**			
	67%	26%	7%	<1%
	Intermediate goods	Capital goods	Consumer goods	Other
Potential Response to Phase 3:	**$ 53 billion list (The rest)**			
	52%	33%	5%	10%
	Intermediate goods	Capital goods	Consumer goods	Other

Source: Chad P. Bown, Euijin Jung and Zhiyao (Lucy) Lu, September 20, 2018.

Since the establishment of GATT, America has been a pioneer in the liberalization of trade, and after China became a leader in world trade after its WTO membership, tensions and disputes between USA and China started. In 2018, America decided to adopt protectionist policies against China due to China's unfair competition. United States' tariff imposition against China is a protectionist measure and China's retaliation measures are obstacles to trade liberalization as the two world trade leaders have great world shares. China and the United States account for 22.6% of world merchandise trade (WTO, 2018, p. 23).

If the two countries continue their trade war, these protectionist policies can turn into non-tariff barriers. The protectionism by adopting tariffs in fact is a looser way of protectionism. As the tariff is a tax on imports, the importer country can import by bearing the extra cost of tariffs. The impact of tariffs to protect domestic production is uncertain. But non-tariff barriers like quotas, import bans have great impacts, in that, the import is restricted despite the domestic demand. Non-tariff barriers are the hardest and the strictest way of protectionism. So, the trade war should not be deepened and not endanger the trade liberalization in the world.

FUTURE RESEARCH DIRECTIONS

This study examined the trade relations between the USA and China. The protectionist measures that both sides pursue to each other and the trade disputes between both sides are discussed in this study. The strong and the significant aspects of this study are the examination of the trade problems between USA and China. The constraint of the study is that the impact of the trade wars on the other macro-economic indicators like GDP, GDP growth, investments etc. are not taken into account. The trade war is analyzed only from the trade perspective. A research about the impact of trade wars on macro-economic indicators in both countries would be beneficial. A further research might also include the impact of these trade wars on world trade.

CONCLUSION

Establishment of GATT was a milestone for world trade liberalization which was initiated by the United States. Protectionist policies lessen in time but China had stayed out of the system. The United States supported China's WTO membership to achieve a fair and more market-oriented trade in the world, as China was one of the largest traders. After China's WTO membership, trade disputes between China and the USA began. According to the United States Representatives, China was not a responsible member of the WTO by pursuing unfair trade policies. The United States increased tariffs against Chinese imports and the trade war between the countries started. For every tariff increase by the United States, China undertook retaliation measures.

United States of America has always been the pioneer for the liberalization of world trade. Without reaching the desired level of liberalization in trade yet as expected in the WTO Doha Tour, these protectionist measures of the United States of America and also of China are disappointing since all the efforts to liberalize trade from the 1995 Uruguay Round onwards, could fail. Both countries have to reach an agreement, and have to change their trade policies. The USA and China had better end the trade war. Otherwise, the United States' efforts for trade liberalization would be wasted. The two countries are the world trade leaders. It will be their benefit to end the trade war.

REFERENCES

Bown, C., Jung, E., & Lu, Z. (September 20, 2018). Trump and China Formalize Tariffs on $260 Billion of Imports and Look Ahead to Next Phase. *Peterson Institute for International Economics*. Retrieved from https://piie.com/blogs/trade-investment-policy-watch/trump-and-china-formalize-tariffs-260-billion-imports-and-look

Chen, E. I. H. (2014). US-China trade relations and economic distrust. *Chinese Economy*, *47*(3), 57–69. doi:10.2753/CES1097-1475470304

Diliberto, M. (2015). Why are products from China so cheap? *Quora*. Retrieved from https://www.quora.com/Why-are-products-from-China-so-cheap

Donnan, S. (2018). US says China WTO membership was a mistake. *Financial Times*. Retrieved from https://www.ft.com/content/edb346ec-fd3a-11e7-9b32-d7d59aace167

FXStreet. (2018, September 17). Breaking News: Trump: If countries will not make fair deals with us, they will be "Tariffed!" Retrieved from https://www.fxstreet.com/news/breaking-news-trump-if-countries-will-not-make-fair-deals-with-us-they-will-be-tariffed-201809171020

GATT. (1987, February 18). *China's Status as a Contracting Party (Publication no: L/6125)*. Switzerland. Retrieved from https://docs.wto.org/gattdocs/q/GG/L6199/6125.PDF

GATT. (1987, March 4). *Minutes of Meeting*. Retrieved from https://docs.wto.org/gattdocs/q/GG/C/M207.PDF

He, C., Li, C., & Lin, C. (2018, March 22). Economic Impacts of the Possible China–US Trade War. *Emerging Markets Finance and Trade*, *54*(7), 1557-1577. Retrieved from https://www.tandfonline.com/doi/abs/10.1080/1540496X.2018.1446131

Kim, M. H. (2014, January 02). The U.S.–China Trade Deficit. *The International Trade Journal*, *28*(1), 65–83. doi:10.1080/08853908.2013.814555

Lardy, N. R. (1999, April 1). China's WTO Membership. *Brooking Policy Brief Series*. Retrieved from https://www.brookings.edu/research/chinas-wto-membership/

Liu, T., & Woo, W. T. (2018, October 04). Understanding the U.S.-China Trade War. China. *Economic Journal (London)*, *11*(3), 319–340. doi:10.1080/17538963.2018.1516256

Macrotrends. (2018). *Dollar Yuan Exchange Rate - 35 Year Historical Chart.* Retrieved November 11, 2018, from https://www.macrotrends.net/2575/us-dollar-yuan-exchange-rate-historical-chart

National Bureau of Statistics China. (2018). *China Labor Costs.* Retrieved from https://tradingeconomics.com/china/labour-costs

A quick guide to the US-China trade war. (2019, January 7). BBC News. Retrieved from https://www.bbc.com/news/business-45899310

Office of the United States Representative. *China, Mongolia and Taiwan.* Retrieved from https://ustr.gov/countries-regions/china-mongolia-taiwan

Office of the United States Trade Representative. (2018). *2017 Report to Congress on China's WTO Compliance.*

Office of the United States Trade Representative (2018, March 22). *Findings of the Investigation into China's Acts, policies, and Practices related to Technology Transfer, Intellectual Property, and Innovation under Section 301 of the Trade Act of 1974.*

Office of the United States Trade Representative. (2018, June 15). *USTR Issues Tariffs on Chinese Products in Response to Unfair Trade Practices.* Retrieved from https://ustr.gov/about-us/policy-offices/press-office/press-releases/2018/june/ustr-issues-tariffs-chinese-products

Office of the United States Trade Representative. (2018, September 18). *USTR Finalizes Tariffs on $200 Billion of Chinese Imports in Response to China's Unfair Trade Practices.* Retrieved from https://ustr.gov/about-us/policy-offices/press-office/press-releases/2018/september/ustr-finalizes-tariffs-200#

Office of the United States Trade Representative. (2018, June). *USTR Finalizes Tariffs on $200 Billion of Chinese Imports in Response to China's Unfair Trade Practices.* Retrieved from https://ustr.gov/about-us/policy-offices/press-office/press-releases/2018/june/ustr-issues-tariffs-chinese-products

Office of the United States Trade Representative. (2018, June 29). *Section 301 Product List Fact Sheet.* Retrieved from https://ustr.gov/about-us/policy-offices/press-office/fact-sheets/2018/june/section-301-product-list-fact-sheet

Qing, K. G. (April 14, 2012). Timeline: China's reforms of yuan exchange rate. *Reuters.* Retrieved from https://www.reuters.com/article/us-china-yuan-timeline/timeline-chinas-reforms-of-yuan-exchange-rate-idUSBRE83D03820120414

Rosyadi, S. A., & Widodo, T. (2018). Impact of Donald Trump's tariff increase against Chinese imports on global economy: Global Trade Analysis Project (GTAP) model. *Journal of Chinese Economic and Business Studies*, *16*(2), 125–145. doi:10.1080/14765284.2018.1427930

Santana, R. (2017). 70th Anniversary of the GATT: Stalin, the Marshall Plan, and the Provisional Application of the GATT 1947. *Journal of Trade Law and Development*, *9*(2).

Skonieczny, A. (2018). Trading with the enemy: Narrative, identity and US trade politics. *Review of International Political Economy*, *25*(4), 441–462. doi:10.1080/09692290.2018.1448879

Tan, H. (2018, August 22). Beijing retaliates as new US tariffs kick in on $16 billion of Chinese goods. *CNBC*. Retrieved from https://www.cnbc.com/2018/08/23/us-china-trade-war-new-round-of-american-tariffs-on-chinese-imports.html

Tan, R. (2018, July 6). The U.S.-China trade war has begun. Here's how things got to this point. *The Washington Post*. Retrieved from https://www.washingtonpost.com/news/worldviews/wp/2018/07/05/a-timeline-of-how-the-u-s-china-trade-war-led-us-to-this-code-red-situation/?noredirect=on&utm_term=.70088ed928df

United States Census Bureau. (2018). *Trade in Goods with China*. Retrieved from https://www.census.gov/foreign-trade/balance/c5700.html

U.S. Department of Commerce. (2018). *U.S. Department of Commerce Announces Steel and Aluminum Tariff Exclusion Process.* Retrieved from https://www.commerce.gov/news/press-releases/2018/03/us-department-commerce-announces-steel-and-aluminum-tariff-exclusion

Wang, H. (1999). The Asian Financial Crisis and Financial Reforms in China. *The Pacific Review*, *12*(4), 537-556. Retrieved from https://www.tandfonline.com/doi/pdf/10.1080/09512749908719305

World Bank. (2018). *China, Exports of goods and services (% of GDP).* Retrieved from https://wits.worldbank.org/CountryProfile/en/Country/CHN/StartYear/1992/EndYear/2016/Indicator/NE-EXP-GNFS-ZS#

World Trade Organization. (2001, September 17). *WTO successfully concludes negotiations on China's entry*. Retrieved from https://www.wto.org/english/news_e/pres01_e/pr243_e.htm

World Trade Organization. (2018). *China Trade Profile*. Retrieved from from https://www.wto.org/english/res_e/statis_e/daily_update_e/trade_profiles/CN_e.pdf

World Trade Organization. (2018). *World Trade Statistical Review 2018*. Retrieved from https://www.wto.org/english/res_e/statis_e/wts2018_e/wts2018_e.pdf

World Trade Organization. (n.d.). *Disputes by Member States*. Retrieved from https://www.wto.org/english/tratop_e/dispu_e/dispu_by_country_e.htm

Yu, Y. (2018). *The reform of China's exchange rate regime*. Canberra, Australia: ANU Press, The Australian National University.

KEY TERMS AND DEFINITIONS

Most Favored Nation (MFN): MFN clause provides that if any country grants a privilege to a GATT member country, then this privilege will be granted also to all GATT members unconditionally.

Retaliation Measures: When a country's trade policy is inconsistent with the WTO rules, the consultations. If after these consultations, the losing country does not change its policy, WTO grants the other country to apply equivalent trade barriers.

Trade Disputes: Conflicts in trade occur, when a country does not remove its trade policy which is inconsistent with the WTO rules and harms other country's trade.

Trade Liberalization: Reducing of trade barriers like quotas, customs tariffs, etc., to ease trade between countries.

Trade Protectionism: Implementation of trade policies by a country that restrict or limit trade against the other countries.

ENDNOTES

1 Renminbi is the official currency of the Republic of China. Yuan is the unit of account. The expression of the prices is generally in yuan.

2 Protocol of Accession: to become a WTO member, applicant country signs a Protocol of Accession which includes the details about the regulations that an applicant country

3 European Community (EC) pursued protectionist policies like production payments, import levies and export subsidies to support its producers and to ensure stability in production level and in the products prices. The United States criticised the EC because of these trade-distorting policies.

Chapter 5
Trade Protectionism:
Pros and Cons

Birgül Cambazoğlu
Aydın Adnan Menderes University, Turkey

ABSTRACT

The increased commercial protection of countries as a result of the Great Depression caused the effects of the global crisis to deepen and last longer. Many countries took short-term steps to minimize the negative social impacts of the crisis by implementing protectionism. However, the crisis was gradually deepened and exerted long-term impacts on macroeconomic variables. The international platform made several attempts to reduce protectionism. However, following the global economic crisis in 2007-2009, the barriers to international trade have increased in many countries, especially in the USA. In many countries, inward-looking protectionist economic policies have been increasingly preferred. Thus, the global impact of countries' adoption of protectionism in their international trade policies has begun to be discussed in terms of the pros and cons for partners. This study analyzes the pros and cons of international trade protectionism on the basis of the impact of trade on macroeconomic variables. The results show that not only protectionism but also free trade produces both winners and losers.

DOI: 10.4018/978-1-5225-9566-3.ch005

INTRODUCTION

International trade and trade theories are among the oldest branches of economic thought. From the ancient Greeks to the present day, the determinants of trade between countries, their impacts on the parties, and the question of which trade policies are best have been the subject of considerable debate. Depending on the gains from trade or on the losses of those damaged by imports, researchers have put forward different views (Irwin, 2001). It can be said that these views are basically divided into two opposite camps. The first camp focuses on the benefits of free international trade to the parties, especially on its contribution to economic growth and technological progress, while the second focuses on the idea that domestic industries, laborers and cultures are damaged by foreign competition. As it is seen, there is no consensus that free trade is the best trade policy.

With respect to these two main perspectives, the first has been influenced by Classical thought and the second by Mercantilist thought. According to the Mercantilist thought prevailing in Western Europe in the 17th and 18th centuries, the most profitable situation, that is the source of wealth, is the case where the value of exported domestic goods exceeds the value of imported foreign goods. In other words, the case of foreign trade surplus was considered the most profitable situation. The Mercantilists camp stated that the export of industrial products is beneficial (their import is harmful), while the exports of raw materials are harmful (their import is beneficial). They justified this view by arguing that the increased volume of raw materials in a country provides a cost advantage and by extension leads to an increase in production and employment; thus, the export of high value-added products contributes to the country's economy. They further noted that for the proper functioning of this process, it is necessary to support it with government policies. They, therefore, proposed a highly interventionist system by using trade taxes that change the commodity composition of trade in favor of its homeland. Thus, the entry of gold into the country is supported, while the exit of gold from the country is hindered. One-way free trade in favor of the home country is advocated in line with the basic tenets of Mercantilist thought, which is consistent in itself. In other words, the dominant view is trade protectionism for the main country. However, how is this strategy supposed to work if all partner countries of international trade behave the same? In other words, not every country can have a foreign trade surplus, export only high value-added products or import raw materials. Mercantilism has been subjected to the following criticism: "How can trade be done between countries if each country tries to enjoy a foreign trade surplus?".

The Mercantilist thought that held sway over international trade lost its dominance with the acknowledgment of Adam Smith's book "An Inquiry into the Nature and Causes of the Wealth of Nations" published in 1776. In this work, anti-mercantilist thought was based on important grounds. Thus, the foundations of a new world were laid, which is based on individuality, has no need for government intervention, and is enriched by the dominance of free trade. It was argued that the individual interests of rational people lead to an increase in productivity with the increased division of labor and specialization in the economy, thereby multiplying the capital savings of countries. To put it differently, the "invisible hand" which operates according to the law of nature ensures social order and paves the way for enrichment; thus, there is no need for government intervention. An intervention disrupts the natural functioning. David Ricardo, one of the advocates of the same thought system, supported and advanced Adam Smith's theory of "Absolute Advantage" with his theory of "Comparative Advantages". In his "On the Principles of Political Economy and Taxation" published in 1817, David Ricardo defended the advantages of foreign trade to countries. Firstly, he emphasized that the expanding market and the resulting increase in production lead to an increase in specialization and labor force, thereby boosting productivity and reducing the cost of production per unit. Secondly, he underscored that international competition reduces the monopoly power of domestic producers and force them to design and achieve higher production yields. Finally, he noted that consumers are able to buy a wide range of products at low prices and benefit from the increased purchasing power for their limited incomes (Abboushi, 2010). The advocates of free foreign trade from Ricardo to the present day have highlighted the advantages of the aforesaid liberalization of foreign trade to the parties and sustained their efforts into the removal of obstacles to the liberalization of trade. In a nutshell, the Mercantilist understanding that total wealth is stable and all countries cannot gain in the foreign trade (one country's gain is another's loss) was replaced by the understanding that total wealth is unstable and all countries may gain with the liberalization of foreign trade. This thought held sway until the Great Depression of 1929.

Although David Ricardo's views have been sidelined for a certain period of time, they are still valid and indispensable for the advocates of free trade. In modern times, especially since the establishment of the General Agreement on Tariffs and Trade (GATT), countries involved in international trade have enjoyed increased economic welfare and ensured political stability. The increased awareness of the advantages of international trade to the parties has led to an increase in countries' demand for membership in international commercial organizations (Abboushi, 2010). However, it has been observed that apart from its positive effects, foreign trade has negative cultural, social and economic impacts on countries. This observation has led to the reappearance of protectionist orientations. Additionally, due to the steadily growing disparity between developed and developing countries, developing countries have been unable to make full use of foreign trade and countries' openness has increased their vulnerability to international crises. This observation has also strengthened protectionist trends. In this regard, it can be said that the support for protectionist trade policies is generally bolstered periodically in periods of slow economic and income growth. The tendency to use tariffs and other protectionist measures, especially in the G20 countries, has been resurrected since the Global Financial Crisis. In other words, protectionism has increased in G20 countries since the Global Financial Crisis. Therefore, the growth in world trade has become stagnant over the past few years. These developments bear clear risks and signs that the trend toward more protectionist policies may be accelerated. More protectionist policies have been signaled especially by US President Donald Trump's stance toward protectionist trade policy[1], tendencies to employ protectionism to help a country survive the economic crisis, and strengthening advocates of protectionism in some parts of Europe (Productivity Commission [PC], 2017). In other words, the idea has been gaining strength that protectionism, which has reappeared as a controversial tactic between policymakers and economists, can be used as an important trade policy to increase the economic welfare of a country. Some policy-makers and economists put the following interpretation as to the growing strength of advocates of trade and investment barriers: foreign trade and economic growth will slow down, thereby lowering living standards. For example, it has been argued that the US trade war on China and Mexico will reduce economic growth in three countries, especially in Mexico, and the increased protectionism toward China and Mexico will not narrow the US trade deficit in the long run but will lead to a significant restructuring of world trade. The uncertainty as to what may result from the growing tendency of protectionism has been influencing global trade and investment. Those who argue that uncertainties will narrow production and negatively affect economic growth have been strongly emphasizing that increasing protectionist measures around the world will lead to a global recession and by extension unemployment and lowering living standards (PC, 2017; Kommerskollegium National Board of Trade [KNBT], 2016). On the other hand, they consider an increasing tendency toward more free markets to be the best response to preventing protectionist trends. It is thus evident that the trend toward protectionism in foreign trade has been becoming strong simultaneously with the trend toward the liberalization of foreign trade. It is now unclear which trend will be stronger, depending on which course countries will follow. Having said that, it is surprising that some countries that advocate for protectionist measures are developed countries (primarily the US), thereby causing concern that protectionist measures will be widespread. In some developed countries, policymakers make use of the public belief that foreign trade is beneficial, as well as of the increasing public awareness that there are both winners and losers.

In this context, it is important to understand the effects of protectionism in foreign trade, especially on the economic structure. According to this background, the aim of this study is to address both positive and negative aspects of these effects. To this end, the study first provides a concise overview on the conceptual dimension and effects of free foreign trade to better understand the effects of protectionism in foreign trade.

BACKGROUND

Free Trade

In order to better understand the effects of protectionism, it is necessary to understand the basics of views on trade liberalization. Thus, it is of importance to define the concept of free trade. The international trade literature has reached no consensus on the conceptual definition of free trade. The main reason for this is that in determining the conceptual dimension of free trade, some studies focus on only the flow of goods and services, while others refer to all cross-country flows. The narrow-scoped definition of free trade based only on the flow of goods and services involves the removal of unfair obstacles to the flow of goods and services. In other words, free foreign trade is a system in which the national and international flow of goods and services is not subject to interventions and restrictions by political decision-makers. Free trade, an integral part of the broad series of economic reforms initiated after World War II, refers to the reduction of tariffs, the abolition of quotas and restrictions on capital flow (Drozdz & Miškinis, 2011). The concept of free trade has been slightly expanded with the inclusion of capital flows in this definition. According to Foudo (2012), free foreign trade refers to the case when there is no intervention in trade, such as taxes, tariffs, and non-tariff barriers (regulatory legislation and quotas and even inter-state governed trade agreements such as the North American Free Trade Agreement and The Central America Free Trade Agreement). It seems that the definitions are often intended for the flow of goods and services.

Free trade is also defined as a system in which individuals, regions and countries, namely trade partners, benefit from the comparison of different cost advantages in production What benefit-oriented approaches ignore is that free trade also has important costs. If the benefits of free trade outweigh costs and threats, it results in disagreement among economists (Drozdz & Miškinis, 2011). Therefore, this study first discusses the advantages of free foreign trade and then its disadvantages.

Building on the arguments put forward by David Ricardo, free trade advocates point to the various advantages offered by the liberalization of foreign trade to the parties and use them as the basic premise of their argument for the removal of barriers to trade liberalization. The advantages that free trade offers to trade parties are as follows: (Amadeo, 2019; Drozdz & Miškinis, 2011):

1. It brings a more dynamic structure to local industries by ensuring them to adopt a more competitive structure, steering them to R&D, minimizing costs and encouraging productivity growth; thus, it prevents the formation of monopoly structures;
2. It reduces government spending by reducing and/or abolishing the subsidization of local businesses by national decision makers of free foreign trade; thus, it helps use funds in more efficient areas. This situation also ensures that institutions have a strong structure;
3. With the increasing amount of direct foreign capital entering the country through free trade, local companies have easier access to technology and transfer technology. Thus, local companies become familiar with effective production methods and utilize local resources optimally. Eventually, the scale structure of local companies is expanded. Increased scale efficiency shows that local companies minimize their costs and maximize their profits. In particular, this situation applies to the mining, oil drilling, and manufacturing industries;
4. Free foreign trade contributes to the formation and development of new international networks for production and marketing, thereby paving the way for an expansion of the market and a strong growth of trade and investment.
5. Free inter-industry trade changes intra-industry trade, which gives a comparative advantage. Thus, intra-industry trade enables countries to make use of larger markets;
6. With free trade, local companies grow by using new technological developments and thus create new lines of business. The emergence of new business lines also increases the rate of labor force employment. Labor force employment also increases through the growth of the scale structure of local companies. In other words, when the local sector, which has a comparative advantage with the division of labor and specialization, takes a price advantage, it leads to an increase in export figures and by extension in the employment rate in the relevant sector. Thus, it raises the purchasing power of individuals and improves the total welfare at the national level;

7. Consumers gain access to goods of different quality and variety at lower prices when imported goods enter the country. The real power created by the price advantage, namely the increase in purchasing power caused by the low price of goods, has a positive knock-on effect on other lines of business;
8. After all, all these positive effects (especially increased labor and specialization, and quick access to new technologies) accelerate the economic growth of trading countries, thereby creating higher standards of living.

In a nutshell, free foreign trade facilitates the spread of information and technology, the proliferation of innovations, the increase in competition, access to less expensive and more efficient input goods and services, the increased division of labor and specialization, the prevention of waste of resources, and the proliferation of companies that produce optimum outputs. Thus, these positive developments at the micro level contribute to the strengthening and growth of national economic structures at the macro level. Therefore, it creates a higher standard of living.

Although there is a wide range of studies on international trade theory and its projected advantages, there is little research on the threats of free trade. A considerable amount of literature on free trade generally focuses on the positive aspects of trade. However, trade liberalization has both economic benefits and costs. In other words, free foreign trade provides parties with these apparent advantages, as well as disadvantages (Drozdz & Miškinis, 2011). These are as follows: (Amadeo, 2019; Drozdz & Miškinis, 2011):

1. The fact that foreign companies generally enter an aggressive competition in free trade causes domestic companies to reduce prices to protect their national market against such competitive companies. In other words, domestic companies are forced to adopt non-price-based strategies to compete with imported goods and protect sales. This makes domestic companies have to accept low profits. The possibility that domestic companies do not maintain low profitability for a long period of time leads to the risk of unemployment.
2. If countries adopt price-based strategies to protect or increase their market share in free trade, it leads to different prices in the market. Thus, the probability of trade diversion in countries remaining outside this competitive environment increases and the welfare of these countries decreases.
3. Multinational companies transfer labor force to countries where they directly invest through parent companies (especially the transfer of senior executives). Thus, external labor supply increases, thereby causing domestic managers to be deprived of such positions.

4. Since developing market countries do not have adequate labor protection, multinational companies see the labor force in these countries as cheap outsourcing and employ women and children in factory jobs under substandard conditions.
5. Many developing countries have no laws to protect patents, inventions, and new processes. The current laws are not always fully enforced. Therefore, the ideas of multinational companies are often stolen and they fail to compete with local producers who produce at lower prices.
6. Many developing countries have traditional agriculture-based economies. When subsidized farming enterprises in developed countries enter the local markets of such countries and the local markets fail to compete, it leads to the contraction of the sector's production and unemployment. Thus, migration from agricultural areas to cities is quickened. Therefore, internal migration with unprepared infrastructure distorts the structure of urbanization. In addition, the accumulation of excessive labor force in cities and the lack of sufficient knowledge and skills of the agricultural labor force to adapt to new conditions lead to structural unemployment. All these developments increase the rate of poverty and crime in cities. It should also be noted that these countries become importers of agricultural products due to the contraction of the agricultural sector. External dependence on agricultural products is an important macroeconomic problem.
7. Although developing countries generally have environmental protection laws, they are not practiced effectively. This situation causes multinational companies to see it as an advantage. Therefore, companies use timber, minerals and other natural resources in their own favor, thereby leading to the depletion of resources. Thus, fertile lands turn into waste areas.
8. The fact that international companies transfer consumption behaviors in the country of the parent company to trade partner countries leads to the deterioration in social, cultural and consumption habits in those countries, and as well as the deformation of their economic structure.
9. Since each country has different standards of quality, allowing low-quality and low-priced foreign goods to enter local markets leads to the misinformation of local consumers and the deterioration in perceived quality. Thus, poor-quality goods spread widely across local markets. Various health problems arise.
10. The dominance of the goods of foreign companies adopting an aggressive pricing policy causes domestic consumers to develop consumption habits toward foreign goods. If there is a demand for imported goods and domestic producers fail to compete with these prices and to stimulate the demand for

domestic goods, it leads to the contraction of the sector. Decreasing scale efficiency isolates companies from the national market and the unemployment rate rises. Increasing unemployment rate influences other sectors by producing a multiplier effect. As a result of the domino effect, the production capacity of the country shrinks; thus, the total welfare decreases.

11. Tariffs both facilitate promoting the competitiveness of local producers and enable countries to acquire tax revenues. Attempts to reduce tariffs and remove barriers particularly make developing countries vulnerable to external competition. It also deprives governments of such tax revenues. In order to cover the cost of tax losses, governments resort to alternative methods that challenge local producers. Therefore, local producers are harmed on all sides.
12. If a country fails to concentrate on the production of goods with a comparative advantage in free foreign trade and the relative importance of other sectors decreases, it makes the country dependent on trade partners. If the economic, political or social status of trade partners deteriorates, it may cause damage to the export-based industrial branches of the country. Therefore, all the following macroeconomic indicators of the country in question deteriorate: decline in total production, increased unemployment rate, and the loss of welfare.
13. Developing countries often export low value-added products. However, foreign companies exporting to these countries export high value-added products in contrast to local companies. Thus, local producers lose their competitiveness in their own markets and withdraw from both domestic and foreign markets. Therefore, the dominance of foreign companies over the national market becomes increasingly widespread and the country in question happens to constantly import these goods. This leads to a steady rise in the external dependence of that country.
14. The constant foreign exchange outflow from the country as a result of its external dependence causes that country to have a current account deficit. Therefore, the country increasingly searches for foreign funds, thereby leading to an increase in borrowing trends.
15. In order to make the current account deficit, countries tend to attract portfolio investments; the profit-driven nature of portfolio investments leaves countries open to negative internal and external shocks. Constant exposure to negative shocks leads to a decline in the credibility of the country and the confidence in the national currency, thereby leads to an increased orientation toward foreign currencies with high convertibility.

It is clear that foreign trade has positive and negative impacts on the economies of countries. It is worth noting that the degree of development of countries determines whether negative impact or positive effects will be greater. Small countries, which are generally developing countries, are often negatively influenced by international trade in the long run. However, some developed countries focus on some of the negative effects of free trade and resort to trade protectionism to protect themselves. To sum up, countries have turned to protectionist measures by citing the negative effects of free trade as the reason.

MAIN FOCUS OF THE CHAPTER

Trade Protectionism

An Overview of the Modern History of Trade Protectionism

The British Corn Laws in the 19th century was considered the first modern political action on protectionism and the origin of fear of protectionism. Landowners in the UK urged to keep prices of grain products high in favor of domestic producers in order to reduce the power loss against industrial patrons. With the enactment of the British Corn Laws, grain import was limited by tariffs and other trade restrictions. In 1846, the British Corn Laws were repealed as a result of the activities of industry patrons for repeal, who claimed that labor costs were increased by laborers' demand for higher wages due to their inability to make ends meet as a result of the increased grain prices. The second important development in protectionism is the US Tariff Act, also known as the Smoot-Hawley Tariff, which entered into force on June 17, 1930. By the law enforced to protect businesses and farmers, customs duties were increased to 45% on average (Irwing, 2011). The fact that this caused retaliatory wars led to the further deepening of the Great Depression of 1929. The volume of foreign trade between the US and Europe was significantly damaged from 1929 to1932. It seems that when countries resort to protectionist measures in foreign trade by putting up these valid and consistent rationales, it brings about a risk of retaliation. In this case, all countries are likely to be adversely affected by this retaliatory war. US President F. D. Roosevelt, who forecast the effects of this possible situation, took a step toward trade liberalization in 1934, reduced customs duties and signed the Reciprocal Trade Agreements Act (RTAA) into law on the cooperation with trade partners (VakıfBank Economic Research Department [VEAM], 2018).

Following World War II, the Bretton Woods System was adopted in view of the negative effects of protectionism, which laid the foundations of the current international trade system. Protectionist measures for foreign trade deeply influenced countries in macroeconomic terms, thereby increasing trends toward the liberalization of international trade. By signing the General Agreement on Tariffs and Trade (GATT)[2] in 1948 by 23 countries, the parties thereto assumed their obligations for the liberalization of trade. Further developments were in the direction of the further liberalization of world trade. However, the increasing dominance of Japanese goods in the US market led the US to resort to protectionist measures against Japanese goods in 1991. When US President G. W. Bush raised customs duties on steel in 2002, it resulted in shrinking production and employment problems. This practice ended in December 2003 due to a threat of retaliation by the European Union (VEAM, 2018).

The Global Financial Crisis (GFC) in 2008 revived protectionist trends. The fear has arisen that the potential negative effects of the wave of protectionism (the end of prosperity and the prevention of economic growth) would reappear. To stop these fears, in November 2008, the G20 countries declared that they would not impose new protectionism-oriented trade restrictions and adhere to the rules of the World Trade Organization (WTO). Shortly thereafter, a surveillance system mutually conducted by the WTO, the Organization for Economic Co-operation and Development (OECD) and the United Nations Conference on Trade and Development (UNCTAD) was established to monitor the G20 commitment. An independent non-government initiative, the Global Trade Alert (GTA), was also initiated for a similar purpose. Shortly after these monitoring mechanisms were established, the OECD launched a services trade restrictiveness index (OECD STRI). The World Bank also launched another project with the same title (WB STRI). Additionally, the OECD has begun to inform countries by publishing the FDI regulatory restrictiveness index (FDI Index) with annual updates since 2010. The World Bank has published the overall trade-restrictiveness Index (OTRI) since 2009 (KNBT, 2016). The objective of all these steps was to inform the countries about the course of international trade. All these indices are important indicators for the direction of the effects of trade barriers.

In addition to all the developments, US President Donald Trump's protectionist trade policy stance[3], the exclusion of the statement of the refusal of protectionist policies from the final declaration of the G20 meeting of 2017[4], and strengthening advocates of protectionism in some parts of Europe suggest that the steps taken so far are not disincentive and the wave of protectionism will become gradually widespread. According to a study conducted by the International Monetary Fund (IMF), which reflects the cost of this wave, if the US imposes a 10% increase in tariffs on imports from all over the world, it will lead to a permanent 1% decline in real GDP (Guarino, 2018).

In consideration of the foregoing discussions, it seems that developed countries resort to more protectionist measures than developing countries. However, in a study in 2013, Panagariya expressed the opposite. Panagariya (2003) argues that on average, poor countries have higher tariff barriers than high-income countries.

In order to grasp this globally emerging picture, it is first necessary to understand what trade protectionism is and how it affects international trade parties. An insight into these questions allows a deeper understanding of how policymakers drive the system.

Conceptual Dimension of Trade Protectionism

According to the concept of a free market economy; free competition constitutes the basis of economic activity. In order to compete in international markets, companies need to ensure economic efficiency; the division of labor and specialization contributes to the achievement of efficiency in production. Ensuring efficiency in production is also indicative of effectiveness in resource distribution. Thus, the free functioning of the price mechanism ensures effectiveness in the division and distribution. Therefore, economic efficiency is achieved through the free price mechanism. The competitiveness of countries in foreign trade increases. As a result of the non-stationary nature of total wealth, producers of a country with high competitiveness make more profit. Otherwise, the opposite is also true. Although the view of free trade is based on theoretically strong grounds, it seems that the international transfer of goods and services is unlikely to be possible without any limitations in practice. In other words, it is impossible to speak of completely free trade. As a matter of fact, political decision-makers cannot ignore the pressure of domestic producers and often resort to protectionist measures in international trade. It is then necessary to clarify the question "What is protectionism?".

Protectionism is defined as practices involving the opposite methods of free trade practices and promoting economic growth and wealth formation within the borders of a country (Guarino, 2018). In a broad sense, protectionism refers to the fact that policymakers of a country limit the flow of goods and services between countries through economic policies by putting up various reasons. According to Guarino (2018), protectionism means that a country or sometimes member countries of a trade bloc resorts to trade barriers in order to protect their economies from the potential dangers of international trade. In order to protect the economic interests of key industries, commodities, and employment of laborers, political decision-makers subsidize domestic production within the framework of protectionist measures and impose tariffs on foreign products with high competitiveness against domestic products (Sagar, 2017; Guarino, 2018). However, as noted by Foudo (2012), foreign trade can also be limited by high tariffs on imported or exported goods, restrictive quotas, various import-restrictive government regulations, and anti-dumping laws designed to protect local industries from foreign takeover or competition. In addition, the restriction of non-tariff imports, particularly voluntary export restraints of all kind, is called "new protectionism" measures (Ruggie, 1994). However, these definitions indicate that the concept of protectionism has not been addressed from a wide range of perspective.

In the international literature, there is no consensus on what the concept of protectionism is and on its content. To put it differently, there is no official definition of protectionism accepted by academics or international institutions. The main reason for this is that the concept of foreign trade is today defined under a broader perspective. Considering the history of foreign trade theories, they focus solely on the flow of goods and services outside the borders of the country. Today, foreign trade is defined under a wider perspective. The wide range of relations of foreign trade includes the following (KNBT, 2016): the cross-border sale of finished goods, intermediate goods, and capital goods; services delivered through various supply modes; the cross-border movement of persons needed for the production or sale of goods or services; investments in the form of foreign organizations; the movement of data needed for the cross-border transactions of goods or services; technology transfer; and the collection and dissemination of knowledge about process and production methods.

In a nutshell, the expansion of the size of the concept of foreign trade has brought about the problem of what will be evaluated within the scope of protectionism. According to the survey conducted by KNBT (2016), the concept of protectionism is defined in line with six different views:

1. The view focusing on policy instruments affecting commodity trade: The definition of protectionism with a focus on customs tariffs and commercial defense policies that prevent commodity trade.
2. The view focusing on the scope and/or legality of the WTO: The definition of protectionism within the scope of all means of protectionism established by the WTO.
3. The view focusing on intention-based approaches: The definition of protectionism in line with policy-makers' protectionist trends by consciously asserting various macroeconomic problems such as unemployment and sectoral problems.
4. The view focusing on public-driven trade restriction: The definition of protectionism within the framework of non-tariff barriers such as various subsidies and export support measures.

5. The view focusing on discrimination: The definition of protectionism within the framework of discrimination against foreign companies or others in line with commercial interests.
6. The view focusing on market deterioration: The definition of protectionism that analyzes the negative impact exerted by the deterioration of market competition on welfare.

It appears that there is no consensus on the definition of protectionism since the concept is addressed from different angles. Thus, a more detailed discussion of rationales for protectionism helps clarify the content of protectionism.

The Pros of Trade Protectionism

Countries put up certain rationales for implementing protectionist measures. The benefits, namely advantages, underlie the rationales for protectionist measures. An important rationale and advantage of protectionist measures is the restoration of trust of governments. The Global Financial Crisis in 2008 has revived anti-globalization trends by taking different forms such as economic crisis, commercial crisis, employment crisis, and a crisis of confidence. Some studies indicate that the most important of this whole process is the crisis of confidence. The loss of confidence in the system causes the system to be re-questioned. Policymakers who truly grasp this situation often foreground protectionist rhetoric through patriotism in order to restore the confidence of their citizens in times of crisis. Such rhetoric is generally not questioned but quickly accepted by citizens and consolidate the authority of political power. It has been discussed that in most of the public-choice models, public officials resort to these policies to maximize the possibility of re-election (Kaempfer, Tower, & Willett, 2004). In other words, policymakers make protectionism look understandable, rational and preferable (Fung, 2009). The work of some researchers supports the understandable and justifiable rationales put forward by political decision-makers. These rationales are the arguments proposed for the acceptance of protectionism. These rationales also represent the advantages that a country will gain. The primary reasons include national security, economic development, increasing competitiveness, reducing unemployment, making up a balance of payments deficit, and reducing external dependence.

One of the most common rationales and advantage of protectionist measures is that they ensure national security. It is argued that free trade increases external dependence; thus, it is of key importance to protect sectors of strategic importance such as defense industry in order to prevent the country from running into trouble in a state of emergency such as a war in which the flow of goods and service may be interrupted. In other words, in protectionism based on national security, political decision-makers tend to protect the defense industry and sectors of specific importance from external competition in order to increase their resilience to war in the case of the emergence of national security-related situations such as the state of war. The necessity and continuity of these policies are advocated for the protection of the existence of the state.

Another rationale for protectionist trends is increasing competitiveness. The "Infant Industry Argument" offers developing countries and the "Strategic Trade Theory" offers developed countries solutions to increase competitiveness. These theories include practices to protect industries that might have a comparative advantage and by extension competitiveness in the future from customs tariffs, other restrictions, and foreign competition. According to the infant industry argument, industries that might enjoy a comparative advantage and become capable of producing optimum outputs are temporarily protected until they attain this level (Seyidoğlu, 2013). If these practices are successful, the competitiveness of the country in question increases, thereby leading to an increase in the volume of production. However, this means a loss to manufacturers of other countries. The basis of another protectionist policy implemented with the rationale of competitiveness is the "Strategic Trade Theory". According to this theory, in order for technology-based industries (computer, communication tools, etc.) to have a comparative advantage, it is necessary to resort to protectionist measures so that the scales structure of scale can be allowed to expand. The whole nation benefits from the emerging external benefit, thereby allowing rapid growth in the future and increasing national welfare (Seyidoğlu, 2013).

Blocking the entry of dumped goods into the country is another rationale and advantage of protectionist measures. In general, countries tend to undersell or sell at a loss to increase their market share in other countries or to hold sway over the market. The aggressive pricing strategy impairs the competitiveness of producers in other countries. Seeing that domestic producers fail to compete, policy-makers impose anti-dumping duties as high as dumped prices in order to protect domestic producers that lose their competitive advantage against low-priced imported goods. Thus, domestic producers are given the opportunity to compete.

Fair trade, namely the equalization of conditions, is another rationale and advantage of protectionist measures. In other words, conditions are equalized between countries through the methods of protectionism. It is discussed that the difference in production and cost resulting from the non-equality of some conditions, such as countries' technology, labor force, and environment leads to unfair competition in foreign trade. It is argued that it is necessary to resort to protectionism in order to overcome this inequality (Acar, 2004). As a result, barriers used for the elimination of the difference ensure that trade is fair.

Another reason and advantage of protectionist measures is the solution to important macroeconomic problems of countries. Countries struggling with macroeconomic problems such as unemployment problem and a balance of payments deficit use this rationale to resort to protectionist measures in foreign trade. In order to solve the social problems caused by continuous unemployment, countries try to shift the demand from abroad to domestic markets by resorting to import-restrictive measures. Thus, the increase in demand for domestic goods is intended to increase the volume of domestic production, thereby increasing the volume of labor employment. Another macroeconomic problem that countries fight against is the balance of payments deficit. Countries that have a balance of payments deficit try to solve this problem through protectionist measures. Due to the domestic demand for low-priced imported goods in and the inability of domestic producers to compete with the prices of foreign goods, these countries have a balance of payments deficit. Central banks of these countries constantly use foreign exchange reserves to make up the foreign trade deficit, which eventually leads to the meltdown of foreign exchange reserves. Thus, the search for outsourcing is quickened, thereby resulting in borrowing. Thus, the fluctuation in all macroeconomic indicators of these countries leads to a decrease in their credibility. Policymakers of these countries raise tariffs and restrict imports to prevent these undesired situations. However, policymakers can resort not only to tariffs but to other protectionist measures. As a result, the reduced import volume impedes the outflow of foreign currency outside the country and the balance of payments deficit is reduced to some extent. [5]

The abuse of the labor force is another rationale and advantage of protectionist measures. In other words, it is argued that protectionist measures prevent. Free trade leads to the worsening of working conditions of employees and the abuse of labor force in countries where the labor force is not under the protection of legal regulations. Multinational companies regard the labor force in emerging market economies only as cheap outsourcing and can make employees work without adequate labor protection. Women and children are often employed in factory jobs under substandard conditions. Therefore, political decision-makers need to protect their citizens by resorting to various protectionist measures in order to prevent the abuse of labor. The working conditions of employees are improved if necessary protectionist measures are achieved.

Bargaining power is another rationale and advantage of protectionist measures. If a country imposes or maintains high tariffs due to its weakness in international markets compared to other countries, it can occupy an advantageous position in international markets. In negotiations with other trade partners to abolish or reduce protectionism, the country tries to gain some benefits in return for the abolition or reduction of protectionist measures. This practice is slightly different from the others. The country uses protectionist measures to force its trade partners to create advantages in its own favor (Seyidoğlu, 2013). The fact that if this country is a big country or a single buyer or seller, then it achieves success should also be excluded.

It is an undeniable fact that countries' resort to protectionist measures in foreign trade for these valid and consistent reasons brings about many possible risks. In view of the foregoing discussions, the disadvantages of protectionist measures in foreign trade are addressed in the following section of the study.

The Cons of Trade Protectionism

A debate on the costs of protectionism reflects, to some extent, the debate on the gains from trade liberalization (KNBT, 2016). The disadvantages of protectionist measures are stronger than the advantages (Coughlin, Chrystal, & Wood, 1988). Foreign trade protectionism can negatively affect the macroeconomics of a country and often the global economy in the short and long run. These effects are discussed in detail below.

Protectionist measures can negatively affect consumers' choices and by extension their consumption. Consumers are unable to access the quantity, quality, and variety of products after the introduction of protectionism, which they previously access at lower prices before protectionist measures. In other words, after protectionism, consumers have very limited options for the quantity, quality, and type of product. Therefore, consumers choose from a limited basket and pay more for them. To put it another way, some consumers who are unable to change their consumption habits in a short period of time have to pay more for a limited amount of goods and products, thereby causing a huge increase in inflation. Some consumers are unable to get through or have difficulty getting through the price increase due to the narrowing of the supply of goods and services in the domestic market. Therefore, they stop consuming or consume less of these goods and services. Protectionism implies that producers transmit the effects of increased prices to consumers, which result from the shrinking basket of goods and services as opposed to the global competitive environment. Thus, the spending power of consumers is restricted. This situation negatively affects the welfare of consumers (Guarino, 2018; Lombardo, n.d.).

Countries that resort to currency control by keeping their national currency low to sell their products at lower prices in foreign markets face the problem of inflation and high interest rates in the long run (Malpass, 2005). There will be an increase in the prices of all foreign products sold in the domestic market of countries that resort to foreign currency control; therefore, consumers will have to pay more to buy these products. Especially in cases where consumers cannot stop consuming medical goods with low price elasticity, they will obtain these goods by paying higher prices. This situation applies especially to other necessary groups of goods. The key point to highlight is that political decision-makers offer the country's industry the opportunity to compete through foreign currency control, thereby causing consumers to bear the burden of costs (Guarino, 2018; Lombardo, n.d.)

If countries that use the rationale of the infant industry argument, one of the most important arguments of protectionism, to justify their protectionist measures, achieve their expectations, their economies are negatively affected. Newly industrialized countries temporarily protect certain branches of industry until the maturation period. If these industries rest on the laurels of their protectionist measures, it may interrupt their attempts to minimize their costs and may reduce their productivity. In other words, since industry branches under the protection by tariffs (and other measures) fail to assess cost benefits, that is, to determine the optimal production method, they are unlikely to compete when the protection ends. In fact, this situation is indicative of adverse selection. Adverse selection brings about the moral danger. Therefore, these branches of industry resist ensuring that temporary support does not end. It should be noted that infant industries, which are considered to be competitive in the future and protected until the maturation period, cost a considerable amount of money and financial resources to states. In order to afford this cost, countries tend to borrow as a result of their search for resources. All these costs are felt throughout society. Although what happens fails to achieve what is targeted, the resulting costs are likely to be undeniably huge and produce a social welfare-reducing effect (Guarino, 2018; Lombardo, n.d.).

The biggest danger of protectionist measures, namely their biggest disadvantage is that they can lead to retaliatory wars (trade wars). Retaliation (trade retaliation or retorsion) can be defined as follows: if a foreign trade partner country takes protectionist measures such as tariffs, quotas, subsidies, and exchange rate controls on the grounds that its exports are adversely affected, the other partner country counteracts using trade policies similar to trade restrictions, regardless of whether they are political and military allies. The main reason for countries to retaliate is that they can no longer sell their raw materials, finished goods or intermediate goods in markets where they can normally do (Guarino, 2018). If only tariffs are used as means and there is retaliation, this is called tariff war. As a result, the trade volume between two countries shrinks and completely ends. Therefore, both countries suffer from a loss of welfare. This might negatively affect not only the two countries but also other countries. The global supply chain is disrupted by retaliatory wars; thus, countries lose their market share, and global trade volume shrinks. Therefore, the total volume of production is narrowed, thereby causing the unemployment problem to worsen. Eventually, global economic growth is interrupted. The best example of this situation is the Smoot-Hawley Act. With the enforcement of the Smoot-Hawley Act, other countries suffered from this situation have resorted to retaliation. As a result of retaliatory wars, global trade decreased by 67% and U.S. exports decreased by 75% (Guarino, 2018).

The greatest possible danger of retaliatory wars is the possibility of turning into real wars. Countries that are dependent on each other are often less prone to wars. However, countries with a low degree of dependence are more likely to fight each other (Lombardo, n.d.). As a result, this situation indicates that there is always a possibility for a real war to break out.

CONCLUSION

Protectionism, seen as one of the means of surviving the economic crisis, resurrected with the rhetoric of policymakers after the Global Financial Crisis in 2008. Advocates of protectionism have recently strengthened in some parts of Europe especially due to US President Donald Trump's protectionist trade policy stance. Strengthening protectionist trends have led to a globally growing wave of fear. The main reason behind this fear is the negative experiences of countries.

Although there have been comments about the possible consequences of recent developments, the uncertainty of the outcome still remains. This uncertainty is due to the impossibility of a simple assessment of the results of policymakers' foreign trade decisions in the national and international arena, as well as the necessity to adopt a versatile perspective. If a country resorts to protectionism in foreign trade for understandable and justifiable reasons and benefits from it, it might have a negative impact on other countries. It is still uncertain which counter-attacks will be made by countries that are negatively affected. Therefore, the potential global effects of this domino effect are very hard to clearly estimate. Preferring protectionism to reverse the negative effects of free trade might not produce the expected effect. To put it another way, the above-discussed gains of countries that resort to protectionism can turn into losses. In this case, countries should get to the core of the rationales they put forward to implement protectionist measures. In other words, countries should gain a deeper insight into the matter and come up with solutions to their structural problems. Solving structural problems will increase the competitiveness of countries, thereby reducing their external dependence. It is also impossible to speak of fair trade in the case of external dependence. If there is no fair trade, it is understandable that countries resort to protectionism. However, protectionist methods should be used at an optimal level. In a nutshell, it can be said that countries should choose optimal protectionist measures so that they will not turn into retaliatory wars.

REFERENCES

Abboushi, S. (2010). Trade protectionism: Reasons and outcomes. *Competitiveness Review*, *20*(5), 384–394. doi:10.1108/10595421011080760

Acar, M. (2004). İktisadın ezelî sorunsalı: serbest ticaret mi, korumacılık mı? Retrieved from http://www.liberal.org.tr/sayfa/iktisadin-ezeli-sorunsali-serbest-ticaret-mi-korumacilik-mi-mustafa-acar,165.php

Amadeo, K. (2019). Free trade agreements with their pros and cons. *The Balance*. Retrieved from https://www.thebalance.com/free-trade-agreement-pros-and-cons-3305845

Coughlin, C. C. K., Chrystal A. & Wood, G. E. (1988). Protectionist trade policies: a survey of theory, evidence and rationale. *Federal Reserve Bank of ST. Louis Paper*.

Drozdz, J., & Miškinis, A. (2011). Benefits and threats of free trade. *Economics*, *2*(14), 40–49.

Fouda, R. A. N. (2012). Protectionism and free trade: A country's glory or doom? *International Journal of Trade. Economics and Finance*, *3*(5), 351–355.

Fung, V. K. (2009). Jobs, global trade and the perils of protectionism: the imperative of restoring confidence. In R. Baldwin & S. J. Evenett (Eds.), The Collapse of Global Trade, Murky Protectionism and the Crisis: Recommendations for the G20 (pp. 25-28). London: Centre for Economic Policy Research (CEPR).

Guarino, A. S. (2018). The economic effects of trade protectionism. *Focus Economics*. Retrieved from https://www.focus-economics.com/blog/effects-of-trade-protectionism-on-economy

Irwin, D. (2001). *A Brief History of International Trade Policy*. Retrieved from https://www.econlib.org/library/Columns/Irwintrade.html

Irwin, D. (2011). *Peddling protectionism: Smoot-Hawley and the Great Depression*. Oxford, UK: Princeton University Press.

Kaempfer, W. H., Tower, E., & Willett, T. D. (2004). Trade protectionism. In C. K. Rowley & F. Schneider (Eds.), *The Encyclopedia of Public Choice* (pp. 570–590). Boston: Springer.

Kommerskollegium National Board of Trade. (2016). Protectionism in the 21st Century.

Lombardo, C. (n.d.). 13 most valid protectionism pros and cons. Retrieved from https://vittana.org/13-most-valid-protectionism-pros-and-cons

Malpass, D. (2005). Exchange rate protectionism: A harmful diversion for trade and development policy. *The Cato Journal*, *25*(1), 107–110.

Panagariya, A. (2003). International trade. *Foreign Policy*, *139*(139), 20–28. doi:10.2307/3183727

Productivity Commission. (2017). Rising protectionism: challenges, threats and opportunities for Australia.

Ruggie, J. G. (1994). Trade, protectionism and the future of welfare capitalism. *Journal of International Affairs*, *48*(1), 1–11.

Sagar, A. (2017). Free global trade v/s protectionism- a critical review. *International Journal of Engineering Sciences & Research Technology*, *6*(4), 252–254.

Seyidoğlu, H. (2013). *Uluslararası iktisat teori politika ve uygulama (19. Baskı)*. İstanbul: Güzem Can Yayınları.

VakıfBank Economic Research Department (2018). Ticaret Savaşları Endişeleri Artırıyor. *VakıfBank Haftalık Rapor*.

ENDNOTES

1 During the presidential campaign, Donald Trump promised a tariff of 45% on imports from China and 35% on imports from Mexico (PC, 2017).

2 Following the Uruguay Round negotiations, which ended on December 15, 1993, the World Trade Organization (WTO) was established in 1995 by the countries which signed the General Agreement on Tariffs and Trade (GATT). WTO members adopted a whole set of rules for the development of international trade and the free movement of goods and services.

3 Apart from the tariffs imposed in the line with protectionist policies, US President Donald Trump decided to impose additional taxes and trade sanctions on China.

4 See VEAM (2018).

5 However, the country's dependence on imported inputs hinders the expected effect.

Chapter 6
Forms and Mechanisms of Economic Cooperation Between Russia and Belarus Within the Union State:
Tasks, Problems, Achievements

Natalia Eremina
St. Petersburg State University, Russia

ABSTRACT

On December 8, 2019, the Union State will celebrate its twentieth anniversary. During this time, a fairly long way has been covered - the main institutions were built, the tools for deepening and intensifying integration were defined, the people of Russia and Belarus acquired new opportunities. The Union State of Belarus and Russia is an actual research topic, since regional integration is now the trend of global development. And it is the Union State that is viewed by experts as the basis of the integration processes in the post-Soviet space. The Union State acts as a tool for enhancing integration processes in general in the post-Soviet space and explains to the citizens of the countries the advantages of these processes. The purpose of this study is to analyze the dynamics of the integration process within the framework of the Union State, to determine its factor in the intensification of regional integration in the post-Soviet space.

DOI: 10.4018/978-1-5225-9566-3.ch006

INTRODUCTION

The post-Soviet space is a complex geopolitical, economic, social and cultural phenomenon. This is the "Large Space", which records a long historical experience of interaction and coexistence of different peoples within the framework of Russia, the Moscow kingdom, the Russian Empire, the USSR. History shows that centripetal and centrifugal tendencies constantly interacted and dynamically replaced each other, always preserving the basic connections between peoples, regardless of changes in the state structure. And now, considering the development of the post-Soviet space, we are witnessing an interweaving of integration and disintegration tendencies within the framework of the "Large Space", which unites not only Russia and Belarus, but also the Eurasian Economic Union (EAEU) member states.

Exploring the development of this macro-region (post-Soviet space) in historical dynamics, it is impossible not to note the tendency of mutual attraction of many peoples of the post-Soviet space to each other and, above all, to Russia. For these deep reasons, regional integration in the post-Soviet space has a special historical, cultural and geopolitical uniqueness. Especially if we are talking about the Union State of Russia and Belarus, which is formed, in fact, by one people, because the Russians and Belarusians come from the same root and have a common history, a common mentality, common ideas about the structure of the world, etc. It also explains why within the framework of the USSR one of the most successful examples of economic cooperation was the cooperation between the Belarusians and the Russians. That is why the economic integration of Russia and Belarus is based on the cultural interaction of peoples and the political dialogue, which must be mentioned in our study.

The peculiarities of the post-Soviet space for the first time fully manifested themselves in the framework of the Union State, for this reason, the movement to further integration formats in the post-Soviet space, for example, within the Eurasian Economic Union (EAEU), is justified. And already the development of the EAEU raises the question of promoting the integration movement towards China (conjugation of the Eurasian integration with the Silk Road) and in the direction of the European Union within the framework of the idea of "Greater Europe from Lisbon to Vladivostok". In the Union State for the first time, the question of the harmonization of norms and standards was raised, which, in particular, is carried out by Russia and Belarus together and in accordance with international standards. In this regard, the Union State is also perceived as a test model for testing different versions of economic regional integration, based on political dialogue.

In the Union State, close and strong economic ties are formed, which have not been affected by the global financial crises. Russia is the main economic, trade and strategic partner of Belarus. It represents the main market for Belarusian industry and agriculture, and is the main supplier of the necessary energy resources for the country. In turn, Belarus significantly strengthens the position of Russia, providing it with additional access to the borders of European states through Belarusian transport corridors. Today, for Russia and Belarus, the priority direction for integration in the post-Soviet region is the Customs Union and the development of a single economic space. From 1999 to the present, countries have achieved a lot on this path, and their trade is constantly growing, which confirms the effectiveness of regional economic integration within the Union State.

The experience of the Union State has shown that institutions in the processes of regional economic integration play a key role. They act as a system-forming factor, determine the format and development of the integration movement. But their very formation in the post-Soviet space requires a long time. It is important that the cooperation of the parties within the framework of the Union State has shown that the desire for a multi-vector foreign policy of the participants of the integration movement also imposes its imprint on the formation of institutions. At least, the states, forming a single economic and social space, a security space, do not raise the question of a single political space with a single foreign policy orientation. Also, the Union State has set the competition dilemma of two principles in financing common projects. Thus, the principle of "proportional parity" in financing in some cases contradicts the principle of "parity" in obtaining benefits from the integration process. Another important conclusion of cooperation within the framework of the Union State is the recognition of Russia's special role in the strategy of the integration movement, which at the same time seeks to realize parity in setting its goals.

Therefore, the Union State identified the possibilities of regional integration in the post-Soviet space and activated it. The Union State is a successful economic integration model, a test platform for the development of Eurasian integration as a whole, since within this model not only economic, social, but also political, geopolitical issues and the problem of security are solved.

The goal of this study is to analyze the dynamics of the integration process within the framework of the Union State, to determine its factor in the intensification of economic regional integration in the post-Soviet space. To achieve this goal it is necessary to study positive and negative aspects and results of Belarusian-Russian economic and trade interaction.

BACKGROUND

Literature Review

To date, there are certain scientific approaches to study the problems of economic and trade interaction between Russia and Belarus within the framework of the Union State. Scientific literature on the topic can be divided into groups. First, a number of authors explore the problems of regionalization in economic cooperation between Belarus and Russia, emphasizing the need to develop economic institutions for interaction and for increasing trade (Nikulina, 2016; Greenberg, 2019).

Secondly, special attention of researchers was devoted to the issues of trade and economic cooperation in the context of political integration, linking the success of economic activities with the political dialogue of the parties (Valovaya, 2016; Vardomsky, 2011; Lisovolik, 2016; Kuzmina, 2017; Koktysh, 2004). These authors also investigated the institutional features of the integration of Russia and Belarus. Interestingly, the Belarusian authors, for instance V.A. Melnik, call the economic interaction of Belarus and Russia the result of a common history and the need for economic survival (Melnik, 2004). A.I. Suzdaltsev proves that the pace of economic integration does not correspond to the achieved level of political unity of the two states, though bases on the political dialogue (Suzdaltsev, 2007). These authors also argue that the different potential of the economies of Belarus and Russia is not an insurmountable obstacle to the integration processes in bilateral relations.

Thirdly, researchers of the economic interaction of Belarus and Russia believe that it depends on the general integration processes in the post-Soviet space. So, I. Azar and V. Mashko write about new opportunities for economic and trade cooperation between the two countries in the context of the Eurasian integration (Azar, 2007; Mashko, 2009).

Fourthly, it is important to note that Western European researchers critically consider Belarusian-Russian interaction. For example, K.D. Martinsen and A. Wilson believe that Russia in this interaction puts economic pressure on Belarus, making it its military-political springboard. Moreover, Western European researchers are more concerned with the negative features of the economic and commercial interaction between Russia and Belarus, rather than with its positive aspects (Martinsen, 2002; Wilson, 2011).

Methodology

The research is based on the two conceptual approaches that are equally effectively applicable to the study of regional integration in the post-Soviet Space, in particular, to analyze the development process of the Union State. The use of these concepts simultaneously reveals the sustainability factors and the main obstacles to the deeper integration.

Firstly, a competitive concept is applied, within which we examine how integrating countries realize their interests, seek to get maximum benefits, here we analyze the obstacles articulated by national interests and the desire of states to secure their sovereignty.

Secondly, a cumulative concept is used, focusing on interregional cooperation and on the joint approaches of states to deriving benefits from the integration movement. Within the framework of this concept, researchers should evaluate inter-regional cooperation, first of all, cross-border cooperation. It allows for the "merging" of integrating states and brings integration tasks closer to a population that is starting to feel itself part of the integration movement. In this case, we say that integration acts as a tool to increase the sustainability of regional and national economies. Here it is important to pay attention to the so-called parameters of the interdependence of states, which clearly indicate the effectiveness of the integration process. Among these parameters, we analyze the legal foundations of the integration movement, socio-economic indicators of integration in dynamics, vertical and horizontal relations, indicators of import growth, exports, and entry into new markets of member states.

Analysis of these processes requires monitoring statistics in the following areas: the total budget of the Union State, statistics on the development of national economies in the framework of integration processes.

THE UNION STATE AS A TEST ECONOMIC INTEGRATION MODEL

The Union State in Development of Economic Interaction Between Russia and Belarus (The Legal Framework)

Integration processes in the post-Soviet space began almost immediately after the collapse of the USSR. The new independent states that emerged in the post-Soviet space were connected to each other by numerous economic ties that could not be broken without significant damage to the national economies. It is not surprising that, for example, the Commonwealth of Independent States appeared simultaneously with the dissolution of the USSR. However integration processes manifested themselves most clearly due to cooperation between Russia and Belarus. From the very beginning, this union was provided with economic ties, while it was based on political dialogue between Russia and Belarus.

The Union State was developing at a rapid pace. On February 21, 1995, Russia and Belarus signed the Treaty of Friendship, Good Neighborhood and Cooperation. On April 2, 1996, the Treaty on the Formation of the Community of Russia and Belarus was concluded between the countries. On April 2, 1997, the Treaty on the Union of Belarus and Russia was signed. The Treaty on the Establishment of the Union State of Russia and Belarus was signed on December 8, 1999. It entered into force on January 26, 2000. It was preceded by the Treaty on the equal rights of citizens and the Agreement on the creation of equal conditions for business entities (December 25, 1998). The Union State's competencies include foreign policy, defense and security, budgetary, monetary and tax systems, customs, energy, transport and communications. Each state within the Union retains sovereignty, independence, territorial integrity, state structure, the Constitution, the state flag, the coat of arms (Soyuznoye gosudarstvo Belarusi i Rossii, 2018).

According to the Treaty 1999, the Supreme body of the Union State – The State Council- was made up of heads of the states, governments and parliaments. The executive body of the Union State is the Council of Ministers, which consists of the Chairman of the Council of Ministers, the heads of governments, the Secretary of the State, the ministers of foreign affairs, economics and finance of the member states, and the heads of the main sectoral and functional governing bodies of the Union State. The Treaty also provided for the creation of a common legislative institution of the Union State - a bicameral Parliament. However, the Parliamentary Assembly of the Union State is currently acting instead of it. According to the Treaty, the Court of the Union State and the Court of Accounts should be created, which have not yet been formed (Dogovor O sozdanii Soyuznogo gosudarstva, 1999).

The Treaty on the Union State provided for the creation of the necessary legal grounds for the full-fledged interaction of the countries. The economic and trade cooperation between Belarus and Russia within the framework of the Union State is determined by all the normative treaties defining the format of the development of the Union State.

Firstly, it is the Treaty on the Establishment of the Union State, the Program of Actions for the implementation of its provisions of December 8, 1999, and other normative legal acts, which aimed at creating a single economic and customs space, integrated energy and transport systems, harmonizing national legislations in the economic sphere. Besides that Russia and Belarus have signed about 200 contracts and agreements so far. At the same time, this experience has a beneficial effect on different forms of interaction between states in the post-Soviet space, for example, within the framework of the Eurasian Economic Union (EAEU). All these agreements have turned the Union State into the most advanced form of an integration association in the post-Soviet space. Thanks to regulatory law, a single migration space has been created in the Union State, there are no customs and border controls between the states, and citizens of both countries travel within the Union State using national documents. Citizens of the two countries have equal opportunities for free education and in employment, they can stay on the territory of another state without registration for 30 days (Mezhgosudarstvennyye otnosheniya Rossii i Belarusi, 2018).

Secondly, the interaction of the states is defined by the provisions of the foreign policy concepts of Russia and Belarus, which have defined a strategy for further deepening integration. Thirdly, this interaction is based on the personal meetings of the heads of the states, which have become regular. For example, in 2016 the presidents of Russia and Belarus held seven meetings. In 2017 there were four meetings (at the same time, the prime ministers of the countries met 9 times). In 2018 eight meetings were held.

The documents and meetings of the leaders of Belarus and Russia provided the beginning of the economic integration of Russia and Belarus from 1995 to 1999 (the first stage of economic integration within the Union State). During this period, the Customs Zone was created, the Russian market was opened for Belarusian goods, and the Belarusian market was opened for Russian goods. However, from the very beginning it became obvious that the economic decisions depend on the political component in the dialogue between Minsk and Moscow. Besides that often in matters of relations with third countries, Russia and Belarus act individually. Not completing the process of forming the Customs Union, since tariff disputes between the parties were not fully resolved, since 2000, Belarus and Russia have begun to create the Common Market, which means elimination of restrictions on movement of production factors in the Union State - investments, workers, information (the second stage of economic integration within the Union State). In 2005, the parties began the process of coordinating the activities of credit and financial institutions to convene a basis for harmonizing and unifying social, fiscal and monetary policies (the third stage of economic integration within the Union State). However, this process is slow since Belarus and Russia maintain significant differences in tax and legislative systems (Suzdaltsev, 2007).

A positive factor in enhancing economic integration was the adoption of a common budget of the Union State. In 2000, the first budget of the Union State was approved, which is a solid basis for financing joint projects in various fields. Judging by the budget, the Union State is developing steadily. For example, for 2018, the total income of the budget of the Union State is about 7 billion Russian rubles; the total expenditure of the budget of the Union State is about 5 billion Russian rubles; the surplus of the budget of the Union State is 2 billion rubles. Russia in 2018 contributed more than 3 billion rubles to the total budget, the Republic of Belarus - about 2 billion rubles. Other types of income are also included in the budget revenues of the Union State (for example, income derived from the use of the property of the Union State, as well as income from its sale - in the amount of

100 percent) and others (Parlamentskoye Sobraniye prinyalo byudzhet Soyuznogo gosudarstva, 2018).

In 2019, the budget of the Union State increased. The income is determined in the amount of more than 7 billion rubles. The revenue part was formed due to gratuitous transfers of the member states in the amount of about 5 billion rubles. Deductions by the Russian Federation amounted to more than 3 billion rubles, the Republic of Belarus transferred about 2 billion, as in the previous year. The budget of the Union State for 2019 provides funding for 36 programs, projects and activities: among them, 11 programs, 23 events and 2 projects. It is of special importance in the context of global economic slowdown (Parlamentskoye Sobraniye prinyalo byudzhet Soyuznogo gosudarstva, 2018).

Thus, despite the problems of forming the common market within the Union State, dependence of economic activities on political dialogue between Moscow and Minsk, the global slowdown in economic growth, the weakening of economic opportunities and the limitation of resources, the economic and trade cooperation between Russia and Belarus is developing quite successfully.

Examples of Economic and Trade Cooperation Between Russia and Belarus in the Union State

Russia is the main and most important trade and economic partner of Belarus. Belarus is in the first place among all countries of the Commonwealth of Independent States (CIS) in terms of trade with Russia, and ranks fourth among all of Russia's global partners. At the same time, not only Russia is the main investor in the economy of Belarus, but also Belarus almost 70% of all its investments abroad is investing in the Russian economy. Trade between Russia and Belarus has been growing on a permanent basis since 1999 (Soyuznoye gosudarstvo Belarusi i Rossii, 2018).

Thus, from 1999 to 2010, Russian exports to Belarus in terms of money increased by 4.8 times, and exports of Belarusian goods to the Russian Federation increased by 3 times in terms of money. The structure of Russia's exports to Belarus during this period was dominated by fuel and energy products. Thus, the key role of Russia in the trade balance of Belarus was largely determined by the success precisely in the field of energy supplies. In the structure of Russia's exports to Belarus, in addition to fuel and energy products, ferrous metals can be distinguished, as well as chemical products, fertilizers, automobiles (Mashko, 2011).

In the structure of Belarusian exports to Russia, goods with a high degree of processing occupied the leading position in this period, i.e. machinery, equipment and vehicles. Their share in the commodity structure of exports in 2010 amounted to 31.7%. The second largest group in the structure of Belarusian exports to Russia remained food products and agricultural raw materials. In the period, Belarus managed to significantly increase exports of meat and dairy products. For example, from 2000 to 2009, export of beef to Russia increased by 15.7 times, butter and other milk fats – by 3.8 times, milk – by 4 times.

The third largest group in the structure of Belarusian exports were metals and products from them. Meanwhile, the structure of Belarusian exports to Russia was significantly different from the general export commodity structure of Belarus, where the share of high-tech products at that time was significantly inferior to the commodity group. So, in 2009, the total share of mineral products, chemical products, as well as metals and products from them in the total structure of Belarusian exports was 63% (Mashko, 2011).

This trend was continued further. Thus, in the period from 2010 to 2016 there were no changes in the trade relations between Russia and Belarus and in the structure of export-import. In the period from 2010 to 2016 Belarus retained its share in exports to Russia, and Russia retained the volume of exports to Belarus. Although it should be noted that in 2013 the share of mutual exports and imports decreased by one percent. However, since 2015, an intensive growth has been observed, which led to a significant improvement in trade interaction in 2017 (Dinamika vneshney torgovli Rossii v 2010 – 2017, 2018).

In 2017, trade grew by 26% compared to 2016 ($ 32.4 billion). Both in Russia and in Belarus, measures were taken to develop the production base and expand the range of goods. It is important to pay attention to the structure of the Russian-Belarusian trade in 2017. According to the National Statistical Committee of Belarus, the supply of industrial goods from Belarus to the Russian market grew in quantitative volumes: electric transformers (2.2 times), tires (2.1 times), shoes (+ 93.8%), tractors (+ 15.8%), railway cars (+ 35.4%), parts and accessories for automobiles and tractors (+ 13.9%), household and electric heaters (+ 17.5%), furniture (+ s30.2%). Export of some food products from Belarus to Russia also expanded, for example, flour products, cereals and starch (+ 77.7%) (Kuz'mina, 2018).

The same is true of export from Russia to Belarus. The volume of deliveries of petroleum products to Belarus increased by 95.6%, liquefied gas by 56.5%, electric generator engines by 48.6%, parts for automobiles and tractors by 44.0%, acyclic alcohols by 51.0%, ferrous metals by 20.4%, pipes by 11.2%. The growth of deliveries from Russia to Belarus was observed in all major commodity groups: non-precious metals and their products - by 46%, to $2.3 billion, cars and vehicles - by 29.9%, to $2.9 billion, chemical industry and related industries - by 25.3%, up to $2 billion, food products and agricultural raw materials - by 18.6%, up to $1.1 billion. Foreign trade in services between the countries also showed steady growth - by 24%, to $3.59 billion. First of all, these are transport and transit services, as well as banking and communication services (Kuz'mina, 2018).

In 2018, the trade turnover of the Republic of Belarus with the Russian Federation amounted to about $36 billion and increased by 9.4 percent compared to 2017 (Ob itogakh vneshney torgovli Respubliki Belarus' s Rossiyskoy Federatsiyey v 2018 godu, 2018).

In 2018 Russia mainly exported mineral resources to Belarus (more than 50%), as well as machinery, equipment (about 14%), metals and products from them (12%). In small quantities, it supplied products of the chemical industry, food, agricultural raw materials. At the same time, food products and agricultural raw materials came from Belarus to Russia (33%); Belarus also exported to Russia machinery, equipment and vehicles (30%); chemical products (12%); metals and products from them (7%); textiles and footwear (7%). Practically for all enterprises of Belarus, the Russian market remains the largest and most reliable. For example, the main export of products of the largest automotive giant of Belarus - BELAZ - accounts for Russia (almost 60% of all products) (Ob itogakh vneshney torgovli Respubliki Belarus' s Rossiyskoy Federatsiyey v 2018 godu, 2018).

Other examples of successful economic cooperation include the construction of the Belarusian Nuclear Power Plant, the first unit of which will be launched in 2019. Besides that the interregional cooperation between Russia and Belarus has a very large potential. More than 80 subjects of Russia are developing trade and economic cooperation with Belarus. In Russia, there are more than 200 subjects of trading networks with Belarusian capital. More than 3 thousand enterprises with Russian capital are organized in Belarus. In the production sphere, more than 8 thousand enterprises are connected with each other, more than 1 thousand joint ventures are established and operate (Mezhgosudarstvennyye otnosheniya RF i Belorussii, 2018).

Therefore, by now we already can argue that within the framework of the Union State, the economies of the two countries are developing in parallel, they are interdependent, though Russia remains the economic leader in this Union. However, the heads of Russia and Belarus set the tasks of further intensifying mutual development, activating the interaction of the business circles of the two countries, as well as encouraging young people to develop joint projects, paying attention to various forms of interregional cooperation.

In the development of this idea, Russia and Belarus signed an agreement on the creation of Russian-Belarusian and Belarusian-Russian business councils. The business councils include 27 Belarusian businessmen and 44 representatives of Russian business circles. Business councils must address complex issues: the lifting of restrictions and ensuring equal conditions for doing business; interaction within the framework of import substitution policy (Praktika provedeniya belorussko-rossiyskikh molodezhnykh biznes-inkubatorov, 2018).

In addition, the Belarusian-Russian youth business incubators became a regular practice. Thanks to this program, young representatives of Russia and Belarus aged from 18 to 35 years are trained on the basis of leading economic universities of the two countries. Youth business incubators have become another platform for communication between Russian and Belarusian citizens, for sharing experience and searching for like-minded people for business development (Praktika provedeniya belorussko-rossiyskikh molodezhnykh biznes-inkubatorov, 2018). The governments of both countries also support common projects in the development of new technologies.

However, at present, it is the cooperation of the Republic of Belarus with the Russian regions that belongs to the priority areas of the Belarusian-Russian interaction and creates a platform for trade and economic relations.Cross-border and interregional cooperation is provided with a common cultural and historical foundation, mentality, infrastructure, and complementarity of economic interests.

On May 29, 2015, the Concept of interregional and cross-border cooperation of the CIS member states for the period up to 2020 and the Plan of measures for its implementation were adopted. On their basis, the development of interregional and cross-border cooperation within the Union State is carried out. The Concept establishes the principles and objectives of the activities of the executive authorities of the CIS member states and their regions, as well as of organizations and citizens in the field of interregional and cross-border cooperation of the CIS member states.

The border area of Russia with Belarus is 140 thousand square km. Cross-border cooperation develops in parallel with interregional cooperation. This interaction is assisted by various forums contributing to the establishment of relations between the regions of Russia and Belarus. For example, the Forums of Regions are held annually, starting in 2014. Within the framework of the Forums of Regions, the interaction of regions in the development of technology and innovations is discussed. And in 2018, the first Forum of the border regions of Russia and Belarus took place in Bryansk (Russia). The main idea of this event was the opportunity for participants to make proposals for the development of all areas of activity within the framework of the Union State, which will contribute to the effective integration of the two countries. In 2019, it is planned to hold the Second Forum of the border regions of Russia and Belarus (Podvedeny itogi Foruma prigranichnykh territoriy Rossii i Belarusi, 2018).

If we consider economic and trade cooperation at the regional level, the leading positions in the mutual trade of the Republic of Belarus with the regions of the Russian Federation are presented by the Central, Ural, Volga and Northwestern Federal Districts. For example, cooperation of Belarus with the Tyumen, Moscow, Smolensk, Orenburg, Bryansk, Nizhny Novgorod, Kaluga regions, the Republic of

Tatarstan is effectively developing. The volume of foreign trade with these regions exceeds 70 percent of the Belarusian-Russian trade. The interaction of the Belarusian regions with Russian megacities - Moscow and St. Petersburg is actively developing. To build up cooperation between the Russian and Belarusian regions, business cooperation councils of Belarus with Moscow, St. Petersburg, Nizhny Novgorod and Sverdlovsk were created. An effective tool for regulating bilateral relations are joint working groups on cooperation established in more than 40 regions, as well as the Belarusian-Russian Council for Long-Term Cooperation of Regions, Ministries, and Government Bodies in Kaliningrad Region (Soyuznoye gosudarstvo Belarusi i Rossii, 2018).

One of the main aspects in the interaction of trade control of Belarus and Russian regions are also 11 branches of the Embassy of the Republic of Belarus in the Russian Federation (in the cities of Nizhny Novgorod, Novosibirsk, Ufa, Kazan, Kaliningrad, Krasnoyarsk, St. Petersburg, Yekaterinburg, Khabarovsk, Rostov-on-Don, Smolensk), whose activities contribute to the rapid solution of issues of bilateral trade and economic relations with supervised constituent entities of the Russian Federation.To date, quite a lot of examples of interregional cooperation of Belarusian and Russian regions have been accumulated.

So, Mogilev (Belarus) and Novosibirsk (Russia) regions actively cooperate. Novosibirsk Region supplies various technological products to Belarus, being interested in importing equipment and food products from Mogilev. Cooperation is accompanied by a mutual exchange of delegations (Mogilevskaya i Novosibirskaya oblasti, 2018).

Cooperation between Tula region (Russia) and various regions of Belarus and its enterprises is fruitfully developing, for example, in the framework of the infrastructure project “Industry 4.0”, which provides for the electrification of urban transport. The project has already proved high economic efficiency in Minsk and other cities. Agreements on the development of cooperation in the areas of transport, light industry, and agriculture have been concluded (Gubernator Tul’skoy oblasti, 2018).

Ulyanovsk region of Russia cooperates with Belarus in the production of medical equipment and in the construction of livestock farms (Belarus’ i Ul’yanovskaya oblast’ Rossii, 2018). Interestingly, the interaction of Belarus and Russia is carried out in all areas, including on the organization of labor. For example, Belarusian Vitebsk region signed an agreement on cooperation of trade unions between Vitebsk, Pskov and Smolensk regions for 2019–2020 (Profsoyuzy Vitebskoy, Pskovskoy i Smolenskoy oblastey podpisali soglasheniye, 2019).

In general, joint Russian-Belarusian projects are being implemented in 60 regions of Russia, more than three thousand organizations with Russian authorized capital are registered in Belarus, and more than 50 joint ventures have been established in Russia. Only in 2018, business contracts worth 500 million rubles were signed (Soyuznoye gosudarstvo Belarusi i Rossii, 2018).

At the same time, cross-border cooperation remains the most significant part of the permanent cooperation between Belarus and Russia.

Currently, economic cooperation between the regions of Belarus and Russian Bryansk region is very active. Almost 50 percent of the commodity turnover of Bryansk region falls on the Republic of Belarus. The foreign trade turnover of Bryansk region with the Republic of Belarus for the first 9 months of 2018 amounted to $ 438 million. Of all the diversity of industrial relations, it is worth to single out successfully operating joint Russian-Belarusian enterprises for the production of agricultural equipment (plants Bryanskselmash and Amkodor-Bryansk) (Pravitel'stvo Bryanskoy oblasti, 2018).

Belarusian and Russian regions also hold joint exhibitions and fairs of production achievements. We will mention such events as the "Day of the Bryansk field", "Svenskaya fair", "Belagro", as well as exhibitions and fairs held in Gomel, Vitebsk, Mogilev and other Belarusian regions. The cooperation of the regions of Russia and Belarus every year reaches a higher and higher level and adds not only in quantitative indicators, but also in qualitative ones. Joint working groups for the development of business cooperation have been established in 60 regions of the Russian Federation. Regions, farms and small and medium-sized businesses actively cooperate (Pravitel'stvo Bryanskoy oblasti, 2018).

Obstacles to the Economic and Trade Interaction of Russia and Belarus

Despite many tools used, developing the interaction between Russia and Belarus, some problems remain that impede the deepening of integration processes within the Union State. First of all, the provisions of the Union State Treaty were not fully implemented. Thus, the Parliament, the Court and the Accounts Chamber of the Union State were not formed. Also, the general statistical service has not yet been established. Accordingly, there is no question of adopting the Constitution of the Union State, although its project was created in 2005.

In addition, it should be said about the socio-economic problems of the Union State. The economic benefits of the Union State for Belarus are greater than for Russia. Thus, Belarus's exports to Russia account for about one-third of Belarus's GDP. Also, Russia is the main donor of many development projects of the Union State. Among other problems we should mention differences in taxation, rules for labeling goods; insufficient state support for small and medium-sized businesses, which prevents equal competition between Russian and Belarusian entrepreneurs.

These problems impede the introduction of a single currency. At the same time, the single currency is specified in the Agreement "On the unification of the monetary system of the Republic of Belarus with the monetary system of the Russian Federation and on the conditions for the functioning of a common monetary system", as well as in the Union State Treaty of 1999. Russia, which is aware of increasing financial and economic burden on the country, is still not satisfied with the idea. And in Belarus they are discussing the problem of losing sovereignty (Soyuznoye gosudarstvo Belarusi i Rossii, 2018).

The supply of not always high-quality foodstuffs of Belarus to the Russian market also becomes a negative factor, which leads to the so-called "milk" and "meat" wars.

Periodically, political rhetoric also affects interaction, primarily in the area of prices for Russian energy sources supplied to Belarus. In some critical moments on these subjects, the President of Belarus did not defiantly participated in 2016 in EAEU summits.

In addition, Belarus, adhering to the concept of a multi-vector foreign policy, does not always support Russia's foreign policy decisions. For example, Belarus has not yet recognized Abkhazia and South Ossetia. Different views on international problems impede the attainment of integrity by the Union State. Given that certain problems arise periodically, the Union State cannot reach a higher level of integration.

However, both countries face the challenge to solve the problem of lack of investment and increase product competitiveness, more effective participation in economic and trade competition in the global market. And it is in a joint way that these problems are easier to solve. And there is understanding of this at the highest management level.

The Union State as a Factor in the Development of the Eurasian Economic Space

Today, Russia and Belarus are leaders in the Eurasian integration processes in the post-Soviet space. There are many reasons for this. During the period of the Soviet Union, Russia and Belarus were advanced republics in the sphere of economics and technology, developed numerous interactions even within the framework of the

USSR. It is for this reason that Belarus and Russia literally immediately after the collapse of the USSR began to form a common economic space (Eremina, 2016).

The Union State, being the first sustainable integration project in the post-Soviet space, has become the basis of other integration processes. The Union State has created a set of agreements and arrangements that became the basis for the development of the EAEU. In this respect, the Union State is considered as a model for the EAEU. However, within the framework of the EAEU, solutions that influence the development of the Union State are also being tested.

Belarus, for example, is interested in the single energy market, which will become operational in the EAEU in 2025, which should affect the interaction between Russia and Belarus within the framework of the Union State. All experts agree that the Union State has a positive impact on the development of the EAEU.

With regard to the future strategy of the Union State in the post-Soviet space, two points of view are expressed.

A number of researchers believe that over time the Union State can be integrated into the Eurasian Economic Union, and within its framework it will finally become the core of Eurasian integration (Rakhimov, 2017), will fulfill a progressive mission - to consolidate and increase the stress resistance of the entire post-Soviet space. In this case, the Union State is perceived as an integral part of larger integration projects (Soyuz Belarusi i Rossii yavlyayetsya yadrom YEAES, 2017).

Another point of view is that, on the contrary, the EAEU can be an example in some aspects for the Union State, in terms of individual issues in the legislation, terminology used, for example, in the energy sector, antitrust law, and the Union State should take into account the realities of the EAEU (Yanikeyeva, 2018).

Parallel participation in several integration projects brings the maximum benefit to the participating States, primarily to Belarus. Thus, thanks to inter-branch relations, Belarus was able to secure the largest volume of imported raw materials and materials from the EAEU countries (Lukashenko: sozdaniye EAES ne otmenyayet perspektiv Soyuznogo gosudarstva, 2015). Although, unlike the Union State, the EAEU focuses more on the development of foreign trade relations (more than 86% of the trade relations of member countries). The EAEU confirms the complementarity of countries, the influence of the experience of the USSR.

The Union State as a Factor of Strengthening the Positions of Russia and Belarus in the Global Economy

Participation in integration projects, such as the Union State and the EAEU, allows states to act more confidently on the world market and increase exports, despite individual and even systemic economic problems.

For example, Belarusian exports of goods in 2018 amounted to 33.7 billion, primarily due to engineering products (Obzor itogov vneshney politiki Respubliki Belarus', 2018). This means that by the same period of 2017, the turnover of foreign trade in goods amounted to 115% (Belarus' v 2018 godu bol'she prodavala i pokupala, 2019). According to Belarusian data, more than 60% of the production was exported (59.7% in January-October 2017). And the export flow of Belarusian products has gained a steady upward trend. Deliveries of investment goods to the EU market have almost doubled, mainly due to the growth in truck exports. Growth in exports is also noted in traditional sales markets. In Russia, the share of Belarusian machinery in the segment of agricultural machinery occupies a leading position and amounts to almost 60%. In recent years, considerable work has been done in the Republic of Belarus to create a technical regulation system that meets the requirements of the EAEU and the WTO, based on modern technical regulations and standards. Today in Belarus, about 30% of state standards are harmonized with international and European analogues (Boleye 60% belorusskoy produktsii, 2018).

However, out of the total volume of Belarusian exports, the share of the EAEU countries accounted for 46.5% (of which the Russian Federation accounted for 44%), and the largest buyers of Belarusian products, besides Russia, were Ukraine, the United Kingdom, Germany, the Netherlands, Poland, Lithuania, Kazakhstan, Brazil (due to large-scale supply of potash fertilizers) and China. At the same time, the main volumes of imports were supplied by Russia, China, Germany, Poland, Ukraine, Turkey, Italy, the USA, Lithuania and the Netherlands (Vneshnyaya torgovlya Belarusi, 2018).

Russian exports in conditions of sanctions grew at a moderate pace. Exports from Russia for the period from December 2017 to June 2018 amounted to $ 251 billion. Mineral products were mainly exported (52%). In the structure of exports by countries, China is in the first place (12%), the Netherlands is second (9%), followed by Germany (about 8%), Belarus (5%) and Turkey (5%) (Eksport iz Rossii, 2018). And in the structure of imports by countries (goods from the group "Food products, drinks") Belarus ranks first (10%) (Eksport iz Rossii, 2018).

It is interesting, at the same time, that Russia in 2018 itself increased the supply of products of the agro-industrial complex to Belarus by 20% compared with 2017 (RF v 2018 godu uvelichila eksport produktsii APK, 2019). Among the importing countries, the main partners of Russia are China, Germany, the United States and Belarus, with Belarus slightly lagging behind the United States (Eksport i import Rossii po tovaram i stranam, 2018).

An additional global incentive for improving relations between Belarus and Russia and the growth of their joint positions in the global market will be the Silk Road, which should soon begin its work, and in which Belarus is the only hub outside of China. In this situation, Belarus and Russia will be able to jointly earn and attract investments in various projects under the Silk Road. Russia and Belarus are the economic partners of China, representing the most important elements of the transport system of Eurasia. This is all the more justified in the context of the idea proposed by Russia and supported by China for linking the Chinese concept of the Belt and the Road and the integration project of the EAEU.

In addition, thanks to the harmonization of legal and managerial decisions of Belarus and Russia, not only Russia, but also Belarus, which is not a member of BRICS, got the opportunity to enter the markets of the BRICS member countries, while Russia and China are now the main economic and strategic partners of Belarus. It is Russia, which occupies the first place in the geographical structure of Belarusian exports and imports, determines the high share of participation of the BRICS countries in the foreign trade of the Republic of Belarus. The second BRICS country in terms of turnover with the Republic of Belarus is China, which accounts for 3% of Belarusian exports and 7% of imports (Vneshnyaya torgovlya Belarusi v yanvare-iyune, 2018).

Belarus exports to China mainly raw materials - potash fertilizers, polyamides, timber, as well as combine harvesters and others. Telephones, computers, equipment, parts of vehicles, footwear parts, etc. are imported from China. Brazil is the third trade partner with the Republic of Belarus among the BRICS states. Belarus exports to Brazil 2% of exports and imports around 0.4% (Vneshnyaya torgovlya Respubliki Belarus', 2015). The main export positions of Belarus in the Brazilian market are potash and nitrogen fertilizers; X-ray equipment; fabrics, etc. (Istoriya dvustoronnikh otnosheniy Belarusi i Brazilii, 2018). Belarus imports from Brazil mainly fruits (apples, pears, citrus fruits, apricots, cherries, peaches, and tomatoes), sugar, pork, leather, etc. (Rutko, 2017). However, the export opportunities of Belarus in the markets of the BRICS countries have not yet been realized.

Thus, due to the stability of the positions of Belarus and Russia within the integration groups in the post-Soviet space, they are able to diversify exports and to a lesser extent depend on imports from third countries. First of all, this concerns Belarus, which, thanks to its cooperation with Russia, was able to enter new markets. The joint work of countries within the framework of the Union State is also an additional factor providing a positive view on the issue of accession of the Republic of Belarus to the World Trade Organization (Eksport belorusskikh tovarov vyros na $4,5 mlrd, 2019).

SOLUTIONS AND RECOMMENDATIONS

Russia remains the main trading partner of Belarus. The share of Russia in the foreign trade turnover of the Republic of Belarus exceeds 50%, while Belarus is among the five largest trading partners of Russia (4th place), accounting for 5% in the Russian foreign trade turnover. Since these positions are maintained from 1999 to the present, in spite of certain problems, it is necessary to pay attention to the following aspects:

1. The issues of energy, supply and transit of energy resources require a constant dialogue of the parties for the prevention of gas pricing disputes.
2. In order to intensify trade between the parties, it is necessary to diversify the goods produced, while emphasizing joint production. Accordingly, it is necessary to create a new production, as well as to modernize the existing production by joint efforts of the two countries. For this, it is necessary to develop the scientific and technical potential in cooperation, thanks to the coordination of scientific research, the creation of Russian-Belarusian technical design bureaus.
3. There is a task to combine the activities of Russia and Belarus in joint promotion to foreign markets, including the markets of the EU countries and China. This is relevant in connection with China's implementation of the "One Belt, One Road" strategy.
4. It is also necessary to form close cooperation between Russian and Belarusian entrepreneurs, promoting equal opportunities for business development.
5. It is very important to fully support interregional cooperation between Russia and Belarus. Cross-border and interregional cooperation will allow creating a socio-economic integrated space and will denote common economic interests.
6. A strategically valuable step in strengthening the Union State will be the intensification of cooperation between Russia and Belarus within the framework of the Eurasian Economic Union.

FUTURE RESEARCH DIRECTIONS

The Union State remains a hot topic for many scientific papers. However, at present one can talk about the need to continue exploring the development of the Union State in the context of global and regional processes. This will determine the role and place of the Union State as a special integration model in the Eurasian space and elaborate criteria for assessing the prospects for the development of economic partnership between Belarus and Russia.

It is also necessary to study the development trends of the world economy and to conduct a comparative analysis of the institutional forms of economic cooperation between Russia and Belarus with other integration entities.

In addition, there are currently quite a lot of studies analyzing the problems of cooperation between Russia and Belarus, but there are not enough works that offer mechanisms for solving problems that arise. Therefore, further development of the theme of the Union State should be related to the analysis of interinstitutional interaction in the formation of a common economic space. These data will allow to elaborate a strategy for the development of the Union State.

CONCLUSION

In 2019 twenty years have passed since the signing of the Treaty on the Establishment of the Union State of Belarus and Russia. The Union State proposes new parameters of economic development based on the implementation of new industrialization, the high role of the state as a major player in the national market. The Union State not only helps states to jointly defend their interests at the global level, but also protects their economies from the negative aspects of globalization. The Union State, also realizing common interests, inspires confidence to citizens who fully appreciate the advantages of the common market, the absence of customs and the border between Russia and Belarus. In recent years, Belarus and Russia have significantly advanced in the formation of a single economic space, ensuring equal rights of citizens of countries, harmonization of legislation to ensure equal conditions for enterprises. Most of the significant tasks within the framework of the Union State have already been implemented - a common legal space for mutual guarantees and the rights to education and health care for Russians in Belarus and Belarusians in Russia.

The Union State created special opportunities for trade interactions between Russia and Belarus, which had previously developed within the framework of the USSR. It is important that mutual trade has a particularly beneficial effect on the development of border regions of the two countries. In addition, Russia and Belarus have formed a single transport corridor, important for the development of trade in Eurasia. Note that the volume of mutual trade, as well as the variety of imports and exports, is gradually increasing. This proves that the Union State really promotes the growth of trade interaction.

The Union State suits everyone, from the political establishment, to the citizens of the two states, despite the fact that some projects have not yet been fully or completely implemented. Although the principle of parity between countries is not always respected. On the way of integration, measures are being taken to solve the obstacles. Among them, such as the establishment at the legislative level of a special regime for border areas (Rossiya i Belorussiya budut sotrudnichat' po obshchemu zakonu, 2018), as well as the transition to uniform statistical indicators, which will positively affect the socio-economic forecasting (Gronskiy, 2018).

At the same time, unevenness in every sense of Belarus and Russia makes a more significant contribution to the Union State of Russia, and for this reason brings great economic benefits to Belarus, creating additional opportunities for both parties.

REFERENCES

Azar, I. (2007). Perspektivy sozdaniya soyuza Rossii i Belorussii [Prospects for the creation of a union of Russia and Belarus]. *Mirovaya ekonomika I mezhdunarodnyie otnosheniya*, *3*, 10-19.

Belarus' i Ul'yanovskaya oblast' Rossii otmechayut polozhitel'nuyu dinamiku vzaimnogo tovarooborota (2018, December 5). [Belarus and the Ulyanovsk region of Russia note the positive dynamics of mutual trade]. *Sotrudnichestvo regionov.* Retrieved from http://www.soyuz.by/news/region/42507.html

Belarus' v 2018 godu bol'she prodavala i pokupala chem godom raneye (2019, January 10). [Belarus sold and bought more in 2018 than in the previous year]. *Informatsionnoye Agentstvo Sputnik.* Retrieved from https://sputnik.by/economy/20190110/1039526637/Belarus-v-2018-godu-bolshe-prodavala-i-pokupala-chem-godom-ranee.html

Boleye 60% belorusskoy produktsii v 2018 godu otpravleno na eksport (2018, December 20). [More than 60% of Belarusian products in 2018 were sent for export]. *Informatsionnyy Portal Soyuz Belarus'/Rossiya.* Retrieved from https://rg.ru/2018/12/20/bolee-60-belorusskoj-produkcii-v-2018-godu-otpravleno-na-eksport.html

Dinamika vneshney torgovli Rossii v 2010 - 2017 godakh [Dynamics of Russian foreign trade in 2010–2017]. (2018). *Vneshnyaya Torgovlya Rossii na osnove dannykh Federal'noy tamozhennoy sluzhby Rossii.* Retrieved from http://russian-trade.com/reports-and-reviews/2018-03/dinamika-vneshney-torgovli-rossii-v-2010-2017-godah/

Dogovor O sozdanii Soyuznogo gosudarstva [*Treaty Establishing the Union State*]. (1999). Moscow. Retrieved from http://base.garant.ru/1155132/#ixzz5hc0JB3j4

Eksport belorusskikh tovarov vyros na $4,5 mlrd [Exports of Belarusian goods grew by $4.5 billion]. (2019, February 4). *Informatsionno-analiticheskiy portal Soyuznogo gosudarstva.* Retrieved from http://www.soyuz.by/news/finance/43243.html

Eksport i import Rossii po tovaram i stranam [Export and import of Russia by goods and countries]. *Statistika vneshney torgovli. Po dannym FTS Rossii.* (2018). Retrieved from http://ru-stat.com/

Eksport iz Rossii «Vse tovary» [Export from Russia "All goods"]. (2018). *Statistika vneshney torgovli. Po dannym FTS Rossii.* Retrieved from http://ru-stat.com/date-M201712-201812/RU/export/world/

Eremina, N. (2016, July). Advent of a new civilization project: Eurasia in – U.S. out? *Journal of Eurasian Studies*, *7*(2), 162–171. doi:10.1016/j.euras.2016.02.001

Grinberg, R. S. (2019). *Rossiyskaya sotsial'no-ekonomicheskaya Sistema: realii i vektory razvitiya: monografiya* [*Russian socio-economic system: realities and vectors of development: monograph*]. Moscow: INFRA-M.

Gronskiy, A. (2018). *Soyuznoye gosudarstvo Rossii i Belarusi: problemy i perspektivy.* [*The Union State of Russia and Belarus*]. Retrieved from http://zapadrus.su/rusmir/pubru/1880-soyuznoe-gosudarstvo-rossii-i-belorussii-problemy-i-perspektivy.html

Gubernator Tul'skoy oblasti: region gotov k dal'neyshemu ukrepleniyu vzaimodeystviya s Belarus'yu po vsem napravleniyam [Governor of the Tula Region: the region is ready to further strengthen cooperation with Belarus in all areas]. (2018, December 26). *Informatsionno-analiticheskiy portal Soyuznogo gosudarstva.* Retrieved from http://www.soyuz.by/news/region/42779.html

Istoriya dvustoronnikh otnosheniy Belarusi i Brazilii [History of Belarus-Brazil bilateral relations]. (2018). *Posol'stvo Respubliki Belarus' v Federativnoy respublike Braziliya.* Retrieved from http://brazil.mfa.gov.by/ru/bilateral_relations/

Koktysh, K. Ye. (2004). *Dinamika mezhdunarodnykh i mezhregional'nykh vzaimodeystviy* [*Dynamics of international and interregional interactions*]. Moscow: ROSSPAN.

Kuz'mina, Ye. (2018). *Rossiysko-belorusskaya torgovlya: vozmozhen li proryv?* [*Russian-Belarusian trade: is a breakthrough possible?*]. Retrieved from http://eurasia.expert/rossiysko-belorusskaya-torgovlya-vozmozhen-li-proryv/

Kuz'mina, Ye. M. (2017). Ekonomicheskoye razvitiye stran YEAES i perspektivy ekonomicheskoy integratsii do 2025 g. [Economic development of the countries of the EAEU and the prospects for economic integration until 2025]. Analiticheskaya zapiska RSMD. Moscow.

Lisovolik, Ya. (2016). Geoekonomika i naslediye yevraziytsev. [Geoeconomics and the legacy of Eurasians Russia in global politics]. *Rossiya v global'noy politike,* 6, 61-69.

Lukashenko: sozdaniye EAES ne otmenyayet perspektiv Soyuznogo gosudarstva Rossii i Belorussii [Lukashenko: the creation of the EAEU does not cancel the prospects of the Union State of Russia and Belarus]. (2015, March 3). *Informatsionnoye Agentstvo TASS*. Retrieved from https://tass.ru/mezhdunarodnaya-panorama/1805062

Martinsen, K. D. (2002, October). The Russian Takeover of Belarus. *Comparative Strategy*, *21*(5), 401–416. doi:10.1080/01495930290043119

Mashko, V. V. (2009). Iz istorii Soyuznogo gosudarstva Belarusi i Rossii: Byudzhet i byudzhetnaya politika. [From the history of the Union State of Belarus and Russia: budget and budget policy]. *MGIMO*, *17*, 182–190.

Mashko, V. V. (2011). *Dinamika razvitiya rossiysko-belorusskikh torgovykh otnosheniy* [*Dynamics of development of Russian-Belarusian trade relations*]. Retrieved from http://economicarggu.ru/2011_2/mashko.pdf

Mel'nik, V. A. (2004). Gosudarstvennaya ideologiya Respubliki Belarus': kontseptual'nyye osnovy [State ideology of the Republic of Belarus: conceptual framework]. Minsk.

Mezhgosudarstvennyye otnosheniya RF i Belarusi (2018, December 25). [Interstate relations of the Russian Federation and Belarus. *RIA Novosti*. Retrieved from https://ria.ru/20181225/1548544649.html

Mezhgosudarstvennyye otnosheniya Rossii i Belarusi [Interstate relations of Russia and Belarus]. (14 May 2018). *RIA Novosti*. Retrieved from https://ria.ru/20180514/1520366481.html

Mogilevskaya i Novosibirskaya oblasti namereny razvivat' mezhregional'noye sotrudnichestvo [Mogilev and Novosibirsk regions intend to develop interregional cooperation]. (2018). *Informatsionno-analiticheskiy portal Soyuznogo gosudarstva*. Retrieved from http://www.soyuz.by/news/region/43081.html

Nikulina, Yu. V. (2016). *Regionalizatsiya v globaliziruyushchemsya mire: problemy i perspektivy*. [*Regionalization in a Globalizing World: Problems and Prospects*]. Retrieved from http://elib.bsu.by/bitstream/123456789/156751/1/276-279.pdf

Ob itogakh vneshney torgovli Respubliki Belarus' s Rossiyskoy Federatsiyey v 2018 godu (2018). [On the results of foreign trade of the Republic of Belarus with the Russian Federation in 2018]. *Posol'stvo Respubliki Belarus' v Rossiyskoy Federatsii*. Retrieved from http://www.embassybel.ru/trade-relations/

Obzor itogov vneshney politiki Respubliki Belarus' i deyatel'nosti Ministerstva inostrannykh del v 2018 godu. [Review of the results of the foreign policy of the Republic of Belarus and the activities of the Ministry of Foreign Affairs in 2018]. *Doklady Ministerstva inostrannykh del*. Retrieved from http://mfa.gov.by/publication/reports/b7fe6b330b96c9b7.html

Parlamentskoye Sobraniye prinyalo byudzhet Soyuznogo gosudarstva na 2019 god v razmere 7 mlrd 245 mln rossiyskikh rubley [The Parliamentary Assembly adopted the budget of the Union State for 2019 in the amount of 7 billion 245 million Russian rubles]. (2018, December 22). *Informatsionno-analiticheskiy portal Soyuznogo gosudarstva*. Retrieved from http://www.soyuz.by/news/finance/42747.html

Podvedeny itogi Foruma prigranichnykh territoriy Rossii i Belarusi [The results of the Forum of the border areas of Russia and Belarus]. (2018, November 30). *Informatsionno-analiticheskiy portal Soyuznogo gosudarstva*. Retrieved from http://www.soyuz.by/news/region/42442.html

Praktika provedeniya belorussko-rossiyskikh molodezhnykh biznes-inkubatorov budet prodolzhena v 2019 godu [The practice of conducting Belarusian-Russian youth business incubators will be continued in 2019]. (2018, December 5). *Informatsionno-analiticheskiy portal Soyuznogo gosudarstva*. Retrieved from http://www.soyuz.by/news/finance/42512.html

Pravitel'stvo Bryanskoy oblasti [*Government of Bryansk region*]. (2018, December 4). Retrieved from http://www.bryanskobl.ru/news/2018/11/28/9393

Rakhimov, K. (2017). Soyuznoye gosudarstvo seychas nakhoditsya v tupike [The Union State is now at a dead end]. *SONAR 2050*. Retrieved from https://www.sonar2050.org/publications/v-blijayshee-vremya-soyuznoe-gosudarstvo-nujno-rassmatrivat-sugubo-v-kontekste-evraziyskoy-integracii/

RF v 2018 godu uvelichila eksport produktsii APK v Belorussiyu na 20% [*The Russian Federation in 2018 increased exports of agricultural products to Belarus by 20%*]. (2019, February 14). Retrieved from http://www.dairynews.ru/news/rf-v-2018-godu-uvelichila-eksport-produktsii-apk-v.html

Rossiya i Belorussiya budut sotrudnichat' po obshchemu zakonu [Russia and Belarus will cooperate under the general law]. *Parlamentskaya gazeta*. (2018, November 29). Retrieved from https://www.pnp.ru/politics/rossiya-i-belorussiya-budut-sotrudnichat-po-obshhemu-zakonu.html

Rutko, D.F. (2017). *Razvitiye vneshneekonomicheskogo sotrudnichestva Respubliki Belarus' so stranami BRIKS* [*Development of foreign economic cooperation of the Republic of Belarus with the BRICS countries*]. Retrieved from ukros.ru/wpcontent/uploads/2017/03/Рутко_Радюк.doc

Soyuz Belarusi i Rossii yavlyayetsya yadrom YEAES – Al.A. Gromyko. [Union of Belarus and Russia is the core of the EAEU - Al.A. Gromyko]. (2017, November 29). *Analiticheskiy Portal Yevraziya Ekspert*. Retrieved from http://eurasia.expert/soyuz-belarusi-i-rossii-yavlyaetsya-yadrom-eaes-gromyko

Soyuznoye gosudarstvo Belarusi i Rossii. Ot Soobshchestva k Soyuznomu gosudarstvu [*Union State of Belarus and Russia. From the Community to the Union State*]. (2018). Moscow: YUNITI-DANA.

Suzdal'tsev, A.I. (2007). Postsovetskoye prostranstvo: ukhodyashchaya real'nost' [Post-Soviet space: a passing reality]. *Mir vokrug Rossii. Kontury nedalekogo budushchego*. Moscow: Kul'turnaya revolyutsiya, 124-137.

Valovaya, T. (2016). Vremya dlya yedinoy valyuty yeshcho ne prishlo [Gross: The time for a single currency has not yet come]. *Mezhdunarodlnaya zhizn'*. Retrieved from https://interaffairs.ru/news/show/16157

Vardomskiy, L.B. (2011). Ekonomicheskiy rost i regional'naya integratsiya na postsovetskom prostranstve. [Economic growth and regional integration in the post-Soviet space]. *Zhurnal novoy ekonomicheskoy assotsiatsii*, *11*, 142-143.

Vitebskoy, P. Pskovskoy i Smolenskoy oblastey podpisali soglasheniye o sotrudnichestve [Trade unions of Vitebsk, Pskov and Smolensk regions signed a cooperation agreement]. (2019, January 18). *Sotrudnichestvo regionov*. Retrieved from http://www.soyuz.by/news/region/43039.html

Vneshnyaya torgovlya Belarusi [Belarus' foreign trade]. (2018, January-July). *Ministerstvo inostrannykh del Respubliki Belarus*. Retrieved from http://mfa.gov.by/export

Vneshnyaya torgovlya Belorussii [Foreign trade of Belarus]. (2018, March 24). *EurAsia Daily*. Retrieved from https://eadaily.com/ru/news/2018/03/24/vneshnyaya-torgovlya-belorussii-ocherednaya-diversifikaciya-ocherednoy-proval

Vneshnyaya torgovlya Respubliki Belarus' (2015). [Foreign Trade of the Republic of Belarus]. S*tatisticheskiy sbornik. Natsional'nyy statisticheskiy komitet Respubliki Belarus*'. Minsk: Nats. statisticheskiy komitet Resp. Belarus.

Wilson, A. (2011). *The last European dictatorship. Yale*. Belarus: Yale University Press.

Yanikeyeva, I. (2018, November 30). Uglubleniye integratsii v ramkakh Soyuznogo gosudarstva [The deepening of integration within the framework of the Union State]. *Mezhdunarodnaya zhizn'*. Retrieved from https://interaffairs.ru/news/show/21126

ADDITIONAL READING

Karatkevich, A. G., & Golovin, Yu. A. (2014). Protsess integratsii Rossiyskoy Federatsii i Belarusi v ramkakh Soyuznogo gosudarstva [The process of integration of the Russian Federation and Belarus in the framework of the Union State]. *Vestnik KGU im. N.A. Nekrasova*, *6*, 290–296.

Kosov, A. P. (2018). Soyuznoye gosudarstvo Belarusi i Rossii v 1999-2018: Geopoliticheskiy aspekt [The Union State of Belarus and Russia in 1999-2018: The Geopolitical Aspect]. *Postsovetskiye Issledovaniya*, *1*(6), 537–549.

Kuznetsova, O. V. (2016). Pryamye inostrannye investitsii v rossiiskikh regionakh v usloviyakh sanktsii [Foreign direct investments in Russian regions under the sanctions conditions]. *International Trends*, *14*(3), 132–142.

Lazorkina, O. I. (2018). Gumanitarnoye izmereniye Soyuznogo gosudarstva Rossii i Belarusi [The humanitarian dimension of the Union State of Russia and Belarus]. *Postsovetskiye Issledovaniya*, *1*(6), 550–551.

Pastukhova, N. B. (2017). Osobennosti gosudarstvennogo suvereniteta uchastnikov Soyuznogo gosudarstva Rossii i Belorussii [Features of state sovereignty of the participants of the Union State of Russia and Belarus]. *Lex Russica*, *1*(122), 198–206.

Shamakhov, V. A., & Mezhevich, N. M. (2018). Analiz ekonomicheskoy modeli Respubliki Belarus': Kontekst gosudarstv Pribaltiki [Analysis of the economic model of the Republic of Belarus: the context of the Baltic states]. *Upravlencheskoye Upravleniye*, *11*, 35–43.

Smishchenko, R.S. (2014). Perspektivy formirovaniya federativnogo ustroystva Soyuznogo gosudarstva [Prospects for the formation of a federal structure of the Union State]. *Izvestiya Altayskogo Gosudarstvennogo Universiteta*, 4-2 (84), 305-308.

Tomashevsky, K.L. (2017). Unifikatsiya trudovogo zakonodatel'stva Rossiiskoy Federatsii I Respubliki Belarus' v ramkah Soyuznogo gosudarstva [Unification of labour law between the Russian Federation and Republic of Belarus' in the Union State]. *Aktual'nye problemy rossiiskogo prava*, *1*(74), 151-158.

KEY TERMS AND DEFINITIONS

Cross-Border Partnership: The cooperation of neighboring regions of different states, especially often in the context of an integrated construction, which includes these states.

Globalization: Strengthening of the interdependence of international actors at all levels, globalization provides the conditions for the formation of integration associations.

Interregional Cooperation: Cooperation of non-border regions.

Joint Production: A form of a country's participation in the international division of labor by creating an enterprise on the basis of jointly contributed property by participants from different countries, joint management, joint distribution of profits and risks.

Large Space: A large economic and political territorial unit, which includes several states.

Post-Soviet Space: The territory of the former Republics of the USSR.

Regional Integration: The interaction of states that form a common economic space and implement political forms of integration.

The Common Market: A single economic zone formed by several states united in an economic union; in this zone, a coordinated economic policy is carried out, uniform customs duties are in effect, etc.

The Eurasian Economic Union: An integration project in the Eurasian space, the goal of which is the economic and political rapprochement of the post-Soviet countries, consists of Russia, Belarus, Kazakhstan, Armenia, Kyrgyzstan.

The Union State: Economic, social, political, cultural, military alliance of Russia and Belarus.

Chapter 7
The United States' Interests in the Middle East During the Obama Administration:
Jordan – A Case Study

Ayman Al Sharafat
Eötvös Loránd University, Hungary

ABSTRACT

This chapter aims to analyze the US's foreign policy priorities toward Jordan in the communications of Obama, through the period from 2009 to 2017. It answers the questions: what were the US's priorities in Jordan during the Obama administration? And how Jordan was described by Obama's communications. This work is a creative one, it uses qualitative and quantitative to investigate Obama's activities toward Jordan. In order to classify the US interests in Jordan, we use Byman and Molle's classification of the US's foreign policy interests in the Middle East: counterterrorism, security of Israel, democratization, nuclear proliferation, and oil. This chapter finds that Obama's foreign strategy and approach had been driven by the maxim of 'multilateral retrenchment', which designed to achieve the United States foreign commitments, reshape its standing among the world powers, and transfer burdens onto foreign partners. The United States of America under the Obama administration substantially depended on Jordan to solve many regional complex issues and crisis.

DOI: 10.4018/978-1-5225-9566-3.ch007

INTRODUCTION

The United States of America has a long history in the Middle East, and its role has grown since the Cold War. The energy supply from the Middle East to US during the Cold War rendered it as the United States-Soviet Union chessboard (Byman & Moller, 2016). In the 1990s the United States continued its presence in the Middle East with its concern about Saddam Hussein and Iran regime ambition to play a role in the region. The efforts of Arab-Israel peace were unsuccessful, that has made the US intensify its presence in the region. After the shock of 11 September attacks, the US involvement in the Middle East has grown once again. In order to curtail terrorism in the Middle East, it deepened on cooperation with allies like Jordan.

BACKGROUND

In 2009 Barack Obama was elected as the first African-American president and he had the highest winning percentage (79%) among all presidents in the twenty years before his election, and in 2012 he was reelected for the second time, he served as the U.S. president from 2009 to 2017 (Al-Sarhan, 2016). President Obama inherited a complex situation in the Middle East; the war in Iraq, Palestine-Israel conflict, Iran's nuclear ambition, Gulf's oil, democratizing of the dictatorship systems and later Arab Spring. All of these hot issues were crucial for Obama's foreign policy in the Middle East. Obama administration put a large-scale of military commitment in the Middle East after terrorist groups started showing up in Iraq and Syria, and it stepped up a lot of efforts to work with allies in the region, Obama asked his partners in the region to participate in a coalition against terrorist militias, the main reason of that coalition was to keep the region security and protect the U.S.'s interests. Jordan was a main player in the coalition and it contributed along with the US in many air strikes in the region. Many politicians considered Obama foreign policy totally different from Bush foreign policy; during the Bush administration, the US believed it could solve all the overseas issues unilaterally. But Obama foreign policy appeared non-interventionist and he focused more on the domestic issues (Lindsay, 2011). In general, the US interests in the Middle East can be broken down into five fields: counterterrorism, keeping Israel security, prohibiting nuclear spread, democratizing of the region and ensuring the flow of oil from the Middle East (Byman & Moller, 2016).

Jordan is a small country in the heart of the Middle East; poor in its sources, surrounded by Syria in the north, Iraq in the east, Saudi Arabia in the south and Israel-Palestine in the west. Due to its Geographic Location, it has enabled Jordan to play an important role in its region and has made it an attractive partner for the

United States. Even Though Jordan and the United States have never been shared an official treaty, but they have cooperated in many issues, inside and outside the Middle East. The geographic location of Jordan is more than important for the supporters (Sharp, 2018). For example, the United States during Obama administration offered $3.75 billion to Jordan as loan guarantee (Sharp, 2018). Due to Jordan's economic problems, Jordan depended on the US aid programs and other Western Countries aids; this continues support has enabled Jordan to deal with its crises and to survive. Many people argue the miserable economic situation of Jordan, hosting a huge number of refugees from its neighbors, its crucial location on the west of oil producers, its long border with Israel and its historic-religion relation with Palestine issue, have made the US wishful to keep Jordan in its basket (Al-Sharafat, 2016).

This chapter analyzes the US's foreign policy priorities towards Jordan in the Obama Era, during the period from 2009 to 2017. The US's foreign policy priorities in Jordan during the Obama administration have not existed in the previous researches widely, and many researchers indicate Obama foreign policy in Jordan as a part of the Middle East in general. Obama era was a turning point in the US foreign policy toward Jordan, and it is so important to examine Obama priorities in Jordan. Therefore, this gives current work an advantage as it is the first work addressing the United States' interests in Jordan by using the data obtained from the interaction between the two countries. This work also is a creative one; it uses qualitative and quantitative research to investigate Obama's activities toward Jordan. This chapter examines documents of Obama during his work as the president of the United States. It answers the questions: what were US's priorities in Jordan during the Obama administration? And how Jordan played a role in the Middle East during the Obama's administration? It hypothesizes that Israel security and counterterrorism were on the top of Obama's priorities in Jordan.

This chapter starts with an introduction to provide a background on the topic, and then it presents its method and procedure. Section three includes the main quantitative findings of the examined documents and it contains a discussion of the study's data. In order to provide more details of the United States interests in Jordan, finding's part (Section three) separates to five subsections: terrorism and counterterrorism, security of Israel, democratization, nuclear proliferation, and fifth subsection is oil. Finally, section four is the conclusion, offers the main results of the work and answering the article questions.

The Obama administration was a turning point in the US foreign policy toward Jordan. This study is the first one addressing the United States' interests in Jordan by using data obtained from the interactions between the two countries. This work is a creative one as I mentioned before; it uses both qualitative and quantitative research to investigate Obama's policies and its impact in Jordan.

In order to examine and analyze the United States of America's foreign policy and priorities in the Hashemite Kingdom of Jordan, during the period from 2009 to 2017. We use data from the searchable "Public Papers" archive of "The American Presidency Project" (http://www.presidency.ucsb.edu/ws/), maintained by John Woolley and Gerhard Peters. The search string was "Jordan", which returned 129 different documents containing the word "Jordan" for the target period. By sorting using relevant and irrelevant hints, there were 24 results returned as irrelevant. "Jordan" returned as irrelevant when it did not refer to the Hashemite Kingdom of Jordan, for example, the ones that referred to a Human name were sorted as irrelevant such as Michael Jordan, Lance Corporal Jordan or and Jordan Denice. To analyze the remaining 105 relevant symbolic or substantive texts which referred to the Hashemite Kingdom of Jordan, this study uses Byman and Moller (Byman & Moller, 2016) classification of the US's foreign policy priorities in the Middle East, in "Sustainable Security: Rethinking American National Security Strategy" book, edited by Jeremi Suri and Benjamin Valentino. Byman and Moller argue that the US interests in the Middle East are: terrorism and counterterrorism, security of Israel, democratization, nuclear proliferation, and oil.

These five priorities are considered by many scholars as the most important interests for the US's national security in the Middle East since 11 September attacks. Therefore, this work examines how much of these five interests appeared in US-Jordan relation under Obama administration. Moreover, this study uses discourse analysis method and provides many quotes from Obama communications to clarify the United States priorities in Jordan from 2009 to 2017. It also uses primary and secondary sources to give full answers to the study's questions.

MAIN FOCUS OF THE CHAPTER

The Obama Administration's strategy and approach in the Middle East had been driven by the maxim of 'multilateral retrenchment' which is designed to achieve the United States foreign commitments, reshape its standing among the world powers, and transfer burdens onto foreign partners (Drezner, 2011). The United States of America substantially has depended on Jordan to solve many regional complex issues and crises, particularly, Arab-Israeli peace negotiations, training Iraqi and Syria forces and counterterrorism (Al-Sarhan, 2016).

The fact that more than half of Jordan's citizens originate from Palestine has made the Palestine-Israeli conflict resonate with Jordanians (Sharp, 2018). Furthermore, through Jordan, the US has able to curtail anti-Israeli powers spread and their role in the Middle East. Jordan is considered as a safe source for the Gulf countries on their western borders. Obama administration used surrogate warfare method in the Middle East; this means it provides states and organizations with facilities and logistics services to fight instead of the United States. The US military assistance which was delivered to its allies in the Middle East is a form of surrogate warfare, this assistance notably Jordan (Krieg, 2016).. The stability of the Gulf countries and their area will definitely leave lasting implications to the whole of US economy, as it depends on Gulf oil (Momayezi & Rosenburg, 2011), Jordan was the key to stability during Obama administration. The Middle East also has served as the main purchaser of the US weapons and military equipment, Jordan has been one of the US weapons buyers in the region as well.

The figure below shows the statistics of US priorities in the Middle East, the numbers show the levels of these priorities targeted at Jordan by Obama's Administration.

Figure 1 shows that Jordan was cited (44) times in the documents, in relation to security and as a partner to the United States of America in countering terrorism. He looked to Jordan as a strategic assistant to fight terrorism in the region, especially after the appearance of ISIS in Iraq and Syria. The second most noticeable interest of Obama in Jordan was the security of Israel. He referred to Jordan as a tool to achieve Palestine-Israeli peace in (31) documents. Al Sharafat (2016) argues that Obama had a lot of interests in the security of Israel, based on three factors: Israel is

Figure 1. The number of hints of the US's interests in the Middle East found in Obama's communications referring to Jordan

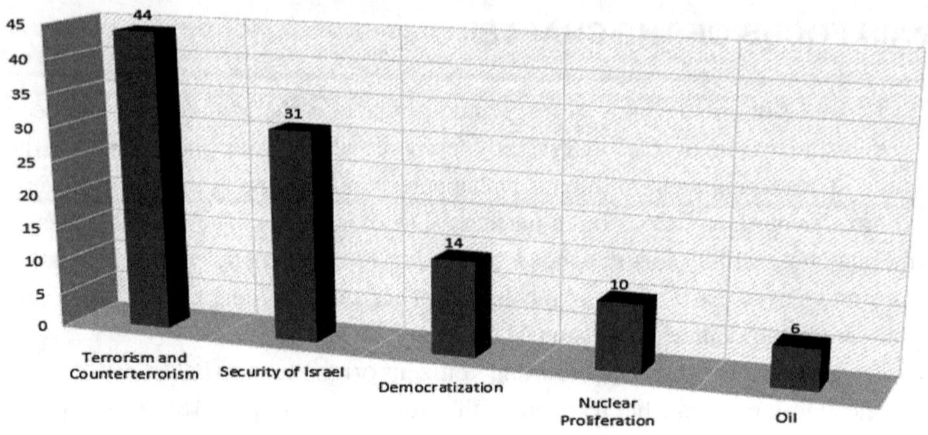

considered a strategic partner for critical reasons, such as: Israel is the only country in the region considered as a strong ally to most of the western countries, Israel also shares common interest with United States of America in relation to economy and security, lastly there is the power of the pro-Israel lobby in United states of America.

Democratization and political reforms in Jordan were mentioned in (14) occasions in the documents with regards to Obama's Policies. He spent a lot of money on democracy promotion and assistance to Jordan, and he praised Jordan's constitutional reforms during Arab spring through several diplomatic meetings and diplomatic visits. Also, Obama administration exerted a lot of efforts against the spread of Mass Destruction Weapons in the region, especially in Iran. He referred to Jordan as a reliable partner in this issue (10) times. Obama believed that security of oil depends on the stability of the region, he referred to Jordan in (6) occasions as the source of oil countries' stability. The following subsections are dissociation and details of the US interests in Jordan during Obama administration.

Terrorism and Counterterrorism

Since the 11/9 attacks the United States has prioritized in countering terrorism in the Middle East to protect itself and its interests there, it has tried to find strong allies inside the region to fight against terrorism. Through allies' cooperative work, the United States has access to military services, intelligence, agents, airports, free moving and the ability to target terrorists everywhere (Dreazen, 2012). The Jordanian Foreign Minister, Nasser Judeh during a conference with Hillary Rodham Clinton Secretary of State, said:

... our presence in Afghanistan today is ... to combat terrorism and the root causes of terrorism ... to help out in the humanitarian effort that is needed there.... our presence in Afghanistan will be enhanced and increased in the coming phase. This is something that is ongoing. Jordan was one of the first countries there. We are not only part of a network of countries that are trying to assist Afghanistan and Afghanis, but also trying to combat terror and terrorism (Sharp, 2015).

The United States during Obama administration repeated many times the importance of burden-sharing and using multilateral strategy toward the Middle East crises. This point found clearly in the National Security Strategy 2015:

The threshold for military action is higher when our interests are not directly threatened. In such cases, we will seek to mobilize allies and partners to share the burden and achieve lasting outcomes (The White House, 2015).

As Obama also repeatedly mentioned in one way or another:

Ultimately, it is not the job of the United States to solve every problem in the Middle East. The people in the Middle East are going to have to solve some of these problems themselves (CNN, 2015).

After Syrian War has started and the fight against terrorist groups was needed, the US increased its military aid to Jordan through Defense Department and other agencies to ensure that Jordan would be a successful warrior against terrorism in the region. Obama on December 11, 2015 through his letter to congressional leaders on the global deployment of United States Combat-Equipped Armed Forces, stated:

U.S. Armed Forces elements, including Patriot missile systems, artillery, fighter aircraft, and related support, command, control, and communications personnel and systems, are deployed to Jordan to support the security of Jordan and promote regional stability (Obama, 2015b).

Later with the appearance of ISIS, Jordan found itself dealing with a host of state and non-state players, including the Syrian system, Syrian rebel organizations, the United States, Israel, Iran, Hezbollah, and ISIS. In order to stop the flow of chaos, prohibit terrorist infiltration, Jordan has expanded its partnership with the US (Sharp, 2018). Jordan has continued to Cooperate and share intelligence about terrorism with the United States to maintain its local security interests and to keep the stability of the ever-turbulent Middle Eastern states. Jordan h joined the US's international coalition against ISIS. Jordan participated by the Royal Jordanian Air Force (RJAF) which conducted many airstrikes in Syria. However, the death of the Jordanian pilot Muath Al-Kasassbeh in 2014 made Jordan suspend its airstrikes against ISIS (Al-Sarhan, 2016). On February 3, 2015, President Obama in a special statement offered his condolences to Jordan and al-Kasasbeh' family on behalf of American people. Moreover, during an interview with Jon Sopel of BBC on July 24, 2015, Obama said:

In combination with the Turks and the Jordanians and others, what we are trying to do is not only shrink the environment in which ISIL can operate, but also to create an environment in which we stop the border flows of foreign fighters into Syria, we've made progress there (Obama, 2015a).

There is no doubt the US presence in Jordan and its generous aid during Obama administration kept Jordan's internal and external stability, particularly during Arab Spring; one of the most serious popular attempts to find democracy in Arab world. Despite Obama and his partner, Jordan in the Middle East efforts, Obama administration appeared unable to settle Syrian's Civil War. The results behind his position toward Syria did not involve directly in a new war was very complicated. It has caused instability in the Middle East, presented new powers and players in the region. Although, many reports indicate the extremist groups have been hit strongly and they are weak nowadays. The setback in Iraq, the Arab Spring and the death of Bin Ladin are all pieces of evidence of the groups' decline. But that decline cannot apply in Syria, as Syrian War had no serious action of Obama administration.

Security of Israel

The United States of America and Israel have a history of strong bilateral relation, and they have cooperated in many issues in the region, particularly security. Many of the US's administrations had announced that security of Israel means a national security of the US. This relation is based on three principles: shared same values, security interests and internal support (Drezner, 2011). Therefore, a poll in 2015 found that more than 70% of Americans see Israel favorably-much higher than support for all states in the Middle East (Gallup, 2015). President Obama was clear during his remarks following a meeting with the prime minister of Israel Benjamin Netanyahu on September 1, 2010, when he stated:

The United States is going to be unwavering in its support of Israel's security, and we are going to push back against these kinds of terrorist activities. And so the message should go out to Hamas and everybody else who is taking credit for these heinous crimes that this is not going to stop us (Obama, 2010a).

But on another hand, Obama administration in February 2011 had voted a proposal to U.N. Security Council resolution (UNSCR) - approval by fourteen other members of the council- that would have considered the activities of Israeli settlements in East Jerusalem and West Bank as illegal. Although Obama backed off his draft to freeze the activity of settlement within a short time, there was US-Israel tension through most of Obama presidency (Zanotti, 2017).

Jordan has shown a significant interest, more than any other Arab in resolving the situation in Jerusalem, a very sensitive issue to the Kingdom of Jordan. Jordan maintains custodial role over the holy sites in Palestine. The holy site is the third-holiest in Islam religion (Macca and AL Medina in Saudi Arabia are in the first and second positions respectively) (Lederman, 2017). The spokesperson of the government of Jordan in January 2017 warned that a move of the US embassy to Jerusalem would mean cross a "red line" and it would cause catastrophic outcomes on many levels, and the spokesperson indicated such this decision would affect Jordan-Israeli relation and perhaps other Arab countries (Moore, 2017). Also, the Palestinians issue and their rights resonate with most of the population because over half of Jordan's residents originate from Palestine (Sharp, 2018). Furthermore, Jordan is considered as a buffer between Israel and Arab countries, it has the longest border with Israel and West Bank (Al-Sarhan, 2016). In remarks following a meeting with King Abdullah II of Jordan on May 17, 2011, Obama said:

Jordan, obviously, with its own peace with Israel, has an enormous stake in this. The United States has an enormous stake in this (Obama, 2011).

Also, On February 21, 2016, there was a four-way meeting between Netanyahu, King Abdullah of Jordan and Egypt's leader Abdel Fattah al-Sisi to consider Israel's security (B, 2017). Israel has a concern about Iran's nuclear program; it fears that if Iran develops nuclear weapons, it will threaten Israel's national security, as Iranian's leaders usually promise to destroy Israel in a day. Therefore, the US with its partners in the region such as Jordan have offered a lot of effort to stop this program. Also, Israel has a concern about Iran's allies in the region who threaten Israel national security such as Hizballah and Hamas. By cooperating with the US, Israel has developed the "Iron Dome" and "Arrow" defense systems to improve its defenses against rockets and missiles (Sharp, 2012).

Democratization

The Obama administration pressured Middle Eastern regimes to start making democratic and political reforms through many diplomatic meetings and support through its economic aid program. Throughout the Obama administration, the United States and Jordan economic relations remained strong. On September 22, 2008, the non-binding five years Memorandum of Understanding (MOU) was signed. The US's Department of State Archive mentions that:

The MOU is a step forward in our already strong bilateral relationship and reinforces our commitment to work together on a range of important issues – including advancing security and stability in the region and encouraging economic development and political reform (US Department of State Archive, 2008).

In a democratic scope, The United States of America under president Obama supported capacity-building projects for the Jordanian Judicial Council, the parliament's support offices, the Judicial Institute, and justice sector. Also, the National Democratic Institute and The International Republican Institute got U.S. aids to train members of parliament and political parties in Jordan (Sharp, 2018). On January 17, 2012, during remarks following a meeting with King Abdullah II of Jordan, President Obama stated:

We discussed, as well, the extraordinary efforts that have been made by His Majesty, as well as the Prime Minister, in guiding political reform inside of Jordan. I think His Majesty has been ahead of the curve in trying to respond to the legitimate concerns and aspirations, both politically and economically, of the Jordanian population. And so we have said that we want to be as helpful as we can in encouraging this ongoing reform process that's taking place (Obama, 2012).

The occurrence of the unexpected Arab Spring put democracy promotion to center stage, although democratization and political reforms ardor cooled when the Arab Spring resulted to wars and caused a coup in Egypt (Byman & Moller, 2016). Al Sarhan (2016) argues that the United States during the Arab Spring recognized that Jordan's stability was crucial to its interests in the Middle East; the United states of America understood that any protests in Jordan's regime could bring about an anti-Western authority. Therefore, the US intensified its support to the Kingdom. During Syrian refugees' waves to Jordan, the United States prevented Jordan from being overwhelmed by refugees.

Many people believe that the United States of America is standing behind autocrats in the Middle East in order to focus on its major priorities which are supply of oil, security of Israel, and counterterrorism. These interests are impediments to the United States commitment to promoting human rights, democracy, and freedom. In fact, Obama continued his support for dictatorships in the Middle East because democratization was not on the top of his priorities in the region. During remarks prior to a meeting with King Abdullah II of Jordan, on April 26, 2013, President Obama confirmed the importance of working with Jordan to investigate Syrian's crisis:

So we're going to be working with countries like Jordan to try to obtain more direct evidence and confirmation of this potential use. In the meantime, I've been very clear publicly, but also privately, that for the Syrian Government to utilize chemical weapons on its people crosses a line that will change my calculus and how the United States approaches these issues (Obama, 2013).

There were several weaknesses in Obama's democratization policy in the Middle East. First, under President Obama, the US promotion of democracy won little support in the Arab countries. Second, many of the autocrats were staunch supporters of United States and its Allies. So, the Obama administration was, in essence, abandoning partners if it would support democracy seriously. Third, many people argue that countering terrorism needs strong regimes, and democracy for the short-term in particular weakens regimes while the threat of civil strife gives opportunities to extremist groups. Thus, the US's support of the dictatorships regimes in the Middle East has tarnished the image of the US in the Arab's eyes; democracy is so popular in the region.

Nuclear Proliferation

The United States leaders often cite that the prevention of the development of Nuclear weapons in the Middle East is of vital importance. Although Israel has its own nuclear weapons, which dates back to the 1960s, the United States did not consider it as a threat because Israel is one of the closest allies to the United States of America. The concern about nuclear in the Middle East is so-called "reactive" or "tit-for-tat" proliferation: That means when one country succeeds in the development of nuclear weapons, the neighbors of this country will be encouraged to do so, thus increasing the countries which have nuclear weapons (Byman & Moller, 2016). Another concern is the possession of nuclear weapons by a country will make it a regional leader, a good example of this is Iran, any success by Iran in the development of nuclear weapons will make it dominate the region, it will also threaten the security of Israel, an important ally to the United States of America. Possession of Nuclear Weapons by Iran will also increase the dominance and regional strength of Russia due to its close relationship with Iran. It will also serve as a catalyst in the development of nuclear weapons by the neighboring and close countries in the region such as Jordan, Saudi Arabia, Turkey and Qatar.

The Obama Administration argued that international nuclear cooperation would provide additional transparency into Iran's nuclear program. Obama supported a variety of opposition movements against Iran and exerted a lot of efforts to isolate it from the international community, it was important for Obama to keep Jordan with his campaign against Iran's program. In a private meeting between President Obama and King Abdullah II of Jordan during a nuclear summit in Washington, on April 12, 2010, the two leaders discussed Iran's nuclear ambition. According to US officials, both leaders shared the importance of strengthening the Nuclear Non-Proliferation Treaty (Los Angeles Times, 2010). Also, President Obama in his participation on sustaining action to strengthen global nuclear security, on April 1, 2016, stated:

We need sustained action and ambition on nuclear security after the 2016 Nuclear Security Summit to address continuing and evolving nuclear security challenges, with the objectives of advancing implementation of nuclear security commitments and building a strengthened, sustainable and comprehensive global nuclear security architecture. The Governments of Argentina, Armenia, Australia, Belgium, Canada, Chile, China, Czech Republic, Denmark, Finland, France, Georgia, Germany, Hungary, India, Italy, Japan, Jordan..., aiming to facilitate cooperation and sustain activity on nuclear security after the 2016 Nuclear Security Summit (Obama, 2016).

Obama success in 2015 to sign with Iran the Joint Comprehensive Plan of Action which aimed to disband the nuclear weapons program of Iran and the sanctions on Iran would release as an exchange process. Although Obama did a significant progress in preventing nuclear proliferation by using his diplomacy, many experts argue that there was a suspicious relation between Obama's decision to not involve in Syria crisis and his nuclear deal with Iran, as Bashar al-Assad, the leader of Syria regime is the patron of Iran.

Oil

Since the 1970s the United States has a strategic interest in the Middle East oil, it was involved in securing easy access to the oil sources for itself and others. The Middle East oil producers export far more from what they consume of the Black Gold. The oil statistic in 2015 indicated that oil producers in the Middle East produce about 30% of total oil production in the World (US Energy Information Administration, 2015). President Obama in his response to a question about the Middle East oil during a Question-and-Answer session in Seattle, in Washington, on October 21, 2010, answered:

Unfortunately, we haven't weaned ourselves off Middle East oil ... (Obama, 2010b)

Many experts argue that dependence on foreign energy and crude, especially in the Middle East, was viewed as a risk to the United States national security and economic growth (Momayezi & Rosenburg, 2011). According to Roger J. Stern, crude's security in the Middle East region cost the United States $7.3 trillion dollars between 1976 and 2007 (Momayezi & Rosenburg, 2011). Also, the State Department in the US considers one in five barrels of oil which come to the US as unstable or dangerous (Lyon, Lefton, & Daniel Weiss, 2010). The real danger for the US's national security comes from an invading state or organization could invade oil area in the Middle East, and that means the occupier might deprive the US of getting oil easily, and a significant percentage of energy sources would require the possibility to manipulate oil market or creating price spikes, like what happened when Saddam Hussien invaded Kuwait in 1990. Another danger that Iran might block the Strait of Hormuz, which is considered as the most important chokepoint for oil flow in the world (Byman & Moller, 2016). Therefore, During Obama administration, Jordan was a main player in the oil region stability, there was a US military presence in its land to close the oil producing countries; also, Jordan is one of the Gulf States that have a close relationship with United States of America. Jordan was a keeper of Gulf internal and external security, many times Jordan was involved in military action in Gulf countries against rebels, particularly in Bahrain.

SOLUTIONS AND RECOMMENDATIONS

In the whole Middle East and Jordan, for instance, there are economic corruption, diplomatic failure, an inability of the military, slouch administrative and most of the states depend on foreign aids and imports. Lack of democracy, ethnicity and nationalism, the prevalence of authoritarianism, religious extremism along with economic stagnation, are the primary factors that have imbalanced nations power and authority in the Middle East countries. The Arab-Israeli conflict also posed a dilemma to all Middle East countries, and this conflict created a permanent unsafe region. All this open the area for the United States to intervene in its internal and external affairs. Therefore, Jordan should find new allies in order to get economic growth and sustainable development, as the United States cares only about its interests in the Middle East and how it could protect these interests as long as possible.

FUTURE RESEARCH DIRECTIONS

Future research might investigate the factor behind democracy failure in the Middle East, what is the role of the United States in creating the Middle East's political systems in the current forms. Is the United States serious in democracy promotion in the region or not and if not, when it will allow for full democracy in the Middle East? The military coup in Egypt might consider as a case study.

CONCLUSION

The United States of America under Obama administration substantially depended on Hashemite Kingdom of Jordan to solve many regional complex issues and crisis. Particularly, regarding Arab-Israeli peace negotiations, and counterterrorism, the Obama administration put a large-scale of military commitment in the Middle East after terrorist groups started appearing in Iraq and Syria, and it stepped up a lot of efforts to work with its allies in the region. Jordan was a main player in the campaign against terrorism; it contributed along with the US in many airstrikes around the region. Many politicians consider Obama foreign policy was totally different than Bush foreign policy, during Bush administration the US believed that it could solve all the overseas issues unilaterally. The United States during the Arab Spring recognized that Jordan's stability was crucial to its interests in the Middle East, the US understood that any protests in Jordan's regime could bring an anti-Western-Israeli authority. Therefore, the US intensified its support to the Kingdom. Also, during Syrian refugees' waves to Jordan, the United States prevented Jordan from being overwhelmed by refugees.

REFERENCES

Al-Sarhan, A. (2016). *United States' Foreign Policy toward the Hashemite Kingdom of Jordan: 1990-2014*. Atlanta University.

Al-Sharafat, A. (2016). *US's strategy in the Middle East during Bush administration*. The University of Jordan.

Byman, D., & Moller, S. B. (2016). The United States and the Middle East: Interest, Risks and Costs. In J. S. and B. Valentino (Ed.), Sustainable Security: Rethinking American National Security Strategy. Oxford: Oxford University Press.

CNN. (2015, July 15). President Obama continues his news conference on the Iran deal. USA.

Dreazen, Y. J. (2012, May 9). Foiled Bomb Plot Highlights Growing CIA-Saudi Arabian Ties. CNN.

Drezner, D. W. (2011). Does Obama have a grand strategy? Why we need doctrines in uncertain times. *Foreign Affairs*, *90*(4), 58.

Gallup. (2015, February 23). Seven in Ten Americans Continue to View Israel Favorably. Retrieved from http://www.gallup.com/poll/181652/seven-americans-continue-view-israel-favorably.aspx

Krieg, A. (2016). Externalizing the burden of war: The Obama Doctrine and US foreign policy in the Middle East. *International Affairs*, *92*(1), 97–113. doi:10.1111/1468-2346.12506

Lederman, J. (2017, January 30). Trump courts Jordan's king amid embassy, refugee concerns. *Associated Press*. Retrieved from http://www.dailymail.co.uk/wires/ap/article-4173794/Trump-courts-Jordans-king-amid-embassy-refugee-concerns.html

Lindsay, J. M. (2011). George W. Bush, Barack Obama and the future of US global leadership. *International Affairs*, *87*(4), 772. doi:10.1111/j.1468-2346.2011.01003.x

Los Angeles Times. (2010, April 12). Obama discusses Mideast peace prospects with Jordan's King Abdullah. Retrieved from http://latimesblogs.latimes.com/dcnow/2010/04/obama-discusses-mideast-peace-prospects-with-jordans-abdullah.html

Lyon, S., Lefton, R., & Daniel Weiss. (2010, April 23). Quenching Our Thirst for Oil: Growing Global Oil Demand Harms U.S. Security and Economy. *American Progress*. Retrieved from https://www.americanprogress.org/issues/green/news/2010/04/23/7657/quenching-our-thirst-for-oil/

Momayezi, N., & Rosenburg, R. B. (2011). Oil, the Middle East and U.S. National Security. *International Journal of Humanities and Social Science*, *1*(10), 1–7.

Moore, J. (2017, January 6). Jordan Tells Trump: Moving U.S. Embassy to Jerusalem a 'Red Line.' *Newsweek*.

Obama, B. (2010a, September 1). Remarks Following a Meeting With Prime Minister Benjamin Netanyahu of Israel. Retrieved from http://www.presidency.ucsb.edu/ws/?pid=88375

Obama, B. (2010b, October 21). Remarks and a Question-and-Answer Session in Seattle, Washington. Retrieved from http://www.presidency.ucsb.edu/ws/index.php?pid=88609&st=Jordan&st1=

Obama, B. (2011, May 17). Remarks Following a Meeting With King Abdullah II of Jordan. Retrieved from http://www.presidency.ucsb.edu/ws/index.php?pid=90389&st=Jordan&st1=

Obama, B. (2012, January 17). Remarks Following a Meeting With King Abdullah II of Jordan. Retrieved from http://www.presidency.ucsb.edu/ws/?pid=98978

Obama, B. (2013, April 26). Remarks Prior to a Meeting With King Abdullah II of Jordan and an Exchange With Reporters. Retrieved from http://www.presidency.ucsb.edu/ws/?pid=103550

Obama, B. (2015a, July 24). Interview with Jon Sopel of BBC. Retrieved from http://www.presidency.ucsb.edu/ws/?pid=128836

Obama, B. (2015b, December 11). Letter to Congressional Leaders on the Global Deployment of United States Combat-Equipped Armed Forces. Retrieved from www.presidency.ucsb.edu/ws/?pid=111236

Obama, B. (2016, April 1). Joint Statement on Sustaining Action To Strengthen Global Nuclear Security. Retrieved from http://www.presidency.ucsb.edu/ws/?pid=117319

Ravid, B. (2017, February 19). Exclusive: Kerry Offered Netanyahu Regional Peace Plan in Secret 2016 Summit with al-Sissi, King Abdullah. *Haaretz*. Retrieved from www.haaretz.com/israel-%0Anews/.premium-1.772531?=&ts=_1487969163123

Sharp, J. M. (2012). *US Foreign Aid to Israel.* Washington, D.C.: Congressional Research Service. Retrieved from http://www.fas.org/sgp/crs/mideast/RL33222.pdf%3E

Sharp, J. M. (2015). *U.S. Foreign Aid to Israel.* Washington, D.C.: Congressional Research Service. Retrieved from http://securityassistance.org/sites/default/files/RL33222.pdf

Sharp, J. M. (2018). *Jordan : Background and U.S. Relations.* Washington, D.C.: Congressional Research Service.

The White House. (2015). *National Security Strategy.* Washington, D.C.

US Department of State Archive. (2008, September 22). The United States and the Hashemite Kingdom of Jordan Sign Memorandum of Understanding on Assistance.

US Energy Information Administration. (2015). Monthly Energy Review October 2015. Retrieved from 3Cwww.eia.gov/totalenergy/data/monthly/pdf/sec11_5.pdf%3E

Zanotti, J. (2017). *Israel : Background and U.S. Relations in Brief.* Washington, D.C.: Congressional Research Service; Retrieved from https://fas.org/sgp/crs/mideast/R44245.pdf

ADDITIONAL READING

Al Sharafat, A. (2016). *US's strategy in the Middle East during Bush administration*. The University of Jordan.

Amawi, A. M. (1996). USAID in Jordan. *Middle East Policy*, *4*(4), 76–89. doi:10.1111/j.1475-4967.1996.tb00238.x

Anderson, J. E. (2003). *Public Policymaking*. Boston, New York: Houghton Mifflin Company.

Cooley, A. (2008). *Base Politics: Democratic Change and the U.S. Military Overseas*. New York: Cornell University Press.

Crabb, C. V. Jr. (1983). *American Foreign Policy in the Nuclear Age*. New York: Harper & Row, Publishers.

Eisenstadt, M., & Pollock, D. (2012). Friends with Benefits: Why the U.S.-Israeli Alliance Is Good for America. *Foreign Affairs*.

Gelvin, J. L. (2005). *The Modern Middle East: A History*. New York: Oxford University Press.

Sandars, C. T. (2000). *America's Overseas Garrisons: The Leasehold Empire*. New York: Oxford University Press. doi:10.1093/acprof:oso/9780198296874.001.0001

KEY TERMS AND DEFINITIONS

Interests: The feeling of a human or the concern of a country about something. In international relations, interests mean a nation aims or objectives towards another nation and they are not necessary to be announced.

Israel-Palestine Conflict: The ongoing conflict between Palestinians and Israelis. It began in 1948. It started when Israel has occupied the West Bank and the Gaza.

Jordan: A kingdom located on the heart of the Middle East with size 89,342 square kilometers, it considering as an entrance between the Middle East and North Africa, Mediterranean countries and Gulf countries. Jordan is an ally of the United States since its independence from Great Britain in 1946.

Nuclear Weapon: An explosive device, it derives its strong force from nuclear reactions. Israel is the only state in the Middle East has this destructive power, while Iran is struggling to get it.

President Obama: Barack Obama who was born on August 4, 1961, he served as 44th president of the United States from 2009 to 2017.

The Middle East Oil: Oil or petroleum is a very important energy source use in all human life aspects. The Middle East is the largest oil producer in the world and it holds enormous reserves of oil.

The Middle East Region: An area that includes Palestine, Israel, Jordan, Egypt, Lebanon, Syria, Iraq, Saudi Arabia, Sudan, Oman, Yemen, Qatar, Turkey, Bahrain, Libya, Kuwait, United Arab Emirates, and Iran.

Chapter 8
Globalization in the Ottoman Empire:
An Evaluation Through the Naval Institutions and International Trade Policies

Büşra Karataşer
Tekirdağ Namık Kemal University, Turkey

ABSTRACT

The purpose of this chapter is to examine how globalization has played a decisive role in the Ottoman Empire and how it created reform through international trade policies and institutions. The first part will examine the concept of globalization and the integration of the Ottoman Empire into the West, the fundamentals of the Ottomanmentality and the effects of globalization on the Ottoman Empire in the 19th century. The second part will examine how globalization played a decisive role in the Ottoman Empire, the 19th century Ottoman economy, Ottoman international trade, and Ottoman external loans. The third part examines the institutionalization and modernization of the Ottoman Empire, reforms in naval affairs during the reign of Abdul Hamid II, and the organization of the navy. The fourth part will examine the institutional relations in the Ottoman Empire after globalization. Institutions will be examined in terms of how they were restructured or how new ones were created to adapt to a new world order.

DOI: 10.4018/978-1-5225-9566-3.ch008

INTRODUCTION

The 19th century is a different era for Ottoman society and its economy than the previous periods. Although important changes were made in the traditional Ottoman order, the basic features of the 17th and 18th centuries were preserved. While the power of the central state decreased in the Ottoman Empire, the efficiency of the Ayans began to increase. The ayan provided economic support by collecting taxes on behalf of the state, not by reorganizing production or transforming production relations. There were both struggles and cooperation between the central state and the ayan. From the 1820s onwards the Ottoman Empire was faced with the military, political and economic power of the West. After the Industrial Revolution, the new economy in the era of globalization carried out its economic activities within a new world order. The increasing independence of the ayan in the Ottoman hinterlands, and, on the other hand, the increased power of the West, led the Ottoman Empire to reform its social and economic structures and strengthen the power of the central state in many areas. In the face of these developments, radical changes were made to the economic structure of Ottoman society and different institutions were created from the 18th century onwards. The origins of the societal and economic changes in the social structure of Turkey in the 20th century is to be found in the 19th century, and this came about through changes in the structure of the state as a whole (Pamuk, 2002).

The Industrial Revolution began in the UK and then developed in other countries in Western Europe, transforming their economies through the production of a substantial amount of goods manufactured at a low cost. By the second half of the 19th century, European countries were searching for new markets for their products and looking for inexpensive and abundant sources of raw materials. After the Industrial Revolution, the commercial and economic bonds between the industrialized countries were strengthened, while the trade in products and agricultural goods between Western European countries and developing countries expanded. By the end of the 19th century, technological developments had also caused an increase in maritime trade worldwide (Pamuk, 2017).

BACKGROUND

In this article the concept of 'globalization' refers to the 'First Wave of Globalization', which, according to the World Bank, occurred between 1870 and1914. The main factors in globalization were the general global situation and the changes and expansion happening in the world economy. Those who have contributed to the literature on globalization have been interested in the economic aspects of globalization, including, for example, "The Other Side of Globalization is Poverty" (Şenses, 2001) and "Was Neoliberal Globalization an Opportunity or Obstacle to Development?" (Şenses, 2004). Öniş et al. (2014) discussed inequality of income in globalization; Aydınlı (2007) explained how globalization caused institutionalization in the late Ottoman Empire; Seyidoğlu (2003) discussed the concept of globalization in terms of economics; Pamuk (2017) approached globalization through the economic growth of the Ottoman Empire. With regard to maritime affairs, the institutionalization of the Ottoman Empire was evaluated in terms of 'Naval Organization' (Düzcü, 2009). This study uses the concept of globalization to refer to the First Wave of Globalization and investigates for the first time how it occurred in the Ottoman Empire in terms of maritime reforms and international trade policies. The processes of modernization and globalization in the Ottoman Empire are evaluated in the context of maritime reforms and international trade through the institutions that were created after the First Wave of Globalization. The changes which began in these institutions allowed the Ottoman Empire to adapt to the changing world and to continue to exist.

MAIN FOCUS OF THE CHAPTER

The aim of this section is to explain how the Ottoman Empire perceived globalization after the First Wave of Globalization and how it changed its institutions. The Ottoman Navy was modernized by taking the leading countries in the world as models and this situation revived the Ottoman economy. This section aims to explain the Ottoman Empire's adjustments in international trade policies, its position regarding debt, the meaning of the Ottoman Empire's borrowing according to the European governments and how the Empire continued to function through modernizing its institutions after globalization.

GLOBALIZATION AND THE VIEW OF GLOBALIZATION IN THE OTTOMAN EMPIRE

Globalization

Globalization refers to the extension and development of relations between countries, the dissolution of antagonistic positions due to ideological differences, and the dissemination of wealth to other countries as a result of going beyond the borders of the country and the beliefs and expectations of different societies (Aktel, 2001).

The emergence of the concept of globalization also leads to discussion of the high number of poor people in the world (Şenses, 2004).

In recent years, the concept of globalization has attracted great attention from all sectors of society. The interest has brought with it, discussions of the widespread effects of globalization. The main reason for these discussions is that the world has undergone many changes as a result of these long-term effects. Globalization has not only allowed for a faster circulation of products worldwide. In addition, borders have lifted in the domains of culture, the law, education and politics (Çeken et al., 2008). The concept of globalization has thus been described in different ways by various authors and opinions of globalization have changed over time. Globalization not only refers to the deregulation of trade but also the globalization of production, the spread of multinational corporations around the world and the deregulation of financial markets (Seyidoğlu, 2003). Globalization led to a significant slowdown in the growth of productivity in industrialized capitalist countries. As a result of the changing balance in the industrialized world, industrialized nations increased their production and turned towards industrializing countries as new markets (Şenses, 2004).

Although there are different definitions of globalization, there are various groups opposed to it and others who support it. The reasons cited by those who oppose globalization are ongoing problems such as unemployment and loss of income that occur alongside an increase in trade, as well as decreases in the revenues of developing countries (Konukman et al., 2008). Globalization can indicate are-organization of human activity, leading to a greater internationalization and regionalization, as well as a re-arrangement of the relations between the center and the regions (Çelik, 2012). It has, however, also been found that globalization increased income inequality. This situation has caused frustration in the mass of people in the industrialized countries (Öniş, 2014).

The period between 1870 and 1914 is called the 'First Globalization Era.' This period is considered to be the period when capitalism established world domination (Savaş, 2004). The main characteristic of the period is that the gold standard was accepted as the norm in financial markets and trade relations (Danışoğlu, 2004). In the 16th and 17th centuries, Spain and Portugal accelerated their military colonization of world by virtue of the superiority of their weapons' technology and their dominance in the maritime sphere, supplying cheap raw materials and a labor force from their colonies. They transported gold and silver obtained from mining to the West. This was the beginning of a policy called mercantilism, in which wealth was measured in gold and silver. Many of the goods subject to trade in mercantilism were luxury goods such as spices and tobacco. This first period of globalization ended with the outbreak of the First World War (Savaş, 2004).

Integration of the Ottoman Empire Into the West

With the transition to capitalism in Europe in the 16th and 17th centuries, the history of the other regions in the world (with the exception of Japan) needs to be examined in terms of the interrelation of capitalist and non-capitalist modes of production. As one specific state which needed to integrate with the world economy, the integration of the Ottoman Empire with the West can be seen as a specific kind of transformation (Pamuk, 1994).

While the world economy was developing rapidly in the 19th century, many regions underwent processes of encirclement. The process by which a country is encircled can be both similar and different to that undergone by other countries. In examining the Ottoman state, we first need to understand the Ottoman mentality in order to understand how it adapted to the West (Pamuk, 1994).

Foundations of the Mentality of the Ottoman Empire

The Islamic states played an important role in the formation of the Ottoman mentality and the institutions of the Ottoman Empire. The Ottoman Empire was the heir to these states. The main aim of the old Turkish economic and social traditions was to provide for the welfare of the people. The reason for the existence of the state was public service; in this respect, the Ottoman economic structure was highly traditional. In the Ottoman Empire, under the influence of local traditions, a number of more or less different economic regions were formed. The system was based around the idea of 'Justice'; therefore, it was believed that policies designed to increasing the income necessary for the state to survive should just. Another aspect of justice was social welfare; the reason for the economic decisions taken by the state should be 'ibadullahın terfih-i ahvallerini,' that is, the provision of social welfare. When this balance of justice and well-being is disturbed due to the need to increase state revenues, crisis emerges (Tabakoğlu, 2005). Fiscalism is another important principle in the mentality of the Ottoman Empire. According to this principle, the state wishes to both raise revenues and to reduce spending (Genç, 2000).

The Effects of Globalization on the Ottoman Empire in the 19th Century

The Industrial Revolution, which originated in England in the second half of the 18th century, was the result of a long scientific and technological process that had lasted for centuries. Although it started in England, it brought the whole world under its influence in a short period of time. The effects of the Industrial Revolution included the formation of bourgeois classes engaged in trade and banking, the expansion of trade worldwide, developments in transportation and production techniques, and the creation of new forms of production; all of these were examples of the development of new behaviors and ideas (Erdem, 2016).

With the Industrial Revolution, becoming richer was no longer a matter of manufacturing and selling products through free trade. Until the Industrial Revolution, the exploitation of the world's most precious mines and international trade and commercial capital were provided for and production continued (Erdem, 2016). The increase in industrial production was significantly reflected in the general level of welfare in the UK. Until the Industrial Revolution, the national income per capita was less than 1000 dollars in 1776, when *The Wealth of Nations* was published, but rose from the year of publication to 2000 dollars by the 1830s.The rise in per capita income was actually due to the change in economic thinking in the world. At the time of the publication of this work, the view was that universal wealth and financial independence could only be achieved by accumulating gold and silver. This was a turning point in human history (Skousen, 2003).

While these developments were being experienced around the world, the Ottoman Empire was experiencing internal and external political and economic problems. Industrialization was not only a matter of production but also a legal, political and sociological phenomenon (Dumrul and Dumrul, 2014). The Ottoman state continued its restructuring work for a long time, but was not successful because of heavy defeats in war and territorial losses. The Ottoman-Russian wars led to great difficulties in the Ottoman Empire. Similarly, the prolonged Ottoman-Iranian wars, the Ottoman-Austrian War and the Ottoman-French War caused heavy losses to the country's productivity. The fact that the wars took place on different fronts in the same period weakened the military and economic power that existed in the Ottoman Empire. Financial losses resulted in an inability to allocate a budget for restructuring and innovation (Erdem, 2016).

While the Ottoman Empire was dealing with the wars, there were also problems with the land system. This was the sector that kept the Ottoman economy alive, and which had its own unique structure. The Ottoman land system consisted of 'Miri,' or foundation land, and property land. Any conquered land was taxed to pay salaries. Soldiers called cavalryman lived in the villages where the tax was dedicated to them by a commander, and they carried out their services at the call of the state (Tabakoğlu, 2013).

The largest part of the land system was 'Miri land'. Miri land belonged to the state and was given over for cultivation by 'rayahs' (subjects). In the 18th century, the masses began to take Miri lands as property in contradiction to the existing rules. On the other hand, the cavalryman confiscated the Miri land where the state's power was weak. Thus, the largest regions of the Ottoman Empire emerged in time (Kenanoğlu, 2005).

There were other lands beside Miri lands. These were the lands allocated as foundation lands, for income, mosques, social complexes, madrasas, roads, bridges and educational institutions (Karataşer, 2018). These areas were in the ownership of private individuals to a much smaller extent than other land (Erdem, 2016).

After the establishment of the Kanun-ı Esasi in 1876, the 1877-1878 Ottoman-Russian War broke out and led to the dissolution of parliament. This situation was an obstacle to the institutionalization of the Ottoman Empire (Aydınlı, 2007). In the 19th century, there was a significant change in the land ownership of the Ottoman Empire. In 1858, land reform was carried out under the name of the 'Land Code.' According to this law, the state recognized private ownership of land and allowed for the sale of land. The aim of the state was to increase the revenues of the central state and to reduce the power and authority of the provinces. With the Land Code, the big landowners were empowered and the share of the state in the agricultural surplus decreased. While small producers, who were the cornerstones of the Ottoman Empire, were easily taxable, this sector lost importance with the Land Code (Kenanoğlu, 2005). The designation of private property, which began in the 18th century in the West, led to the loss of power of the Ottoman Empire. Ottoman subjects living in the Balkans were directly affected by the private property practices used in the West. In order to avoid damage to the right of sovereignty in these lands, the Ottoman rulers decided to loosen the application of private property over time (Erdem, 2016). The power of large landowners in rural areas meant that this sector expanded its share in agriculture against the state. However, small producers could easily be taxed and constituted the financial base of the central government. One development affecting the financial power of the Ottoman Empire was the economic consequences of migrations to Anatolia. Throughout the 19th century the population of the areas within the borders of Turkey today was eight to nine million; by the time of the First World War this was thought to have reached sixteen to seventeen million. The population migrating to Anatolia was concentrated in three regions. The first was the migration from Crimea to Rumelia and Anatolia, the second was the Circassian migration from the Caucasus to Rumelia and Anatolia, and the third was the migration from the Balkans to Macedonia and Anatolia. These three migration movements increased the total population by one million. The Ottoman Empire migrated and led the population to agriculture. As Istanbul was supplied with cereal crops by the Balkan regions, a large need for cereals emerged with the loss of these lands (Pamuk, 2017). It even became very difficult to meet the needs of Istanbul; for this reason, grain was imported from other countries (Karataşer, 2013).

GLOBALIZATION AND MODERNIZATION IN THE OTTOMAN EMPIRE

19th Century Ottoman Economy

The economy of the Ottoman Empire in the early 19th century was in a period of decline. Traders, who were representatives of the central state, large landowners and civil servants knew that the central power of the state was at stake and that this could lead to a financial depression. The production levels, capital accumulation and technological change in the early 19th century indicate that the Ottoman economy was in recession. Until the second quarter of the 19th century, the share of European trade in agricultural production or even in the production of agricultural commodities was very small. At the end of the 18th century, both the Empire and the interregional trade with Russia and Egypt were more important than trade with Central and Western Europe (Pamuk, 1994).

When looking at the Ottoman industry in the 19th century, Ottoman artists were able to see the 19th century. Towards the end of the century, factory goods were unable to withstand competition from foreign markets and had to delay their activities and withdraw from production. For this reason, the Ottoman Empire was increasingly subject to foreign markets (Eldem, 1994).

International Trade in the Ottoman Empire

After the Industrial Revolution the structure of international trade changed in Europe and the other countries of the world, including the Ottoman Empire, were shaped in this context. From the beginning of the 19th century, Western European countries began making cheap, mass-produced manufactured goods. In the 19th century, European countries were trying to find markets for these goods, especially cotton textile products, and on the other hand, they were trying to provide themselves with the necessary foodstuffs and cheap and abundant raw materials. The countries we have defined as underdeveloped entered world trade by specializing in agricultural products in this period (Pamuk, 1985).

From the 18th century onwards, the Ottoman Empire was capable of feeding and clothing a population of 20-25 million. The trade volume with the European states was quite limited, in addition to the total production and consumption volume of the country. The intense introduction of European manufactured goods to the Ottoman markets only took place after the Industrial Revolution in the 19th century (Tabakoğlu, 2014).

From the second half of the 18th century, the embassies and consulates of the Western countries in Turkey were engaged in the marketing their industrial property to the Ottoman Empire. They worked in cooperation with minority ethnic populations within the Empire. Minority traders became interpreters in the embassies of those states in order to benefit from the privileges of the European merchants, and they changed the subject matter to exoneration. When the European states began to acquire rights by minorities in the Ottoman Empire with the Treaty of Küçük Kaynarca, this patronage system became widespread. Most of the zimmi traders have become exoneration (Kütükoğlu, 1974). From 1802, when the Ottoman state was unable to take the lead in the Berat issue, the European Merchants Association was established by giving the rights granted to the foreign merchants to the minorities among its own subjects. In this way, the state took the view that foreign trade would remain under its control, and that it would prevent the decline in revenue from the cizye. In the face of this development, the Muslim traders also demanded that these rights be granted to the European merchants and thus, Hayriye merchants were established. The first Hayriye merchant license was granted in 1810. In contrast to the European traders, restrictions on the number of Hayriye Traders were established despite the fact that Muslims had already been established in European trade (İpşirli, 1998).

Some legal regulations and trade agreements also gave direction to the foreign trade in the Ottoman Empire. The treaties signed by the Ottoman Empire with Britain and later with other European states paved the way for profitable trade in the Ottoman Empire. With these treaties, the customs duties imposed by the Ottoman Empire on exports and imports remained at very low levels. However, by signing these treaties, the Ottoman state had waived the right to upgrade customs barriers in order to protect domestic industry in the following years, following an independent external trade policy. The 1838 Trade Treaty can be seen as a turning point in the process of opening the Ottoman economy to the world economy. The trade agreements signed in 1838-1841 also changed the balance of political and military power in Europe after the Napoleonic Wars. The Ottoman Empire signed a treaty with England in 1838, ten years after defeat in the Russian War of 1828-1829. This treaty made the Ottoman markets stronger by making Ottoman raw materials more commercial in the short term. According to this Treaty, the level of tariffs applied to Ottoman foreign trade was pre-determined. Before 1838, a 3 percent customs duty was imposed on imports and exports. In addition, they had to pay an 8 percent tax while carrying their goods from local and foreign merchants to one region within the country. According to the Treaty of 1838, the taxes on exports increased to 12 percent and the taxes on imports were 5 percent. On the other hand, while domestic traders continued to export domestic goods, foreign traders were free of the 8 percent tax burden. With these changes in taxes, foreign traders had great privileges over domestic traders. State intervention on the international trade of the Ottoman Empire, which was more important than the tax rates, was abandoned and did not return again (Pamuk, 1985).

With regard to the Ottoman classical foreign trade policy, an economic understanding was applied to increase the abundance of goods within the country and to encourage economic profitability, in particular in terms of prices, but to limit imports (Savrul, 2013). In addition to the export-promoting foreign trade policy supported by capitulations, agreements signed with European states were granted to foreigners for foreign trade without barriers. These privileges granted to foreigners made the Ottoman Empire an open market for the European states. In addition, the Ottoman Empire provided great benefits to the European economies (Mcgowan, 1981).

The ratio of international trade in Anatolia increased 12-15 times between 1820 and 1914. Between 1820 and the First World War, imports of cotton and cotton yarn in the regions within the borders of the Ottoman Empire in 1911 increased by more than 100 times and the imports of cotton and cotton per person increased by more than 50 times. Between 1820 and1842, imports increased more than ten times and their share in the domestic market exceeded 30%. In the early 1870s, imported goods accounted for more than 80% of total cotton consumption (Tabakoğlu, 2014).

The most important consequence of the Industrial Revolution for the Ottoman Empire was the fact that the state started to be a country that exported raw materials to industrial countries and imported manufactured goods from them. This is why the Ottoman Empire's external trade increased ten times during the period from the 1820s to the First World War. Again, due to technological developments during the Industrial Revolution, the price of industrial goods fell in favor of nations such as the Ottoman Empire specializing in agricultural products, which accelerated the decline of the system of small industries in the Ottoman Empire (Tabakoğlu, 2014).

Exports from the Ottoman Empire increased steadily between 1830 and 1911. Although France, Russia, Germany, England, France, Germany, Austria and Russia all played an important role in this period, the countries that received the most exports were France, Russia and Germany. In terms of imports to the Ottoman empire from 1830-1911, the countries from which the Ottoman Empire imported most were Russia, England, France, Austria, Germany. Despite the increase in imports and exports, the international trade deficits of the Ottoman Empire increased gradually due to the fact that there were more imports than exports (Güven, 1998). Examining 19th-century Ottoman exports, two properties draw attention. The first of these is that the share of any specific commodity was not large. Although the volume of exports more than doubled between 1878 and 1913, the total share of imported goods did not greatly change. According to the Ottoman financial statistics, the percentage of the eight most important commodities in the total export amount of tobacco, wheat, barley, grape, fig, raw silk, mohair and opium was 51% in 1878-1880, while the share of the same goods in 1913 was 44%. The difference was due to the decline in wheat exports. The share of food items in 1911-1913 was 33-35%, the share of raw materials was 56-58%, the share of semi-finished goods was 2-3% and of manufactured goods was 6-7%. Cotton and other textile products accounted for the largest share of manufactured goods (Pamuk, 1985).

External Borrowing in the Ottoman Empire

In the17th and 18th centuries, the Ottoman Empire experienced territorial losses and lost its reputation alongside the land. Military expenditure increased as a result of wars that lasted for many years, which led to an increase in budgets. In the face of the financial difficulties experienced by the Ottoman state, the duration of the contracts with refugees for one year or three years in order to provide long-term and advance income is 17. At the end of the century, it was started to be given to the winners of the tender on condition of "for perpetuity"(Özdemir, 2010).

The process of external borrowing in the Ottoman Empire is in a way the process by which it became integrated with the world. Before examining the first external borrowing process that began in 1854, the Ottoman state had to apply for external loans under various conditions and these conditions should be examined. The government that borrowed from foreign sources in the West experienced a financial crisis going back many years. These loans, which were usually from big banks in Europe, were not regular and were not significant amounts. When looking at the reasons for the financial crisis in the Ottoman state, the situation a few centuries ago needs to be examined. In the Ottoman Empire, which was a bureaucratic agricultural society, the expansion of the central state expansion and financial imbalance was experienced with the dissolution of the system of grooming, which was a characteristic of the decentralized Ottoman Empire. From the end of the 16th century onwards, financial crises deeply affected the Sublime Porte. These financial crises deepened in the 18th century with the defeat of the Ottoman Empire in various (Gürsel, 1985).

The 19th century is very important in terms of Ottoman economic history. The most important feature of the period was reform under the influence of the West in order to increase the power of the central state in the fields of education, law, the economy and finance. Another important feature of this period is that due to the rapid development in European trade the economy was opened to foreign markets.

The Ottoman Empire was gradually becoming a state that specialized in the export of agricultural goods and imported manufactured goods. From the 1770s to the 1840s, there were serious budget deficits due to frequent wars and reforms. In the 1820s and the 1830s, budget deficits reached the highest level. In the face of increasing budget deficits, the state went on to increase its control over tax resources and domestic borrowing. In the case of a financial crisis where other methods were not enough, it also had to resort to adulteration (Pamuk, 2017). The purpose of money adulteration was to transfer the value of money in the state to the treasury. By selling gold and silver goods in the hands of the people to the state over the price of the state, a number of precious metals were collected in the royal mint and sold for more than the actual price (Cezar, 1986). This method, which was initially used to narrow the budget deficits, resulted in counterfeiting over time and had an inflationary effect. This situation made the country's economy worse (Binhan, 2002). In 1775, the Ottoman Empire went into internal debt with the application of Esham in order to escape the financial crisis (Akar, 2001).

First Period of Loans

The first loan was made in the Ottoman Empire in 1854. Insufficient demand for the borrowing attempt through Rothschild was the first sign of the Ottoman Empire's high cost of borrowing from international financial markets through its own means. Rothschild carried out the loan transactions, and Lord Clarendon stated to the French Ambassador to London, Namık Paşa that France's support was necessary for the realization of debts. The loan conditions were made difficult and the Ottoman Empire was asked to borrow from other sources. After these negotiations, Namik Paşa decided that borrowing would not be suitable for the Ottoman state and that the banknote shortage would be met with the export of cash and that it was requested to borrow after receiving a positive opinion from the markets (Akar and Al, 2003).However, from the 1840s until the first loan, the representatives of European financiers and European states were pressuring the headquarters to solve the economic problems of the Ottoman Empire (Yıldız, 2007). In the period of the wars, the power of the money changers in the country was not enough to solve the country's economic crisis. However, in the Ottoman Empire, European foreign capital was formed and acted as an intermediary for the savings of the people. Instead of industry, savings became a mechanism to provide loans to foreign countries (Kazgan, 1991).

The first Ottoman foreign loan was made in 1854.The amount of this foreign debt was 3 million pounds sterling, the issuance of bonds was 80%, the interest rate was 6% and the maturity was 33 years. A specific amount of the Egyptian Tax was given as a guarantee of the loan. Tax guarantee (Akar and Al, 2003). The second external loan was made by London in 1855. The amount of this external loan was five million pounds sterling. The interest rate was4%. Egyptian taxes and some of the income of Damascus and Izmir customs have been shown to correspond to this debt in the direction of Egypt loan. This borrowing was also made due to the Crimean War. 49,263Turkish Lira of this was reserved for the first installment, and 2500 Turkish Lira were left as a commission. The rest was spent on war costs. The debut installment of the debts received has been paid to the war costs. The debts incurred caused the Ottoman Empire to borrow again and again, not by means of investments but by means of warfare (Karamursal, 1989). Another borrowing in the Ottoman Empire was made in 1858. This was received from London. The amount was five million pounds sterling, and the interest rate was six percent. In response to this debt, some of Istanbul's customs and oktruva revenues have been shown, but it is a requirement to be collected under the supervision of a delegation consisting of representatives of this income. In 1860, a new direction was requested by Fuat Paşa from London, but England wanted to lend with heavy conditions. Other loans taken by the Ottoman Empire were eight million sterling in 1862, 50 million francs in 1864, 150 million francs from the Paris Stock Exchange in 1865, and 40 million Turkish lira in 1865.In 1869, Paris loaned 555,555,300 francs. In 1870 the Rumeli Railway was borrowed with the name of the loan. In 1871, 5,700,000 pounds sterling was borrowed from London. In 1872, 10 million pounds sterling was borrowed and in 1873, 30,550,558 Ottoman lira was borrowed at a rate of interest of six percent. Until this date, a total of 250, 273, 924 lira had been borrowed in the period of Abdülaziz (Karamursal, 1989). As the years passed in the Ottoman Empire, it became difficult to enter into debt and financial audits were made. A French and British infrastructure was established as it had become more difficult to borrow. In 1863, the Ottoman Bank was established with the participation of a French group, which provided 50% of the capital to the British Ottoman Bank, which had been active since 1856. This bank was both a private French and British bank and the Bank of the Ottoman Empire. The bank was established to provide guarantees to the debts owed by the Ottoman Empire and maintained its existence within the state for some time. However, after a while, European and local capital holders came together and many credit institutions were born (Thobie, 1985).

In 1876, the Ottoman Empire became unable to repay its external debts and stopped its payments. The negotiations between the Ottoman government and French, British, Austrian, German and other creditors, which were interrupted due to the Ottoman-Russian war, resulted in a treaty signed in December 1881 (Muharram 1299 AH, according to the Hijri calendar). This is called the Muharram decree (Pamuk, 2007). According to the Muharram decree, the Ottoman Empire was not taken, and the Balkan states did not attempt to collect the debts owed to European creditors from these states. The tax to be taken from Eastern Rumeli was determined as 240,000 Ottoman liras, which was first reduced to 180,000 lira in the face of the opposition of the Rumeli Parliament, and this amount was then determined as 130,000 lira, which was not paid on a regular basis. However, this amount was not paid and the income from Cyprus was to be paid to Düyun-ı Umumiye, while the British invasion of Cyprus and the UK surplus was to be paid to the owners of 1855 bonds and the Ottoman State was not able to generate income after this date (Geyikdağı, 2008).

After examining the external loans received by the Ottoman Empire, the Ottoman Empire was founded in the 19th century. it has not been bordered by other alternatives that have financed the budget deficits through external borrowing for centuries. In the 19th century, internal borrowing was not a serious alternative, especially long-term internal borrowing; the reason for this was that the domestic financial markets were too small for the amount the state wanted to borrow. The reason for not borrowing through coin adulteration in the 19th century was that it was not an appropriate method to provide additional financial income. Paper was able to fulfill the function of money borrowing. In the 19th century, the Ottoman Empire had two options, paper money and external loans. Long-term borrowing seemed attractive when borrowing started in the 1850s.Despite the reluctance of the Ottoman bureaucracy to borrow, it seemed attractive to the Ottoman Empire to borrow from European markets for a long time. In 1881, the European creditors were overseen by Ottoman finance, and the Ottoman State made a number of attempts to maintain credibility in order to maintain European debt. The foreign debt of the Ottoman Empire was relatively stable, foreign trade grew faster in Bridge and more foreign investors were formed. Foreign trade grew at an average rate of 5% in the 19th century. Income per capita increased. On the other hand, the fact that the income sources were the European states caused the Ottoman finance to be negatively affected. Increases in international debt led to economic and political dependence (Pamuk, 2007).

INSTITUTIONALIZATION AND MODERNIZATION IN THE OTTOMAN EMPIRE

The Ottoman Empire survived with every wide geographical area and at the crossroads of trade routes for a period of six hundred years; this is a very important issue because many states in Europe have not been able to protect their assets for so long. Other states which expanded and prospered in the 16th century alongside the Ottomans, such as the Safavids in Iran and the Indian Turkish-Mongol State, disappeared in the 17th and 18th centuries under the pressure of financial and military problems. In the same centuries, the Ottoman Empire became stronger in the face of great pressure and recovered despite intense wars and began the process of modernization by increasing the power of the central government. As one of the most important factors in economic development, this brought institutions and institutional changes to the forefront (Pamuk, 2007). One economic perspective, that of 'new institutional economics' which emerged in western Europe, has the thesis that the most important process required for economic development and growth are the institutions that constitute a state. In looking at Ottoman history, it was generally accepted that the Ottoman Empire entered a period of decline from the end of the 16th century. Recent studies have revealed that this period should not be interpreted as an uninterrupted period of regression. In the face of the changes in the Eurasian continent, society was reorganized by adapting and modernizing. In the 19th century, both before and after the society was reorganized, central bureaucracy became more powerful by suppressing any uprisings that emerged and by establishing a tradition of negotiation in the face of domestic and foreign threats. It was flexible and pragmatic to talk about the policies and institutional changes that were being implemented, regardless of the rules, traditions and patterns of behavior of the past. Ottoman society and Ottoman Empire could not achieve institutional changes to capitalism before the 19th century. However, the process of modernization that had begun years before the reorganizations made it easier to adapt the educational system, the Army and Navy, and the bureaucracy in almost every region of the state to the changing world order and allowed the Empire to continue for a longer period of time (Pamuk, 2015).The main area that we will examine as an example of the effects of institutionalization and industrialization in the Ottoman Empire is the Navy. Through innovations in this area, the Ottoman Empire made significant progress both in naval history and trade.

Reforms in Naval Supervision

With the announcement of reorganizations in 1839, important reforms were made in the Navy. After the foundation of the Naval Assembly, the most important reform was the abolition of the Kaptanpaşa, which had continued to exist in the Ottoman state organization for a long time, and instead, the supervision of the Navy was established. The Navy was to separate this supervision from the umur-ı Naval supervision established in 1804. Founded in 1804, supervision was replaced by Shipyard Assurance. The idea of the abolition of the Kaptanpaş was first put forward in 1845. After the establishment of the Naval Assembly, important changes were made to the navy, and the shipyard and the navy could not be managed together in terms of administrative and financial aspects. In 1861, the Under secretariat of the Navy and Shipyards was abolished. All the duties of this institution were placed on the Kaptanpaşa (Gencer, 1991). In this restructuring, the transition from sailing to the use of steamboats, which was a result of the Industrial Revolution, was the main factor. Since the Ottoman navy and maritime trade had begun to use steamboats, the Ottomans tried to change the administrative organization to account for this (Düzcü, 2017).

After the establishment of the Naval supervision, a deputy and an accountant were appointed to this supervision and then arrangements were made to determine the duties of the captain of the Naval Supervision. The Naval administration and command assembly, which carried out shipyard and naval works under the supervision of the Navy. The Navy Guard managed the finances of the shipyard and Navy and acted in partnership with the captain's office in recruiting military personnel for some military issues (Gencer, 1986).

By 1864 significant changes had been made under the supervision of the Naval Meclis-I Bahriye, and the management was divided. In the Abdulhamid period, the Naval Council was again divided by the administration and the Ottoman Naval organization became specialized. In 1876, the Naval Supervision was abolished but was re-established towards the end of the same year (Düzcü, 2009).

Naval Organization Under Abdul Hamid II

When the Sultan Abdülaziz period ended and the reign of Abdul Hamid II began, the effects of the change in administrative, technical and scientific conditions in the organization of the Navy began to be seen. In addition to a few remaining divisions and commissions from the Sultan Abdülaziz period, many different divisions and commissions were established under Abdulhamid II, and changes to the Navy occurred very rapidly. The attempt was made to keep up more quickly with developments in naval affairs occurring around the world (Düzcü, 2013).

During the reign of Abdülhamid II, there were news developments in marine technology thanks to torpedo boats and other changes. This led to the development of the Navy by introducing new units. When looking at the naval offices during the reign of Abdülhamid II, we see an increase in numbers and a rise in specialization. In a decree published in 1877, the Naval Council's name changed to Shura-yı Bahriye. Founded in 1863 as the Erkan-ı Harbiye-i Bahriye Officer Office, the division was reorganized in 1877 and followed the developments in the European navy: The Equipment Department provided personnel with supplies such as coal, medicine, machinery and electricity, lumber and clothes. The Dersaadet Port Administration determined the status and number of military and commercial vessels operating in Istanbul and other places. The Court-Martials Office was the department in which charges and penalties related to the Navy were imposed. The Amire Shipyard officer was responsible for all import and export, manufacturing, construction and repair works of the Amire Shipyard. The Court of Appeals heard appeals of any court-martials. The Medical Department looked after the health of the Naval soldiers and the training of the medical officers. The Port Command Department tried to implement the decisions of the naval council in relation to the discipline and the assignments of the Naval soldiers. The Areli Maden-i Hümayun Supervision provided coal for all ships in the navy. The Naval School was the school that trained all naval admiral and officers. If the administration is offset, it was carrying passengers and cargo to both domestic and foreign ports (Düzcü, 2009).

When looking at the Ottoman naval policy during the First Constitutional Era, it can be seen that the long-term problems of the state negatively affected the economy and finances. Economic bottlenecks were experienced due to capitulations and public debts (Kodaman, 2002).

As in the period of Abdul Hamid II, during the First Constitutional Era, it was the threatening attitudes of Russia and Greece, the neighboring states of the Ottoman Empire, which determined Ottoman naval policy. Russia planned to gain access to the Mediterranean through the Black Sea. The second major threat to the Ottoman Empire was Greece. Since 1829, Greece had been very influential on the Greek people located within the Empire on the islands of the Eastern Mediterranean. Greek boats and ships on each island were encouraged by the Greek Cypriots to rebel to bring the islands under the control of Greece. During the Second Constitutional Era, new policies were implemented in the field of naval affairs. The most important of these policies was the use of British expertise. The world leadership of the British in naval affairs was a known fact. Taking advantage of British naval experts, using British ships and armored ships and installing British machinery and boilers on ships, gave Ottoman ships a great advantage. However, significant steps were also taken in naval affairs by changing the administrative system of the Navy Supervisor (Karataşer, 2016).

In the Second Constitutional Era, foreign expertise in the naval field was utilized, as in many other fields. It was decided that a Naval council would be brought from England, including an admiral with knowledge and experience of artillery and torpedoes. As a result of this decision, Admiral Gamble came from the UK to Turkey with a salary of 3000 English pounds a year for two years of work. Two other English admirals, Admiral Limpus and Admiral Williams were also appointed. As a result of the experience of these admirals, the Naval Supervision was divided into four divisions. The First Division was for the Military Affairs of the Navy, including naval intelligence, and preparation for expedition. The Second Division dealt with the entrance of the officers to the Naval, promotions and retirements, education and student examinations. The Third Division was the Materials Department, which handled the design and construction of new ships. The Fourth Division was for equipment, and managed contracts and equipment, coal, accounting and surveying (Düzcü, 2009). The experts suggested that new warships and torpedoes be made. All three experts also focused on the subject of training and the naval personnel were provided with training. Since the economic conditions of the country were not good, an organization was established in order to support the navy. The name of this society was the Donanma-yı Osmani Muavenet-i Milliye Society. It was based in Istanbul and its most important contribution was to provide new ships to the Ottoman navy with the help it collected. The ships received included the Mithat Paşa, the Reşit Paşa, Giresun ships, torpedo destroyer ships, the numune-i Hamiyet and Gayret-i Vataniye, and the armored destroyer ships Turgut Reis and Barbaros Hayreddin (Langensiepen, 2000).

SOLUTIONS AND RECOMMENDATIONS

The Ottoman Empire became aware of the changing world order and industrialization and modernized its institutions and to continue own existence. The Ottoman Empire made major reforms in the maritime organization, one of the most important areas of the state. Experts were brought from foreign countries, the personnel were trained, and new equipment was obtained. Although the international trade policies were disadvantageous and the economic condition of the country was poor, a great effort was made not to borrow with heavy interest. The reforms carried out in the naval field to improve the economy positively affected industrialization and the economy. Attempts were made to try to implement the international trade policies in favor of the Ottoman State, but the increased burden of international debt did not permit this.

The Ottoman Empire was aware that the world had been industrialized and modernized by globalization and realized that the Empire was not sustainable without industrialization. The Ottoman Empire tried to ensure the continuity of the Empire by making reforms to its international trade policies after reforms in the naval sphere. Important reforms were made in navy and institutions were modernized. New technologies and training for the crews were provided for ships. The Ottoman Empire modernized the institutions of the 18th century and created completely different institutions in the 19th century. If the Ottoman State had not been able to achieve this, it would probably have ceased existence before the end of the First World War. In this way, it continued its existence for many years. However, the Ottoman Empire's failure to implement globalization, modernization and industrialization was no longer due to the insufficiency of the trained labor force, the loss of land and the deterioration of economic conditions day by day.

CONCLUSION

Evaluating the process of globalization in the Ottoman Empire through its international trade policies and institutions shows how important this concept had become in the world. The first wave of globalization affected the Ottoman Empire in a way similar to other nation states. The Ottoman Empire wanted to integrate into the West, saw the innovations and tried to imitate them. However, there were problems in implementing them quickly enough. The main problem was related to the mentality of the Ottoman Empire. The Ottoman Empire privileged the welfare of the people above all. However, when the welfare of the people came up against the effort to increase the revenues of the state, a number of failures occurred. Under the impact of globalization, European nations acted with the idea of finding a new market for emerging industries; they tried to make other states in the world into their markets.

The Ottoman Empire tried to integrate with the reform movements occurring in the West. But on the one hand, these improvements and reforms, and, on the other hand, domestic and foreign political and economic problems led the country into economic and financial difficulties. The Ottoman Empire had to fight on several fronts while dealing with reforms. Economic and financial difficulties meant that they could not be carried out in time. However, because the Ottoman Empire knew the importance of restructuring, it explored various ways to adapt. The new state made changes to the land regime to generate revenues. With the Land Law of 1858, the state recognized private property. Thus, the income obtained from the land, which was the largest source of income of the Ottoman Empire, was significantly reduced.

In order to reduce this loss of income over time, the amount of private property was reduced. Another problem experienced by the Ottoman Empire was the increase of the population due to immigrants who came the Ottoman Empire after the loss of territories. The Balkan regions, which were the grain warehouses of the Ottoman Empire, were lost and this caused the country to face food shortages.

In assessing the role of globalization in the Ottoman Empire, international trade and foreign borrowing should be evaluated. In the 19th century, both wars and reforms left the Ottoman economy in a difficult position. With the aim of increasing the commercial activities of the state, the Ottoman Empire entered into a trade agreement with European states to increase the volume of external trade. However, concessions granted to foreigners prevented Ottoman citizens from trading profitably. After the Ottoman-Russian War, the Ottoman Empire signed a trade treaty with Russia, but this treaty caused the Ottoman State to lose its independence in external trade. However, despite all the negative effects, the international trade of the Ottoman Empire increased between 1830 and 1910.The Ottoman Empire went down the route of external borrowing in order to restore the balance of foreign trade deficit. The Egyptian tax was provided as collateral for foreign loans. But over time, foreign loans were not enough to pay the installments of other foreign debts and could only pay war costs. The inability to use foreign loans for investment and the need to borrow more over time led the Ottoman Empire to find new sources of loans.

When looking at the institutionalization and modernization of the Ottoman Empire, it is necessary to investigate the reasons why the Ottoman Empire survived for so many years. The Ottoman Empire followed and understood all the innovations that had occurred since the Industrial Revolution and took the necessary measures. One of the most important areas that the Industrial Revolution affected and triggered was the naval sector. The Ottoman Empire first established the Naval Assembly; when this assembly was not sufficient, the Naval Supervision was established. When this was established, it was separated into divisions and specialization was implemented. The Naval Supervision was organized with the help of experts from England. The Supervision was divided into different departments and functions. The ships required were ordered immediately. The Ottoman Empire was aware of modernization and made its people aware of it. A relief team was established to supply ships abroad. In areas where the state budget was not sufficient, the people themselves helped to order ships through the society that had been founded.

In general, when looking at how the Ottoman Empire was affected by globalization, it can be said that the Ottoman Empire saw the necessities of the era and tried to adapt. However, being aware of the process and making improvements was a process that required a plan. The improvements desired should be evaluated while considering the economic and political conditions of the country. The Ottoman Empire needed to develop the growth of revenue in the country; in order to achieve this, it tried to increase the trade and succeeded in doing so. However, territorial losses and the inability to convert the loans received into investments caused problems. Even though the Ottoman Empire wanted to solve its economic issues without borrowing, the European states argued that the Ottoman Empire would not be able to overcome these crises without receiving loans. The Ottoman Empire refused to borrow for a long time and even though it wanted to solve the crises by increasing the income obtained from within the borders of the country, the migrations that occurred as a result of wars pushed the Ottoman Empire into the foreign debt. Knowing the importance of improving the state, the Empire tried to adapt the modernization process, starting with its institutions. The historical longevity of the Ottoman Empire was achieved by adapting and modernizing its institutions to the changing condition of the world.

REFERENCES

Akar, Ş. K. (2001). Osmanlı Devleti'nde Kısa ve Uzun Vadeli Borçlanma'nın Gelişimi. İstanbul Üniversitesi İktisat Fakültesi Mecmuası, 51(2), 99-124.

Akar, Ş. K., & Al, H. (2003). *Osmanlı Dış Borçları ve Gözetim komisyonları (1854-1856)*. İstanbul: Osmanlı Bankası Arşiv ve Araştırma Merkezi.

Aktel, M. (2001). Küreselleşme Süreci ve Etki Alanları. Süleyman Demirel Üniversitesi İktisadi ve İdari Bilimler Fakültesi Dergisi, 6(2),193-202.

Aydınlı, E. (2007). The Turkish Pendulum between Globalization and Security: From the Late Ottoman Era to the 1930s'. Middle Eastern Studies, 40(3), 102-133.

Binhan, E. Y. (2002). *Osmanlı İmparatorluğu'nu Dış Borçlanmaya İten Nedenler ve İlk Dış Borç*. Akdeniz İİBF Dergisi.

Çeken, H., Ökten, Ş., & Ateşoğlu, L. (2008). Eşitsizliği Derinleştiren Bir Süreç Olarak Küreselleşme ve Yoksulluk. C.Ü. İİBF Dergisi, 9(2), 79-95.

Çelik, M. Y. (2012). Boyutlarıyla ve farklı algılarıyla küreselleşme. Dumlupınar Üniversitesi Sosyal Bilimler Dergisi, 2(32), 57-73.

Cezar, Y. (1986). *Osmanlı Maliyesinde Bunalım ve değişim Dönemi (18. Yüzyıldan Tanzimat'a Mali Tarih)*. İstanbul: Alan Yayıncılık.

Danışoğlu, A. Ç. (2004). Küreselleşme'nin Gelir Eşitsizliği ve Yoksulluk Üzerindeki Etkileri. İstanbul Ticaret Üniversitesi Dergisi, 3(6), 215-239.

Dumrul, C., & Dumrul, Y. (2014). Osmanlı İmparatorluğu'nu Kapitalist Paternde Sanayileşmesinin Önündeki Engeller Üzerine Bir İnceleme. Yönetim ve Ekonomi Araştırmaları Dergisi, 12(23), 146-170.

Düzcü, L. (2009). Osmanlı Bahriye Teşkilatında Reform Çabaları (1876-1922). *Akademik Bakış*, *3*(5), 3-19.

Düzcü, L. (2013). Osmanlı Sanayi Çağına Adım Atışına Denizcilikten Bir Örnek: Buharlı Gemiye Geçişte Başlıca Parametreler (1828-1856). History Studies, 5(1), 113-127.

Düzcü, L. (2017). *Yelkenliden Buharlıya Geçişte Osmanlı Denizciliği (1825-1855)*. İstanbul: Doğu Kütüphanesi Yayınları.

Eldem, V. (1994). *Harp ve Mütareke Yıllarında Osmanlı İmparatorluğu'nun Ekonomisi*. Ankara: Türk Tarih Kurumu.

Erdem, E. (2016). Sanayi Devriminin Ardından Osmanlı Sanayileşme Hamleleri: Sanayi Politikalarının Dinamikleri ve Zaafiyetleri. *Erciyes Üniversitesi İİBF Dergisi*, *48*, 17-44.

Genç, M. (2000). *Osmanlı İmparatorluğu'nda Devlet ve Ekonomi*. İstanbul: Ötüken Neşriyat.

Gencer, A. İ. (1986). *Türk Denizcilik Tarihi Araştırmaları*. İstanbul: Türkiye Denizciler Sendikası.

Gencer, A. İ. (1991). Bahriye Nezareti. Türkiye Diyanet Vakfı İslam Ansiklopedisi. *Ankara:Türkiye Diyanet Vakfı Yayınları*, 4.

Geyikdağı, V. N. (2008). *Osmanlı Devleti'nde Yabancı Sermaye(1854-1914)*. İstanbul: Hil Yayıncılık.

Gürsel, S. (1985). Osmanlı Dış Borçları. Tanzimattan Cumhuriyete Türkiye Ansiklopedisi. *İstanbul:İletişim Yayınları*, 3.

Güven, T. C. (1998). Cumhuriyetin 75. Yıl Dönümünde Dış Ticaretimizin Geçmişi ve Bugünü. *Dış Ticaret Dergisi*, *3*, 26-41.

İpşirli, M. (1998). Hayriye Tüccarı. Türkiye Diyanet Vakfı İslam Ansiklopedisi. *İstanbul:Türkiye Diyanet Vakfı*, 17.

Karamursal, Z. (1989). *Osmanlı Mali Tarihi Hakkında Tetkikler*. Ankara: Türk Tarih Kurumu.

Karataşer, B. (2013). Birinci Dünya Savaşı ve Mütareke Döneminde İstanbul'un İaşesi. Kahraman Maraş Sütçü İmam Üniversitesi İİBF Dergisi, 3(2), 97-114.

Karataşer, B. (2016). İkinci Meşrutiyet Dönemi Osmanlı Donanma Politikası: Milli Donanmayı Kurma Çabaları. In *VIII. Türk Deniz Ticareti Tarihi Sempozyumu* (pp. 138-143).

Karataşer, B. (2018). *İslam İktisadi Anlayışının Osmanlı'da Kurumsal Yansımaları*. Bursa: Ekin Basım Yayın Dağıtım.

Kazgan, H. (1991). *Galata Bankerleri*. İstanbul: Türkiye Ekonomi Bankası A.Ş Yayınları.

Kenanoğlu, M. M. (2005). Miri. Türkiye Diyanet Vakfı İslam Ansiklopedisi. *Ankara:Türkiye Diyanet Vakfı*, 30.

Kodaman, B. (2002). İkinci Meşrutiyet Dönemi(1908-1914). Türkler. *Ankara:Yeni Türkiye Yayınları*, 13.

Konukman, A., & Çiftçi, C. (2008). Küreselleşmenin Gelir Dağılımı Üzerindeki Etkileri.*Ekonomik Yaklaşım*, *19*, 59-83.

Kütükoğlu, M. S. (1974). Osmanlı-İngiliz İktisadi Münasebetleri (1580-1838). *Ankara. Türk Kültürünü Araştırma Enstitüsü*, 1.

Langensiepen, B. (2000). *Osmanlı Donanması 1828-1923. Çev. Renan Mengü.* İstanbul: Denizler Kitabevi.

Mcgowan, B. (1981). *Economic Life in Ottoman Europe*. Newyork: Cambridge University.

Öniş, Z. (2014). Küreselleşme,Gelir Adaletsizliği ve Demokrasinin Geleceği:Kriz Sonrası Eğilimler. *İktisat ve Toplum*, *4*(47), 13-25.

Özdemir, B. (2010). *Osmanlı Devleti Dış Borçları*. Ankara: Maliye Bakanlığı strateji Geliştirme Başkanlığı.

Pamuk, Ş. (1985). 19.yy'da Osmanlı Dış Ticareti. Tanzimattan Cumhuriyete Türkiye Ansiklopedisi. *İstanbul:İletişim Yayınları*, 3.

Pamuk, Ş. (1994). *Osmanlı Ekonomisinde Bağımlılık ve Büyüme (1820-1913).* İstanbul: Tarih Vakfı Yurt Yayınları.

Pamuk, Ş. (2002). Küreselleşme Çağında Osmanlı Ekonomisi (1820-1914). Türkler Ansiklopedisi. *Ankara:Yeni Türkiye Yayınları*, 14.

Pamuk, Ş. (2015). *Türkiye'nin 200 Yıllık İktisadi Tarihi*. İstanbul: İş Bankası Kültür Yayınları.

Pamuk, Ş. (2017). *Osmanlı'dan Cumhuriyete Küreselleşme, İktisat Politikaları ve Büyüme*. Türkiye İş Bankası Kültür Yayınları.

Savaş, V. (2004). *Dünya Ekonomi Sistemi*. İstanbul: Yeditepe Üniversitesi Yayınları.

Savrul, B. K., Özel, H. A., & Kılıç, C. (2013). Osmanlı'nın Son Döneminden Günümüze Türkiye Dış Ticaretinin Gelişimi. Girişimcilik ve Kalkınma Dergisi, 1(8), 55-78.

Şenses, F. (2001). *Küreselleşmenin Öteki Yüzü: Yoksulluk-Kavramlar, Nedenler,Politikalar ve Temel Eğilimler*. İstanbul: İletişim Yayınları.

Şenses, F. (2004). Neoliberal Küreselleşme Kalkınma İçin Bir Fırsat mı, Engel mi? *ERC*.

Seyidoğlu, H. (2003). Uluslararası İktisat Teori Politika ve Uygulama. İstanbul: Güzem Yayınları.

Skousen, M. (2003). *Modern İktisadın İnşası.Çev.Mustafa Acar, Ekrem Erdem, Metin Toprak*. Ankara: Liberte Yayınları.

Tabakoğlu, A. (2005). *Türkiye İktisat Tarihi*. İstanbul: Dergah Yayınları.

Tabakoğlu, A. (2013). *İslam İktisadına Giriş*. İstanbul: Dergah Yayınları.

Tabakoğlu, A. (2014). *Türkiye İktisat Tarihi*. İstanbul: Dergah Yayınları.

Thobie, J. (1985). *Osmanlı Devletinde Yabancı Sermaye Tanzimattan Cumhuriyete Türkiye Ansiklopedisi*. İstanbul: İletişim Yayınları.

Yıldız, A. (Ekim 2007). Osmanlı İmparatorluğu'nun Borçlanmasında Yabancı Sermaye'nin Etkisi. *İstanbul Üniversitesi Siyasal Bilgiler Fakültesi Dergisi*, *37*, 113-125.

KEY TERMS AND DEFINITIONS

External Borrowing in the Ottoman Empire: It was an effort to finance the poor economic conditions of the Ottoman Empire due to the loss of land.

Fiscalism: One of the fundamentals of the mentality of the Ottoman Empire.

Globalization: The process of industrialization which is defined as the First Globalization.

Institutionalization: The attempt to modernize the institutions of the Ottoman Empire in order to achieve industrialization.

Modernization: The adaptation of the Ottoman Empire to the industrialization process which started in the western countries.

Ottoman Navy Organization: It was the 19th century Ottoman naval organization. In the Ottoman Empire, it was an important area in which experts were brought from Europe in terms of ship, worker and expert to achieve optimization.

The Period of Abdulhamid II: It was the years of 1876-1908, when the Ottoman Empire became modernized and institutionalized.

Chapter 9 An Analysis of Risk Transfer and Trust Nexus in International Trade With Reference to Turkish Data

Aslı Taşbaşı
Işık University, Turkey

Pınar Yeşim Sarıca
Işık University, Turkey

Ahmet Hakan Yüksel
Işık University, Turkey

ABSTRACT

International trade introduces a range of risks, which causes uncertainty over the timing of delivery and payment between exporters and importers. This chapter is a first attempt in dissecting Turkey's trade data in terms of risk allocation and trust between the parties involved. Breaking down Turkish export and import data for the years 2000 to 2018 according to methods of payment and use of currencies, the chapter first finds the risk is distributed unevenly between the exporter and the importer. Then findings are evaluated to open a new avenue of future research, constructed on the inquiry whether emerging economies like Turkey can establish trust in their trade with developed economies by using blockchain technology.

DOI: 10.4018/978-1-5225-9566-3.ch009

INTRODUCTION

In international trade, risk is commonly defined as the possibility of loss of or damage to the goods subject to trade. The transfer of risk, according to this definition, refers to bearing all risks associated with the goods traded. As exporters and importers from all over the world come together to carry out trade transactions despite not only geographical distances but economic, political and cultural differences, the transfer of risk and risk management gain more sensitivity.

Risks in international trade can be economic, country-specific, commercial or cultural. Economic risks are risks that contain economic loss to the sides engaged in trade activity. Country-specific risks imply risks of a wide range, from business to political climate in a specific country. Commercial risks are risks associated with the reliability of partners. Cultural risks are based on cultural differences which may be related with a variety of issues like decision making styles, language barriers or differing ethical concerns. Differences in terminology used, unclear or undefined terms of payment potentially lead future disputes between parties involved.

Estimating the transfer of risk is crucial when setting up the trade contract. Exporters need to receive payment as quickly as time permits, ideally when an order is placed or before the goods are sent to the importer. Importers on the other hand, need to receive the goods at the earliest opportunity, yet to defer payment to the extent that this would be possible, ideally until after the goods are resold to create enough revenue to pay the exporter.

Types of payment in international trade are developed with the intention to characterize and harmonize the methods for payments in return of delivery of goods sold across borders. As such, the payment methods are categorized to clear away disparities in national applications, which otherwise may be deterrent to the smooth functioning of international trade. Varying categories of payment ensure that the risk is moved in various routes between the seller and the buyer. Depending on whether the damage or loss is at the buyer or the seller's risk, each side bears the costs.

This study attempts to diagnose whether Turkey bears a symmetric cost with its partners in bilateral trade in terms of risks undertaken. Assessing Turkish export and import data according to types of payment and use of currencies, the study intends to reveal whether there is a consistent pattern of undertaking risk in favor of the exporter or the importer. If international trade is unevenly structured according to these risk parameters favoring the exporter or the importer, and if the ongoing trade relationship does not at least converge over time to a state relatively even, it is worth examining whether there is an issue resulting from the way countries trade. This paper is a first in the sense that it anatomizes Turkey's international trade as such and links the findings with the trust issue in international trade. The findings are evaluated according to the possibility of Turkey's restoring trust with the help of blockchain technology-based international trade and finance.

MAIN FOCUS OF THE CHAPTER

Risks (and Costs) of Trade and Risk Transfer

A typical firm would like to offer attractive payment terms to encourage its potential markets, but at the same time it would want its money as soon as possible, so it can carry out its day-to-day operations and invest in future growth. While this challenge exists in all commercial transactions, it carries more risk in international transactions. Indeed, engaging in international trade, firms find new markets, yet, it is often riskier than domestic trade. While mutual benefit is assumed to exist in bilateral trade, the sides' interest in payment terms is different. Good payment terms to the exporter may mean bad payment terms to the importer or vice versa. Being engaged in bilateral trade, the exporter or the importer has to take into account several factors before agreeing to a specific payment method. The exporter takes into account the trade history with the buyer, political unrest and economic (in) stability in the country of destination, competitors' offering terms and the risk of price/exchange rate changes. Factors that need attention for the importer on the other hand may be the possible loss or damage during delivery, supplier problems, delays in transport, import tariffs, storage of goods and exchange rate fluctuations.

Most transactions in the world are carried out through 'Open Account' method. This payment method carries the highest risk for the exporter because it does not guarantee payment on time or even the payment itself. On the contrary, cash in advance method implies the highest risk for the importer because the exporter will receive the payment of the goods before they are sent. In this case, the importer trusts that the seller will fulfill the contract and deliver the goods on time and as specified. An alternative widely used method, letters of credit, provides good protection because payment from the importer is guaranteed by the importer's bank.

In international trade, various risks may arise also depending on the volatile nature of exchange rates. Changes in the expected value of a contract between its signing and its execution due to unexpected changes in foreign exchange rates for instance may cause a transaction risk. Converting financial statements from one currency to another to consolidate them may cause a translation risk, while changes in competitive position because of permanent changes in exchange rates may result economic risk. The more stable and stronger the national currency is, the less the risk of business transactions. All kinds of volatility and instability in terms of the currency means taking over the risk for the country concerned. The party that trades on the currencies accepted as reliable by the global markets will transfer this risk on its own even if there is any financial risk related to the currency of the counterparty.

Following two sections evaluate Turkish data in terms of the risks of trade related to payment methods and the risks that may arise regarding the currency used in trade.

Turkey's Trade in Terms of Risk Transfer Indicators

This section deals with Turkish trade data for the years 2000 to 2018 according to risk transfer indicators of payment and exchange rate volatility.

Turkey's Trade by Types of Payment

Using data for a time span covering the 19 years between 2000 and 2018, types of payment in foreign trade have been categorized separately for situations where Turkey is either the exporting or the importing party. Types of payment data in Turkish exports and imports are published in totals by the Ministry of Customs and Foreign Trade. When these data are decomposed according to types of payment which are the leading indicators that show to what manner risk is shared (or transferred) among parties in trade relationship Turkey is found to be undertaking relatively higher risk whether it be in a position of an importer or exporter.

Indeed, historically, the types of payments data for exports and imports of Turkey show that, Turkish firms have low bargaining power with foreign partners in the choice of payment terms. Both exporters and importers are unable to determine the payment terms that are suitable for them, and they bear all the risks associated with international trade transactions.

According to data compiled from the Turkish Ministry of Customs and Trade, most commonly preferred type of payment in Turkey's exports is ''cash against goods, cash on delivery''. Between 2000 and 2018, this method of payment has taken share from total payments at a minimum of 44% and a maximum of 66%.

This method may be preferred when the exporter aims to gain the trust of the importer; however, during the eighteen year long time span investigated in this study, there has not been a shift in Turkish exports from this or alike methods which guarantee the delivery of the good in its perfect timing and form for the importer, to other methods which minimize the risk for the exporter. Indeed, cash against goods is the "riskiest method for the exporter" since "the importer does not make any payment until he receives the purchased good" (Acar, 2009, pp. 3). This method is followed by "cash against documents" whose share has halved, from 28.60% in 2001 to 13.88% in 2018.

Leading type of payment in Turkey's imports on the other hand is ''advance payment''. During the time span taken into consideration, this payment method has consistently taken the lion share, with a maximum of 51.44% in 2010 and a minimum of 31.03% in 2001. Dominance of advance payment method in Turkish imports can give an idea about the risk- taking behavior of the exporters selling goods to Turkey, complimentary to the export data discussed above. In addition to minimizing the risk, this method provides a pre-financing to produce, prepare and ship the goods in terms of exporter.

Advance payment is followed by ''cash against goods, cash on delivery'' and ''letter of credit'' payment methods respectively. Taken together with the weight of cash against goods method in Turkish exports, data suggest that whatever the direction of the trade, Turkey is the party that holds majority of the risk in its trade relations.

These findings demonstrate the importance of well-functioning financial markets in Turkey. To operate efficiently in foreign markets, Turkish firms are required to improve trade financing and risk mitigation tools and develop an efficient financial system in order to trade at lower costs. Appropriate policy actions and measures are needed for new and smaller exporters to maintain business. These actions will not only help Turkish firms to reach the financing they need to export more and diversify their exports at product and destination points, but also eliminate the risk of a trade transaction.

Finally, agreements between importers and exporters should create institutional structures to ensure effective regulation and implementation, as better enforcement of contracts to increase their exports of Turkish firms or enter the market and increase its ability to improve the lives of the newly established bilateral trade relationship. Overall, a combination of these policies, Turkey's product range and geographic scope of diversification, export quality to increase the export growth to increase to, balancing their export earnings and thus will help lead to sustainable long-term economic growth.

Turkey's Trade by Currencies

Transaction costs of a currency would be lower if the volume of transactions in the currency are higher and the exchange rate volatility against other currencies is lower (Hau et al., 2002). As can be seen in Figure 3, most widely used currencies in Turkish exports are US Dollar and Euro. US Dollar has the minimum share of 42.47% in 2007 and the highest share of 50.83% in 2000. With the physical entrance of Euro into circulation in 2002, this currency has not only replaced Deutsche Mark in currencies used but also became the close rival of the US dollar. Since 2002, Euro has been used at a minimum of 44.18% in 2015 and at a maximum of 50.81% in 2018.

Figure 1. Turkey's exports by types of payment (2000-2018)
Source: Authors' calculations based on data compiled from Turkish Ministry of Customs and Trade

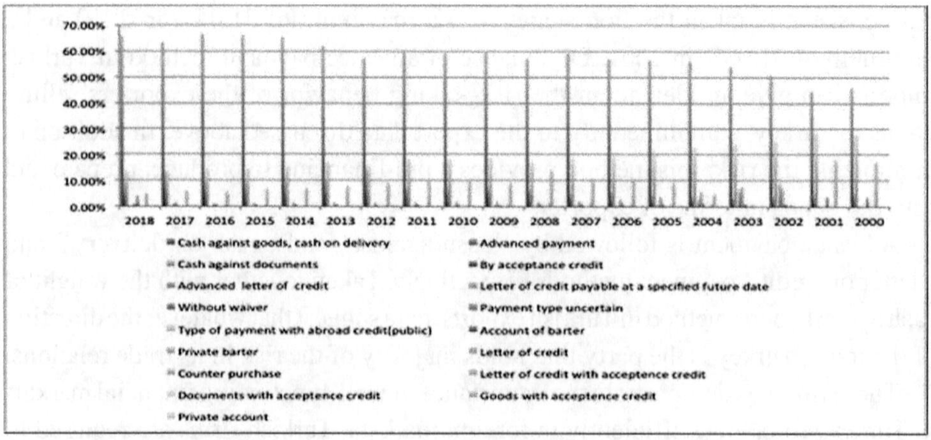

**For a more accurate representation see the electronic version.*

Figure 2. Turkey's imports by types of payment (2000-2018)
Source: Authors' calculations based on data compiled from Turkish Ministry of Customs and Trade

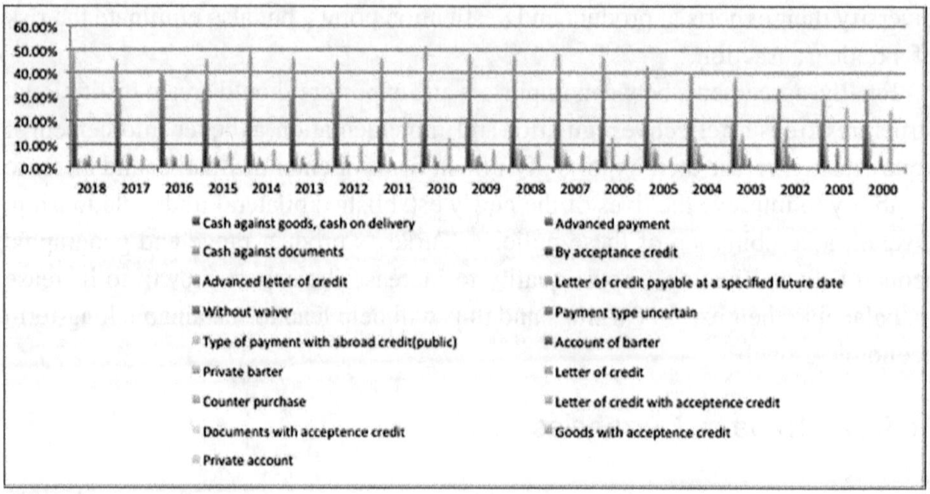

**For a more accurate representation see the electronic version.*

In line with its global dominance as leading international currency, the US Dollar is by far the most widely used currency in Turkish imports (see Figure 4). During 2000 to 2018, it has been the medium of exchange for more than half of the import transactions. It takes a minimum at 55.03% in 2004 and a maximum at 64.23% in 2012. US Dollar is followed by Euro with the lowest ratio of 29.97% in 2012 and the highest ratio is 40.29% in 2004.

Despite the attempts to increase the use of Turkish Lira (TRL) in international trade (among planned bilateral trade in national currencies with Russia, Iran, China and Ukraine, only the first two seem to have agreed upon the idea), a strong shift as in the case of Chinese Renminbi (CNY) cannot be observed. As of 2015, 23% of China's total imports and exports were made with CNY. In the international currency of payments, while CNY ranked 35th in October 2010 it ranked 5th in October 2015. While the share of TRL in imports was 2.84% in 2009, it increased to 7.58% in 2017. Approximately 5% of total exports and approximately 7% of total imports in 2016 are made in TRL. By the year 2018, about 5% of exports and 6% of imports are realized in TRL.

Figures 5 and 6 show that current depreciation process of TRY requires an even more careful look at the foreign currency risk element in the country's foreign trade. In particular,

considering that the TRY has depreciated almost 50% on annual basis and that it has suffered the longest period of consecutive daily losses in the past 20 years, importers are likely to face a payment risk (https://www.ebury.com/blog/ebury_post/whats-next-turkish-lira/).

Figure 3. Turkey's exports by currencies (2000-2018)
Source: Authors' calculations based on data compiled from Turkish Statistical Institute (TURKSTAT)

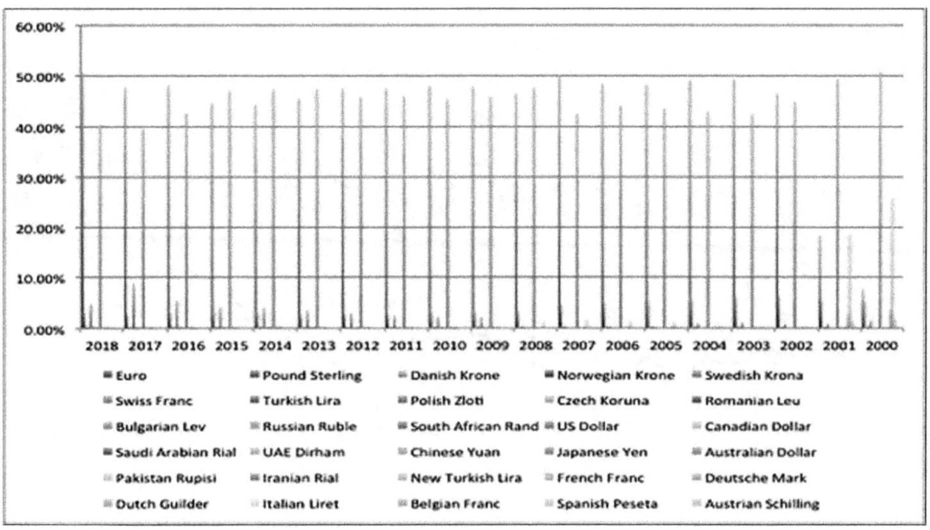

**For a more accurate representation see the electronic version.*

Figure 4. Turkey's Imports by Currencies (2000-2018)
Source: Authors' calculations based on data compiled from Turkish Statistical Institute (TURKSTAT)

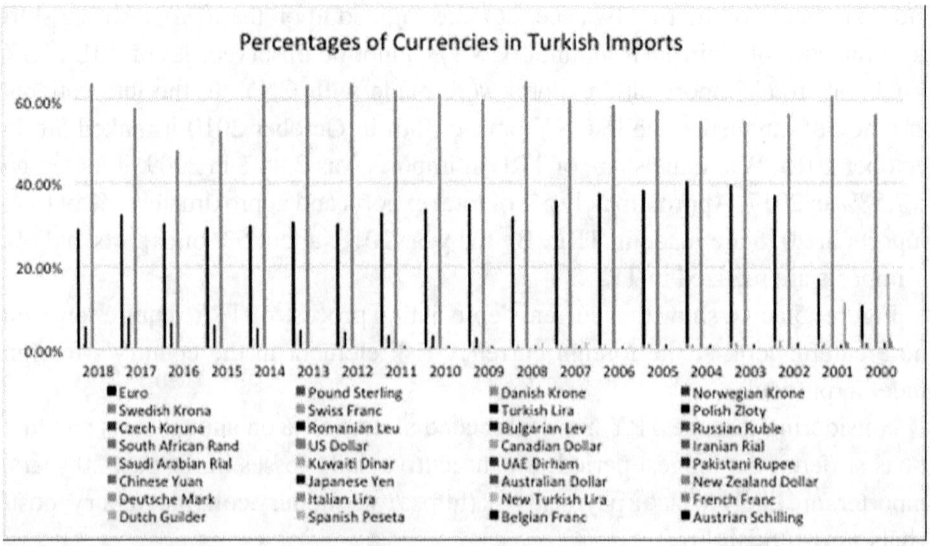

**For a more accurate representation see the electronic version.*

Figure 5. U.S. Dollar/ Turkish Lira over the period January 2017 to October 2018
Source: Trading Economics.com, OTC Interbank

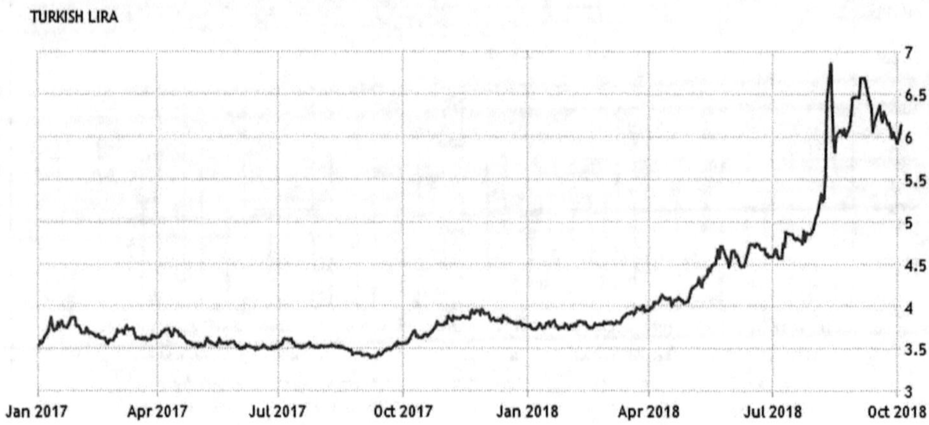

Figure 6. Euro / Turkish Lira over the period October 2017 to October 2018
Source: European Central Bank, Eurosystem, https://www.ecb.europa.eu

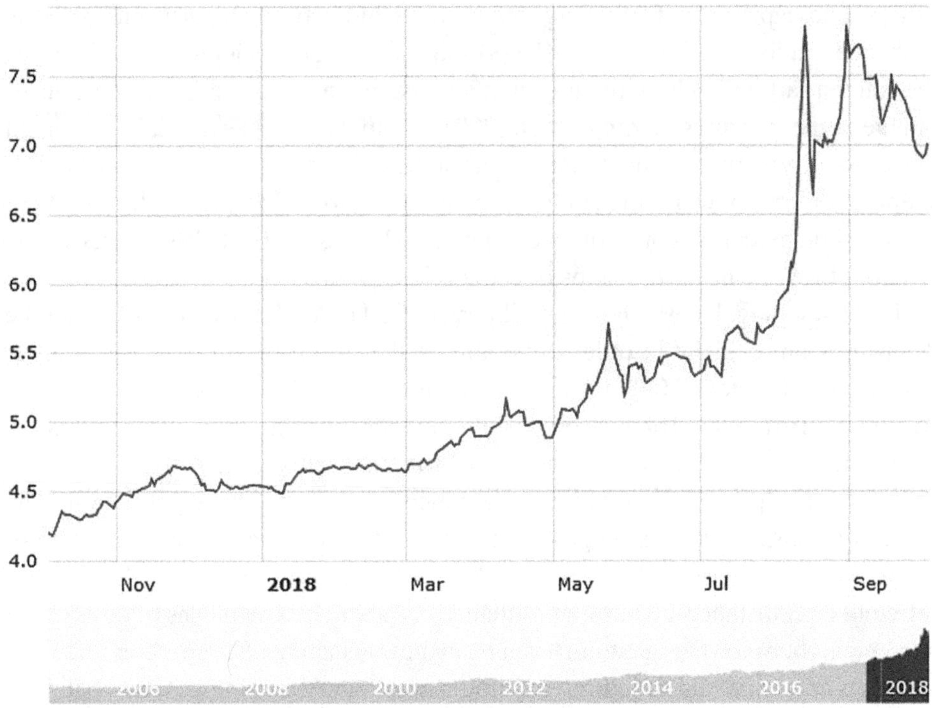

THE ROLE OF TRUST IN INTERNATIONAL TRADE AND IMPLICATIONS FOR FUTURE RESEARCH

Issues connected with concept of trust, have attracted attention of researchers in areas of management and economics due to the concept's capability to identify the efficiency and effectiveness of inter-organizational relationships. The surging importance of collaboration within and between organizations has played an important role in the increasing interest toward inter-organizational trust. Trust is widely heralded as the building block of collaboration (McClellan, 2003), an efficient lubricant to economic exchange (Powell, 1990) and the binding bond between organizations (Rinehart, 2007).

Extant literature furnishes various definitions for the concept of trust. A general approach embodies trust as a "set of expectations shared by all those involved in and exchange" (Zucker, 1986). Further research attempt to delineate these set of expectations via empirical research. Larson (1992) and Gulati (1995) emphasize the role of expectations regarding high reliability, which is also defined as crucial by Moorman et al. (1992) and Ganesan (1994) as they identify trust as "the willingness to rely on an exchange partner in whom one has confidence including expectations of credibility and benevolence". Mohr and Spekman (1994) attest the reliability aspect of trust and capability of fulfilling mutual obligations by both parties involved in exchange relationship. Zaheer et al. (1998) underscore the behavioral expectations that the counterpart will behave reliably, predictably and fairly under the circumstances of potential opportunism. Poppo et al. (2003) deem trust as an essential component of relational governance and define it as a composite concept that includes promise-keeping, information sharing and open communication. Howarth et al. (2004) put emphasis on perception of fairness and justice whereas De Laat (1997) stresses the vitality of loyalty in relationships of economic exchange.

Understanding Transaction Cost Theory (TCT) of Williamson (1979) could be deemed as prerequisite in order to be able to develop savvy about trust in inter-organizational context. TCT, built on the insights of Coase (1937), has made significant contribution to the study of inter-organizational exchange since it enables researchers to elaborate on the nature and degree of risks in transactions and recognized by the grounds it has provided on which governance mechanisms have been built. The theory of transaction costs suggests that the human factor and the actual nature of transactions is determined by cost and "with the aim of minimizing the latter in different circumstances, control of exchanges is postulated by means of developing agreements between the agents intervening in the transactions. These materialize into contracts or contractual structures, minimum cost being the guiding criterion toward the different types of contract" (Pena & Aroyabe, 2002). Three dimensions could be mentioned to characterize transactions. "These are uncertainty, the frequency with which transactions recur and the degree to which durable transaction-specific investments are incurred" (Williams, 2000). There are two behavioral assumptions argued by Williamson (1979) which independently, but in conjunction, create transactions costs, namely opportunism and bounded rationality (Gjalt & Nooteboom, 2000). Opportunism encompasses self-seeking behavior with cunning intelligence (Becerra, 2009). Some economic agents may possess a disposition to cheat, exercise deceptive practices and abuse undisclosed information when asymmetries exist (Williams, 2000). Some people may behave opportunistically when a contract with them leaves some gaps (Becerra, 2009).

Therefore, according to TCT, organizations exist because of the dexterity they offer to mitigate adverse effects of "human opportunism through the exercise of hierarchical controls that are not accessible to the markets" (Ghoshal & Moran, 1996). TCT assumes that "in absence of some form of governance mechanism, agreements between organizations will always be subject to risks from opportunistic behavior" (Hoyt & Huq, 2000). Opportunism leads to higher transaction costs and might emerge when there is an asymmetry between transacting parties (Welty & Becerra-Fernandez, 2001). Given the fact that humans have limited cognitive ability to process all available information human agents tend to select the optimal solution to any given organizational problem (Williams, 2000), which "places a limit in the possibility to write full contracts that could otherwise regulate all relations among independent actors" (Becerra, 2009). This limited ability mainly stems from incomplete information about market conditions, which inhibits the organization form making predictions about the future leading to mistakes (Gjalt & Nooteboom, 2000).

Williamson's is barely among the proponents of the notion of trust and underscores his opposition by arguing that "…it is redundant at best can be misleading to use term "trust" to describe commercial exchanges for which cost-effective safeguards have been devised in support of more efficient exchanges" and deems calculative trust as a contradiction in terms (Williamson, 1993). However, a thorough scanning of the voluminous literature indicates that lack of trust happens to be a stumbling block to success of strategic alliance formation (Kwon & Suh, 2005). Bachmann and Zaheer (2008) postulate the functionality of trust in inter-organizational context and argue that "the role of trust becomes evident under such circumstances when an opportunistic partner can exploit the weakness of the focal party". TCT offers safeguards, however, they are not only heavy-handed, also expensive (Bachmann & Zaheer, 2008). Firms may not develop mutual trust in the beginning of the relationship and might have proclivity for relying on functional tools such as contractual provisions that enable monitoring of experience (Barber, 1983). Early stage relationships can be based on calculativeness (Bachmann & Zaheer, 2008). Trust based on calculation is likely to apply particularly to relationships which are new and hence can only proceed based on institutionalized protection or the reputation of the partner (Child & Faulkner, 2002). During the initial phase of developing trust among transacting firms both parties involved in the relationship calculate the costs and rewards of interacting with one another (Doney & Cannon, 1997). Even if there are opportunities to be dishonest short-term benefit seeking acts must be balanced in a calculus-based way against the longer-run gains of maintaining good reputation.

Lewicki & Bunker (1996) suggest two more types of trust which are knowledge-based trust and identification-based-trust. Knowledge-based trust develops over time and accommodate itself on information rather than deterrence. At this point it would be appropriate to mention the role of time horizon in building trust. The valuation of future plays a critical role in building trust-based relationships. When the organizations' rate of time discount is low they will be inclined to value the future more than will one with a higher rate of discount (Zaheer & Harris, 2006). Knowledge-based trust is based on the other's predictability mostly derived from repeated interactions. At the identification-based level both parties effectively "understand and appreciate each other's priorities and this mutual understanding is developed to the point that each can effectively act for the other" (Lewicki & Bunker, 1996). Trust leads to greater levels of communication frequency between parties involved in the exchange relationship and is expected to contribute to increased investment in the relationship relative to other types of governance mechanisms (Rinehart, 2007). Lack of trust may result in suppression of useful information for problem solving (Dyer & Chu, 2003).

Trust plays a critical for the flow of "open and truthful information especially when proprietary information such as sales orders and inventories or information on future business plans facilitate collaboration" (Sako, 1992). Trust emerges in situations where the trustworthy partner in the exchange relationship (a) is conceded to make good faith efforts to comply with prior pledges, (b) enable adjustments perceived as fair by parties involved in exchange relationship and (c) refrains from taking excessive advantage of an exchange partner even in the presence of opportunity (Dyer & Chu, 2003). Thus, the concept of trust is inevitably reciprocal and relational in nature. In contrast to calculative trust, relational-as-social-trust implies the inclusion of relational elements or possessing a social orientation, nonetheless, relational-as-dyadic trust favors a dynamic and reciprocal view of trust rather than a dispositional one (Zaheer & Harris, 2006). Lack of trust may end up with suppression of relevant information that would be useful for problem solving (Dyer & Chu, 2003).

For foreign trade, the essence of trust is verified by the fact that risk aversion is a dominant behavior for countries engaged. Although empirical studies show that risk aversion has a more decisive role in foreign trade preferences than many other factors, it has received little attention in literature. From early theorists such as Ricardo (1819) and Heckscher (1919) to recent ones like Eaton and Kortum (2002) or Melitz (2003), trade theories have rather identified bilateral trade with production costs.

In fact, many factors that trigger or feed risk avoidance behavior determine the structure of trade relations. Exchange rate volatility, especially when it is associated with demand, suggests the question, to which extent do foreign firms, who are risk averse, change their relations with trade partners.

At the end of a similar questioning path, Esposito (2016) finds that the ability to attract foreign firms looking for benefits of risk diversification is a major determinant in gains from trade. According to Esposito's model, risk diversification behavior dominates higher productivity (lower cost) level in the decision to enter a market. Yet, evidence from Esposito's study shows that the size of the firm matters in the perception of risk while entering a market. That is, while a market may serve to hedge risk for a small firm, larger firm may prefer to sell alternative markets to avoid risk.

In the model, in the exceptional case of risk neutrality, i.e. zero risk aversion, the condition to enter a market is where the productivity of the firm exceeds the following equation.

$$\left(Z_{ij}^{-}\right)^{\sigma-1} = \frac{w_i f_j \tilde{L}_j P_j^{1-\sigma} \sigma}{\bar{\alpha}_j \left(\frac{\sigma}{\sigma-1} \tau_{ij} w_i\right)^{1-\sigma} Y_j}$$

where z_{ij} is productivity, w_i is inelastic (given) wage (price) level, L_j is continuum of workers, σ is elasticity of substitution greater than *1*, $\alpha_j(z)$ is an exogenous demand shock specific to good z in market j, $p_j(z)$ is the price of variety z in j, Y_j is total income spent by consumers in j. In case that the productivity exceeds the equation above, profit maximizing risk neutral firm would not take into account the variance and the above equation would imply the condition of positive profits. Therefore, it can be implied that the reason for a firm to enter a market and engage the related negative expected profits would be where the market in question would serve to hedge for demand risk.

In studies that follow, Esposito's model can be adapted to formulate the asymmetry in the behavior of risk aversion in Turkey's bilateral trade. Investigating if there exists a similar effect of demand shocks for Turkey and the Turkish Lira during periods where there is intensive volatility in exchange rates could be a question worth examining and potentially the results can be matched with data provided in this study.

Alabayır & Muzır (2016) examine the preferences towards types of payment in import and export transactions between Turkey and the EU which constitute approximately 45% share of EU of Turkey's foreign trade. The authors, using TSI (Turkish Statistical Institute) data of 2015, offer an empirical study that investigates the results of a survey face to face carried out with 42 joint-stock companies and companies with above title operating in Turkey's Bursa province. Although the study is limited in terms of the time lag taken and the region in which the firms operate, the results are consistent with the data evaluated in this study. The data presented also in the work of Alabayır and Muzır verify that in cases where Turkey is in the importer status, EU firms choose the least risky payment method, while in cases where Turkey is the importer exactly the opposite occurs. The responses of the Turkish firms to the survey questions on the issue confirm the essence of the lack of trust in the developed countries' trade with developing countries.

Reflecting people's judgment and evaluation (Roy et al., 2014, pp.694), trust is a touchstone in broad economic relations and particularly in international trade. In cases where trust is not established, the pattern of trade may alter completely. Starting from the first stage with the introduction of raw material into the production process, where and how the good is produced, its distribution, maintenance, up until its shipment and final delivery, each phase of trade rests on trust. Is it possible for a country to enable its trade partners change their behavior of risk avoidance by increasing transparency and easing transactions using a universally accepted system's nearly perfect functioning infrastructure?

Through increased visibility and transparency, quick and smooth control of the quality and provenance of goods, reduction of processing time for banking actions and other services, real time view of documents, blockchain technology advocates are assertive to say that the system allows even the least trusting parties to comfortably conduct business. Even more precisely in their own words, blockchain technology "…may promote an unprecedented level of trust" (Lechmacher & Mcwaters, 2017)

Instead of dealing with the technical details of blockchain technology, we choose to leave for further research, within the limited content of the present study, finding out whether adoption of this technological infrastructure may help emerging economies such as Turkey, to establish trust currently lacking in their trade with developed economies.

CONCLUSION

Various methods and instruments are designed to support exporters and importers to make sure international trade runs smoothly. Firms engaged in bilateral trade choose from a wide array of instruments depending on the degree of trust built with their trading partners. Indeed, a closer look on the risk-taking behavior and risk transfer of the parties involved in trade can easily show the essence of trust in bilateral trade, despite the globally binding regulations.

Trust has been proposed as a panacea to inherent risks exposed by organizations engaging in contract-based relationships. If trust is established among parties involved in trade, partners not only meet standards of quantity and quality as agreed upon; also go beyond these and contribute in an innovative fashion whenever this seems necessary to accomplish goals without having to control each other.

Turkish trade data evaluated in the paper show that the country's trade partners have invariably chosen to bear minimum risk in their trade with Turkey, with preferences towards the most guaranteed methods of payment. Risk transfer patterns –in long tradition and in their extremely solid form- are at loss of Turkey, whether the country is in an exporter or an importer status. This fact has formed the basis of the present study, discussing that establishment of trust may be the reason behind.

Data proves that the most commonly preferred type of payment in Turkey's exports is cash on delivery, which is the method preferred when the exporter aims to gain the trust of the importer. Leading type of payment in Turkey's imports on the other hand is cash in advance, which shows that the exporter is in absolute risk avoidance. Normally, it can be expected that the exporters, who insist trading with this payment method, may not compete with alternative markets offering more attractive payment terms to the importer, which seemingly is not the case for Turkish imports. In addition to this stationary risk transfer pattern in terms of payment methods, consecutive losses experienced by Turkish Lira in the global markets signals the importers a currency fragility risks, peculiar to current economic conditions.

The paper is a first in its investigation of risk transfer and trust nexus in Turkish trade data and up to date in mainly two respects; it declares the current currency risk of Turkish Lira as an additional factor that may influence the risk taking behavior of trade partners and it opens the floor for discussion on adoption of blockchain technology in trade finance for bilateral trade among economies asymmetric in nature. We suggest that, given the constantly developing conditions, techniques and practices of international trade, it is worth discussing a new and alternative system based on trust and transparency in the fast and smooth solution of the problems that may arise as a natural result of this evolution process.

REFERENCES

Acar, O. (2009). Evaluations for trade and trade finance in Turkey. *TEPAV Policy Note*, July.

Alabayır, A., & Muzır, E. (2016). Dış ticaret işlemlerinde ticaret yapılan yerlere göre ödeme şekli tercihi ve tercih nedenlerini belirlemeye yönelik ampirik bir çalışma. *İşletme Araştırmaları Dergisi. Journal of Business Research*, *8*(1).

Bachmann, R., & Zaheer, A. (2008). Trust in inter-organizational relations. In S. Cropper, M. Ebers, C. Huxham, & S. Ring (Eds.), *The Oxford Handbook of Inter-organizational Relations* (pp. 533–554). New York: Oxford University Press.

Barber, J. B. (1983). *The logic and limits of trust. New Brunswick, Canada:* Rutgers University Press.

Becerra, M. (2009). *Theory of the firm for strategic management: economic value analysis*. Cambridge: Cambridge University Press. doi:10.1017/CBO9780511626524

Child, J., & Faulkner, D. (2002). *Strategies of co-operation: managing alliances, networks and joint ventures*. New York: Oxford University Press.

Coase, R.H. (1937). The nature of the firm. *Economica*, *4*, 386-405.

de Gjalt, J., & Nooteboom, B. (2000). *The causal structure of long-term supply relationships: an empirical test of a generalized transaction cost theory*. Dordrecht: Kluwer Academic Publishers.

De Laat, P. (1997). Research and Development Alliances: Ensuring Trust by Mutual Commitments. In M. Ebers (Ed.), *The Formation of Inter-Organizational Networks*. New York: Oxford University Press.

Doney, P. M., & Cannon, J. P. (1997). An examination of the nature of trust in buyer-seller relationships. *Journal of Marketing*, *61*, 35–51.

Dyer, J. H., & Chu, W. (2003). The role of trustworthiness in reducing transaction costs and improving performance: Empirical evidence from the United States, Japan and Korea. *Organization Science*, *14*(1), 57–68. doi:10.1287/orsc.14.1.57.12806

Eaton, J., & Kortum, S. (2002). Technology, geography, and trade. *Econometrica*, *70*(5), 1741–1779. doi:10.1111/1468-0262.00352

Ebury. (2018). What is next for the Turkish Lira after its violent sell off? Retrieved from https://www.ebury.com/blog/ebury_post/whats-next-turkish-lira/

Esposito, F. (2016). Risk diversification and international trade. Society for Economic Dynamics. European Central Bank-Europa. Retrieved from https://www.ecb.europa.eu

Ganesan, S. (1994). Determinants of long-term orientation in buyer-seller relationships. *Journal of Marketing*, *58*(2), 1–19. doi:10.1177/002224299405800201

Ghoshal, S., & Moran, P. (1996). Bad for practice: A critique of the transaction cost theory. *Academy of Management Review*, *21*(1), 13–47. doi:10.5465/amr.1996.9602161563

Gulati, R. (1995). Does familiarity breed trust? The implications of repeated ties for contractual choice in alliances. *Academy of Management Journal*, *38*(1), 85–112.

Hau, H., Killeen, W. P., & Moore, J. (2002). Michael John, How has the euro changed the foreign exchange market? *Economic Policy*, *17*(34), 149–191. doi:10.1111/1468-0327.00086

Heckscher, E. F. (1919). The effect of foreign trade on the distribution of national income. *Ekonomisk Tidskrift*, *21*.

Howorth, C., Westhead, P., & Wright, M. (2004). Buyouts, information asymmetry and the family management dyad. *Journal of Business Venturing*, *19*(4), 509–534. doi:10.1016/j.jbusvent.2003.04.002

Hoyt, J., & Huq, F. (2000). From arms-length to collaborative relationships in the supply chain: An evolutionary process. *International Journal of Physical Distribution & Logistics Management*, *30*(9), 750–764. doi:10.1108/09600030010351453

Kwon, G., & Suh, T. (2005). Trust, commitment and relationships in supply chain management: A path analysis. *Supply Chain Management*, *10*(1), 26–33. doi:10.1108/13598540510578351

Larson, A. (1992). Network dyads in entrepreneurial settings: A study of the governance of exchange relationships. *Administrative Science Quarterly*, *3*(1), 76–104. doi:10.2307/2393534

Lechmacher, W., & Mcwaters, J. (2017). How blockchain can restore trust in trade. Weforum. Retrieved from https://www.weforum.org/agenda/2017/02/blockchain-trade-trust-transparency

Lewicki, R. J., & Bunker, B. B. (1996). Developing and maintaining trust in work relationships. In R.M. Kramer & T.R. Tyler (Ed.), Trust in Organizations: Frontiers of Theory and Research (pp. 438-458). Thousand Oaks, CA: Sage Publications. doi:10.4135/9781452243610.n7

McClellan, M. (2003). *Collaborative manufacturing: using real time information to support the supply chain*. Florida: St. Lucie Press.

Melitz, M. J. (2003). The impact of trade on intra-industry reallocations and aggregate industry productivity. *Econometrica*, *71*(6), 1695–1725. doi:10.1111/1468-0262.00467

Mohr, J., & Spekman, R. (1994). Characteristics of partnership success: Partnership in attributes, communication behavior, and conflict resolution techniques. *Strategic Management Journal*, *15*(2), 135–152. doi:10.1002mj.4250150205

Moorman, C., Zaltman, G., & Desphande, R. (1992). Relationships between providers and users of market research: The dynamics of trust within and between organizations. *JMR, Journal of Marketing Research*, *29*(3), 314–328. doi:10.1177/002224379202900303

Oberman, N. G. (1997). *Transfer of risk from seller to buyer in international commercial contracts: A comparative analysis of risk allocation under the CISG*. UCC and Incoterms.

Pena, N. A., & Arroyabe, J. C. F. (2002). *Business Cooperation*. New York: Palgrave Macmillan. doi:10.1057/9780230554696

Poppo, L., Zhou, K. Z., & Zenger, T. (2003). The economic and social embeddedness of relational governance: An empirical study exploring origins and effectiveness. *Paper presented at the Academy of Management 2003 Annual Meetings*, Seattle, WA. 10.5465/ambpp.2003.13793233

Powell, W. W. (1990). Neither market nor hierarchy: Network forms of organization. In B. M. Staw & L. L. Cummings (Eds.), *Research in Organizational Behavior* (pp. 295–336). Greenwich: JAI Press.

Republic of Turkey Ministry of Trade, Customs and Trade. (n.d.). Retrieved from https://ggm.ticaret.gov.tr/

Ricardo, D. (2015). Principles of political economy and taxation. Cambridge: Cambridge University Press. (originally printed in 1819)

Rinehart, L. M. (2007). Negotiating throughout the supply chain. In J. T. Mentzer, B. M. Myers, & T. P. Stank (Eds.), *Handbook of Global Supply Chain Management* (pp. 407–426). Thousand Oaks, CA: Sage Publications. doi:10.4135/9781412976169.n24

Roy, D., Munasib, A., & Chen, X. (2014). Social trust and international trade: The interplay between social trust and formal finance. *Review of World Economics*, *150*(4), 693–714. doi:10.100710290-014-0197-2

Sako, M. (1992). *Prices, quality and trust: inter-firm relations in Britain and Japan*. Cambridge: Cambridge University Press. doi:10.1017/CBO9780511520723

Turkish Statistical Institute (TURKSTAT). (n.d.). Retrieved from http://www.turkstat.gov.tr/

Türkiye B.F.O. (n.d.). Turkish Interbank Rate. (n.d.). Retrieved from https://tr.tradingeconomics.com/turkey/interbank-rate

Welty, B., & Becerra-Fernandez, I. (2001). Managing trust and commitment in collaborative supply chain relationships. *Communications of the ACM*, *44*(6), 67–73. doi:10.1145/376134.376170

Williams, S. (2000). An empirical application of transaction-costs theory to organizational design characteristics. *The Journal of Psychology*, *34*(1), 81–92. doi:10.1080/00223980009600851 PMID:10654849

Williamson, O. E. (1979). Transaction cost economics: The governance of contractual relations. *The Journal of Law & Economics*, *22*(2), 233–261. doi:10.1086/466942

Williamson, O. E. (1993). Calculativeness, trust and economic organization. *The Journal of Law & Economics*, *36*(1, Part 2), 453–486. doi:10.1086/467284

Zaheer, A., & Harris, J. (2006). Inter-organizational trust. In O. Shenkar & J. Reuer (Eds.), *Handbook of Strategic Alliances* (pp. 169–197). Thousand Oaks, CA: Sage Publication. doi:10.4135/9781452231075.n10

Zaheer, A., McEvily, B., & Perrone, V. (1998). Does trust matter? Exploring the effects of inter-organizational and interpersonal trust on performance. *Organization Science*, *9*(2), 141–159. doi:10.1287/orsc.9.2.141

Zucker, L. G. (1986). The production of trust: Institutional sources of economic structure. *Research in Organizational Behavior*, *8*, 53–111.

KEY TERMS AND DEFINITIONS

Blockchain: Blockchain is a meta-technology interconnected with other technologies and consists of several architectural layers: a database, a software application, a number of computers connected to each other, peoples' access to the system and a software ecosystem that enables development. The blockchain runs on the existing stack of Internet protocols, adding an entire new tier to the Internet to ensure economic transactions, both instant digital currency payments and complicated financial contracts.

Exchange Rate Volatility: The volatility of exchange rates is the source of exchange rates risk and has certain implications on the volume of international trade. Higher risk emerges for risk-averse traders as the exchange rate volatility escalades which also diminishes foreign trade. This happens to be the reason why deal on exchange rate is closed at the moment of contract agreement, however, payment is not made until the delivery takes place. Unpredictability of the exchange rates increases uncertainty regarding expected level of profit deteriorating international trade.

International Trade: International trade refers to exchange of capital, goods, and services across international borders including the activities of the government and individual. International trade happens to constitute a significant share of gross domestic product.

Interorganizational Trust: Trust is the essential asset in building long-lasting relationships between organizations engaging in trading operations. It is referred to as a lubricant to economic exchange that dwindles complex realities quickly and economically than prediction.

Risk Transfer: Refers to undertaking of the risk associated with the payment method employed. Payment is put on hold until goods are delivered to the importer when entire risk is owned by the exporter. In other case risk is undertaken by the importer where payment is fulfilled immediately after closing the deal.

Transaction Cost Theory: This theory suggests that the actual nature of transactions with respect to the goods transferred and environments in which they are performed is determined by costs. Parties involved in transactions develop agreements that are materialized into contracts. According to the theory, some form of governance mechanism is necessary for agreements in order to be able to stave potential risk off derived from opportunistic behavior.

Types of Payment: There are various ways to fulfill payment obligations of the goods subject to exports such as letter of credit, advance payment, clean payment, open account method and documentary collection method. Selection of the correct payment method is deemed essential in order to ensure the proper negotiation of contracts.

Chapter 10
Influence of Tariff Liberalization on Bilateral Trade:
Implications for Russia and Its Asian Trade Partners

Ekaterina Arapova
MGIMO University, Russia

Elena Maslova
MGIMO University, Russia

ABSTRACT

The study aims at evaluating and comparing trade effects of tariff liberalization on bilateral trade between Russian and its Asian trade partners: China, India, Thailand and Vietnam. The partial equilibrium model - the Software for Market Analysis and Restrictions on Trade (SMART) model - underlies the research methodology. The authors calculate the trade effects of 1% linear cut of customs duties imposed on key commodity groups of mutual import flows and identify elasticities of bilateral import of different commodity groups on customs duties. On the basis of a comparative analysis of the results obtained, the authors formulated a set of conclusions regarding the efficiency of tariff regulation of imports in different countries and industrial sectors, tracking the changes of the influence of tariff liberalization on the dynamics of import of various categories of goods (depending on the value added and technological effectiveness).

DOI: 10.4018/978-1-5225-9566-3.ch010

INTRODUCTION

Tariffs are the most common kind of barrier to trade. Moreover, they remain the main instrument of trade regulation in Russia (and EAEU on the whole), as the use of non-tariff measures is limited. The number of Russian non-tariff barrier, imposed on import goods accounted for 365 in the early 2019, compared with 2724 in China, 1795 in the Republic of Korea, 1739 in Japan, or 750 in India.

Foreign trade policy conducted by the government, predetermines the country's positions on global markets and in international division of labor and remains one of the key instruments for achieving the country's long-term strategic priorities.

The contemporary strategic priorities of Russia's foreign trade are declared in its main long-term planning documents: The Road Map "Supporting Access to Foreign Markets and Export Support," The Federal programs "Development of foreign economic activity" and "Industrial development and increase of its competitiveness", Priority projects "International cooperation and export in industrial sector" and "Export of agricultural products", The strategy of scientific and technological development of the Russian Federation etc. The long-term goals can be formulated as follows:

- Achieving a geographical balance of Russian foreign trade,
- Increasing exports of manufacturing products, especially engineering products;
- Reducing dependence on the export of raw materials, expanding non-oil and non-energy exports,
- Ensuring the competitiveness of domestic products in global agricultural markets.

The study aims at quantitative evaluating and comparing trade creation effects of tariff liberalization (the elasticities of mutual trade flows on import tariffs) in Russia's relations with its three Asian partners: China, India and Thailand. The authors make an attempt to compare potential effects of tariff liberalization on bilateral trade of different commodity groups (trade creation effects), as well as make conclusions, to which extent the mutual tariff liberalization can contribute to attaining the strategic priorities, declared above.

BACKGROUND

The influence of tariffs on trade flows is widely discussed in academic literature, the effects are evaluated with the use of both qualitative and quantitative instruments.

Import tariffs influence prices of imported goods. According to the classical theories of international trade lower prices on import goods result in higher demand amongst consumers, which stimulate import (Balassa, 1967; Heckscher and Ohlin, 1991).

Falling tariff levels, teamed with lower transportation and communication costs, have cleared away many man-made and natural obstructions to trade, making the international playing fieldflatter than it has ever been (Baldwin and Martin, 1999).

A significant number of studies are devoted to assessing the impact of tariff regulation on the dynamics of foreign trade.

For several decades Leamer (1988) has been engaged in assessing the impact of foreign trade regulatory instruments (tariff and non-tariff) on the dynamics of import flows in the sectoral and geographic aspects. With the dependent variable being a natural logarithm of imports, 2 factors were used in the model as influencing regressors: the average level of customs duties (on the relevant product category) and the quantitatively expressed aggregated indicator of the applied non-tariff restrictions. The researcher came to the conclusion that the impact of customs duties on imports is relatively more significant compared to the impact of non-tariff restrictions.

Feenstra (1995), as many other researchers, wrote about the traditional mechanism of the influence of customs duties on the dynamics of imports: the duties costs are being transferred to the cost of imported products and result in the rising of their price, the decrease of price competitiveness and, accordingly, so does the volume of imported goods supplies. However, his contribution to the theory of international trade lies in the fact that he showed that in the conditions of imperfect competition, the transfer of the cost of increasing the customs tariff may be unequal to the amount of the costs of paying customs duties. That means that a 1% increase in the customs tariff leads to an increase in the price of imported products by less than 1% (reducing the potential net profit of the exporters / trading margin), while the increase in the cost of imported products may significantly vary in different industries (Feenstra, Lipsey, and Bowen, 1997).

Wang (2001), basing the study on cross-country and inter-industry data on average levels of customs duties and trade flows for 70 countries (including both industrialized and developing), proved not only the significance of the influence of tariff regulation on import flows and their inverse relationship in accordance with the provisions of the classical theory, but also proved the high elasticity of imports in terms of the average customs tariff. He quantitatively estimate that a 1% increase in customs tariff leads to a decrease in imports by an average of 2%.

Kee, Nicita and Olarreaga (2005) made a huge contribution to assessing the impact of customs duties on import volumes, calculating a comprehensive system of price elasticity coefficients of imports (more than 300,000 coefficients for 117 countries using 6-digit Harmonized System codes (HS codes)).The average coefficient of elasticity for all countries and groups of goods amounted to -1.67, the median level is -1.08.

Despite a significant number of domestic studies on Russia's foreign trade policy, the number of works based on a quantitative assessment of the effects of trade protectionism or liberalization and the impact of customs duties on the dynamics of Russian imports, is limited. (Knobel, 2010) empirically proved the negative dependence of the demand for imports on their own price and the positive dependence of the demand for imports on the price of domestic substitutes, while depending on the product category, the resulting elasticity coefficients vary from -0.61 to -1, 63 and 0.25 and 2.53, respectively. Afontsev (2016) also comes to a general conclusion about the effectiveness of the use of customs duties for the reduction of competition from imported goods. The positive effect of tariff liberalization on Russian trade was proved by Arapova and Isachenko (2019).

In their scientific works, Russian and foreign researchers empirically proved that the potential impact of foreign trade policy instruments (including customs duties) on import dynamics depends on the starting conditions: the level of import penetration and import dependence of individual industries; the overall level of development of a particular country and its growth rate); the structure of domestic production and the specialization of the country in the international division of labor, and so on. The gains from tariff removal are positive and only the magnitude remains to be determined (Feenstra, 1995). The resulting changes in the home and foreign prices, production, consumption, and imports and exports will depend on the positions and shape of the home and foreign demand and supply schedules (Stern, 1973).

The effectiveness of tariff regulation is determined by differences in price elasticity of domestic demand, as well as differences in the nature of the interchange of imported and domestic goods (the theory of perfect and imperfect substitutes that has been developed by Rhomberg, 1973; Isard, 1977; Goldstein and Khan, 1985).

Thus, the positive impact of tariff liberalization on the dynamics of foreign trade flows is confirmed by empirical results of a significant number of authors. However, differences in quantitative estimates confirm, that it's highly important to evaluate quantitatively the effects of tariff liberalization for every particular trade partner and commodity group, as the elasticity of substitution between home and foreign produced goods can vary.

METHODOLOGY

The research bases on the partial equilibrium model - the Software for Market Analysis and Restrictions on Trade (SMART) model, which is commonly used in academic literature for analyzing effects of trade liberalisation, mainly within integration blocks (see Guei, Mugano and Le Roux, 2017; Cheong, 2010; Arapova, 2015).

The SMART-model, being a part of the World Integrated Trade Solution system allows to calculate three types of tariff liberalization effects:

Trade Effects: (1) trade creation effect – increasing demand for imports from the partner country because of lower tariffs rates, and (2) trade diversion effect – redirecting import flows from traditional trade partners in favor of those with lower customs duties (applicable for non-MFN cases – economic integration scenarios or non-WTO members).

Welfare Effects - gains of national consumers because of cheaper import,

Revenue Effects - losses of the national budgets because of lowering incomes in form of customs duties.

Using the SMART Simulation tool the authors calculate the trade creation effects of 1% linear cut of customs duties imposed on key commodity groups of mutual import flows and identify elasticities of bilateral import of different commodity groups on customs duties. The calculations base on the UNCTAD TRAINS database, which allows to retrieve all tariff types together or separately for a selected reporter, commodity group of the Harmonised System and year. The elasticity of substitution used for the simulation model was 99%. The base year is 2016.

MAIN FOCUS OF THE CHAPTER

Issues, Controversies, Problems

The objects of the SMART-modeling were the product categories that form the basis of Russia's foreign trade with Asian partners (about 75-80% of mutual trade). The calculation results are shown in Tables 1-6.

The price elasticity of Chinese imports has been gradually decreasing in recent years, which entails a relative decrease in the efficiency of tariff regulation of foreign trade and its possibility to influence import flows. This trend is confirmed by the calculations of imports from Russia. For all of the studied commodity groups, imports were inelastic in terms of the value of customs duties, i.e. a 1% reduction in customs duty rates can potentially give a cumulative trade effect of less than 1% of the volume of imports of the relevant product group as of 2016 (see Table 1).

Table 1. Results of a quantitative assessment of the likely increase in Chinese imports of Russian goods with a 1% linear reduction of customs duties on goods from Russia

Product Code (HS)	Product Label	Import Growth in Case of 1% Linear Cut of Tariff Rates, %*
0303	Frozen fish (excluding fish fillets and other fish meat of heading 0304)	0.05
1204	Linseed, whether or not broken	0.00
1213	Cereal straw and husks, unprepared, whether or not chopped, ground, pressed or in the form ...	0.02
2710	Petroleum oils and oils obtained from bituminous minerals (excluding crude); preparations containing ...	2.80
3104	Mineral or chemical potassic fertilizers (excluding those in tablets or similar forms, or in ...	0.03
3105	Mineral or chemical fertilizers containing two or three of the fertilizing elements nitrogen, ...	0.56
7102	Diamonds, whether or not worked, but not mounted or set (excluding unmounted stones for pick-up ...	0.08
7110	Platinum, incl. palladium, rhodium, iridium, osmium and ruthenium, unwrought or in semi-manufactured ...	0.02
7403	Copper, refined, and copper alloys, unwrought (excluding copper alloys of heading 7405)	0.00
7502	Unwrought nickel	0.00
8401	Nuclear reactors; fuel elements "cartridges", non-irradiated, for nuclear reactors; machinery ...	0.00
8411	Turbojets, turbopropellers and other gas turbines	0.00
8419	Machinery, plant or laboratory equipment whether or not electrically heated (excluding furnaces, ...	0.89
8479	Machines and mechanical appliances having individual functions, not specified or included elsewhere ...	0.00
8481	Taps, cocks, valves and similar appliances for pipes, boiler shells, tanks, vats or the like, ...	0.00
8703	Motor cars and other motor vehicles principally designed for the transport of persons, incl. ...	0.00
8708	Parts and accessories for tractors, motor vehicles for the transport of ten or more persons, ...	0.07
8711	Motorcycles, incl. mopeds, and cycles fitted with an auxiliary motor, with or without side-cars; ...	0.14
8802	Powered aircraft "e.g. helicopters and aeroplanes"; spacecraft, incl. satellites, and suborbital ...	0.00
8803	Parts of aircraft and spacecraft of heading 8801 or 8802, n.e.s.	0.00
9013	Liquid crystal devices not constituting articles provided for more specifically in other heading; ...	0.02
9032	Regulating or controlling instruments and apparatus (excluding taps, cocks and valves of heading ...	0.03
Total		0.37

* In "zero" cases the effect of tariff liberalization was positive, but negligible

Source: author's calculations

The only exception was petroleum oil and oils obtained from bituminous minerals (HS 2710). Imports of this product group from Russia could grow by 2.8% if the customs duty rates were reduced by 1%. Tariff liberalization with respect to imports from Russia may comparatively favorably affect the supply of mineral or chemical fertilizers of the HS 3105, as well as machinery, plant or laboratory equipment (HS 8419). The potential increase of Chinese imports due to the trade creation effects may be 0.89% and 0.56%, respectively. However, it should be take into account that both positions account for less than 1% of Russian exports to China, moreover, laboratory and industrial equipment is actively imported by Russia from China, taking the second line in the structure of Russian imports in 4-digit HS. In all other cases, the positive effect of the liberalization of customs duties rates is minimal.

A possible increase in Russian imports from China with a symmetrical reduction in customs duty rates by 1% may turn out to be several times lower than the increase in Chinese imports of goods from Russia.

In absolute terms, the largest increase in Russian imports of electric instantaneous or storage water heaters (HS 8516) and articles of plastics and other materials (HS 3926) can be expected (see Table 2). Although for all commodity groups, the elasticity of imports at an average level of customs duties is less than 1, for these categories, the elasticity coefficient was relatively higher - 0.75 according to the HS 3926 (the maximum rate among all the commodity groups under study) and 0.35 according to the HS 8516. A relatively higher elasticity of imports at the rates of customs duties is typical for certain types of textile products (HS 6115), a reduction of the rates of import customs duties by Russia by 1% may contribute to the growth of Chinese exports by 0.46% due to the growth of domestic demand for China products.

In absolute terms, the largest increase of Indian imports from Russia is possible for diamonds (HS 7102), since it is this product group that occupies the first position in the structure of domestic exports to India. At the same time, the elasticity of imports of the corresponding category on the average level of customs duties remains low: a 1% reduction in duties will increase imports from Russia by only 0.08% due to trade creation effects (see Table 3). In the case of tariff liberalization on the part of India, Russia will have the opportunity to expand the supply of unwrought and semi- manufactured silver (HS 7106), since the elasticity of Indian import demand for silver at the average level of customs duties is much higher: a 1% reduction of the latter will stimulate import growth by 0,41%.

A reduction in Indian import duties on Russian products may, to the greatest extent, affect the volume of imports of chemical products, organic, inorganic chemical compounds and fertilizers. The highest coefficient of import elasticity in terms of the average level of customs duties is typical for the commodity group of HS 2835 - phosphinates, phosphonates and phosphates, a 1% reduction in customs duties

Table 2. Results of a quantitative assessment of the likely increase in Russian imports of goods from China with a 1% linear reduction of the rates of customs duties on goods from China

Product Code (HS)	Product Label	Import Growth in Case of 1% Linear Cut of Tariff Rates, %*
2922	Oxygen-function amino-compounds	0.04
2933	Heterocyclic compounds with nitrogen hetero-atom[s] only	0.02
3907	Polyacetals, other polyethers and epoxide resins, in primary forms; polycarbonates, alkyd resins, ...	0.06
3920	Plates, sheets, film, foil and strip, of non-cellular plastics, not reinforced, laminated, ...	0.08
3921	Plates, sheets, film, foil and strip, of plastics, reinforced, laminated, supported or similarly ...	0.08
3926	Articles of plastics and articles of other materials of heading 3901 to 3914, n.e.s.	0.75
6115	Pantyhose, tights, stockings, socks and other hosiery, incl. graduated compression hosiery ...	0.46
6402	Footwear with outer soles and uppers of rubber or plastics (excluding waterproof footwear of ...	0.00
7318	Screws, bolts, nuts, coach screws, screw hooks, rivets, cotters, cotter pins, washers, incl. ...	0.07
7323	Table, kitchen or other household articles, and parts thereof, of iron or steel; iron or steel ...	0.24
7326	Articles of iron or steel, n.e.s. (excluding cast articles)	0.11
8407	Spark-ignition reciprocating or rotary internal combustion piston engine	0.06
8419	Machinery, plant or laboratory equipment whether or not electrically heated (excluding furnaces, ...	0.00
8443	Printing machinery used for printing by means of plates, cylinders and other printing components ...	0.01
8471	Automatic data-processing machines and units thereof; magnetic or optical readers, machines ...	0.00
8473	Parts and accessories (other than covers, carrying cases and the like) suitable for use solely ...	0.00
8516	Electric instantaneous or storage water heaters and immersion heaters; electric space-heating ...	0.35
8517	Telephone sets, incl. telephones for cellular networks or for other wireless networks; other ...	0.00
8528	Monitors and projectors, not incorporating television reception apparatus; reception apparatus ...	0.06
8529	Parts suitable for use solely or principally with transmission and reception apparatus for ...	0.03
8708	Parts and accessories for tractors, motor vehicles for the transport of ten or more persons, ...	0.04
9503	Tricycles, scooters, pedal cars and similar wheeled toys; dolls' carriages; dolls; other toys; ...	0.14
Total		0.04

* In "zero" cases the effect of tariff liberalization was positive, but negligible
Source: author's calculations

rates can increase their import by 2.6%. Imports of mineral or chemical nitrogenous fertilizers (HS 3102) may increase by 0.41%.

The import elasticity petroleum oils and oils obtained from bituminous minerals (HS 2710) is only -0.08, therefore tariff liberalization on the part of India will not contribute to the growth of this commodity position in the structure of domestic exports.

Table 3. Results of a quantitative assessment of the likely increase in Indian imports of goods from Russia with a 1% linear reduction of the rates of customs duties on goods from Russia

Product Code (HS)	Product Label	Import Growth in Case of 1% Linear Cut of Tariff Rates, %*
0713	Dried leguminous vegetables, shelled, whether or not skinned or split	0.14
0909	Seeds of anis, badian, fennel, coriander, cumin or caraway; juniper berries	0.00
2524	Asbestos (excluding products made from asbestos)	0.12
2701	Coal; briquettes, ovoids and similar solid fuels manufactured from coal	0.01
2704	Coke and semi-coke of coal, of lignite or of peat, whether or not agglomerated; retort carbon	0.14
2710	Petroleum oils and oils obtained from bituminous minerals (excluding crude); preparations containing ...	0.08
2814	Ammonia, anhydrous or in aqueous solution	0.08
2835	Phosphinates “hypophosphites”, phosphonates “phosphites” and phosphates; polyphosphates, whether ...	2.60
2933	Heterocyclic compounds with nitrogen hetero-atom[s] only	0.07
3102	Mineral or chemical nitrogenous fertilisers (excluding those in pellet or similar forms, or ...	0.41
3104	Mineral or chemical potassic fertilisers (excluding those in tablets or similar forms, or in ...	0.18
3105	Mineral or chemical fertilisers containing two or three of the fertilising elements nitrogen, ...	0.00
3904	Polymers of vinyl chloride or of other halogenated olefins, in primary forms	0.00
3908	Polyamides, in primary forms	0.08
4002	Synthetic rubber and factice derived from oils, in primary forms or in plates, sheets or strip; ...	0.10
4703	Chemical wood pulp, soda or sulphate (excluding dissolving grades)	0.03
4801	Newsprint as specified in Note 4 to chapter 48, in rolls of a width > 36 cm or in square or ...	0.07
7102	Diamonds, whether or not worked, but not mounted or set (excluding unmounted stones for pick-up ...	0.08
7106	Silver, incl. silver plated with gold or platinum, unwrought or in semi-manufactured forms, ...	0.41
7202	Ferro-alloys	0.04
7208	Flat-rolled products of iron or non-alloy steel, of a width >= 600 mm, hot-rolled, not clad, ...	0.06
7209	Flat-rolled products of iron or non-alloy steel, of a width of >= 600 mm, cold-rolled “cold-reduced”, ...	0.06
7225	Flat-rolled products of alloy steel other than stainless, of a width of >= 600 mm, hot-rolled ...	0.04
7407	Bars, rods and profiles, of copper, n.e.s.	0.61
7408	Copper wire (excluding surgical sutures, stranded wire, cables, plaited bands and the like ...	0.14
7502	Unwrought nickel	0.07
7601	Unwrought aluminium	0.13
8487	Machinery parts, n.e.s. in chapter 84 (excluding parts containing electrical connectors, insulators, ...	0.02
8803	Parts of aircraft and spacecraft of heading 8801 or 8802, n.e.s.	0.04
Total		0.11

* In “zero” cases the effect of tariff liberalization was positive, but negligible
Source: author’s calculations

Increasing the supply of copper products may have a high potential, in particular, Indian imports of copper wire (HS 7408) from Russia may grow.

At the same time, the opportunities to increase Russian supplies to India of more technologically advanced products with a higher added value, which are strategically important to Russia, remain very limited.

The participants' decision to purchase relatively more technologically advanced products, in particular, parts of aircraft and spacecraft (HS 8803) is largely due to non-price characteristics, quality indicators, reliability and the level of export information support.

The elasticity of Indian imports at the average level of customs duties remains extremely low (-0.04), therefore, trade liberalization will not lead to a significant increase in the share of more technological products in the structure of Russian exports to India.

Russian import from India is significantly more diversified than export. While the average coefficient of import elasticity in terms of customs duty rates for Russia is similar to that of India for imports from Russia, the influence of price factors on foreign trade decisions considerably varies depending on the industry and product group. A relatively higher import elasticity at the rates of customs duties is typical for articles of cement, concrete or artificial stone (HS 6810), at 0.79 (see Table 4). The reduction of import duties can expand the demand for these categories of Indian goods in the Russian market due to trade creation effects.

In absolute terms, the largest increase in imports can be seen in the import of medicaments (HS 3004), which currently holds the first position in the structure of Russian imports from India and surpasses the average level of imports from India in general, albeit having a significantly lower import elasticity at the rates of customs duties (at the level of 0.11). In the case of a tariff liberalization on the part of Russia (as part of the EAEU), Russian imports of extracts, essences and concentrates of coffee, tea, etc. (HS 2101), may increase.

The largest benefits can be obtained by Russian exporters of mineral or chemical fertilizers (HS 3105) and frozen fish (HS 0303) (see Table 5). In both cases, trade liberalization, accompanied by a decrease in import prices, may increase the demand for Russian products (trade creation effects).

Comparatively smaller benefits can be obtained by Russian producers of synthetic rubber (HS 4002), however, given the growing demand for the relevant product group from Thailand in the long term (provided the intensive liberalization regarding the import of these products), potential trade effects may increase.

Table 4. Results of a quantitative assessment of the likely increase in Russian import of goods from India with a 1% linear reduction of the rates of customs duties on goods from India

Product Code (HS)	Product Label	Import Growth in Case of 1% Linear Cut of Tariff Rates, %*
0304	Fish fillets and other fish meat, whether or not minced, fresh, chilled or frozen	0.02
0306	Crustaceans, whether in shell or not, live, fresh, chilled, frozen, dried, salted or in brine, ...	0.06
0806	Grapes, fresh or dried	0.03
1207	Other oil seeds and oleaginous fruits, whether or not broken (excluding edible nuts, olives, ...	0.00
1301	Lac; natural gums, resins, gum-resins, balsams and other natural oleoresins	0.08
1302	Vegetable saps and extracts; pectic substances, pectinates and pectates; agar-agar and other ...	0.05
2101	Extracts, essences and concentrates, of coffee, tea or maté and preparations with a basis of ...	0.10
2401	Unmanufactured tobacco; tobacco refuse	0.04
2925	Carboxyimide-function compounds, incl. saccharin and its salts, and imine-function compounds	0.01
2933	Heterocyclic compounds with nitrogen hetero-atom[s] only	0.02
3004	Medicaments consisting of mixed or unmixed products for therapeutic or prophylactic uses, put ...	0.11
3204	Synthetic organic colouring matter, whether or not chemically defined; preparations based on ...	0.01
3304	Beauty or make-up preparations and preparations for the care of the skin, incl. sunscreen or ...	0.02
4011	New pneumatic tyres, of rubber	0.03
4203	Articles of apparel and clothing accessories, of leather or composition leather (excluding ...	0.07
6810	Articles of cement, concrete or artificial stone, whether or not reinforced	0.79
7219	Flat-rolled products of stainless steel, of a width of >= 600 mm, hot-rolled or cold-rolled ...	0.05
7222	Other bars and rods of stainless steel; angles, shapes and sections of stainless steel, n.e.s.	0.05
8409	Parts suitable for use solely or principally with internal combustion piston engine of heading ...	0.07
8481	Taps, cocks, valves and similar appliances for pipes, boiler shells, tanks, vats or the like, ...	0.03
8517	Telephone sets, incl. telephones for cellular networks or for other wireless networks; other ...	0.01
8526	Radar apparatus, radio navigational aid apparatus and radio remote control apparatus	0.01
8708	Parts and accessories for tractors, motor vehicles for the transport of ten or more persons, ...	0.03
Total		0.08

* In "zero" cases the effect of tariff liberalization was positive, but negligible

Source: author's calculations

Table 5. Results of a quantitative assessment of the likely increase in Thai imports of goods from Russia with a 1% linear reduction of the rates of customs duties on goods from Russia

Product Code (HS)	Product Label	Import Growth in Case of 1% Linear Cut of Tariff Rates, %*
0303	Frozen fish (excluding fish fillets and other fish meat of heading 0304)	0.08
3105	Mineral or chemical fertilisers containing two or three of the fertilising elements nitrogen, ...	0.08
4002	Synthetic rubber and factice derived from oils, in primary forms or in plates, sheets or strip; ...	0.03
Total		0.08

* In "zero" cases the effect of tariff liberalization was positive, but negligible
Source: author's calculations

In absolute terms, Thai producers of articles of jewellery (HS 7113) can benefit the most from the liberalization of tariff regulation by the EAEU as a whole and Russia, in particular: a 1% reduction in customs duty rates will provide an increase in exports from Thailand to 0.8%. In terms of the percentage of the 2016 import value, the maximum increase can be achieved in imports of refrigerators, freezers and other refrigerating and freezing equipment (HS 8418), their exports to Russia may increase by 1.13%. Thai manufacturers will also be able to increase supplies of transmission apparatus for radio-broadcasting or television (HS 8525) to Russia.

Thai producers of certain categories of agricultural products will also have the opportunity to expand their supplies to the Russian market. This primarily concerns the producers of prepared and canned fish (HS 1604), fruits and nuts (HS 2008).

SOLUTIONS AND RECOMMENDATIONS

The calculations of elasticity coefficients allow suggesting a range of recommendations for policy-making. Firstly, it makes sense for Russia to negotiate with its EAEU partners lower pace of tariff liberalization on textile and apparel, as well as on table, kitchen or other household articles, as these emerging Russian sectors are relatively more vulnerable to import price competition and need higher protection. Secondly, lowering customs duties, imposed on parts of jewellry, may increase competitiveness

Table 6. Results of a quantitative assessment of the likely increase in Russian imports of goods from Thailand with a 1% linear reduction of the rates of customs duties on goods from Thailand

Product Code (HS)	Product Label	Import Growth in Case of 1% Linear Cut of Tariff Rates, %
1604	Prepared or preserved fish; caviar and caviar substitutes prepared from fish eggs	0.18
2008	Fruits, nuts and other edible parts of plants, prepared or preserved, whether or not containing ...	0.13
3004	Medicaments consisting of mixed or unmixed products for therapeutic or prophylactic uses, put ...	0.00
3901	Polymers of ethylene, in primary forms	0.08
4011	New pneumatic tyres, of rubber	0.01
5601	Wadding of textile materials and articles thereof; textile fibres with a length of <= 5 mm ...	0.01
7113	Articles of jewellery and parts thereof, of precious metal or of metal clad with precious metal ...	0.80
8418	Refrigerators, freezers and other refrigerating or freezing equipment, electric or other; heat ...	1.13
8429	Self-propelled bulldozers, angledozers, graders, levellers, scrapers, mechanical shovels, excavators, ...	0.01
8443	Printing machinery used for printing by means of plates, cylinders and other printing components ...	0.00
8517	Telephone sets, incl. telephones for cellular networks or for other wireless networks; other ...	0.01
8525	Transmission apparatus for radio-broadcasting or television, whether or not incorporating reception ...	0.38
8542	Electronic integrated circuits; parts thereof	0.01
8704	Motor vehicles for the transport of goods, incl. chassis with engine and cab	0.19
8708	Parts and accessories for tractors, motor vehicles for the transport of ten or more persons, ...	0.11
Total		0.19

* In "zero" cases the effect of tariff liberalization was positive, but negligible

Source: author's calculations

of national producers of final jewelry items. Thirdly, while negotiating free trade areas in the framework of EAEU+1, Russia must insist on gradual lowering of India's customs duties, imposed on chemical products (organic chemicals and fertilizers, medicines, etc.) from the EAEU countries, liberalization of China's tariff regulation of import of mineral oils, as well as mineral and chemical fertilizers from the EAEU members.

FUTURE RESEARCH DIRECTIONS

The proposed methodology and the obtained results can be used in further research for solving applied issues of Russia's foreign trade policy (as a part of the Eurasian Economic Union).

In May 2018, during the EAEU summit in Sochi, the President of Russia stressed the strategic importance of expanding the integration links of the EAEU with non-regional partners. All the three explored countries (China, India and Thailand) are among the potential integration partners. In September 2016, Thailand submitted an official request to start a joint study on the feasibility of establishing a FTA with the EAEU; the 6 countries discussed plans to form a FTA at the APEC summit in 2017. At the 2017 St. Petersburg Economic Forum, the official negotiations on the establishment of an FTA between the EAEU and India started, the parties signed a joint statement. In May 2018 EAEU and China signed a multilateral Agreement on Trade and Economic Cooperation.

Being the effects of 1% linear cut of customs duties, the calculations in this chapter provide a necessary basis for simulating potential economic integration effects in the framework of three integration blocks and modelling various scenarios of multilateral negotiations. The results of the future research underlie a set of practical recommendations on the Russia's position in the negotiating process on each of the potential agreements on economic integration.

CONCLUSION

The results of SMART-modelling proved and inverse dependence of trade flows on tariff regulation consistently with the theoretical models. Tariff liberalization results in higher trade flows, the current research confirms the findings in the most of previous fundamental studies, including Leamer (1988), Feenstra (1995), Wang (2001) etc.

At the same time elasticities of import flows on customs duties seemed to be very different. The sample average import demand elasticities vary from -0,04 to -0,37 for the 1%-linear cut scenario and the variation of coefficients is very high dependently on the commodity group.

The price elasticity of Russian imports turns out to be on average relatively lower than that of Chinese or Indian imports from Russia. In the case of Thailand, the situation is reversed - Russian imports are relatively more sensitive to changes in Thai import value.

To the greatest extent, the expansion of foreign trade flows in absolute terms can be advanced by accelerated tariff liberalization by China. How ether, this can hardly be considered to be in Russia's strategic interests, since it will lead to an increase in Russian exports of the traditional product category — petroleum oil and its products — and will contribute to the growth of these product positions in the structure of Chinese imports from Russia.

ACKNOWLEDGMENT

This research received no specific grant from any funding agency in the public, commercial, or not-for-profit sectors.

REFERENCES

Afontsev, S. A. (2016). Perspektivy importozameshcheniya v rossijskoj ehkonomike [Prospects for import substitution in the Russian economy]. *Vestnik Omskogo universiteta Seriya. EHkonomika, 1*, 13–19. (in Russian)

Arapova, E. (2015). Measuring "Integration Potential" of the Free Trade Area of the Asia Pacific. *Malaysian Journal of Economic Studies, 2*, 157–185.

Arapova, E. Y., & Isachenko, T. M. (2019). Russian trade policy: Main trends and impact on bilateral trade flows. *International Journal of Economic Policy in Emerging Economies, 1*(1), 26–48. doi:10.1504/IJEPEE.2019.098684

Balassa, B. (1967). *Trade Liberalization Among Industrial Countries: Objectives and Alternatives*. New York: McGraw Hill.

Baldwin, R., & Martin, P. (1999). *Two Waves of Globalisation: Super-ficial Similarities, Fundamental Differences*. Cambridge, MA: National Bureau of Economic Research. doi:10.3386/w6904

Cheong, D. (2010). Methods for Ex Ante Economic Evaluation of Free Trade Agreements. *ADB*.

Feenstra, R. (1995). Estimating the Effects of Trade Policy. *NBER*. Retrieved from http://www.nber.org/papers/w5051.pdf

Feenstra, R., Lipsey, R., & Bowen, H. (1997). World Trade Flows, 1970-1992, with Production and Tariff Data. *NBER*. Retrieved from http://www.nber.org/papers/w5910.pdf

Goldstein, M., Khan, M. S., & Officer, L. H. (1980). Prices of Tradable and Nontradable Goods in the Demand for Total Imports. *The Review of Economics and Statistics, 2*(62), 190–199. doi:10.2307/1924744

Guei, K. M. A., Mugano, G., & Le Roux, P. (2017). Revenue, welfare and trade effects of European Union Free Trade Agreement on South Africa. *South African Journal of Economic and Management Sciences.*, *20*(1). doi:10.4102ajems.v20i1.1655

Heckscher, E. F., & Ohlin, B. G. (1991). *Heckscher-Ohlin trade theory*. The MIT Press.

Isard, P. (1977). The Price Effects of Exchange Rate Changes. U.S. Treasury.

Kee, H., Nicita, A., & Olarreaga, M. (2005). Import Demand Elasticities and Trade Distortions. *The World Bank. The European Trade Study Group (ETSG)*. Retrieved from http://www.etsg.org/ETSG2005/papers/olarr.pdf

Knobel, A. Yu. (2010). *Zakonomernosti formirovaniya urovnya tarifov v mezhdunarodnoj torgovle* [Regularities of the formation of the tariffs in international trade]. Moscow: Gaidar Institute. (in Russian)

Leamer, E. E. (1988). Cross-Section Estimation of the Effects of Trade Barriers. In R. Feenstra (Ed.), *Empirical Methods for International Trade*. The MIT Press.

Rhomberg, R. R. (1973). Toward a General Trade Models. In R.J. Ball (Ed.), The International Linkage of National Economic Models.

Stern, R. M. (1973). Tariffs and Other Measures of Trade Control: A Survey of Recent Developments. *Journal of Economic Literature*, *3*(11), 857–888.

Wang, Q. (2001). Import-Reducing Effect of Trade Barriers: a Cross-Country Investigation. *IMF*. Retrieved from https://www.imf.org/external/pubs/ft/wp/2001/wp01216.pdf

WTO. (2012). A Practical Guide to Trade Policy Analysis. Retrieved from https://www.wto.org/english/res_e/publications_e/wto_unctad12_e.pdf

ADDITIONAL READING

Calvo-Pardo, H., Freund, C., & Ornelas, E. (2009). The ASEAN Free Trade Agreement: Impact on Trade Flows and External Trade Barriers. *CEP*.

Cheong, D. (2008). The Effects of AFTA: A Disaggregated Analysis. *Johns Hopkins University, SAIS Bologna Center.* Retrieved from http://www.jhubc.it/facultypages/dCheong/3CheongAFTAEffects.pdf

Estrada, G., Park, D., Park, I., & Park, S. (2011). ASEAN's Free Trade Agreements with the People's Republic of China, Japan, and the Republic of Korea: A Qualitative and Quantitative Analysis. *ADB Working Paper Series on Regional Economic Integration, 75,* 3-28.

Estrada, G., Park, D., Park, I., & Park, S. (2012). The PRC's Free Trade Agreements with ASEAN, Japan, and the Republic of Korea: A Comparative Analysis. *ADB Working Paper Series on Regional Economic Integration, 92,* 3-32.

Nakawiroj, W. (2016). Trade and sustainability: How strong are the empirical linkages between trade structures and sustainability performance? *International Journal of Economic Policy in Emerging Economies, 3*(3), 272–289. doi:10.1504/IJEPEE.2016.079127

KEY TERMS AND DEFINITIONS

EAEU: Eurasian Economic Union, integration block on the Post-Soviet space, which includes 5 countries – Russia, Kazakhstan, Armenia, Belarus and Kyrgyzstan.

Economic Integration: Arrangement at multilateral level that includes reduction and elimination of trade barriers, as well as unification of economic policies.

SMART: The Software for Market Analysis and Restrictions on Trade, a simulation tool, proposed by the World Integrated Trade Solution to measure the effects of tariff liberalization.

Tariff: Special tax, imposed on imported goods.

Trade Liberalization: Gradual cancellation of trade regulations (tariff and non-tariff barriers to trade).

Chapter 11
The Efficiency of Corporate Tax Incentives in Developing Countries Based on Foreign Direct Investments

Simla Güzel
Namık Kemal University, Turkey

ABSTRACT

During the last quarter century, a remarkable global growth was experienced in Foreign Direct Investment (FDI), especially the developing countries, considered FDIs as an important factor in overall economic development strategies. The developing countries aim to attract foreign capital to strengthen their local economy, increase market opportunities, and provide better services to the society. For this purpose, these nations implement various types of tax incentives. Although there are several studies on the effectiveness of tax incentives in FDI, the issue has not been tackled with respect to developing countries. The present study scrutinized the effectiveness of corporate tax incentives in developing countries based on FDI. In conclusion, it could be suggested that tax incentives may be effective in increasing FDI; however, in this group of countries with low level of investments and complex laws in taxation and other fields and could not cope with innovations, red tape and poor governance, it is also important to develop the organizational infrastructure for investments.

DOI: 10.4018/978-1-5225-9566-3.ch011

INTRODUCTION

Foreign direct investments are considered among the most significant contributors to economic growth. Higher capital accumulation and additional economic activity could benefit economic growth in the short term. In comparison with the local corporations in the receiving economy, foreign investing firms could have higher overall productivity. Hence, a composition effect might come into play. By means of human capital and technological advancements and product and process innovations, FDI results in positive productivity spillover to local corporations in the long-run.

During the last quarter century, a remarkable global growth was experienced in FDI, since several nations, especially the developing countries, considered FDIs as an important factor in overall economic development strategy. FDI is important in achieving economic growth not only in developed but also in developing countries. Foreign capital is used by the developed countries for a more stable growth, while developing countries aim to increase investments and to strengthen the economy.

Several policy instruments are used to attract FDI to a country. These policies include economic, political and social stability, entrance and functioning rules, treatment of foreign affiliate standards, market operation and structure policies, international FDI agreements, privatization and trade policies, coherence of FDI and tax policies. In order to increase FDI, countries began to utilize tax incentives widely, especially in recent years, and policy makers constantly re-evaluate the present tax regulations.

In developing countries particularly, it was noted that the importance of tax incentives in growing foreign investments became prevalent in the globalization period. On the one hand, the requirement to abandon most important source of income for the state, the tax revenues, forces the countries to implement relevant tax policies. Developing countries usually adopt corporate tax incentives such as, preferential or very low general tax rates, tax allowances and tax holidays.

In addition to the generosity of the incentives provided to attract foreign investments, the effectiveness of these incentives is also important. The success of tax incentives is associated with good incentive design and general economic characteristics of the country. Externalities, public goods, liquidity problems and coordination problems within the economic system lead to market failures and failure of effective investments. Furthermore, tax incentives could be effective if they could be used for their original purposes. In particular, the cost of tax incentives grows as a consequence of the budgetary constraints and the corruption in developing countries. Also, weaknesses in tax management capacity in developing countries lead to tax avoidance and evasion. In investment decisions, factors such as political stability, organizational quality, and market size play a role in addition to tax incentives.

The aim of this study is to evaluate the significance of corporate tax incentives for FDI in developing countries. Accordingly, the first section of the study covers definitions of tax incentives and corporate tax incentive types. In the second section, information on corporate tax incentives in developing countries and related problems are presented. In this section, primarily the definition of developing countries and information on the corporate tax incentives implemented in this group of countries are provided. In the third section of the study, the significance of FDI for developing countries is discussed. With the aim of rating the effectiveness of tax incentives in terms of FDI, general information is provided initially, and then the relevant literature is addressed and the last section included the results.

BACKGROUND

The correlation between taxation and FDIs has been a major focus in tax policy studies. The findings in econometric studies have changed significantly over time. Historically, it was determined that fiscal considerations had an insignificant impact on FDIs. More recent research, however concluded that taxes could be effective on investment decisions under certain circumstances (Kransdorf, 2010, p.71). Wilson (1999) maintained that in the event that a government increases the tax rate, a decline occurs in the net return and capital relocates elsewhere in line with the perfectly mobile capital assumption. Accordingly, the conclusions encourage the use of tax incentives in order to decrease tax rates and attract FDIs. Gastanaga, Nugent and Pashamova (1998) examined the factors determining FDIs. They saw that in case the country fixed effects remain controlled, marginal CIT rates adversely affect FDI flows. Tung and Cho (2000) aimed to ascertain the direct impact of tax incentives in China on FDI. The results they obtained demonstrated that tax incentives successfully attracted FDI to China, and furthermore, affected the selection of a particular FDI type. Wei (2000) investigated the impact of corruption and tax variables on FDI flows taking place from OECD countries to host countries in developed as well as developing nations. The findings of that study demonstrated that both variables were significant in explaining FDI flows. Benassy-Quere Fontagne and Lahreche-Revil (2005) determined the factors that affected foreign direct investments between 1984 and 2000 in 11 OECD counties with panel data analysis. Study findings demonstrated that differences in corporate tax rates had significant impact on investment decisions. Bellak, Leibrecht and Damijan (2009) reported that high corporate tax rates in Central and East European countries had negative effects on foreign direct investments. A study conducted by Bellak and Leibrecht (2009) indicated that tax-reduction strategies by CEEC governments had a significant impact on foreign corporations' location decisions.

Klemm and Van Parys (2010) took into account how effective the incentives are to attract investment in Latin American, Caribbean and African countries for the 1985–2004 period. They utilized the dynamic panel data econometrics and concluded that decreased CIT rates and extended tax holidays were able to attract FDIs in Latin America and the Caribbean but not in Africa.

Effiok, Tapang and Eton (2013) analyzed the effects of tax policies and tax incentives on FDI. The results showed that taxes have a significant effect on FDI.

Olaleye, Riro and Memba (2016) determined the effectiveness of tax incentives on FDI in terms of the production companies in Nigeria. According to the results obtained from the analysis, incentives for corporate tax have a positive effect on FDI in terms of firms.

Ugwu (2018) stated that the reduction of corporate tax rate in Nigeria, Ghana and South Africa affected the FDI positively when supported by other tax incentives.

Slusarczyk (2018) evaluated the impact of tax incentives on FDI in Poland. Special Economic Zones and exemption from property tax incentives provided by the Polish Government have a positive effect on FDI.

There are also studies, which argued that factors other than the tax incentives were more effective on the FDIs.

Loree and Gusinger (2009) investigated the influence of policy and non-policy factors on the new U.S. direct investment targets. In one case, policy variables were found to be "important" because governments were able to change policies swiftly, whereas non-policy determinants such as market size and infrastructure could be changed after years. Tax policies changes might spur changes in domestic as well as foreign investments in a couple of years. James (2010) demonstrated that both tax and non-tax incentives can be implemented by policy makers to boost investments. He also concluded that the investment climate in an economy was critical for the impact of tax incentives.

In transition economies in OECD (1995), the effect of tax incentives on industrialization and investments was positive in East Asia, Taiwan, Korea and Singapore, while in Malaysia, Indonesia, Thailand and Philippines, tax incentives did not demonstrate a similar success. However, there are more important factors that affect FDIs when compared to tax incentives. The quality of the economic and institutional system and the infrastructure required for investments are also quite important. The comparative analysis conducted by Beyer (2002) indicated that although FDIs positively affected the transition process, the implementation of tax concessions were of little value. No correlation was found by the study between tax concessions and FDI influx in transitional economies.

In a SADC technical report, Bolnick (2004) argued that evidence in other developing nations including those in the SADC indicated that tax incentives remained inadequate to attract foreign investors to turn to these countries. The study indicated that economies such as Mauritius, Costa Rica, Ireland and Malaysia were successful in using non-tax incentives to attract FDIs. These countries implemented sound economic reforms, assured political stability, a qualified labor force, developed sufficient infrastructure and applied investment promotions to create higher interest among investors.

Zee, Stotsky and Ley (2002) examined the efficiency of tax incentives on FDIs, especially in developing countries and argued that evidence was limited on the effectiveness of tax incentives in attracting FDIs, particularly in developing countries. They doubted the significance of tax incentives in attracting FDIs in comparison with non-tax factors that increase the attractiveness of an economy.

Van Parys and James (2010) investigated the extent of the effectiveness of tax incentives on attracting investments in Sub-Saharan Africa in their study. They analyzed the neo-classical investment theory arguing that investments are increased by tax incentives by decreasing the user cost of the capital. Along with tax incentives, they also predicted the effect of other investment climate variables that are controlled by the state including the transparency and complexity of the tax system, and the legal protection of foreign investors on investments. In developing countries, these variables are equally important with or even more important in comparison with tax variables.

Kinda (2014) used corporate data for 30 Sub-Saharan Africa (SSA) countries. The study showed that FDIs were influenced by infrastructure, human capital, and institutions; however, the taxes did not play a role in attracting FDIs. It was found that the taxes were ineffective in attracting both vertical (exports industry FDI) and horizontal FDIs (where foreign corporations produce for the host market).

A study by Peters and Kiabel (2015) investigated the impact of tax incentives on the FDI investment decisions in Nigeria. The findings demonstrated that FDI response to tax incentives was negative and significant, that is, increase in tax incentives did not lead to a corresponding increase in FDIs. Based on the findings, the paper recommended, amongst others, that dependence on tax incentives should be reduced and other incentive strategies such as stable economic reforms and stable political climate should be prioritized. Antonakakis and Tondl (2015) investigated the factors that determined FDI outflow from four major OECD countries, which are the US, Germany, France, and the Netherlands to 129 developing countries groups as five different regions during 1995–2008 period. They found that there was no single theory but a wide variety of theories that shaped the decision of OECD FDIs in developing countries. OECD investors seek destinations which have deep-rooted strong trade relations and present a qualified labor force. Important investment criteria also encompassed low wages and attractive tax rates.

Baggerman-Noudari and Offermanns (2016) stated that in their study that, the issues related to taxation are not effective on their own in the FDI investment decisions to be made in developing countries and that investors take into consideration bilateral, multilateral or regional tax treaties.

MAIN FOCUS OF THE CHAPTER

With the globalization period starting in 1980's, developing countries which have lacks especially in capital accumulation have started to realize the importance of attracting foreign investments to their countries. In today's world, FDI is in the centre of development programmes. Accordingly, the effectiveness of tax incentives implemented in order to increase FDI has an important role. As being the most important source of income, taxes are also used as an important tool of incentive policy.

In this study, the effectiveness of corporate tax incentives used to increase FDI was evaluated. The most common corporate tax incentives that developing countries use in order to support FDIs are preferential or very low general tax rates, tax allowances, and tax holidays. One of the most important factors which affect the effectiveness of tax incentives is that incentives are structured in accordance with economic conditions of the country. Economic and social problems, and administrative weaknesses of developing countries may negatively affect the effectiveness of incentives.

TAX INCENTIVES

Tax incentives are one of the important economic intervention instruments of the state. Taxes have significant impact on entrepreneurs' investment decisions. Developed countries commonly utilize these incentives to increase investments, global competitiveness with the integration of global trade activities, and to ensure economic stability. Most developing countries, in addition to the above-mentioned objectives, benefit from several tax incentives to strengthen the national industry and attract foreign investments (United Nations, 2018, p. 3).

Definition of Tax Incentives

In the Turkish Dictionary published by Turkish Language Association, the concept of "incentive" is defined as "motivation" and "encouragement" (TDK).

Tax incentives are among important economic intervention instruments of the state. Tax incentives are as measures to reduce or eliminate tax burden in a certain industry in the economy (Giray, 2016, p. 27).

Tax incentives are practices that aim to reduce tax burden of the entrepreneur taxpayers to improve their investments in the industry. Applications such as preferential tax practices, exceptions, credits, and postponement of tax liabilities are among the tax incentive policies.

Tax incentives can be classified in different groups: tax holidays implemented for a certain period of time, deduction of certain expenditures from tax liabilities, or reduced export tariffs or customs obligations. A tax incentive should aim a specific purpose. It is sometimes difficult to distinguish this requirement. For example, corporate tax can be applied for both national and foreign investors with a low rate of 10% on production revenues. Since this application covers all taxpayers, it could be accepted as a general practice in the tax system or as tax incentive since it only covers production revenues. However, tax incentives could also be enacted to reduce the tax burden in a specific project (United Nations, 2018, p. 5).

Tax systems could be used to achieve various political objectives. However, studies in the literature report three basic functions of tax systems. The most important of these functions is the use of taxes in financing the public expenditures. The second function is the redistribution of taxes. Taxes are used to provide income distribution justice at both individual and institutional levels. And the third is the distribution function of taxes. Accordingly, taxes prioritize productivity impartially and without harming the economy (United Nations, 2017, p. 1).

Today, it is suggested that investment decisions are influenced more by tax incentives when compared to the previous years. There are several reasons behind this development. First, current tax incentives are more generous when compared to previous incentives. Second, the level of trade liberalization and capital mobility are higher today. The removal of obstacles to tax incentives has led to an increase in investment activities. Third, it can be argued that corporations experience significant changes in organizational structure today. Changes in modes of production and distribution, product variety, sales method, and the increase in mobile services have made tax incentives more important (United Nations, 2018, p.6).

Types of Tax Incentives

It is possible to group tax incentives in two categories as direct and indirect tax incentives. The most common tax incentives are as follows (Tekin, 2006, pp. 303-309; OECD, 2007, pp. 21-22; Holland and Vann, 1998, pp. 4-9; Zee, Stotsky & Ley, 2002, pp. 1503-1507; Giray 2016, pp. 72-78):

- **Direct Tax Incentives:** Direct tax incentives on corporate tax are implemented with two methods. The first method is to reduce the normal corporate tax rate on profits. And the other method includes regulations that aim to reduce investment costs when compared to the current rate.
    - **Corporate Tax Rate Incentives:** In this type of incentive, a rate lower than the current corporate tax rate is determined or practices such as full exemption from corporate tax obligation (tax holidays) or low corporate tax on certain qualified projects are implemented.
        - **Tax Holiday:** This type of incentive exempts newly established companies from corporate tax over their earnings at a specific time (e.g. 5 years) in order to improve their investments. Also, it could be implemented as the exemption of companies from corporate tax until they recover the investment costs. This type of incentive is very attractive for foreign investors and is frequently used in developing countries. The administration of this type of incentive is simple and strengthens the relationship between the taxpayers and the tax administration. Besides these advantages, this incentive also has disadvantages such as the fact that it is more oriented towards short-term projects, the use of methods as presenting existing investments as new investments, and increase in tax avoidance.
        - **Preferential Corporate Tax Rates:** This method is also mostly utilized in developing countries. Preferential corporate tax rates are applied to qualified investment projects when compared to other projects. This type of incentive could be considered as a part of the holiday. Also, while having the disadvantages of the tax holiday system, this method also has advantages such as lower revenue loss costs and it is more transparent.

- **Incentives to Reduce Investment Costs:** This type of incentive is used with a view to lowering investment costs in developed as well as developing countries. Incentives to reduce investment costs aims at investments in a particular industry such as tools, equipment, machinery investments.
    - **Investment Tax Credits***:* This type of incentive is used to influence investment costs. It is implemented as a partial deduction of a certain percentage or total deduction of investment cost from the taxable base in certain circumstances. Investment tax credits are more transparent and more efficient when compared to tax holidays. However, when the depreciated assets are replaced by new assets, these new assets can also benefit from the tax credit, leading to the preference of short-term assets, which in turn leads to economic deviation. Furthermore, qualified companies can buy and sell the same assets multiple times in order to benefit from the investment tax credit several times.
    - **Accelerated Depreciation:** Depreciation the accounting of the losses on the fixed assets of the enterprises that accrue over time due to aging, wear, innovations, etc. The loss on the asset value is accounted as expenses. This type of incentive has an effect on investment profits. In this method, the loss of the fixed asset value is depreciated as an expense with a large rate initially and then in decreasing rates. In addition to the high administrative costs of accelerated depreciation, it could be argued that it has the disadvantages of corporate tax incentives and the advantages of investment tax credits.
    - **Investment credits:** This type of incentive has the advantages that it is more comprehensible than the investment tax credits and provides the same credit to all taxpayers, regardless of the marginal rates. Investment credit is a subsidy granted to entrepreneurs who invest. While the investment tax credits reflect a tax that is forfeited when the investments become profitable, these credits are the expenditures that the state has forfeited in advance.

- **Indirect Tax Incentives:** Indirect tax incentives include full or partial exemption from import tariffs and sales taxes (zero VAT rate). These incentives are usually for export businesses. However, several countries could also use indirect incentives in non-export-oriented industries. These incentives are provided as exports incentives and export processing zones (free trade zone) (Zee, Stotsky & Ley, 2002, pp. 1505-1507):

- **Export Incentives:** These incentives are extensively implemented in many countries. They include the exemption of the material used in the export goods manufacturing from indirect taxes and application of the principle of destination country. Export tax incentives are implemented as customs duty and value added tax exemptions.
    - **Customs Duty Exemption:** There are two different implementations for the exemption of the material used in the in the export goods manufacturing from customs duty. In the first implementation, custom duties are excised on the material used in the production of export goods. The taxes paid for these materials are then returned, depending on the inputs in imported goods ratio. In the other implementation, the customs duties of the imported goods by certain exporters, whose exports rates are high in total trade are postponed. When these imports are utilized in the production of goods to be offered to the domestic market, the taxes are then excised. When imported goods are used while exported goods are produced, they are completely free the duties.
    - **VAT Exemption:** In countries that implement the principle of destination country in value added tax basis, the VAT rate is determined as zero. Thus, exporters do not experience any tax burden on imported goods. However, the refund of taxes paid by major exporters on the products they import could take some time, leading to operating capital problems. To address this issue, several countries impose postponement incentives in Value Added Tax. This method, which has the risk of leakage of imported goods into the domestic market, is preferred mostly by the developed countries.
- **Free zones:** These zones are implemented extensively throughout the world, especially in developing countries. In addition to direct tax incentives, indirect ones are also implemented in tax-free production zones. Export products could benefit from tax incentives as long as they are not sold to the domestic market. However, in countries without a developed tax system, it is considered as a risky incentive due to high probability of leakage of the export goods to the domestic market from these zones.

TAX INCENTIVES IN DEVELOPING NATIONS AND RELATED PROBLEMS

The taxes that constitute the most important state revenues do not represent only the economy of a country, but also the state's approach to justice and its authority. Tax policy choices are related to the administrative capacity of the state as well as to the economic structure of a country (Bird & Zolt, 2008, p. 75). The primary objective of tax incentives is to increase investments; however, they contribute to economic growth by increasing investments, and turn into significant costs for the state.

In developed and developing countries, tax incentives are used with various techniques and their effects may vary. This section will address the definition and general properties of tax incentives in developing countries and the concept of developing countries will be defined and their general attributes will be addressed before the problems related to tax incentives.

Definition of Developing Countries

It is useful to define the concept of development before making the definition of developing countries. However, it is not possible to argue that there is a consensus on the definition of the concept of development. Classical economists defined development as an increase in real income per capita, and neo-classical economists considered the concept from a wider perspective. After the Second World War, the emergence of some independent countries led to the consideration of developmental economy separately from the economy in general. Bell (1989) defined the newly independent countries as "latecomer" poor countries and previously independent powerful countries as "pioneer" and rich countries. Economic development is described as the process of latecomer countries catching up with pioneer countries. When the economists define economic development, they consider differences such as cultural, social, production systems in addition to income disparities among countries. Underdevelopment is considered as a multidimensional problem (Nielsen, 2011, p. 5).

In line with the definition of development by the World Bank, when the national per capita income is under USD 12,476, the country is considered as a developing country. The International Monetary Fund (IMF) defined development based on three basic criteria. These criteria were (1) Income per capita, (2) Export diversity (Thus, even the countries that export oil are rich countries, since 70% of their exports are oil-related, they are not considered as developed countries), (3) Integration to the global financial system (Brodzka, 2013, p. 27; Quora).

According to the Global Investment Competitiveness Report (2018), developing countries are classified as presented in Table 1.

Table 1. Developing countries

Low-income countries	Lower-middle-income countries	Upper-middle-income countries
Haiti (LAC)	Tanzania (EAP)	China (EAP)
Afghanistan (SAR)	Indonesia (EAP)	Fiji (EAP)
Nepal (SAR)	Lao PDR (EAP)	Malaysia (EAP)
Burundi (SSA)	Mongolia (EAP)	Thailand (EAP)
Chad(SSA)	Myanmar (EAP)	Albania (ECA)
Congo, Dem. Rep. (SSA)	Papua New Guinea (EAP)	Azerbaijan (ECA)
Ethiopia (SSA)	Philippines (EAP)	Belarus (ECA)
Gambia (SSA)	Samoa (EAP)	Bosnia and Herzegovina (ECA)
Guinea (SSA)	Sri Lanka (EAP)	Bulgaria (ECA)
Liberia (SSA)	Timor-Leste (EAP)	Georgia (ECA)
Madagascar (SSA)	Vietnam (EAP)	Kazakhstan (ECA)
Malawi (SSA)	Armenia (ECA)	Macedonia (ECA)
Mozambique (SSA)	Moldova (ECA)	Montenegro (ECA)
Rwanda (SSA)	Tajikistan (ECA)	Romania (ECA)
Senegal (SSA)	Ukraine (ECA)	Serbia (ECA)
Sierra Leone (SSA)	Uzbekistan (ECA)	Turkey (ECA)
South Sudan (SSA)	Bolivia (LAC)	Turkmenistan (ECA)
Tanzania (SSA)	Guatemala (LAC)	Argentina (LAC)
Uganda (SSA)	Honduras (LAC)	Belize (LAC)
Zimbabwe (SSA)	Nicaragua (LAC)	Brazil (LAC)
	Egypt, Arab Rep. (MENA)	Colombia (LAC)
	Morocco (MENA)	Costa Rica (LAC)
	Tunisia (MENA)	Dominica (LAC)
	Bangladesh (SAR)	Dominican Republic. (LAC)
	India (SAR)	Ecuador (LAC)
	Pakistan (SAR)	Grenada (LAC)
	Cameroon (SSA)	Guyana (LAC)
	Cabo Verde (SSA)	Jamaica (LAC)
	Congo, Rep (SSA)	Mexico (LAC)
	Côte d'Ivoire (SSA)	Panama (LAC)
	Gana (SSA)	Paraguay (LAC)
	Kenya (SSA)	Peru (LAC)
	Lesotho (SSA)	Saint Lucia (LAC)
	Mauritania (SSA)	Suriname (LAC)
	Nigeria (SSA)	Venezuela (LAC)
	São Tomé and Príncipe. (SSA)	Algeria (MENA)
	Sudan (SSA)	Iraq (MENA)
	Swaziland (SSA)	Jordan (MENA)
	Zambia (SSA)	Lebanon (MENA)
		Libya (MENA)
		Maldives (SAR)
		Angola (SSA)
		Botswana (SSA)
		Equatorial Guinea (SSA)
		Gabon (SSA)
		Mauritius (SSA)
		Namibia (SSA)
		South Africa (SSA)

Data Source: Andersen, Kett, & Uexkull, 2018, p. 90.

Note: EAP = East Asia and Pacific: ECA = Europe and Central Asia; LAC = Latin America and Caribbean; MENA = Middle East and North Africa; SAR = South Asia; SSA = Sub-Saharan Africa.

Today, around 80% of the world population live in developing regions. The least developed regions are generally located in Africa, Asia and the Pacific. These poverty-stricken regions, which constitute one of the most important global problems, require financial assistance and funds to meet their basic needs for development. General characteristics of these regions and countries include an agriculture-based economy, uncompetitive economy, and the presence of exploitable natural resources (Brodzka, 2013, p. 28). The fact that the markets in developing countries, which lack sufficient capital, are not sufficiently developed lead to a level of domestic production that does not have the potential to meet the requirements of economic growth and the society (Bazo, 2008, p. 1). In a study titled Capital, Piketty (2013) emphasized the possibility of the investments by capital-abundant countries in poor countries to improve both their revenues and contribute to the production capacity of poor countries and lead to capital accumulation among the factors that affect the convergence between rich and poor countries (Piketty, 2013, p.74). Thus, tax incentives are considered to be particularly important in establishing the conditions in underdeveloped and developing countries that would create investment opportunities.

Corporate Tax Incentives in Developing Countries

Developing countries aim to attract foreign capital in order to strengthen their local economy, increase market opportunities and provide better services to the society. For this purpose, these countries implement various types of tax incentives.

Tax incentives vary from one country to another in developing countries based on the industry, regions and income level. Frequently implemented tax incentives include tax holidays, preferential or very low general tax rates and tax allowances.

The rate of performance is indicated in Table 2, tax incentives are common in construction, information technology (IT) and electronics, machinery and equipment, and other manufacturing industries. Certain developing countries provide tax incentives especially for manufacturing industries in order to increase investments, while others extend incentives to all industries. Approximately 30% of developing countries provide incentives for a specific manufacturing industry. Incentives are not preferred in the service and natural resource industries. Furthermore, incentives are implemented in 40% of the countries and very low corporate tax rates are implemented in almost every industry (Andersen, Kett & Uexkull, 2018, p.75).

The corporate tax rate applied at a lower percentage than the standard corporate tax rate for a particular industry or a group of investors in Table 2 is the preferential tax rate incentive. This type of incentive is preferred by at least 40% of developing countries for at least one industry. The industries where the preferential corporate tax incentive is implemented include manufacturing, information technology and

Table 2. Global use of preferential tax rates, 2015

	East Asia and Pacific	Europe and Central Asia	Latin America and the Caribbean	Middle East and North Africa	South Asia	Sub Saharan Africa	Low income	Lower middle income	Upper middle income	Total
Number of countries covered in database	15	18	23	8	6	37	20	39	48	107
Prevalence of preferential rates by sector and region (share of countries offering concessions in a given sector, percent)										
Food and beverages	40	33	22	25	67	27	25	46	21	31
IT and electronics	33	39	22	25	67	27	25	46	21	31
Air- and spacecraft	33	33	22	25	67	27	25	44	21	30
Automotive industry and other transport	33	33	22	25	67	27	25	44	21	30
Biotechnology, pharmaceuticals and me	33	33	22	25	67	27	25	44	21	30
Machinery and equipment	33	33	22	25	67	27	25	44	21	30
Construction and building material	40	33	22	13	50	27	25	38	23	29
Other manufacturing	33	33	22	25	50	27	25	41	21	29
Apparel, textiles, and footwear	27	33	22	25	50	27	25	38	21	28
Agriculture and fishing	33	33	13	0	67	14	20	31	15	21
Power, utilities, and telecommunications	27	28	17	0	50	19	20	28	17	21
Tourism and hospitality	27	28	17	13	50	16	20	28	17	21
Education and health	20	28	17	13	50	16	20	23	19	21
Financial services	27	28	17	0	33	19	26	26	17	21
IT services	33	28	17	0	50	14	26	26	19	21
Transport and logistics services	20	28	17	13	50	16	23	23	19	21
Entertainment	27	28	17	0	50	14	23	23	19	20
Extractive industries	13	22	13	13	50	22	23	23	13	20
Recycling	20	28	17	0	50	16	23	23	17	20
Renewable energy	20	28	17	0	50	16	23	23	17	20
Business services	20	28	17	0	50	14	23	23	17	19
Trade and retail	13	28	17	0	50	14	21	21	17	18
Trade and retail	60	39	26	38	67	38	56	56	27	40

Data Source: Andersen, Kett, & Uexkull, 2018, p. 92.

electronics industries. The preferential tax rate incentive implemented in these sectors is 31% (Andersen, Kett & Uexkull et al., 2018, p.75).

In developing countries, tax holidays manifest themselves as the most extensively used incentive. While this incentive does not include regulations that would fully affect investments that would enable macroeconomic stability and adequate public infrastructure, it is preferred because it is considered as an open and easy to implement type of incentive (United Nations, 2017, p.1).

In tax holidays, new companies are exempted from income taxes for some time. In particular circumstances, it is possible to extend the grace period to the following tax period at a lower rate. Tax holidays have a significant advantage since they provide a simple solution for foreign investors, since there is no need to calculate taxes in the early years of operation in such as regime, when the tax systems are not yet fully developed. Thus, investors perceive tax holidays as an uncomplicated incentive which relieves the burden of compliance. This perception is inclined to make this incentive attractive, particularly in countries that are in the early years of establishing a corporate tax system. New businesses in a specific region and/or industry could also be the target of a tax holiday (Brodzka, 2013, p. 31).

As seen in Table 3, more than 50% of the countries implement the tax holiday in at least one industry. While 46% of the countries implement tax holiday in construction and manufacturing industries, retail trade is the industry that benefits from tax holidays the least. The average tax holiday period in developing countries is 10 years (Andersen, Kett & Uexkull, 2018, p. 75)

Table 3. Global use of tax holidays, 2015

	East Asia and Pac	pe and Central	erica and the C	East and North	South Asia	bSaharan Afri	Lowincome	wemiddleinco	permiddleinco	Total
Number of countries covered in database	15	18	23	8	6	37	20	39	48	107
Prevalence of tax holidays by sector and region (share of countries offering tax holidays in a given sector, percent)										
Construction and building materials	71	56	48	50	50	32	35	47	52	47
Machinery and equipment	71	56	48	50	50	30	30	47	52	46
Air- and spacecraft	64	56	48	50	50	30	30	47	50	45
Automotive industry and other transport	64	56	48	50	50	30	30	47	50	45
IT and electronics	71	56	48	50	33	30	30	45	52	45
Apparel, textiles, and footwear	64	56	48	50	33	30	30	45	50	44
Food and beverages	64	56	48	50	33	30	30	45	50	44
Other manufacturing	64	56	48	50	33	30	30	45	50	44
Biotechnology, pharmaceuticals, and medi	57	56	48	50	33	30	30	42	50	43
Agriculture and fishing	64	39	30	13	33	32	30	42	33	36
Tourism and hospitality	50	33	35	38	33	24	25	37	33	33
Extractive industries	29	39	26	25	33	24	20	32	29	28
Transport and logistics services	43	33	22	13	33	24	20	29	29	27
Education and health	50	28	22	13	50	19	15	32	27	26
IT services	50	39	22	13	17	19	15	26	31	26
Financial services	29	39	26	13	17	19	15	21	31	25
Power, utilities, and telecommunications	36	28	22	13	50	19	15	29	25	25
Renewable energy	29	33	26	13	33	19	15	26	27	25
Business services	43	28	26	13	17	16	15	24	27	24
Entertainment	43	28	22	13	17	19	15	24	27	24
Recycling	29	28	22	13	17	22	15	24	25	23
Trade and retail	29	33	22	13	17	19	15	21	27	23
Total (countries with tax holidays in at least one sector	71	61	48	50	50	41	40	55	52	51

Data Source: Andersen, Kett, & Uexkull, 2018, p. 91.

Table 4. Global use of tax allowances and credits, 2015

	East Asia and Pacific	Europe and Central Asia	Latin America and the Caribbea	Middle East and North Africa	South Asia	Sub-Saharan Africa	Low-income	Lower-middle-income	Upper-middle-income	Total
Number of countries covered in database	15	18	23	8	6	37	20	39	48	107
Prevalence of tax allowances by sector and region (share of countries offering tax allowance in a given sector, percent)										
Construction and building materials	20	11	4	13	17	14	20	10	10	12
Apparel, textiles, and footwear	20	11	4	13	0	14	20	10	8	11
Automotive industry and other transport	13	11	4	13	0	14	20	8	8	10
Biotechnology, pharmaceuticals and medical products	20	11	4	13	0	11	20	10	6	10
Construction and building materials	20	11	4	13	0	11	20	8	8	10
Food and beverages	20	11	4	13	0	11	20	10	6	10
IT and electronics	13	11	4	13	0	14	20	8	8	10
Air- and spacecraft	13	11	4	13	0	11	20	8	6	9
Other manufacturing	13	11	4	13	0	11	20	8	6	9
Tourism and hospitality	13	11	0	13	0	14	20	8	6	9
Renewable energy	13	11	4	13	0	8	15	5	8	8
Education and health	13	11	0	13	0	8	10	5	8	7
Entertainment	13	11	0	13	0	8	5	8	8	7
Power,utilities and telecommunications	13	11	4	13	0	5	10	5	8	7
Agriculture and fishing	13	11	0	13	0	5	10	5	6	7
IT services	20	11	0	13	0	3	5	5	8	7
Recycling	13	11	0	13	0	5	10	5	6	7
Perakende ticaret	20	11	0	13	0	3	5	8	6	7
Transport and logistics services	13	11	0	13	0	5	10	5	6	7
Business services	13	11	0	13	0	3	5	5	6	6
Financial services	13	11	0	13	0	3	5	5	6	6
Extractive industries	13	11	0	0	0	3	5	3	6	5
Total	33	11	9	13	17	16	25	13	15	16

Data Source: Andersen, Kett, & Uexkull, 2018, p. 94.

And as seen in Table 4, in developing countries, tax allowances and credits enabling the investors to subtract investment expenses from taxable income or offer credits towards payable taxes are less prevalent. Solely, 16% percent of these countries provide these incentives in at least one industry. Receiving allowances or credits is generally linked with investments which include R&D or the purchase and assembly of new equipment or technology (Andersen, Kett & Uexkull, 2018, p. 76).

As seen in Figure 1, policy makers went on lowering CIT rates in developing countries. A decrease was recorded in average CIT rates between 2009 and 2015 in Middle East and North Africa, East Asia and Pacific, Latin America and the Caribbean, Sub-Saharan Africa, and South Asia. On the contrary, European and Central Asian countries introduced a slight raise in mean CIT rates. Mean tax rates across regions varied substantially and ranged between 38 percent in South Asia and 15 percent in Europe and Central Asia. Concurrently, developing countries maintained introducing new tax incentives and offered incentives more extensively. Especially, 46 percent of countries implemented novel tax incentives or boosted the present incentives in at least one industry between 2009 and 2015. In contrast, 24 percent of developing countries abolished or decreased tax incentives in at least one industry over the same period. The biggest increase in incentives was recorded in Sub-Saharan Africa, where 65 percent of countries implemented more recent or higher incentives, while only 21 percent discontinued existing incentives or decreased support rates. The only region where more countries reduced tax incentives when compared to the countries that increased them is South Asia . (Andersen, Kett & Uexkull, 2018, p. 77)

Figure 1. Cutting CIT Rates in Most Regions
Data Source: Andersen, Kett, & Uexkull, 2018, p. 78.

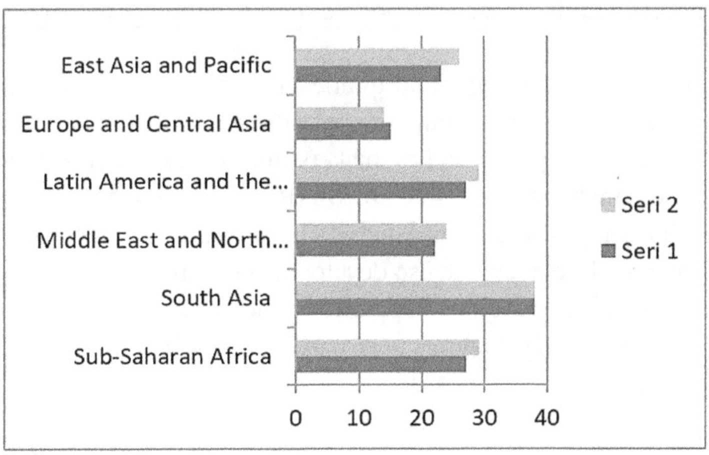

Cambridge Dictionary defines foreign direct investment (FDI) as "money that is invested in companies, property, or other assets by people or organizations from other countries" (Cambridge Dictionary)

Organization for Economic Cooperation and Development (OECD) Benchmark Definition of FDI is "FDI reflects the objective of establishing a lasting interest by a resident enterprise in one economy (direct investor) in an enterprise (direct investment enterprise) that is resident in an economy other than that of the direct investor. The direct or indirect ownership of 10% or more of the voting power of an enterprise resident in one economy by an investor resident in another economy is evidence of such a relationship" (Francis, 2018, p. 31). This definition is important because it serves as a criterion for the target audience and users of FDI statistics (OECD, 2008, p. 15).

FDI is necessary in terms of developed and developing countries as well. The economic importance of FDI could be itemized as follows (Balasubramanyam, Salisu & Sapsford, 2006, p. 28):

1. FDI is a complex formation requiring capital, technical knowledge and technology.
2. It contributes to growth by means of technology transfer and technology and skill diffusion in FDIs receiving countries.
3. The ability of FDI to encourage growth is governed by the trade regime kind applied in the host country in addition to the other benefits. In a protectionist regime, it is probable that FDI undermines economic growth, whereas a liberal trade regime might support it.
4. Many empirical studies put forward that the productivity of foreign corporations functioning in compatible industry groups is higher in comparison with that of local corporations in most efficiency criteria. However, whether the social rate of returns of FDI is on par with private rate of return is a topic of discussion.

In order to offer employment opportunities, introduce sophisticated knowledge and advanced technologies, reach out to global value chains, and expand and improve economic production capacity, policy makers aim to raise interest towards FDI, leading to a more inclusive economic growth (Reyes, 2018, p.51).

In conclusion, it is possible to argue that FDI has an impact on the economic growth process not only in developed but also developing countries. While foreign capital inflows are essential for developed countries to achieve sustainable growth, they are required for developing countries to promote growth and investment. Indirectly,

FDI is an alluring option to exploit for both developed and developing countries. Globally, organizations such as WTO and IMF strive for expanding investment inflows through lowering restrictions imposed on fund transfers. Likewise, from national perspective, some governments come up with policies that can achieve higher capital inflows so as to accelerate economic growth (Saini & Singhania, 2018, pp. 348-49).

In a regional review of FDI, it is possible to see a global decline in FDI flows by 23 percent in 2017 to $1.43 trillion from $1.87 trillion in 2016. The decline basically contradicts with other macroeconomic variables including GDP and trade, in which marked increases were observed in 2017 (United Nations, 2018, p. 1).

Figure 2 demonstrates a decline in FDI flows in developed and transition economies. However, FDI flows to developing economies did not show a change. Consequently, developing economies represent an increasing percentage in global FDI inflows in 2017. FDI inflows accounted for 47 per cent of the total FDI inflows in 2017, which was 36 per cent in 2016, when developing economies achieved almost zero growth rate. Considering that a slight increase is projected in 2018, this negative trend is a source of concern for policymakers all around the world, in developing countries particularly, for which international investment is of vital importance to achieve sustainable industrial advancement (United Nations, 2018, p. 1).

Figure 2. Deduction Rates in Corporate Income Tax (CIT) Rates in Most Regions
Data Source: United Nations, 2018, p. 2

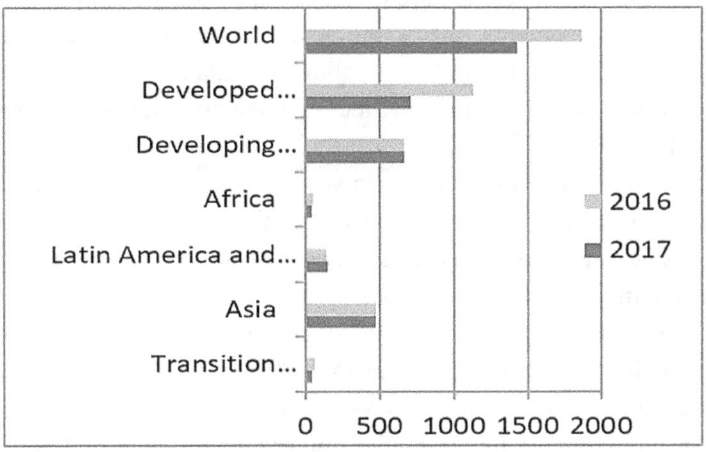

Corporate Tax Incentives With Respect to Foreign Direct Investments in Developing Countries

The share of FDIs is generally bigger in developed countries. Among these countries, the European Union countries and the United States are at the forefront. From the 1980s onwards, progress has been achieved slowly towards attracting FDI to the developing countries (Yavuz & Çiçek, 2010, pp. 71-72).

Foreign investors are reluctant to invest in developing countries for some reasons. This might be attributed to the inadequacy of infrastructure (road, port facilities, communication, etc.) and the poor legal and institutional structure in developing countries. Developing countries are willing to attract these investments to the country since they take into account the effect of FDIs on economic growth (Hines, 1998, p.1). FDIs are of particular importance for developing countries with low growth rates (Blomstrom & Kokko, 2003, p.20). FDIs create higher wages and employment opportunities, as well as economic growth, and have a positive impact on tax revenues to be obtained. Accordingly, economic development is positively affected (Becker, Fuest & Riedel, 2012, p. 1495).

From a policy perspective, attracting FDI is widely considered to be beneficial for the host country because this investment is thought to provide new growth opportunities, higher wages and employment, larger tax revenues—in short, a higher welfare level.

Countries that aim to attract foreign direct investments implement a variety of policies. Economic, political, and social stability, entry and operational regulations, foreign affiliates treatment standards, market function and structure policies, international FDI agreements, privatization and trade policies and harmony of FDI and tax policies are among these policies (Mallampally & Sauvant, 1999). Although there are several factors that affect FDI, the present study scrutinized how tax policies affected FDI.

In order to improve the investment climate with the aim of increasing FDI while setting the development goals, the central and local governments in countries raised their awareness of the importance of financial incentives such as tax deductions (Christiansen, Oman & Charlton, 2003, p. 3).

The effect of taxes on the determination of FDI decisions has grown with the growth of globalization, especially after the 1990s. The fact that export-oriented firms are faced with the competitive pressure emerged in the international markets as a result of globalization increases the importance of tax incentives and cause the firms to tend to compare the tax system and policies of the countries when making an evaluation among investment alternatives (Aktan & Vural, 2010, p. 36). Foreign direct investments prefer countries with low tax burden and high public goods production. On one hand, taxes, which constitute the most important source of public revenues, and on the other, foreign investments affect national policy choices. Developed country investors prefer developing countries as investment areas for various reasons. For example, low market competition, cheap labor force and low exchange rates are among the reasons for this choice (Bazo, 2008, pp. 1-2). Studies based on surveys and econometric analyses conducted by World Bank Group on various investors, which investigated the effects of tax incentives on FDI, show that a 10% increase in tax rates in developing countries reduced FDI by 0.45 points (Peters & Kiabel, 2015, p. 13).

Taxes, especially corporate tax, are one of the factors affecting net profit. High tax rates may cause the investments to be directed towards countries with low effective tax rates (Aktan & Vural, 2010, p. 37). Thus, the role of tax incentives in increasing FDI and capacity of tax incentives to attract FDI is still a matter of debate in public finance (Munongo, Akanbi & Robinson, 2017, p. 152).

Various problems could be encountered in the overall effectiveness of tax incentives, which are considered as an important policy tool in attracting FDI.

Certain costs arise due to tax incentives and these costs significantly affect the efficiency of the tax incentives. There are generally four cost categories. These are (Zee, Stotsky & Ley, 2002, p. 1501):

1. Deviations between non-subsidized and subsidized investment,
2. Loss of state revenues due to subsidized taxes
3. Administrative costs related to tax incentives
4. The fact that tax incentive benefits that could lead to abuse and corruption.

There are also certain structural problems that could lead to increased inefficiency in tax incentives that are considered an important policy instrument for achieving economic growth and development that are among the main objectives in developing countries. These problems include poverty, problems in education and health services, low job opportunities, poor infrastructure and rampant corruption, economic instability, and political and social risks, as well as regional conflicts (Bazo, 2008, pp. 1-8).

Developing countries should be careful about what kind of tax incentives at which weight they should use. Indeed, tax incentives tend to create a burden on the budget if not properly used (Christiansen, Oman & Charlton, 2003, p. 3).

It is not clear which type of tax incentive is more effective in developing countries. There is no prescription on which incentives should be implemented to achieve the economic targets set for these nations. Thus, most countries that aim to increase tax revenues while increasing investments develop their tax incentive systems usually through trial and error (IMF, 2015, p. 3; Bazo, 2008, p. 3).

Although the effect of cost-based instruments, such as tax allowances and credits on new investments is significant, these are not preferred by developing countries. These incentives require superior design features. Contrary to profit-based incentives, the cost of a specific input or production factor can be lowered through cost-based incentives. Regarding investment allowances or credits, a firm might be entitled by the government to subtract a certain percentage of investment costs from the taxable income. The extent of the benefit for the receiving corporation is not associated with its profit level; however, it is linked to the size of the investment. These kinds of tools present a couple of advantages. They are free from the bias of profit-based incentives aimed at highly profitable corporations, and therefore, it is less probable for them to be biased toward corporations that would have made investment anyway. Abuse is also less likely in these ones because of profit shifting, and their magnitude is directly connected to the policy outcome that constituted their basis. Tax holidays and income tax exemptions are extensively used, although these are costly incentives that allow avoidance. This is often due to the weaknesses in tax administration structures in developing countries (Andersen, Kett & Uexkull, 2018, p. 77). These weaknesses make it difficult for the enterprises to invest, while allowing tax avoidance and evasion. (Munongo, Akanbi & Robinson, 2017, p. 154).

The fact that there are economic and political differences among the developing countries leads to several problems in the implementation of tax incentives. For example, the growth-oriented creation of tax policies is appropriate for a country, while the other may not be compatible. The tax policies implemented in developed countries or countries where tax incentives were successful in increasing investments may not be adequate for other countries. Investment incentives in countries with strong investment potential such as Hong Kong, China and Singapore provided the desired results. However, it is not possible for all developing countries to acquire the necessary infrastructure and human resources in a short period of time, thus countries are required to implement tax incentives based on specific national conditions (United Nations, 2017, p. 3).

In efficiency and productivity, the important factor is to design the tax incentives implemented globally so that these would not damage tax competition, rather than with an effective design (IMF, 2015, pp. 3-4).

Furthermore, tax practices in other countries are also important for attracting investments (Zolt, 2014, p.25). In addition, non-tax factors are considered to be more effective in increasing foreign direct investments rather than the tax incentives (Munongo, Akanbi & Robinson, 2017, pp. 153-154). For this purpose, a good infrastructure, macroeconomic stability and improvement of laws are considered as prerequisites (IMF, 2015, p. 4).

Moreover, this group of countries generally is not completely independent for political reasons to create their own tax regimes. Organizations such as the G20 and the OECD also have an impact on national tax systems. From a technical point of view, it could be argued that developing countries have inadequate governance capacity in the implementation of global tax regulations that are shaped by strong economies (Hearson, 201, pp. 3-4).

When the effectiveness of tax incentives is assessed with respect to FDI, another factor emerges. The performance of tax incentives might also show variation according to FDI motivation. FDIs are completely the same; among other things they differ from each other depending on the investor motivation. It is challenging to observe investor motivation in global FDI data available for review, and a singular categorization of industries by FDI motivation is not achievable. As a matter of fact, different motivations within different countries or even within the same country might trigger FDI in the same industry. Nevertheless, a fundamental distinction can be made between mainly market-seeking versus efficiency-seeking FDI industries in line with the share of the revenues acquired from exports versus domestic sales for illustration purposes. Natural resource–seeking FDI, which is the third type of motivation, could be distinguished with the extractive and agricultural industries. FDI in natural resource or efficiency-seeking industries are linked to a large export share, whereas market-seeking investments, by definition, essentially generate domestic sales (Andersen, Kett & Uexkull, 2018, pp. 80-82).

In developing countries, FDI has underwent a transformation from market-seeking and resource-seeking FDIs to more efficiency-seeking (vertical) FDIs (Nunnenkamp, 2002, p. 5).

FDIs in predominantly market-seeking industries constitute 48 percent of the projects in developing countries. They are followed by efficiency-seeking (47 percent) and natural resource–seeking (5 percent) projects. Nevertheless, FDI projects in natural resources, are likely to be bigger in capital investment, and therefore cover a higher share of overall FDI value in comparison with their share in the number of projects (Andersen, Kett & Uexkull, 2018, p.82).

Efficiency-seeking FDIs are export-oriented, and are of critical importance to export diversification. While efficiency-seeking FDIs are basically more difficult to be attracted, they can serve as more than a source of capital by means of creating new and more various employment opportunities which have greater productivity and value. They can also help the acquisition of expertise and the realization of technology transfers by increasing R&D and economic developments in the process (Fruman, 2016).

In industries with mainly efficiency-seeking FDI, competitiveness for FDIs is high, and developing countries widely introduce incentives. In industries like IT and electronics, machinery and equipment, automotive, air- and spacecraft, and biotechnology and pharmaceuticals which seek efficiency, most FDI projects concentrate on a limited number of host countries. Tax incentives should aim to attract efficiency-seeking investors, but it is essential to deal with the basics of the investment climate (Andersen, Kett & Uexkull, 2018, p. 82).

While the importance of tax incentives to increase FDI in developing countries is recognized, the importance of market size and transparency in choosing a country as an investment location should not be neglected. It should be noted that it is essential to prioritize human resources and infrastructure quality, and the incentives should be carefully constructed based on detailed calculations in a way not to disrupt the internal economic environment (Kaymak, 2005, pp. 101-102).

SOLUTIONS AND RECOMMENDATIONS

FDI has positive effects on economic growth and development of all countries, especially developing countries. Weaknesses of developing countries such as lower capital accumulation and lack of substructure are among most important reasons which restrict their competitiveness in international markets. From this perspective, increasing FDIs of developing countries has a distinct importance. The effectiveness of corporate tax incentives used in order to attract FDIs to the country has an important role in the success of these incentives. Tax incentives which are generally used in developing countries are tax holidays and preferential tax rates. Although incentives which directly decrease the cost of investment such as tax allowances and credits aim at investors who are looking for activity, and hence become more effective, they are rarely used. The reason why these types of incentives are not preferred much by developing countries is that it requires a strong tax management. As a result, it is possible to state that instead of implementing general tax incentives, it is important to use incentives which aim at directly increasing FDIs and attracting investors. Additionally, when investors prefer a place as the place of investment, it is also related to that country's macroeconomic stability and the investment climate emerging as a result of this. Strong tax managements and successful governances of developing countries shall be effective in the increase of FDIs.

FUTURE RESEARCH DIRECTIONS

In this study, types of corporate tax incentives generally used in developing countries towards FDI and the effectiveness of these incentives were evaluated. This study includes only developing countries. Accordingly, for further studies, developed countries can also be included and a comparative evaluation can be made.

CONCLUSION

In view of the positive impact of FDIs on economic growth, it is quite common for all countries to pursue efforts to increase FDIs by implementing various policies. FDIs have short term effects on capital accumulation and increase in economic activities and affect long-term economic growth due to external effects by contributing to technological advances, human capital and innovation in domestic corporations.

In general, the significance of FDIs for developing countries with low national investments and production due to lack of capital increased to achieve the goal of economic development.

Developing countries utilize various tax incentives to increase FDIs. Considering the tax competition in international markets, it is important to utilize the incentives effectively. Tax incentives vary based on industries, regions and income levels among developed countries.

Many developing countries remain heavily dependent on tax holidays and preferential tax rates. Actually, only a few developing countries use tax allowances and credits directly reducing the investment costs. This is due to the insufficient tax administration capacity of developing countries. Furthermore, efficiency-seeking investors should be the target of tax incentives. Since efficiency-seeking FDIs improve competitiveness, these are preferred by host countries. Thus, it is important for developing countries to utilize cost-based instruments to increase efficiency seeking investments rather than profit-based incentives. However, investment climate is also significant for this type of investments. It was determined that macroeconomic conditions, infrastructure and strong institutions were significant factors for the investment climate that improve the attractiveness of an economy for FDIs.

In conclusion, it is not possible to suggest that tax incentives, which are important in increasing FDIs in developing countries, are sufficient alone. Goal-oriented tax incentives should be enforced by a strong administrative capacity. Incentive design, transparency, and management is important. It is also necessary to highlight the effectiveness of tax policies and policies on sufficient infrastructure, macroeconomic stability, rule of law, etc.

REFERENCES

Aktan, C. C., & Vural, İ. Y. (2010). Globalleşme ve yabancı sermaye rekabeti. *Hukuk ve İktisat Araştırmaları Dergisi*, *2*(2), 24–48.

Andersen, M. R., Kett, B. R., & Uexkull, E. V. (2018). Corporate tax incentives and FDI in developing countries. *Global Investment Competitiveness Report*.

Antonakakis, N., & Gabriele, T. (2015). Robust determinants of OECD FDI in developing countries: Insights from Bayesian model averaging. *Cogent Economics & Finance*, *3*(1), 1–25. doi:10.1080/23322039.2015.1095851

Baggerman-Noudari, K., & Offermanns, R. (2016). Foreign direct investment in developing countries: Some tax considerations and other related legal matters. *Bulletin for International Taxation*, *70*(6), 310–321.

Balasubramanyam, V. N., Salisu, M., & Sapsford, D. (2006). Foreign direct investment as an engine of growth. *The Journal of International Trade & Economic Development*, *8*(1), 27–40. doi:10.1080/09638199900000003

Bazo, A. E. (2008). Tax incentives offered by developing countries: Attracting foreign investment or creating disaster? *Tax Notes International*, *52*(4), 1–23.

Becker, J., Fuest, C., & Riedel, N. (2012). Corporate tax effects on the quality and quantity of FDI. *European Economic Review*, *56*(8), 1495–1511. doi:10.1016/j.euroecorev.2012.07.001

Bellak, C., & Leibrecht, M. (2009). Do low corporate income tax rates attract FDI? Evidence from eight central and east European countries. *Applied Economics*, *41*(21), 2691–2703. doi:10.1080/00036840701320217

Bellak, C., Leibrecht, M., & Damijan, J. P. (2009). Infrastructure endowment and corporate income taxes as determinants of foreign direct investment in central and eastern European countries. *World Economy*, *32*(2), 267–290. doi:10.1111/j.1467-9701.2008.01144.x

Benassy-Quere, A., Fontagne, L., & Lahreche-Revil, A. (2005). How does FDI react to corporate taxation? *International Tax and Public Finance*, *12*(5), 583–603. doi:10.100710797-005-2652-4

Beyer, J. (2002). Please invest in our country. How successful were the tax incentives for foreign investment in transition countries? *Communist and Post-Communist Studies*, *35*(2), 191–211. doi:10.1016/S0967-067X(02)00007-7

Bird, R. M., & Zolt, E. M. (2008). Tax policy in emerging countries, environment and planning C. *Government and Policy.*, *26*(1), 73–86. doi:10.1068/cav3

Blomström, M., & Kokko, A. (2003). *The economics of foreign direct investment incentives*. CEPR.

Bolnick, B. (2004). *Effectiveness and economic impact of tax incentives in the SADC region*. Gaborone: SADC Tax Subcommittee, SADC Trade, Industry, Finance and Investment Directorate.

Brodzka, A. (2013). Tax incentives in emerging economies. *Business Systems and Economics*, *3*(1), 26–36.

Cambridge Dictionary. (n.d). Retrieved from https://dictionary.cambridge.org/tr

Christiansen, H., Oman, C., & Charlton, A. (2003). *Incentives-based competition for foreign direct investment, the case of Brazil.* OECD Publishing.

Effiok, S. O., Tapang, A. T., & Eton, O. E. (2013). The impact of tax policy and incentives on foreign direct investment and economic growth: Evidence from export processing zones in Nigeria. *European Journaal of Commerce and Management Research*, *2*(9), 191–197.

Francis, S. (2018). Foreign direct investment concepts: Implications for negotiations. *Economic and Political Weekly*, *45*(22), 31–36.

Fruman, C. (2016). Why does efficiency-seeking FDI matter? World Bank. Retrieved from https://blogs.worldbank.org/psd/why-does-efficiency-seeking-fdi-matter

Gastanaga, V. M., Nugent, J. B., & Pashamova, B. (1998). Host country reforms and FDI inflows: How much difference do they make? *World Development*, *26*(7), 1299–1314. doi:10.1016/S0305-750X(98)00049-7

Giray, F. (2008). *Vergi teşvik sistemi.* Bursa: Ezgi Kitabevi Publishing.

Hearson, M. (2017). The challenges for developing countries in international tax justice. *The Journal of Development Studies*, *54*(10), 1932–1938. doi:10.1080/00220388.2017.1309040

Hers, J., Witteman, J., Rougoor, W., & Buiren, K. (2018). *The Role of Investment Hubs in FDI, Economic Development and, Trade Ireland, Luxembourg, Mauritius, the Netherlands, and Singapore.* Investment Facilitation Forum.

Hines, J. R. (1998). *"Tax sparing" and direct Investment in developing countries.* NBER.

Holland, D., & Vann, R. J. (1998). Income tax incentives for investment. Tax Law Design and Drafting, 2, 2-9.

International Monetary Found (IMF). (2015). *Options For Low Income Countrıes' Effective And Efficient Use Of Tax Incentives For Investment.*

James, S. (2010). *Incentives and investments: Evidence and policy implications. World Bank.* Washington, DC: Investment Climate Advisory Services of the Word Bank Group.

Kaymak, H. (2005). Yabancı doğrudan yatırımları artırmak için teşvikler gerekli ve/veya yeterli mi?.*Maliye Dergisi, 149*(Mayıs-Aralık), 74-104.

Kinda, T. (2014). *The quest for non-resource-based foreign direct investment: Do taxes matter?* Washington, D.C: IMF.

Klemm, A., & Parys, S. V. (2010). *Empirical Evidence on the Effects of Tax Incentives.*

Kransdorff, M. (2010). Tax incentives and foreign direct investment in South Africa. *Journal of Sustainable Development, 3*(1), 68–84.

Llambi, C., Rius, A., Carbajal, F., Carrasco, P., & Cazulo, P. (2017). *Are taxes credits effective ın developing countries? The recent Uruguayan experience.* Development Bank of Latin America Working Paper, No 2017/5.

Mallampally, P., & Sauvant, K. P. (1999). Foreign direct investment in developing countries. *Finance & Development, 36*(1), 1–3.

Morisset, J., & Pirnia, N. (2000). *How tax policy and incentives affect foreign direct investment a review.* The World Bank and International Finance Corporation Foreign Investment Advisory Service.

Munongo, S., Akanbi, O. A., & Robinson, Z. (2017). Do tax incentives matter for investment? A literature review. *Business and Economic Horizons, 13*(2), 152–168. doi:10.15208/beh.2017.12

Nielsen, L. (2011). *Classifications of countries based on their level of development: How it is done and how it could be done.*

Nunnenkamp, P. (2002). *Determinants of FDI in developing countries: Has globalization changed the rules of the game?*

OECD. (1995). *Taxation and foreign direct investment: The experince of the economies in transition.* Paris: OECD.

OECD. (2007). Tax incentives for investment – A global perspective: Experiences in MENA and non-MENA countries. Retrieved from http://www.oecd.org/mena/competitiveness/38758855.pdf

OECD. (2008a). *OECD Benchmark definition of foreign direct investment* (4th ed.).

OECD. (2008b). *Policy brief, tax effects on foreign direct investment.* Retrieved from https://www.oecd.org/investment/investment-policy/40152903.pdf

Olaleye, M. O., Riro, G. K., & Memba, F. S. (2016). Effect of reduced company income tax incentives on foreign direct investment in listed Nigerian manufacturing companies. European Journal of Business. *Economics and Accountancy*, *4*(1), 39–54.

Peters, G. T., & Kiabel, B. D. (2015). Tax incentives and foreign direct investment in Nigeria. *IOSR Journal of Economics and Finance*, *6*(5), 10–20.

Piketty, T. (2013). *Yirmi birinci yüzyılda kapital.(Çev: Hande Koçak)*. İstanbul: Türkiye İş Bankası Kültür Publishing.

Quora. (n.d.). *How does the International Monetary Fund judge a country as having a developing or developed economy?* Retrieved from https://www.quora.com/How-does-the-International-Monetary-Fund-judge-a-country-as-having-a-developing-or-developed-economy

Reyes, J. D. (2018). *Effects of FDI on high growth firms in developing countries. Global Investment Competitiveness Report*. Foreign Investor Perspectives and Policy Implications.

Saini, N., & Singhania, M. (2017). Determinants of FDI in developed and developing countries: A quantitative analysis using GMM. *Journal of Economic Studies (Glasgow, Scotland)*, *4*(2), 348–382. doi:10.1108/JES-07-2016-0138

Slusarczyk, B. (2018). Tax incentives as a main factor to attract foreign direct investments in Poland. *Administratie si Management Public*, *30*(30), 67–81. doi:10.24818/amp/2018.30-05

TDK. (n.d.). Retrieved from http://www.tdk.gov.tr

Tekin, A. (2006). Vergi teşvikleri ve ekonomik etkileri. *Dumlupınar Üniversitesi Sosyal Bilimler Dergisi*, *16*, 301–316.

Tung, S., & Cho, S. (2000). The impact of tax incentives on foreign direct investment in China. *Journal of International Accounting, Auditing & Taxation*, *9*(2), 105–135. doi:10.1016/S1061-9518(00)00028-8

Ugwu, J. I. (2018). Tax incentives and foreign direct investment (fdı): Implication for export promotion in Nigeria, Ghana and South Africa, post ifrs adoption. *International Journal in Management and Social Science*, *6*(9), 31–52.

United Nations. (2018). *Design and assessment of tax incentives in developing countries*. New York.

United Nations ESCAP. (2017). *Tax incentives and tax base protection in developing countries*. Retrieved from https://www.unescap.org/sites/default/files/S3_Tax-Incentives-and-Tax-Protection-Base.pdf

Van Parys, S., & James, S. (2010). The effectiveness of tax incentives in attracting investment: Panel data evidence from the CFA Franc zone. *International Tax and Public Finance*, *17*(4), 400–429. doi:10.100710797-010-9140-1

Wei, S. J. (2000). How taxing is corruption on international investors? *The Review of Economics and Statistics*, *82*(1), 1–11. doi:10.1162/003465300558533

Wilson, J. (1999). Theories of tax competition. *National Tax Journal*, *5*(2), 269–304.

Yavuz, A., & Çiçek, S. (2010). Doğrudan yabancı yatırımlar-vergi ilişkisi: Bazı Avrupa Birliği ülkeleri ve Türkiye. *Gaziantep Üniversitesi Sosyal Bilimler Dergisi*, *9*(1), 69–85.

Zee, H. H., Stotsky, G. J., & Ley, E. (2002). Tax incentives for business investment: A primer for policy makers in developing countries. *World Development*, *30*(9), 1497–1516. doi:10.1016/S0305-750X(02)00050-5

Zolt, E.M. (2014). Tax incentives: Protecting the tax base, papers on selected topics in protecting the tax base of developing countries.

ADDITIONAL READING

Alzaidy, G., Bin Niaz Ahmad, M. N., & Lacheheb, Z. (2017). The impact of foreign-direct investment on economic growth in Malaysia: The role of financial development. *International Journal of Economics and Financial Issues*, *7*(3), 382–388.

Ateş, L. (2017). *Yatırım vergi teşvik politikasının hukuki çerçevesi*. İstanbul: Oniki Levha Yayıncılık.

Barcena, A., Prado, A., Cimoli, M., & Perez, R. (2016). *Foreign direct investment in Latin America and the Caribbean*. Santiago: United Nations.

Chaudhuri, S., & Mukhopadhyay, U. (2014). *Foreign direct investment in developing countries: A theoretical evaluation*. New Delhi: Springer. doi:10.1007/978-81-322-1898-2

Hattari, R., & Rajan, R. S. (2011). How different are fdi and fpi flows?: Distance and capital market integration. *Journal of Economic Integration*, *26*(3), 499–525. doi:10.11130/jei.2011.26.3.499

Öner, E. (2018). *Vergi hukuku*. Ankara: Seçkin Yayınları.

Quazi, R. M. (2014). Corruption and foreign direct investment in East Asia and South Asia: An econometric study. *International Journal of Economics and Financial Issues*, *4*(2), 231–242.

Şenyüz, D., Yüce, M., & Gerçek, A. (2019). *Vergi hukuku*. Bursa: Ekin Yayınevi.

KEY TERMS AND DEFINITIONS

Corporate Tax: An objective, direct and flat-rate income tax excised on the revenues of economic units considered as corporations.

Developing Country: The countries that are yet to achieve the status of a socially rich, developed and powerful nation, but strive in that direction.

Direct Tax Incentives: Incentives such as low corporate tax rate, tax holidays, investment allowances, and accelerated depreciation provided for economic entities.

Effectiveness of Tax Incentives: A tax incentive is a part of a national tax system designed to promote an economic activity. Tax incentives could have positive and negative impacts on an economy. Resource allocation refers to government tax revenue losses due to tax incentives.

Foreign Direct Investments (FDIs): Investments in corporations located in another country by corporations in a country by purchasing a corporation, providing the initial capital for a new corporation or increasing the capital of an existing corporation.

Indirect Tax Incentives: Incentives generally provided to certain export-oriented industries or selected non-export-oriented industries. Export incentives could be implemented via customs duty exemption and Value Added Tax Exemption, while non-export-oriented incentives are implemented via free trade zone incentives.

Tax Incentives: Tools that aim to reduce or remove the tax burden excised by the state on economic entities.

Chapter 12
The Impact of Devaluation on Balance of Trade:
The Case of Ethiopia

Suadiq Mehammed Hailu
https://orcid.org/0000-0003-3270-1357
Cukurova University, Turkey

Abdela Yasin Saliya
Cukurova University, Turkey

ABSTRACT

The aim of this chapter is to investigate the short and long-run impact of devaluation of the trade balance of Ethiopia. Devaluation has been used as a measure to improve trade balance. The data was collected from the World Bank for the years 1990 to 2017 and analyzed by applying an Autoregressive Distributed Lag (ARDL) approach and an Error Correction Model (ECM). The empirical findings show that the long run Real Effective Exchange Rate (REER) significantly and negatively correlated with the trade balance. The error correction coefficient which shows the adjustment of disequilibrium in the subsequent year is also significant. The empirical result indicated that devaluation of the Birr can improve the trade balance of Ethiopia. However, in reality, the trade balance of Ethiopia is not improved through a consecutive Birr devaluation. This may be resulted from the non-responsiveness of import to devaluation of the Birr, shortage of import substitute domestic products and the dependency of exports on primary agriculture products.

DOI: 10.4018/978-1-5225-9566-3.ch012

INTRODUCTION

In the globalization era, countries in trade deficit are applying different measures to adjust their trade deficit. Among these measures, devaluation is one of the well-known methods to improve trade deficit. The relationship between balance of trade and devaluation has been explaining by J-curve effect and Marshall-Lerner Condition. The Marshall-Lerner condition implies that if the sum effect of elasticities for import and export is greater than one, devaluation of local currency will improve trade balance in long-run (Bahmani-Oskooee, 1991). J-curve effect is used to explain the reduction and gradual corrections of a country`s trade balance deficit as a result of home currency devaluation. This effect may be derived from the low level of import and export elasticity immediately after the times of devaluation and higher over some time. Among the reasons of low elasticity after devaluation is the unfinished process of pervious imports and exports. It may need time to adjust imports and exports based on the revised exchange rate (Hacker & Hatemi, 2003).

The J-curve effect holds that a country's currency depreciation causes its trade balance to deteriorate for a short time, followed by a flattening-out period, and then a significant improvement occurs for an extended period. When a country's currency depreciates against the currencies of major trading partners, the country's exports tend to rise, and imports fall, which improves the trade balance. In the short run, however, a country's trade deficit may deteriorate just after its currency depreciates, because the higher cost of imports will more than offset the reduced volume of imports (Kim & Kim, 2006).

Ethiopia is one of fastest growing country in the world. The economy of Ethiopia is depending on agriculture and primary agriculture products are the main source of export income. Even though, the trade balance of Ethiopia is in deficit for serval years, the Ethiopian government is trying to improve the quality and quantity of export by taking different measures. The measures include devaluation of home currency (Ethiopian Birr), eliminating export taxes (excluding coffee), financial supporting to exporters, liberalization of international trade, launching of different export incentives and declaration of an opened investment law with several encouragement actions (International Trade Center, 2001).

The main aim of this chapter is to investigate empirically the short run and long run effects of birr devaluation on Ethiopian balance of trade. This means to assess the existence of Marshall-Lerner condition and J-curve effect in Ethiopia after the end of the socialist Derg regime fixed exchange rate system. The national bank of

Ethiopia (NBE) devalued birr in terms of foreign currencies many times. The main target of devaluation is to encourage export and to shrink balance of payment deficit (Maasho, 2017). In this chapter, the authors examined the effect of devaluation of birr on the trade balance of Ethiopia and based on the empirical result, researchers suggested recommendation to improve the trade balance of Ethiopia.

BACKGROUND

International trade is a backbone for every country's economic development. A country import goods and services which are not available in the home from abroad and export goods and services which are surplus from internal usage to foreign countries (Vijayasri, 2013).

There are different determinates of international trade between countries. According to studies done by Warner & Kreinin (1983), Ratnayake (1994), Bahmani-Oskooee (1986), Boskov & Lazaroski (2011), Márquez-Ramos (2007) and Bialynicka-Birula (2014) factors which affect trade flows between countries are exchange rate between country`s currency, real income, price of imported/ exported goods and services, transportation cost, tariff, quota, quality of imported/ exported goods and services, trade infrastructure, geographical factors, technological innovation, distance, political stability and culture.

Every country records their international trade transactions. This record is called balance of payment. In the balance of payment record primarily countries record their exported and imported goods and services. The difference between export and import is known as balance of trade. Export exceeded import means a country is in trade surplus and the reverse is in trade deficit. Based on their comparative advantages in political, social, economic and technological factors, countries struggle to export more than their import from abroad. As stated by United Nations Conference on Trade and Development (UNCTAD) in 2017, key statistics and trends in international trade report, China and Germany achieve the highest trade surplus. On the other hand, the developed nations including USA and UK, and several developing countries are in trade deficit position.

Countries with trade deficit position are taking different measures to correct their balance of trade. Among these measures, devaluation of local currency in terms of foreign currency is the well-known strategy to improve trade deficit. When a country`s local currency devaluated against foreign currency, a country`s goods and services will be cheap in international market and it facilitates to increase export.

On the other hand, foreign goods and services will be expensive in local market and import will fall. The total effect will improve trade balance (Eun & Resnick, 2010). For instance, if the exchange rate of the Ethiopian 'Birr' (local money) is increasing in relation to other countries currency, the balance of payments position for the Ethiopian economy will also be growing and as such will lead to an advantageous position in Ethiopia's Balance of Payments. This is possible because as the Exchange Rate of the Ethiopian Birr in relation to other currencies is increasing. So, Ethiopia's exports would be cheaper, and its import products would be more expensive, thus preferable to consume domestic goods and services than foreign products.

In doing of international trade, one county's currency should be converted into another country's currency. The value of a currency in terms of another currency is called exchange rate. In general, exchange rate systems are categorized as fixed, freely floated, managed float and pegged exchange rate system. Freely floated exchange rate system is an exchange rate system, the values of one currency in terms of another currency is determined by market forces i.e. by the demand and supply conditions of that currency. Under managed float exchange rate system, exchange rates are permitted to fluctuate daily by the national banks of the country. In case of pegged exchange rate system, countries pegged their home currency's in to one of another country's currency or an index of currencies (Madura, 2011).

Ethiopia started the process of issuing fiat money currency in 1941. In 1945, the Ethiopian monetary system was launched based on a currency is known as "the Ethiopian dollar" (Mauri, 2010). The monetary and banking proclamation No. 99 of 1976 introduced the new Ethiopia medium of exchange is known as "birr" instead of the previous Ethiopian Dollar. During the socialist Derg regime (1974-1991), Ethiopia applied a fixed exchange rate system with the rate of 1 US $ to 2.07 birr. In this era, Ethiopian birr was overvalued in terms of major currencies including the US dollar (Degefa, 2001). After the failure of the socialist regime, the transitional government of Ethiopia took the power and made a lot of reforms. On October 1992, Ethiopian birr was devalued by 142% from its fixed rate of 2.07 birr/ US dollar to 5 birr/Us dollar (Eshetu, 2017).

The term devaluation and revaluation are usually used to express the adjustments in exchange rates that made by the monetary authorities or formally central banks in fixed or managed float exchange rate system. Devaluation is the reduction of home currency value against foreign currencies. On the other hand, when the exchange rates are allowed to be free and flexible without the interference of government in response to changes in market condition i.e. the demand and supply of a currency is termed as appreciation or depreciation. The diminution of one currency price against other currencies in response to the demand and supply of the currency is called deprecation (Bekaert & Hodrick, 2017). However, the increase of one currency price against the other currencies in reply to the demand and supply of the currency is called appreciation.

According to Mises (1996), the main objectives of devaluation are to encourage exports and to reduce import, to increase farm products price in terms of domestic currency, to decrease sovereign debt burdens, to attract foreign tourists visiting and to discourage state's own citizens to visit foreign country and to maintain high nominal wage rates. In short run, the exchange rate between two currencies is determined by the changes in inflation, interest rate, income level, government control and by the change in expectation of future exchange rate in the two countries (Madura, 2011).

Currently, Ethiopia is one of the countries which applied managed system of floating exchange rates. The National Bank of Ethiopia devalued the birr multiple times starting from 1992 to the recent year 2017. The table below shows the devaluation year and the percentage of devaluation.

As clearly stated in table 1, birr was devalued more than seven times within 26 years. The main reason for devaluation is to expand export and make import more expensive and the total effect of this expected to improve trade balance.

As shown in figure 1, starting from in 1992, Ethiopian birr had been devaluated in terms of US dollar.

The effect of devaluation on the balance of payments will depend on the behavior of the following variables: i) Merchandise exports; ii) invisible earnings; iii) imports; and iv) private capital movement (da Costa, 1966).

Ethiopian economy is deepening on agriculture and agricultural products are took the highest share in total export. Ethiopia's overall balance of payments during the review period was largely dictated by the merchandise trade balance. The main merchandize export items are coffee, oilseeds, leather and leather products, pulses, meat and meat products, fruits and vegetables, live animals, chat, Gold, flower and

Table 1. The birr devaluation years and percentage of devaluation

No.	Devaluation Year	From Birr/1 US $	To Birr/1 US $	Devaluation in%
1	1992	2.0700	5.0000	142.0%
2	1996	6.2900	8.5000	35.14%
3	2008	9.9500	10.9500	10.05%
4	2009	11.3400	12.5600	10.76%
5	2010	13.6935	16.4685	20.27%
6	2017	23.5910	27.2747	15.61%

Source: World Bank Development Indicators (1992-2017)

Figure 1. The birr per dollar exchange rate from 1960 to 2017
Source: Computed by authors

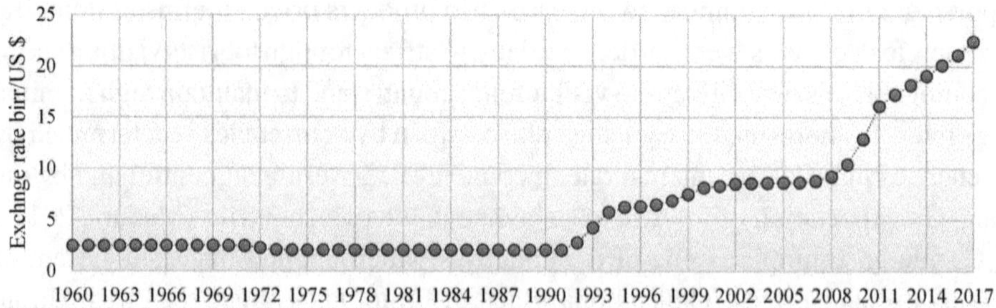

electricity service. According to the national bank of Ethiopia 2016/2017 annual report, out of the total export of Ethiopia to the rest of the world, coffee, oilseeds, pulses, chat, flower and gold took a share of 30.4%, 12.1%, 9.6%, 9.4%, 7.5%, and 7.2%, respectively.

Ethiopia is importing capital goods, consumer goods, fuel and semi-finished products. Capital goods like transportation vehicles, machineries, agricultural and industrial products accounted 38.2%, consumer goods include durable and non-durable goods took 31% and petroleum products accounted 11.5% from the total imports of Ethiopia in 2016/2017.

Figure 2. Import, export and trade balance of Ethiopia
Source: Computed by authors

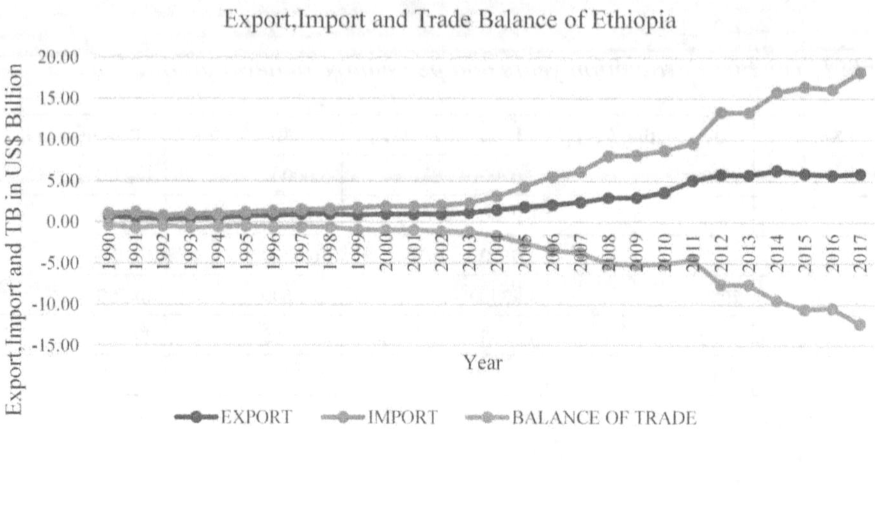

As shown in figure 2, from 1990 to 2017, the total amount of imports of Ethiopia is above the total amount of exports. This shows that Ethiopia is in the position of trade deficit for a long period of time. Theoretically, when countries devalued their currency export will increase and import will decrease. In case of Ethiopia, import is not sensitive to devaluation. The amount of import grows more than the amount of exports. Between 1990-2017 on average, the total amount export increases by 10%[1] and the amount of import grows by 13%[2]. Therefore, the policy applied by Ethiopia to improve trade balance i.e. devaluation of birr is not effective due to the non-sensitivity of import to devaluation. This result is in conformity with Kim and Kim (2006). They stated that, local currency devaluation may not improve a trade deficit due to when products are not sold as expected in international market after devaluation, and when local citizens continue to buy imported foreign products irrespective of their increased prices.

LITERATURE REVIEW

There are several factors which affect trade balance. Among these factors, most of studies concerned with devaluation of local currency. The association between trade balance and devaluation is tested by researchers in different format. Researches conducted in developed country like USA, UK, Japan, Germany and china shows that there is a cointegration between exchange rate and balance of trade. Anju and Uma (1999) tested J-curve effect for Japan using quarterly data from 1975:1 to 1996:4 through error correction model. The finding states that there is a long run relationship between exchange rate and trade balance. This mean J-curve holds for Japan under the studied period. Arize (2017) studied the connection between real exchange rate and trade balance for USA by implementing autoregressive distributed (ARDL) method. He used quarterly data from 1980:1 to 2015:3 and changed in to logarithmic value. The result of the study indicates that the devaluation of US dollar will substantially improve trade balance. Bahmani-Oskooee and Niroomand (1998) by using Johansen and Juselius cointegration technique assessed the existence of long-run Marshall–Lerner condition about 30 countries including USA, UK and Germany. The found that the existence of the condition i.e. in the long run, devaluation could deteriorate balance of trade deficit.

Bahmani-Oskooee (1985) conducted a research on four developing countries (Greece, India, Korea and Thailand) to assess the presence of J-curve effect by collecting quarterly data from 1973 to 1980. The result of the study shows the existence of J-curve. Boyd, Caporale and Smith (2001) analyzed the effects of exchange rate on balance of trade for 8 Organization for Economic Co-operation and Development (OECD) countries through vector autoregressive distributed lag (VARDL) model. They collected quarterly data from IMF for the year 1975 to 1996. The result of the study suggests that Marshall–Lerner condition fulfilled in the long run. Reis Gomes and Senne (2005) conducted a study to assess the effect of devaluation on trade balance in Brazil by using Vector error correction model (VEC-M). They collected 108 monthly data from January 1990 to December 1998. Finally, they found that there is a long run cointegration between exchange rate and balance of trade. The short run J-curve effect also hold.

There are several researches also done to evaluate the connection between exchange rate and devaluation in developing countries. According to Steinherr (1980), the devaluation of local currency in terms of foreign currency for developing countries is an expensive policy measure. Because the decision is taken based on computable past inflation level and optimal structure of production. Otherwise devaluation my not achieve its intended target. Reinhart (1995) studied the effects of devaluation on balance of trade for 12 developing countries from Africa, Asia and Latin America. He used Dickey-Fuller (DF) and Augminted Dickey-Fuller (ADF) for check unit root test. The researcher conclude that devaluation will improve trade balance for Asian and Latin American countries. However, the finding shows that devaluation will not improve African countries trade balance. Because, the dependency of African export on primary commodity products may not be responsive for devaluation.

There are different arguments about the effects of devaluation of birr in Ethiopian economy in general and trade balance in particular. Peter (2010) states that the devaluation of local currency for developing countries like Ethiopia will never improve economic development. It benefits only exporters and everybody else will suffered. For instance, if government is not increase salary in proportion with devaluation, employee`s will harmed by inflation. In addition, the external debt burden also increase as birr devalues. The latest devaluation of birr (15.61%) was done by National Bank of Ethiopia on October 2017 to encourage export and improve balance of trade. This decision was welcomed by both IMF and World Bank (Massho, 2017).

Genye (2011) assessed the relationship between exchange rate and per capita growth in Ethiopia through time serious data for 30 years from 1980-2010.The result of the study shows that there is a negative relationship between devaluation and per capita GDP. Nega (2015) studied the effects of devaluation on Ethiopian balance of trade by using yearly data from 1985/86 to 2012/13. The result shows that there is an increase in export after devaluation but no improvement in balance of trade. This is resulted from non-sensitivity of import with devaluation in case of Ethiopia. The latest study done by Eshetu (2017) applied Vector Error Correction model to check the existence of J-curve effect for Ethiopia. The result shows that J-curve effect exist for Ethiopia.

To summarize, studies done in developed countries to analyze the effect of devaluation on balance of trade are concluded that devaluation of local currency could have a significant effect to improve trade deficit. The authors of this chapter also have similar idea of these research findings. As developed countries have several alternative local products, by devaluing their currency they can make local products cheap in the international market and imported products will be expensive. The final effect will improve trade balance. On the other hand, researches done in developing country shows that devaluation is not a suitable measure to improve their trade balance. This results from the shortage of substitute local products for consumption. Therefore, the local residents may continue to buy imported products without considering the price increment. Furthermore, the side effect of devaluation on local peoples may be more than the intended purpose of trade balance improvement.

MAIN FOCUS OF THE CHAPTER

The focus of the chapter is to check whether devaluation is a correct measure to improve the trade balance of Ethiopia or not. The authors of this chapter believe that, using devaluation as a measure to improve the trade balance is depends on the local production capacity of the country. For instance, for countries that export processed and technological products, if it devalues its home currency will significantly improve its trade balance by expanding its export since its product will be cheap in international market. In case of countries exporting agricultural products like Ethiopia, devaluing the home currency may increase the amount of export but cannot improve trade balance. Because, those countries most of processed products are imported from abroad and even after devaluation, import may not decrease. This is because of processed and substitutable products are not sufficiently produced in the home country.

On the other hand, the measure of devaluation aimed to expand export affects the country by decreasing the power of paying external debts and affect people by creating inflation. According to Federal Reserve Bank of St. Louis (2018) the official external debt of Ethiopia is $30.476 billion. With this amount of external debit using devaluation as a measure to expand export is putting the country in difficulties. This means, as the birr devalued continuously, Ethiopia needs more local currency to pay the interest and principal in terms of foreign currency. In addition to this, as the birr devalued in terms of foreign currency, products in the local market will be expensive and that results inflation. To compensate the inflation, government must increase salary for workers. Unfortunately, until now, with a continuous devaluation of birr government cannot increase the salary. In general, devaluation affects the people negatively by creating life expensiveness in the country. From the abovementioned perspectives, the side effect of devaluation will be more than the intended effect to expand export.

DATA, METHODOLOGY AND MODEL SPECIFICATION

Data

Most of empirical analysis frequently used quarterly data. However, due to unavailability of quarterly data for selected variables, yearly data is collected for the period of 1990 to 2017 from World Bank - Development Indicators (WDI) of 2017 report. All variables are converted in to logarithm form. The name of variables and their descriptions are presented in table 2. *Ln* used to indicate the data are changed in to logarithm format.

Methodology

To assess the short run and long run relationship between real effective exchange rate and balance of trade, the researchers applied Autoregressive Distributive Lag Model (ARDL). Autoregressive Distributive Lag Model (ARDL) is superior for small sample size and for variables combined in different order, I (0), I (1) and a mixture of both orders. Steps to apply ARDL cointegration test are: checking the stationarity and non-stationarity of variables (unit root test), testing the presence of

Table 2. Variable definitions and sources

Variables	Definition	Data Source
*Ln*GDP	Current Gross Domestic Product, PPP (US$ Billion)	World Bank
*Ln*REER	Real Effective Exchange Rate based on CPI	World Bank
*Ln*TB	Trade balance=Export/Import	Own calculation
Export	Total goods and services exported (US$ Billion)	World Bank
Import	Total goods and services imported (US$ Billion)	World Bank
*Ln*EXD	Total External debt (US$ Billion)	World Bank

log run cointegration between variables (cointegration test), selecting the suitable lag length for variables, specifying long term relationship model and short run relationship (Error Correction Model) and finally check the model stability (Nkoro, & Uko, 2016).

Model Specification

From the stated variables in table 2, *Ln*TB is the dependent variable and *Ln*REER, *Ln*GDP and *Ln*EXD are independent variables. Therefore, our trade balance equation estimates as follows:

$$LnTB_t = \alpha_0 + \beta_1 LnREER_t + \beta_2 LnGDP_t + \beta_3 LnEXD_t + \varepsilon_t \tag{1}$$

where, $LnTB_t$ is the logarithm of export to import ratio, $LnREER_t$ is the logarithm of real effective exchange rate, $LnGDP_t$ is the logarithm of gross domestic product, $LnEXD_t$ is the logarithm of total external debt and ε_t is an error term.

If the bond test results show long run cointegration between variables, we can specify the long run and short run ARDL Trade Balance model. The long run ARDL trade balance model presented as follows:

$$\nabla LnTB_t = \alpha_0 + \beta_1 LnTB + \beta_2 LnREER_{t-1} + \beta_3 LnGDP_{t-1} + \beta_4 LnEXD_{t-1} + \sum_{i=1}^{P} \alpha_{1i} \Delta LnTB_{t-1}$$
$$+ \sum_{i=1}^{q} \alpha_{2i} \Delta LnREER_{t-1} + \sum_{i=1}^{r} \alpha_{3i} \Delta LnGDP_{t-1} + \sum_{i=1}^{s} \alpha_{4i} \Delta LnEXD_{t-1} + \varepsilon_t \tag{2}$$

After testing a long run relationship between variables, the subsequent step is the estimation of short run relationship (Error correction model) to determine the speed of recovering disequilibrium to long run equilibrium. The ECM trade balance equation is presented as follows:

$$\Delta LnTB_t = \alpha_0 + \sum_{i=1}^{P} \alpha_{1i} \Delta LnTB_{t-1} + \sum_{i=1}^{q} \alpha_{2i} \Delta LnREER_{t-1}$$
$$+ \sum_{i=1}^{r} \alpha_{3i} \Delta LnGDP_{t-1} + \sum_{i=1}^{s} \alpha_{4i} \Delta LnEXD_{t-1} + \lambda EC + \varepsilon\_t \tag{3}$$

SOLUTIONS AND RECOMMENDATIONS

Unit Root Test

Even though the ARDL cointegration method does not need preliminary test for unit roots, to prevent ARDL model collapse in the existence of combined stochastic trend of I (2), it is necessary to carried out to identify the number of unit roots in the variables under study. To determine the long-term relationship between variables, the ARDL cointegration method used variables in different integration order (Nkoro, & Uko, 2016). There are various unit root test methods. Among them Durbin-Watson (DW) test, Dickey-Fuller test (DF), Augmented Dickey-Fuller (ADF) test, Philip-Perron (PP) tests are used. For this paper, to check the stationary and non-stationarity, authors applied Augmented Dickey-Fuller (ADF) and the result is presented in Table 3.

As shown in table 3, all variables in level I (0) demonstrate non-stationary properties; hence the null hypothesis (Ho) non-stationarity is accepted. When the ADF test is used to the 1st order of differences of the variables, they all become stationary. Thus, it is determined that all the variables in the model are joined of the 1st order.

Cointegration Test

Cointegration is an econometric notion that imitates the presence of a long-run symmetry between time series variables that considered to study. Examining for cointegration is an essential phase to determine whether a model empirically shows significant long run relationships (Nkoro, & Uko, 2016). There are different cointegration tests. In this paper the researchers applied ARDL model. Prior to ARDL model, the authors checked Johansen test of cointegration.

Table 3. Augmented Dickey–Fuller unit root test

Variables	Level I (0)					1st Difference I (1)				
	ADF Test Statistic	Test Critical Values			P-Value	ADF Test Statistic	Test Critical Values			P-Value
		1%	5%	10%			1%	5%	10%	
*Ln*GDP	-2.1497	-4.35	-3.59	-3.23	0.4959	-4.220	-4.37	-3.60	-3.23	0.0042
*Ln*EXD	-0.6290	-4.33	-3.58	-3.22	0.9686	-4.317	-4.35	-3.59	-3.23	0.0109
*Ln*REER	-1.6237	-4.33	-3.58	-3.22	0.7564	-5.623	-4.37	-3.60	-3.23	0.0006
*Ln*TB	-2.5593	-4.33	-3.58	-3.22	0.2999	-5.371	-4.35	-3.59	-3.23	0.0010

Source: Computed by authors using EViews 10,2018

Table 4. Unrestricted Cointegration Rank Test (Trace)

Hypothesized No. of CE(s)	Eigenvalue	Trace Statistic	0.05 Critical Value	Prob.**
None *	0.726071	61.02106	47.85613	0.0018
At most 1	0.533834	27.35399	29.79707	0.0933
At most 2	0.228975	7.510427	15.49471	0.5191
At most 3	0.028417	0.749532	3.841466	0.3866

Trace test indicates 1 cointegrating eqn(s) at the 0.05 level
* denotes rejection of the hypothesis at the 0.05 level
**MacKinnon-Haug-Michelis (1999) p-values
Source: Computed by authors using EViews 10,2018

Table 5. Unrestricted Cointegration Rank Test (Maximum Eigenvalue)

Hypothesized No. of CE(s)	Eigenvalue	Max-Eigen Statistic	0.05 Critical Value	Prob.**
None *	0.726071	33.66706	27.58434	0.0073
At most 1	0.533834	19.84357	21.13162	0.0749
At most 2	0.228975	6.760895	14.26460	0.5178
At most 3	0.028417	0.749532	3.841466	0.3866

Max-eigenvalue test indicates 1 cointegrating eqn(s) at the 0.05 level
* denotes rejection of the hypothesis at the 0.05 level
**MacKinnon-Haug-Michelis (1999) p-values
Source: Computed by authors using EViews 10,2018

As shown in the Table 4 and Table 5, the null hypothesis (Ho) of no long-term relationship between the variables is not accepted because of both the trace statistics at 61.02 and the max-eigen statistics at 33.66 are greater than their respective critical values at 47.85% and 27.58% at 5% level of significance respectively. This shows that there is a long term cointegration between the variables under study.

Table 6. Bounds test

Test Statistic	Value	Signif.	I (0) Asymptotic: n = 1000	I (1)
F-statistic	6.107621	10%	2.37	3.2
K	3	5%	2.79	3.67
		2.5%	3.15	4.08
		1%	3.65	4.66

Source: Computed by authors using EViews 10, 2018

Because of F-Statistic (6.107621) is greater than the critical values of upper bound I (1) 4.66 and lower bound I (0) 3.65 at 1% significant level, there is a long run relationship. Therefore, the null hypothesis of no long run cointegration is rejected.

Based on Johansen test of cointegration and bounds testing, the model has a long run cointegration between variables. After confirming the long run relationship between variables, the next step is estimating long run relationship by error correction model (ECM).

ARDL Long Run Trade Balance Model

Table 7 depicted that the long run ARDL balance of trade model coefficients, P-value, F-statistics and W-statistics. The F-statistics value (6.0944) is greater than the upper bound and lower bound values and w-statistic value (24.3775) also higher than the upper and lower bond values. These two results confirm the availability of long run cointegration between variables.

The variables in the model, exchange rate represented by *Ln*REER and real GDP represented by *Ln*GDP affects trade balance negatively and significantly. External debt represented *Ln*EXD is positively related and insignificant in this model. The variable real GDP with a coefficient -0.195 suggests that there is a log run and negative cointegration between real GDP and Trade balance. The coefficient of *Ln*REER is -0.522. Assume that other things being remain constant, a 1% devaluation of Ethiopian birr will improve trade balance by 0.522% and vice-versa in long run.

The long run cointegration in the model is tested using ARDL model. The result showed that LnREER and LnGDP affects trade balance negatively and significantly. The variable external debt is positively related with trade balance and insignificant in the model. The long run trade balance model result is similar with studies done by Oskooee & Niroomand, (1998), Anju & Uma (1999), Boyd, Caporale & Smith (2001), Reis Gomes & Senne, (2005) and Arize (2017). In addition to this, the result is similar with the previous studies conducted in case of Ethiopia like Gebeyehu (2014), Nega (2015) and Eshetu (2017). This empirical result shows that the existence of Marshall-Lerner condition in case of Ethiopia.

ARDL Error Correction Model

ARDL Error Correction Model represent the short run relationship between dependent and independent variables. The result of ECM is presented in Table 8.

Table 8 shows that all variables in the short run trade balance model is significant. *Ln*REER and *Ln*GDP are affects trade balance negatively, in the same direction in the long run model. *Ln*EXD affect TB positively and significant but, in the long run model affect positively and insignificant. Assume that other things being remain

Table 7. Estimated Long Run Coefficients using the ARDL Approach

ARDL (1,0,0,1) selected based on Akaike Information Criterion, Dependent variable is LNTB 27 observations used for estimation from 1991 to 2017				
Regressor	**Coefficient**		**Standard Error**	**T-Ratio [Prob]**
*Ln*REER	-.52246		.17950	-2.9107 [.008]
*Ln*GDP	-.19536		.054854	-3.5614 [.002]
*Ln*EXD	.12623		.074155	1.7023 [.103]
C	2.1666		.86094	2.5166 [.020]
Testing for existence of a level relationship among the variables in the ARDL model				
F-statistic	95% Lower Bound	95% Upper Bound	90% Lower Bound	90% Upper Bound
6.0944	3.7723	5.0586	3.0460	4.1611
W-statistic	95% Lower Bound	95% Upper Bound	90% Lower Bound	90% Upper Bound
24.3775	15.0891	20.2346	12.1838	16.6443
If the statistic lies between the bounds, the test is inconclusive. If it is above the upper bound, the null hypothesis of no level effect is rejected. If it is below the lower bound, the null hypothesis of no level effect can't be rejected. The critical value bounds are computed by stochastic simulations using 20000 replications.				

Source: Computed by authors using Microfit 5.5, 2018

constant, a 1% devaluation of Ethiopian birr will improve trade balance by 0.277% and vice-versa in short run. The variable real GDP represented by LnGDP with a coefficient -0.10 suggests that there is a short run and negative cointegration between real GDP and Trade balance. The error correction coefficient which shows the adjustment of disequilibrium in the next year is -0.53 and significant at 5% significance level. It means about 53% of imbalance will be adjusted in every year.

The short run relationship between variables in the model is analyzed by using ARDL Error Correction Model. *Ln*REER and *Ln*GDP are affects trade balance negatively, in the same direction in the long run model. *Ln*EXD affect TB positively and significant but, in the long run model affect positively and insignificant. The result of short run ARDL Error Correction Model indicates that the J-curve effect is not existed. Studies conducted by Bahmani-Oskooee (1985), Reis Gomes and Senne, (2005), Gebeyehu (2014), Eshetu (2017) and others found that in short run the J-curve effect is existed.

Error Correction Model Stability

After calculating the short run ECM, the final step is checking the stability of the model. The graphical representation of Cumulative Sum (CUSUM) and Cumulative Sum Squares (CUSUM Square) assumes that if the model is stable, the plot will be inside the critical bounds of 5% significance level.

Table 8. Error Correction Representation for the Selected ARDL Model

ARDL (1,0,0,1) selected based on Akaike Information Criterion			
Regressor	**Coefficient**	**Standard Error**	**T-Ratio [Prob]**
d*ln*REER	-.27693	.075323	-3.6766[.001]
d*ln*GDP	-.10355	.035815	-2.8913[.008]
d*ln*EXD	.17903	.074794	2.3936[.026]
ecm (-1)	-.53005	.14666	-3.6142[.002]
dLNTB = LNTB-LNTB (-1)			
dLNREER = LNREER-LNREER (-1)			
dLNGDP = LNGDP-LNGDP (-1)			
dLNEXD = LNEXD-LNEXD (-1)			
ecm = LNTB + .52246*LNREER + .19536*LNGDP -.12623*LNEXD -2.1666*INPT			
R-Squared	.55839	R-Bar-Squared	.45325
S.E. of Regression	.098317	F-Stat. F (4,22)	6.6384[.001]
Mean of Dependent Variable	-.024455	S.D. of Dependent Variable	.13296
Residual Sum of Squares	.20299	Equation Log-likelihood	27.7094
Akaike Info. Criterion	21.7094	Schwarz Bayesian Criterion	17.8219
DW-statistic	1.8425		

Source: Computed by authors using Microfit 5.5, 2018

Figure 3 shows that the CUSUM and CUSUM square tests of the model is located within the 5% bound tests. Therefore, the model is stable throughout the period of the study.

Ethiopia used devaluation of birr as a measure to improve its trade balance deficit starting from 1992 to present, National bank of Ethiopia devalued birr several times. However, the trade balance of Ethiopia is not improved.

To improve the balance of trade deficit, the government of Ethiopia should use another option in place of devaluations. The authors of this chapter believe that, the first measure should take by the government of Ethiopia is creating conducive environment for private sectors for the purpose of transforming the traditional agriculture-based economy to manufacturing and the agro-industry. This measure is important to participate in the international trade with new products and to provide import substitute local product in the market. Currently most of processed products in Ethiopia is imported from abroad. When Ethiopia start consuming substitute

Figure 3. Plot of CUSUM and CUSUM Square

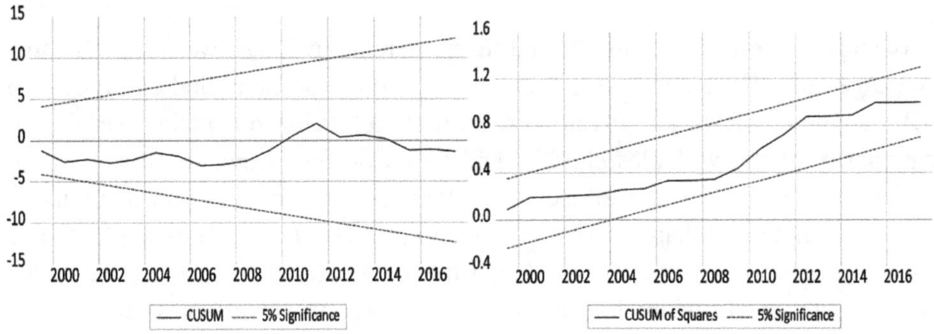

products locally, import may be sensitive to devaluation. Therefore, the government should encourage the private sectors to process the raw agricultural products at least for local consumption. The measure of devaluation to improve trade balance deficit may be appropriate when Ethiopia is being competitive in international market in types as well as quality products and if it is able to produce substitute products for local market. When Ethiopia start substitute products locally, import may be sensitive to devaluation as it is currently not affected by devaluation.

Finally, if the current industrial park projects which starts operation in different regions of the country accomplished effectively and start producing different export-oriented products will have a significant effect on balance of trade.

FUTURE RESEARCH DIRECTIONS

It is suggested that there is a need for deep investigation about how developing countries can compete in the international trade. Technologically advanced countries can compete in the international market using their technology as a comparative advantage. Every country has their own comparative advantage in a specific area and it is very important to formulate their trade policies based on it. Therefore, it is important to every country to identify their advantageous international trade area. On the other hand, some countries identified their comparative advantage and not benefited from it. Therefore, further studies also needed to identify which types of trade policies or measures to be taken by those countries to effectively use their comparative advantage.

CONCLUSION

This chapter assessed the long run and short run relationship between real effective exchange rate (REER) and trade balance of Ethiopia for the period of 1990 up to 2017, applying ARDL and Error Correction Model. Prior to applying ARDL, the stationarity of the variables checked and based on the output the variables are stationery at I (1). In order to decide whether short run or long run relationship between variables, Johansen test of cointegration and Bound tests applied. The result indicates that the model has a long run cointegration between variables. This indicates that short run and long run cointegration between variables can be test.

The empirical findings indicated that there is a long run and short run cointegration between the trade balance of Ethiopia and its birr devaluation. The devaluation of Birr represented by *Ln*REER affects trade balance negatively. The long run coefficient of *Ln*REER is -0.522. This means, considering other things being remain constant, a 1% devaluation of Ethiopian birr will improve trade balance by 0.522% and vice-versa in long run. The error correction coefficient which shows the adjustment of disequilibrium in the next year is -0.53 and significant at 5% level of significance. It means about 53% of imbalance will be adjusted in every year.

Even though, the empirical result shows that the devaluation of Ethiopia`s birr (local currency) can improve the balance of trade, the devaluation of birr many times starting from 1992 to the recent year is not improved the balance of trade even goes to worsen. There are different causes for the non-effectiveness of devaluation strategy for Ethiopia. One of the main reasons is the export of Ethiopia is depending on primary agricultural products. However, all processed products and capital goods are imported from abroad. The shortage of substitute products produced in local market resulted in non-sensitivity of import for devaluation. The total sum effect of this resulted the growth of import exceeded the growth of export and finally Ethiopia is still in trade deficit. Without the availability of adequate substitute products in local market and depending on agricultural commodity export, applying devaluation to improve trade balance may not be a good strategy and cannot improve trade balance deficit.

REFERENCES

Anju, G. K., & Uma, R. (1999). Is there a J-curve? A new estimation for Japan. *International Economic Journal*, *13*(4), 71–79. doi:10.1080/10168739900000045

Arize, A. C. (2017). A convenient method for the estimation of ARDL parameters and test statistics: USA trade balance and real effective exchange rate relation. *International Review of Economics & Finance*, *50*, 75–84. doi:10.1016/j.iref.2017.03.024

Bahmani-Oskooee, M. (1985). Devaluation and the J-curve: Some evidence from LDCs. *The Review of Economics and Statistics*, *67*(3), 500–504. doi:10.2307/1925980

Bahmani-Oskooee, M. (1986). Determinants of international trade flows: The case of developing countries. *Journal of Development Economics*, *20*(1), 107–123. doi:10.1016/0304-3878(86)90007-6 PMID:12268669

Bahmani-Oskooee, M. (1991). Is there a long-run relation between the trade balance and the real effective exchange rate of LDCs? *Economics Letters*, *36*(4), 403–407. doi:10.1016/0165-1765(91)90206-Z

Bahmani-Oskooee, M., & Niroomand, F. (1998). Long-run price elasticities and the Marshall–Lerner condition revisited. *Economics Letters*, *61*(1), 101–109. doi:10.1016/S0165-1765(98)00147-5

Bekaert, G., & Hodrick, R. (2017). *International financial management*. Cambridge University Press.

Bialynicka-Birula, J. (2014). Determinants of International Trade in Art from System Theory Perspective. *International Journal of Business and Management*, *2*(3), 192.

Boskov, T., & Lazaroski, S. (2011). Globalization, trade and business.

Boyd, D., Caporale, G. M., & Smith, R. (2001). Real exchange rate effects on the balance of trade: Cointegration and the Marshall–Lerner condition. *International Journal of Finance & Economics*, *6*(3), 187–200. doi:10.1002/ijfe.157

Buckley, A. (2004). *Multinational finance*. Pearson Education.

Degefa, D. (2001). *The parallel foreign exchange market and macroeconomic performance in Ethiopia*. African Economic Research Consortium.

Eiteman, D. K. (1992). *Multinational business finance*. Pearson Education India.

Eshetu, F. (2017). Birr devaluation and its effect on trade balance of Ethiopia: An empirical analysis. *Journal of Economics and International Finance*, *9*(11), 103–119. doi:10.5897/JEIF2017.0864

Eshetu, F. (2017). Birr devaluation and its effect on trade balance of Ethiopia: An empirical analysis. *Journal of Economics and International Finance*, *9*(11), 103–119. doi:10.5897/JEIF2017.0864

Eun, C. S., & Resnick, B. G. (2010). *International Financial Management (4th ed.)*. Tata McGraw-Hill Education.

Federal Reserve Bank of St. Louis. (2018). *Official External Debt: Debtor Based for Ethiopia*. Retrieved from https://fred.stlouisfed.org/series/ETHDGGDPPT

da Costa, G. C. (1966). Devaluation and balance of payments. *Economic and Political Weekly*, *1*(10), 411–416.

Gebeyehu, A. B. (2014). Exchange Rate and Trade Balance; J Curve Effect in Ethiopia. *Exchange*, *5*(24).

Genye, T. (2011). *Currency Devaluation and Economic Growth: The case of Ethiopia. Departments of Economics*. Stockholm University.

Hacker, R. S., & Hatemi-j, A. (2003). Is the J-curve effect observable for small North European economies? *Open Economies Review*, *14*(2), 119–134. doi:10.1023/A:1022357828945

Hubbard, G. P., & O'Brien, A. P. (2011). Money, banking, and the financial system. Pearson Higher Ed.

Kim, S. H., & Kim, S. H. (2006). *Global corporate finance: text and cases*. John Wiley & Sons.

Maasho, A. (2017). Ethiopia devalues currency by 15 percent to boost exports. *Reuters*. Retrieved from https://www.reuters.com/article/ethiopia-rates/update-1-ethiopia-devalues-currency-by-15-percent-to-boost-exports-idUSL8N1ML40J

Madura, J. (2011). *International financial management*. Cengage Learning.

Márquez-Ramos, L. (2007). *Understanding the determinants of international trade in African countries: An empirical analysis for Ghana and South Africa*. Instituto de Economía Internacional.

Matziorinis, K. N. (2006). *A Brief History of the International Monetary System*. Montreal, Canada: Economics Centre for Continuing Education McGill University.

Mauri, A. (2010). Monetary developments and decolonization in Ethiopia. *Acta Universitatis Danubius Œconomica, 6*(1).

Nega, M.K. (2015) Assessment on Real Effective Exchange Rate and External Sector Development of Ethiopia. *Economics, 4*(4), 64-70. doi:10.11648/j.eco.20150404.12

Nkoro, E., & Uko, A. K. (2016). Autoregressive Distributed Lag (ARDL) cointegration technique: Application and interpretation. *Journal of Statistical and Econometric Methods, 5*(4), 63–91.

Peter, M. (September,2010). Does the devaluation of our currency benefit or hurt Ethiopia? "ECAD forum".Retrieved from https://ecadforum.com/blog/does-the-devaluation-of-our-currency-benefit-or-hurt-ethiopia/

Ratnayake, R. (1994). Determinants of international trade: A simultaneous equation model. *New Zealand Economic Papers, 28*(1), 25–52. doi:10.1080/00779959409544214

Reinhart, C. M. (1995). Devaluation, relative prices, and international trade: evidence from developing countries. *Staff papers, 42*(2), 290-312.

Reis Gomes, F. A., & Senne Paz, L. (2005). Can real exchange rate devaluation improve the trade balance? The 1990–1998 Brazilian case. *Applied Economics Letters, 12*(9), 525-528.

Steinherr, A. (1980). Devaluation in developing countries. *Recherches Économiques de Louvain/Louvain. Economic Review (Federal Reserve Bank of Atlanta), 46*(3), 207–234.

Vijayasri, G. V. (2013). The importance of International Trade in the World. *International Journal of Marketing Financial Services and Management Research, 9*(2), 111–119.

Von Mises, L. (1996). Human action: A treatise on economics. Retrieved from https://mises.org/library/human-action-0/html/c/245

Warner, D., & Kreinin, M. E. (1983). Determinants of international trade flows. *The Review of Economics and Statistics, 65*(1), 96–104. doi:10.2307/1924413

ADDITIONAL READING

Cooper, R. N. (1992). Currency devaluation in developing countries. In *International Economic Policies and their Theoretical Foundations* (pp. 742–770). Academic Press. doi:10.1016/B978-0-12-444281-8.50036-2

Himarios, D. (1989). Do devaluations improve the trade balance? The evidence revisited. *Economic Inquiry*, *27*(1), 143–168. doi:10.1111/j.1465-7295.1989.tb01169.x

Upadhyaya, K. P., & Dhakal, D. (1997). Devaluation and the trade balance: Estimating the long run effect. *Applied Economics Letters*, *4*(6), 343–345. doi:10.1080/135048597355276

KEY TERMS AND DEFINITIONS

ARDL: Autoregressive distributed lag.

Birr: The basic monetary unit of Ethiopia.

Devaluation: It is a monetary policy measure by government to reduce the value of home currency against foreign currencies.

ECM: Error correction model.

GDP: Gross domestic product.

NBE: National Bank of Ethiopia.

REER: Real effective exchange rate. It is the weighted average of a nation's local money in relation to an index of other major currencies.

WDI: World development indicators.

ENDNOTES

1 Estimated by calculating yearly growth rate of export from 1990 to 2017 and divided the sum of all yearly rate by number of years.

2 Estimated by calculating yearly growth rate of import from 1990 to 2017 and divided the sum of all yearly rate by number of years.

Compilation of References

A quick guide to the US-China trade war. (2019, January 7). BBC News. Retrieved from https://www.bbc.com/news/business-45899310

Abboushi, S. (2010). Trade protectionism: Reasons and outcomes. *Competitiveness Review*, *20*(5), 384–394. doi:10.1108/10595421011080760

ABD-Çin Ticaret Savaşı. (2018). Sputnik News. Retrieved from https://tr.sputniknews.com/trend/abd-cin-ticaret-savasi-gumruk-vergisi-ithalat-ihracat/

Acar, M. (2004). İktisadın ezelî sorunsalı: serbest ticaret mi, korumacılık mı? Retrieved from http://www.liberal.org.tr/sayfa/iktisadin-ezeli-sorunsali-serbest-ticaret-mi-korumacilik-mi-mustafa-acar,165.php

Acar, O. (2009). Evaluations for trade and trade finance in Turkey. *TEPAV Policy Note*, July.

Afonso, O. (2001). *The Impact of International Trade on Economic Growth*. Porto: University of Porto.

Afontsev, S. A. (2016). Perspektivy importozameshcheniya v rossijskoj ehkonomike [Prospects for import substitution in the Russian economy]. *Vestnik Omskogo universiteta Seriya. EHkonomika*, *1*, 13–19. (in Russian)

Akar, Ş. K. (2001). Osmanlı Devleti'nde Kısa ve Uzun Vadeli Borçlanma'nın Gelişimi. İstanbul Üniversitesi İktisat Fakültesi Mecmuası, 51(2), 99-124.

Akar, Ş. K., & Al, H. (2003). *Osmanlı Dış Borçları ve Gözetim komisyonları (1854-1856)*. İstanbul: Osmanlı Bankası Arşiv ve Araştırma Merkezi.

Aktan, C. C., & Vural, İ. Y. (2010). Globalleşme ve yabancı sermaye rekabeti. *Hukuk ve İktisat Araştırmaları Dergisi*, *2*(2), 24–48.

Aktel, M. (2001). Küreselleşme Süreci ve Etki Alanları. Süleyman Demirel Üniversitesi İktisadi ve İdari Bilimler Fakültesi Dergisi, 6(2),193-202.

Alabayır, A., & Muzır, E. (2016). Dış ticaret işlemlerinde ticaret yapılan yerlere göre ödeme şekli tercihi ve tercih nedenlerini belirlemeye yönelik ampirik bir çalışma. *İşletme Araştırmaları Dergisi. Journal of Business Research*, *8*(1).

Alekseenkova, E. (2017). EAES k 2025 godu: prioriteti I ozhidaniya gosudarstv-chlenov [The EAEU by 2025: priorities and expectations of member-states]. In *Prospects of the development of the EAEU project by 2025* (pp. 6-37). Russian International Affairs Council.

Al-Sarhan, A. (2016). *United States' Foreign Policy toward the Hashemite Kingdom of Jordan: 1990-2014*. Atlanta University.

Al-Sharafat, A. (2016). *US's strategy in the Middle East during Bush administration*. The University of Jordan.

Amadeo, K. (2019). Free trade agreements with their pros and cons. *The Balance*. Retrieved from https://www.thebalance.com/free-trade-agreement-pros-and-cons-3305845

Analiz perspektivnikh napravleniy razvitiya evraziyskoy integratsii s uchetom strategicheskikh zadach sotsial'no-ekonomicheskogo razvitiya Rossiyskoy federatsii I zadach rossiyskogo predsedatel'stva v EAES v 2018 godu. [The analysis of the perspective directions of development of the Eurasian integration with the strategic objectives of socio-economic development of the Russian Federation and objectives of the Russian chairmanship in the Eurasian Economic Union in 2018]. (2018). *Eurasian panorama*, *3*, 24.

Andersen, M. R., Kett, B. R., & Uexkull, E. V. (2018). Corporate tax incentives and FDI in developing countries. *Global Investment Competitiveness Report*.

Anderson, K., Martin, W., & van der Mensbrugghe, D. (2010). China, the WTO and the Doha Agenda. In D. Greenaway, C. Milner, & S. Yao (Eds.), *China and the World Economy* (pp. 1–20). London: Palgrave Macmillan. doi:10.1057/9781137059864_1

Anju, G. K., & Uma, R. (1999). Is there a J-curve? A new estimation for Japan. *International Economic Journal*, *13*(4), 71–79. doi:10.1080/10168739900000045

Antonakakis, N., & Gabriele, T. (2015). Robust determinants of OECD FDI in developing countries: Insights from Bayesian model averaging. *Cogent Economics & Finance*, *3*(1), 1–25. doi:10.1080/23322039.2015.1095851

Arapova, E. (2015). Measuring "Integration Potential" of the Free Trade Area of the Asia Pacific. *Malaysian Journal of Economic Studies*, *2*, 157–185.

Arapova, E. Y., & Isachenko, T. M. (2019). Russian trade policy: Main trends and impact on bilateral trade flows. *International Journal of Economic Policy in Emerging Economies*, *1*(1), 26–48. doi:10.1504/IJEPEE.2019.098684

Arize, A. C. (2017). A convenient method for the estimation of ARDL parameters and test statistics: USA trade balance and real effective exchange rate relation. *International Review of Economics & Finance*, *50*, 75–84. doi:10.1016/j.iref.2017.03.024

Asian Development Bank. (n.d.). *Agriculture and Food Security Issues in Asia and the Pacific*. Retrieved from https://www.adb.org/sectors/agriculture/issues

Aydınlı, E. (2007). The Turkish Pendulum between Globalization and Security: From the Late Ottoman Era to the 1930s'. Middle Eastern Studies, 40(3), 102-133.

Azar, I. (2007). Perspektivy sozdaniya soyuza Rossii i Belorussii [Prospects for the creation of a union of Russia and Belarus]. *Mirovaya ekonomika I mezhdunarodnyie otnosheniya*, *3*, 10-19.

Bachmann, R., & Zaheer, A. (2008). Trust in inter-organizational relations. In S. Cropper, M. Ebers, C. Huxham, & S. Ring (Eds.), *The Oxford Handbook of Inter-organizational Relations* (pp. 533–554). New York: Oxford University Press.

Baggerman-Noudari, K., & Offermanns, R. (2016). Foreign direct investment in developing countries: Some tax considerations and other related legal matters. *Bulletin for International Taxation*, *70*(6), 310–321.

Bahmani-Oskooee, M. (1985). Devaluation and the J-curve: Some evidence from LDCs. *The Review of Economics and Statistics*, *67*(3), 500–504. doi:10.2307/1925980

Bahmani-Oskooee, M. (1986). Determinants of international trade flows: The case of developing countries. *Journal of Development Economics*, *20*(1), 107–123. doi:10.1016/0304-3878(86)90007-6 PMID:12268669

Bahmani-Oskooee, M. (1991). Is there a long-run relation between the trade balance and the real effective exchange rate of LDCs? *Economics Letters*, *36*(4), 403–407. doi:10.1016/0165-1765(91)90206-Z

Bahmani-Oskooee, M., & Niroomand, F. (1998). Long-run price elasticities and the Marshall–Lerner condition revisited. *Economics Letters*, *61*(1), 101–109. doi:10.1016/S0165-1765(98)00147-5

Bakst, D. (2018). *Agricultural Trade with China: What's at Stake for American Farmers, Ranchers, and Families*. Retrieved from https://www.heritage.org/agriculture/report/agricultural-trade-china-whats-stake-american-farmers-ranchers-and-families

Balassa, B. (1967). *Trade Liberalization Among Industrial Countries: Objectives and Alternatives*. New York: McGraw Hill.

Balasubramanyam, V. N., Salisu, M., & Sapsford, D. (2006). Foreign direct investment as an engine of growth. *The Journal of International Trade & Economic Development*, *8*(1), 27–40. doi:10.1080/09638199900000003

Baldwin, R., & Martin, P. (1999). *Two Waves of Globalisation: Super-ficial Similarities, Fundamental Differences*. Cambridge, MA: National Bureau of Economic Research. doi:10.3386/w6904

Barber, J. B. (1983). *The logic and limits of trust. New Brunswick, Canada:* Rutgers University Press.

Bazo, A. E. (2008). Tax incentives offered by developing countries: Attracting foreign investment or creating disaster*? Tax Notes International*, *52*(4), 1–23.

Becerra, M. (2009). *Theory of the firm for strategic management: economic value analysis*. Cambridge: Cambridge University Press. doi:10.1017/CBO9780511626524

Becker, J., Fuest, C., & Riedel, N. (2012). Corporate tax effects on the quality and quantity of FDI. *European Economic Review*, *56*(8), 1495–1511. doi:10.1016/j.euroecorev.2012.07.001

Bekaert, G., & Hodrick, R. (2017). *International financial management*. Cambridge University Press.

Belarus' i Ul'yanovskaya oblast' Rossii otmechayut polozhitel'nuyu dinamiku vzaimnogo tovarooborota (2018, December 5). [Belarus and the Ulyanovsk region of Russia note the positive dynamics of mutual trade]. *Sotrudnichestvo regionov*. Retrieved from http://www.soyuz.by/news/region/42507.html

Belarus' v 2018 godu bol'she prodavala i pokupala chem godom raneye (2019, January 10). [Belarus sold and bought more in 2018 than in the previous year]. *Informatsionnoye Agentstvo Sputnik*. Retrieved from https://sputnik.by/economy/20190110/1039526637/Belarus-v-2018-godu-bolshe-prodavala-i-pokupala-chem-godom-ranee.html

Bellak, C., & Leibrecht, M. (2009). Do low corporate income tax rates attract FDI? Evidence from eight central and east European countries. *Applied Economics*, *41*(21), 2691–2703. doi:10.1080/00036840701320217

Bellak, C., Leibrecht, M., & Damijan, J. P. (2009). Infrastructure endowment and corporate income taxes as determinants of foreign direct investment in central and eastern European countries. *World Economy*, *32*(2), 267–290. doi:10.1111/j.1467-9701.2008.01144.x

Benassy-Quere, A., Fontagne, L., & Lahreche-Revil, A. (2005). How does FDI react to corporate taxation? *International Tax and Public Finance*, *12*(5), 583–603. doi:10.100710797-005-2652-4

Beyer, J. (2002). Please invest in our country. How successful were the tax incentives for foreign investment in transition countries? *Communist and Post-Communist Studies*, *35*(2), 191–211. doi:10.1016/S0967-067X(02)00007-7

Bialynicka-Birula, J. (2014). Determinants of International Trade in Art from System Theory Perspective. *International Journal of Business and Management*, *2*(3), 192.

Binhan, E. Y. (2002). *Osmanlı İmparatorluğu'nu Dış Borçlanmaya İten Nedenler ve İlk Dış Borç*. Akdeniz İİBF Dergisi.

Bird, R. M., & Zolt, E. M. (2008). Tax policy in emerging countries, environment and planning C. *Government and Policy.*, *26*(1), 73–86. doi:10.1068/cav3

Blomström, M., & Kokko, A. (2003). *The economics of foreign direct investment incentives*. CEPR.

Boleye 60% belorusskoy produktsii v 2018 godu otpravleno na eksport (2018, December 20). [More than 60% of Belarusian products in 2018 were sent for export]. *Informatsionnyy Portal Soyuz Belarus'/Rossiya.* Retrieved from https://rg.ru/2018/12/20/bolee-60-belorusskoj-produkcii-v-2018-godu-otpravleno-na-eksport.html

Bolnick, B. (2004). *Effectiveness and economic impact of tax incentives in the SADC region*. Gaborone: SADC Tax Subcommittee, SADC Trade, Industry, Finance and Investment Directorate.

Boskov, T., & Lazaroski, S. (2011). Globalization, trade and business.

Botta, P. (2017, May 24). *Evraziyskiy soyuz pozvolit Yujnoy Amerike snizit zavisimost ot SSHA – argentinskiy expert [The Eurasian Union will allow South America to reduce its dependence on the US – an Argentine expert].* Eurasia Expert. Retrieved from http://eurasia.expert/evraziyskiy-soyuz-pozvolit-yuzhnoy-amerike-snizit-zavisimost-ot-ssha

Bovdunov, A. (2018, May 17). "Nashi tovari v Irane zhdut": chto dast stranam EAES zona svobodnoy torgovli s Tegeranom ["Our goods are waiting for in Iran": what will the EAEU countries get from the free trade area with Tehran]. *Russia Today*. Retrieved from https://russian.rt.com/world/article/514307-ira-eaes-zona-svobodnoy-torgovli

Bown, C., Jung, E., & Lu, Z. (September 20, 2018). Trump and China Formalize Tariffs on $260 Billion of Imports and Look Ahead to Next Phase. *Peterson Institute for International Economics*. Retrieved from https://piie.com/blogs/trade-investment-policy-watch/trump-and-china-formalize-tariffs-260-billion-imports-and-look

Boyd, D., Caporale, G. M., & Smith, R. (2001). Real exchange rate effects on the balance of trade: Cointegration and the Marshall–Lerner condition. *International Journal of Finance & Economics*, *6*(3), 187–200. doi:10.1002/ijfe.157

Brodzka, A. (2013). Tax incentives in emerging economies. *Business Systems and Economics*, *3*(1), 26–36.

Buckley, A. (2004). *Multinational finance*. Pearson Education.

Byman, D., & Moller, S. B. (2016). The United States and the Middle East: Interest, Risks and Costs. In J. S. and B. Valentino (Ed.), Sustainable Security: Rethinking American National Security Strategy. Oxford: Oxford University Press.

Cambridge Dictionary. (n.d). Retrieved from https://dictionary.cambridge.org/tr

Cass, D. Z., Williams, B. G., & Barker, G. R. (2003). *China and the World Trading System: Entering the Millennium*. New York, NY: Cambridge University Press. doi:10.1017/CBO9780511494482

Çeken, H., Ökten, Ş., & Ateşoğlu, L. (2008). Eşitsizliği Derinleştiren Bir Süreç Olarak Küreselleşme ve Yoksulluk. C.Ü. İİBF Dergisi, 9(2), 79-95.

Çelik, M. Y. (2012). Boyutlarıyla ve farklı algılarıyla küreselleşme. Dumlupınar Üniversitesi Sosyal Bilimler Dergisi, 2(32), 57-73.

Cezar, Y. (1986). *Osmanlı Maliyesinde Bunalım ve değişim Dönemi (18. Yüzyıldan Tanzimat'a Mali Tarih)*. İstanbul: Alan Yayıncılık.

Chang, X., DeFries, R. S., Liu, L., & Davis, K. (2018). Understanding Dietary and Staple Food Transitions in China from Multiple Scales. *PLoS One*, *13*(4), e0195775. doi:10.1371/journal.pone.0195775 PMID:29689066

Chen, E. I. H. (2014). US-China trade relations and economic distrust. *Chinese Economy*, *47*(3), 57–69. doi:10.2753/CES1097-1475470304

Cheng, G. (2007). China's Agriculture within the World Trading System. In I. Sheldon (Ed.), *China's Agricultural Trade: Issues and Prospects* (pp. 81–104). Beijing: International Agricultural Trade Research Consortium.

Cheong, D. (2010). Methods for Ex Ante Economic Evaluation of Free Trade Agreements. *ADB*.

Child, J., & Faulkner, D. (2002). *Strategies of co-operation: managing alliances, networks and joint ventures*. New York: Oxford University Press.

China blasts Trump's new trade tariffs. (2018). CNN. Retrieved from https://money.cnn.com/2018/01/22/news/economy/trump-trade-tariffs-china-reaction/

China exports, imports and trade balance By Country 2017 (2017). World Integrated Trade Solution. Retrieved from https://wits.worldbank.org/CountryProfile/en/Country/CHN/Year/LTST/TradeFlow/EXPIMP/Partner/by-country

Christiansen, H., Oman, C., & Charlton, A. (2003). *Incentives-based competition for foreign direct investment, the case of Brazil*. OECD Publishing.

Chue, B. (2018). Trump's trade war with China will affect all of us – this is how. *Independent*. Retrieved from https://www.independent.co.uk/voices/trump-china-trade-war-tariffs-us-metal-europe-uk-effect-a8543136.html

CNN. (2015, July 15). President Obama continues his news conference on the Iran deal. USA.

Coase, R.H. (1937). The nature of the firm. *Economica, 4*, 386-405.

Coughlin, C. C. K., Chrystal A. & Wood, G. E. (1988). Protectionist trade policies: a survey of theory, evidence and rationale. *Federal Reserve Bank of ST. Louis Paper*.

Cui, K., & Shoemaker, S. (2018). A Look at Food Security in China. *NPJ Science of Food, 2*. doi:. doi:10.103841538-018-0012-x

da Costa, G. C. (1966). Devaluation and balance of payments. *Economic and Political Weekly*, *1*(10), 411–416.

Danışoğlu, A. Ç. (2004). Küreselleşme'nin Gelir Eşitsizliği ve Yoksulluk Üzerindeki Etkileri. İstanbul Ticaret Üniversitesi Dergisi, 3(6), 215-239.

de Gjalt, J., & Nooteboom, B. (2000). *The causal structure of long-term supply relationships: an empirical test of a generalized transaction cost theory*. Dordrecht: Kluwer Academic Publishers.

De Laat, P. (1997). Research and Development Alliances: Ensuring Trust by Mutual Commitments. In M. Ebers (Ed.), *The Formation of Inter-Organizational Networks*. New York: Oxford University Press.

Degefa, D. (2001). *The parallel foreign exchange market and macroeconomic performance in Ethiopia*. African Economic Research Consortium.

Devyatkov, A. (2017). *Mezhdunarodnie svyazi EAES k 2025 godu [International ties of the EAEY by 2025]*. Russian International Affairs Council. June 27. Retrieved from http://russiancouncil.ru/analytics-and-comments/analytics/mezhdunarodnye-svyazi-eaes-k-2025-g/

Diliberto, M. (2015). Why are products from China so cheap? *Quora*. Retrieved from https://www.quora.com/Why-are-products-from-China-so-cheap

Dinamika vneshney torgovli Rossii v 2010 - 2017 godakh [Dynamics of Russian foreign trade in 2010–2017]. (2018). *Vneshnyaya Torgovlya Rossii na osnove dannykh Federal'noy tamozhennoy sluzhby Rossii*. Retrieved from http://russian-trade.com/reports-and-reviews/2018-03/dinamika-vneshney-torgovli-rossii-v-2010-2017-godah/

Dogovor o Evraziyskom ekonomicheskom soyuze [The Treaty on the Eurasian Economic Union]. (2014, May 29). Signed in Astana on May 29. Retrieved from http://www.eaeunion.org/files/history/2014/2014_2.pdf

Dogovor O sozdanii Soyuznogo gosudarstva [*Treaty Establishing the Union State*]. (1999). Moscow. Retrieved from http://base.garant.ru/1155132/#ixzz5hc0JB3j4

Dohmen, H. (1976). China's Foreign Trade Policy. *Inter Economics*, *11*(7), 197–201. doi:10.1007/BF02929005

Doney, P. M., & Cannon, J. P. (1997). An examination of the nature of trust in buyer-seller relationships. *Journal of Marketing*, *61*, 35–51.

Donnan, S. (2018). US says China WTO membership was a mistake. *Financial Times*. Retrieved from https://www.ft.com/content/edb346ec-fd3a-11e7-9b32-d7d59aace167

Dorosh, P. A. (2004). Trade, Food Aid and Food Security: Evolving Rice and Wheat Markets. *Economic and Political Weekly*, *36*(39), 4033–4042.

Dreazen, Y. J. (2012, May 9). Foiled Bomb Plot Highlights Growing CIA-Saudi Arabian Ties. CNN.

Drezner, D. W. (2011). Does Obama have a grand strategy? Why we need doctrines in uncertain times. *Foreign Affairs*, *90*(4), 58.

Drozdz, J., & Miškinis, A. (2011). Benefits and threats of free trade. *Economics*, *2*(14), 40–49.

Dumrul, C., & Dumrul, Y. (2014). Osmanlı İmparatorluğu'nu Kapitalist Paternde Sanayileşmesinin Önündeki Engeller Üzerine Bir İnceleme. Yönetim ve Ekonomi Araştırmaları Dergisi, 12(23), 146-170.

Dünya Ticaret Savaşı Başladı. (2018). Hürriyet Gazetesi. Retrieved from http://www.hurriyet.com.tr/ekonomi/dunya-ticaret-savasi-basladi-40863621

Düzcü, L. (2009). Osmanlı Bahriye Teşkilatında Reform Çabaları (1876-1922). *Akademik Bakış*, *3*(5), 3-19.

Düzcü, L. (2013). Osmanlı Sanayi Çağına Adım Atışına Denizcilikten Bir Örnek: Buharlı Gemiye Geçişte Başlıca Parametreler (1828-1856). History Studies, 5(1), 113-127.

Düzcü, L. (2017). *Yelkenliden Buharlıya Geçişte Osmanlı Denizciliği (1825-1855)*. İstanbul: Doğu Kütüphanesi Yayınları.

Dyer, J. H., & Chu, W. (2003). The role of trustworthiness in reducing transaction costs and improving performance: Empirical evidence from the United States, Japan and Korea. *Organization Science*, *14*(1), 57–68. doi:10.1287/orsc.14.1.57.12806

EAES i ASEAN uglublyaut torgovo-ekonomicheskoe i investitsionnoe sotrudnichestvo [The EAEU and ASEAN deepen their trade-economic and investment cooperation]. (2018, November 14). Eurasian Economic Commission. Retrieved from http://www.eurasiancommission.org/ru/nae/news/Pages/14-11-2018-1.aspx

EAES i Iran v 2019 godu nachnut rabotat v rezhime zoni svobodnoy torgovli [The EAEU and Iran will start working in the free trade zone regime in 2019]. (2018, December 12).. Vesti. Ekonomika. Retrieved from https://www.vestifinance.ru/articles/111681

EAES i MERKOSUR nachinaut sotrudnichestvo v ekonomike (2014). [EEU and MERCOSUR begin cooperation in economy], November 26. Retrieved from https://news2.ru/story/432460/

Eaton, J., & Kortum, S. (2002). Technology, geography, and trade. *Econometrica*, *70*(5), 1741–1779. doi:10.1111/1468-0262.00352

Ebury. (2018). What is next for the Turkish Lira after its violent sell off? Retrieved from https://www.ebury.com/blog/ebury_post/whats-next-turkish-lira/

Eckhouse, B., Natter, A., & Christopher, M. (2018). President Trump Slaps Tariffs on Solar Panels in Major Blow to Renewable Energy. *Time*. Retrieved from http://time.com/5113472/donald-trump-solar-panel-tariff/

Edward, L. (1987). U.S.-Japan Trade War: The Opening Battle.Thomas A. Roe Institute for Economic Policy Studies. Retrieved from:http://s3.amazonaws.com/thf_media/1987/pdf/bg577.pdf

Effiok, S. O., Tapang, A. T., & Eton, O. E. (2013). The impact of tax policy and incentives on foreign direct investment and economic growth: Evidence from export processing zones in Nigeria. *European Journaal of Commerce and Management Research*, *2*(9), 191–197.

Eiteman, D. K. (1992). *Multinational business finance*. Pearson Education India.

Eksport belorusskikh tovarov vyros na $4,5 mlrd [Exports of Belarusian goods grew by $4.5 billion]. (2019, February 4). *Informatsionno-analiticheskiy portal Soyuznogo gosudarstva*. Retrieved from http://www.soyuz.by/news/finance/43243.html

Eksport i import Rossii po tovaram i stranam [Export and import of Russia by goods and countries]. *Statistika vneshney torgovli. Po dannym FTS Rossii.* (2018). Retrieved from http://ru-stat.com/

Eksport iz Rossii «Vse tovary» [Export from Russia "All goods"]. (2018). *Statistika vneshney torgovli. Po dannym FTS Rossii*. Retrieved from http://ru-stat.com/date-M201712-201812/RU/export/world/

Eldem, V. (1994). *Harp ve Mütareke Yıllarında Osmanlı İmparatorluğu'nun Ekonomisi*. Ankara: Türk Tarih Kurumu.

Erdem, E. (2016). Sanayi Devriminin Ardından Osmanlı Sanayileşme Hamleleri: Sanayi Politikalarının Dinamikleri ve Zaafiyetleri. *Erciyes Üniversitesi İİBF Dergisi*, *48*, 17-44.

Eremina, N. (2016, July). Advent of a new civilization project: Eurasia in – U.S. out? *Journal of Eurasian Studies*, *7*(2), 162–171. doi:10.1016/j.euras.2016.02.001

Erokhin, V., & Gao, T. (2018). Competitive Advantages of China's Agricultural Exports in the Outward-Looking Belt and Road Initiative. In W. Zhang, I. Alon, & C. Lattemann (Eds.), *China's Belt and Road Initiative: Changing the Rules of Globalization* (pp. 265–285). London: Palgrave Macmillan. doi:10.1007/978-3-319-75435-2_14

Eshetu, F. (2017). Birr devaluation and its effect on trade balance of Ethiopia: An empirical analysis. *Journal of Economics and International Finance*, *9*(11), 103–119. doi:10.5897/JEIF2017.0864

Esposito, F. (2016). Risk diversification and international trade. Society for Economic Dynamics. European Central Bank-Europa. Retrieved from https://www.ecb.europa.eu

Eun, C. S., & Resnick, B. G. (2010). *International Financial Management (4th ed.)*. Tata McGraw-Hill Education.

Eurasian Economic Union. (2015, May 21). Agreement on trade and economic cooperation between the Eurasian Economic Union and its member States, of the one part, and the People's Republic of China, of the other part. Retrieved from https://docs.eaeunion.org/docs/ru-ru/01417817/iatc_21052018

Evropeyskiy soyuz i Evraziyskiy ekonomicheskiy soyuz: dolgosrochniy dialog i perspektivi soglasheniya [European Union and Eurasian Economic Union: longterm dialog and prospects of agreement]. (2016). St. Petersburg: CII EDB. Retrieved from https://eabr.org/upload/iblock/f28/edb_centre_2016_report_38_eu_eaeu_rus.pdf

Federal Reserve Bank of St. Louis. (2018). *Official External Debt: Debtor Based for Ethiopia*. Retrieved from https://fred.stlouisfed.org/series/ETHDGGDPPT

Fedorov, N. (2016). *The free trade agreement between the Eurasian Economic Union and Vietnam in the context of Russian-Vietnamese relations*. ISA. Retrieved from http://web.isanet.org/Web/Conferences/AP%20Hong%20Kong%202016/Archive/07294803-8c93-4929-9d9d-6e843873e8ce.pdf

Fedorov, N. V. (2018). Soglashenie o zone svobodnoi torgovli mezhdu EAES i V'etnamom kak faktor rossiisko-v'etnamskikh otnoshenii [The Free Trade Agreement between the EAEU and Vietnam as a Factor of Russian-Vietnamese Relations]. *Comparative Politics*, (1), 74–90. doi:10.18611/2221-3279-2018-9-1-74-90

Feenstra, R. (1995). Estimating the Effects of Trade Policy. *NBER*. Retrieved from http://www.nber.org/papers/w5051.pdf

Feenstra, R., Lipsey, R., & Bowen, H. (1997). World Trade Flows, 1970-1992, with Production and Tariff Data. *NBER*. Retrieved from http://www.nber.org/papers/w5910.pdf

Filloon, W. (2018). These Are All the Foods Being Affected by Trump's Trade War. *Eater*. Retrieved from https://www.eater.com/2018/7/18/17527968/food-tariffs-trump-canada-china-mexico-eu

Fouda, R. A. N. (2012). Protectionism and free trade: A country's glory or doom? *International Journal of Trade. Economics and Finance*, *3*(5), 351–355.

Francis, S. (2018). Foreign direct investment concepts: Implications for negotiations. *Economic and Political Weekly*, *45*(22), 31–36.

Frankel, J. A., & Romer, D. H. (1999). Does Trade Cause Growth? *The American Economic Review*, *89*(3), 379–399. doi:10.1257/aer.89.3.379

Free Trade Agreement between the Eurasian Economic Union and its member States, of the one part, and the Socialist Republic of Vietnam, of the other part. (n.d.). Eurasian Economic Commission. Retrieved from http://www.eurasiancommission.org/ru/act/trade/dotp/sogl_torg/Documents/EAEU-VN_FTA.pdf

Fruman, C. (2016). Why does efficiency-seeking FDI matter? World Bank. Retrieved from https://blogs.worldbank.org/psd/why-does-efficiency-seeking-fdi-matter

Fung, V. K. (2009). Jobs, global trade and the perils of protectionism: the imperative of restoring confidence. In R. Baldwin & S. J. Evenett (Eds.), The Collapse of Global Trade, Murky Protectionism and the Crisis: Recommendations for the G20 (pp. 25-28). London: Centre for Economic Policy Research (CEPR).

FXStreet. (2018, September 17). Breaking News: Trump: If countries will not make fair deals with us, they will be "Tariffed!" Retrieved from https://www.fxstreet.com/news/breaking-news-trump-if-countries-will-not-make-fair-deals-with-us-they-will-be-tariffed-201809171020

Gale, F., Hansen, J., & Jewison, M. (2015). *China's Growing Demand for Agricultural Imports*. Washington, DC: U.S. Department of Agriculture, Economic Research Service.

Gallup. (2015, February 23). Seven in Ten Americans Continue to View Israel Favorably. Retrieved from http://www.gallup.com/poll/181652/seven-americans-continue-view-israel-favorably.aspx

Ganesan, S. (1994). Determinants of long-term orientation in buyer-seller relationships. *Journal of Marketing*, *58*(2), 1–19. doi:10.1177/002224299405800201

Gao, T. (2017). Food Security and Rural Development on Emerging Markets of Northeast Asia: Cases of Chinese North and Russian Far East. In V. Erokhin (Ed.), *Establishing Food Security and Alternatives to International Trade in Emerging Economies* (pp. 155–176). Hershey, PA: IGI Global.

Gastanaga, V. M., Nugent, J. B., & Pashamova, B. (1998). Host country reforms and FDI inflows: How much difference do they make? *World Development*, *26*(7), 1299–1314. doi:10.1016/S0305-750X(98)00049-7

GATT. (1987, February 18). *China's Status as a Contracting Party (Publication no: L/6125).* Switzerland. Retrieved from https://docs.wto.org/gattdocs/q/GG/L6199/6125.PDF

GATT. (1987, March 4). *Minutes of Meeting.* Retrieved from https://docs.wto.org/gattdocs/q/GG/C/M207.PDF

Gebeyehu, A. B. (2014). Exchange Rate and Trade Balance; J Curve Effect in Ethiopia. *Exchange*, *5*(24).

Gencer, A. İ. (1986). *Türk Denizcilik Tarihi Araştırmaları.* İstanbul: Türkiye Denizciler Sendikası.

Gencer, A. İ. (1991). Bahriye Nezareti. Türkiye Diyanet Vakfı İslam Ansiklopedisi. *Ankara:Türkiye Diyanet Vakfı Yayınları*, 4.

Genç, M. (2000). *Osmanlı İmparatorluğu'nda Devlet ve Ekonomi.* İstanbul: Ötüken Neşriyat.

Genye, T. (2011). *Currency Devaluation and Economic Growth: The case of Ethiopia. Departments of Economics.* Stockholm University.

Geyikdağı, V. N. (2008). *Osmanlı Devleti'nde Yabancı Sermaye(1854-1914).* İstanbul: Hil Yayıncılık.

Ghoshal, S., & Moran, P. (1996). Bad for practice: A critique of the transaction cost theory. *Academy of Management Review*, *21*(1), 13–47. doi:10.5465/amr.1996.9602161563

Ghosh, I., & Ghoshal, I. (2017). Implications of Trade Liberalization for Food Security under the ASEAN-India Strategic Partnership: A Gravity Model Approach. In V. Erokhin (Ed.), *Establishing Food Security and Alternatives to International Trade in Emerging Economies* (pp. 98–118). Hershey, PA: IGI Global.

Giray, F. (2008). *Vergi teşvik sistemi*. Bursa: Ezgi Kitabevi Publishing.

Goldstein, M., Khan, M. S., & Officer, L. H. (1980). Prices of Tradable and Nontradable Goods in the Demand for Total Imports. *The Review of Economics and Statistics*, *2*(62), 190–199. doi:10.2307/1924744

Grinberg, R. S. (2019). *Rossiyskaya sotsial'no-ekonomicheskaya Sistema: realii i vektory razvitiya: monografiya* [*Russian socio-economic system: realities and vectors of development: monograph*]. Moscow: INFRA-M.

Gro Intelligence. (2018). *China's Road Map to Food Security*. Retrieved from https://gro-intelligence.com/insights/chinas-roadmap-to-food-security

Gronskiy, A. (2018). *Soyuznoye gosudarstvo Rossii i Belarusi: problemy i perspektivy*. [*The Union State of Russia and Belarus*]. Retrieved from http://zapadrus.su/rusmir/pubru/1880-soyuznoe-gosudarstvo-rossii-i-belorussii-problemy-i-perspektivy.html

Guarino, A. S. (2018). The economic effects of trade protectionism. *Focus Economics*. Retrieved from https://www.focus-economics.com/blog/effects-of-trade-protectionism-on-economy

Gubernator Tul'skoy oblasti: region gotov k dal'neyshemu ukrepleniyu vzaimodeystviya s Belarus'yu po vsem napravleniyam [Governor of the Tula Region: the region is ready to further strengthen cooperation with Belarus in all areas]. (2018, December 26). *Informatsionno-analiticheskiy portal Soyuznogo gosudarstva*. Retrieved from http://www.soyuz.by/news/region/42779.html

Guei, K. M. A., Mugano, G., & Le Roux, P. (2017). Revenue, welfare and trade effects of European Union Free Trade Agreement on South Africa. *South African Journal of Economic and Management Sciences.*, *20*(1). doi:10.4102ajems.v20i1.1655

Gulati, R. (1995). Does familiarity breed trust? The implications of repeated ties for contractual choice in alliances. *Academy of Management Journal*, *38*(1), 85–112.

Gürsel, S. (1985). Osmanlı Dış Borçları. Tanzimattan Cumhuriyete Türkiye Ansiklopedisi. *İstanbul:İletişim Yayınları*, 3.

Güven, T. C. (1998). Cumhuriyetin 75. Yıl Dönümünde Dış Ticaretimizin Geçmişi ve Bugünü. *Dış Ticaret Dergisi*, *3*, 26-41.

Hacker, R. S., & Hatemi-j, A. (2003). Is the J-curve effect observable for small North European economies? *Open Economies Review*, *14*(2), 119–134. doi:10.1023/A:1022357828945

Hamrin, C. L., & Zhao, S. (1995). *Decision-Making in Deng's China: Perspectives from Insiders*. Armonk, NY: M.E. Sharpe.

Hau, H., Killeen, W. P., & Moore, J. (2002). Michael John, How has the euro changed the foreign exchange market? *Economic Policy*, *17*(34), 149–191. doi:10.1111/1468-0327.00086

He, C., Li, C., & Lin, C. (2018, March 22). Economic Impacts of the Possible China–US Trade War. *Emerging Markets Finance and Trade*, *54*(7), 1557-1577. Retrieved from https://www.tandfonline.com/doi/abs/10.1080/1540496X.2018.1446131

Hearson, M. (2017). The challenges for developing countries in international tax justice. *The Journal of Development Studies*, *54*(10), 1932–1938. doi:10.1080/00220388.2017.1309040

Heckscher, E. F. (1919). The effect of foreign trade on the distribution of national income. *Ekonomisk Tidskrift*, *21*.

Heckscher, E. F., & Ohlin, B. G. (1991). *Heckscher-Ohlin trade theory*. The MIT Press.

Hers, J., Witteman, J., Rougoor, W., & Buiren, K. (2018). *The Role of Investment Hubs in FDI, Economic Development and, Trade Ireland, Luxembourg, Mauritius, the Netherlands, and Singapore*. Investment Facilitation Forum.

Hines, J. R. (1998). *"Tax sparing" and direct Investment in developing countries*. NBER.

Holland, D., & Vann, R. J. (1998). Income tax incentives for investment. Tax Law Design and Drafting, 2, 2-9.

Howorth, C., Westhead, P., & Wright, M. (2004). Buyouts, information asymmetry and the family management dyad. *Journal of Business Venturing*, *19*(4), 509–534. doi:10.1016/j.jbusvent.2003.04.002

Hoyt, J., & Huq, F. (2000). From arms-length to collaborative relationships in the supply chain: An evolutionary process. *International Journal of Physical Distribution & Logistics Management*, *30*(9), 750–764. doi:10.1108/09600030010351453

Huang, J., & Rozelle, S. (2006). The Emergence of Agricultural Commodity Markets in China. *China Economic Review*, *17*(3), 266–280. doi:10.1016/j.chieco.2006.04.008

Huang, J., Wei, W., Cui, Q., & Xie, W. (2017). The Prospects for China's Food Security and Imports: Will China Starve the World via Imports? *Journal of Integrative Agriculture*, *16*(12), 2933–2944. doi:10.1016/S2095-3119(17)61756-8

Hubbard, G. P., & O'Brien, A. P. (2011). Money, banking, and the financial system. Pearson Higher Ed.

Interim Agreement leading to formation of a free trade area between the Eurasian Economic Union and its Member States, of the one part, and the Islamic Republic of Iran, of the other part. (n.d.). Eurasian Economic Commission. Retrieved from http://www.eurasiancommission.org/ru/act/trade/dotp/sogl_torg/Documents/Interim%20Agreement%20EAEU-Iran_final.pdf

Interim Agreement on a free trade area between the EAEU and Iran. (2018, May 17). *Eurasian panorama*, *3*, 17-18.

International Monetary Found (IMF). (2015). *Options For Low Income Countries' Effective And Efficient Use Of Tax Incentives For Investment.*

Interview of the Chairman of the EAEC Board T. Sargsyan to The Economic Times. (2018, September 7). Retrieved from https://www.alta.ru/ts_news/62670/

İpşirli, M. (1998). Hayriye Tüccarı. Türkiye Diyanet Vakfı İslam Ansiklopedisi. *İstanbul:Türkiye Diyanet Vakfı*, 17.

Irwin, D. (2001). *A Brief History of International Trade Policy*. Retrieved from https://www.econlib.org/library/Columns/Irwintrade.html

Irwin, D. (2011). *Peddling protectionism: Smoot-Hawley and the Great Depression*. Oxford, UK: Princeton University Press.

Isard, P. (1977). The Price Effects of Exchange Rate Changes. U.S. Treasury.

Istoriya dvustoronnikh otnosheniy Belarusi i Brazilii [History of Belarus-Brazil bilateral relations]. (2018). *Posol'stvo Respubliki Belarus' v Federativnoy respublike Braziliya*. Retrieved from http://brazil.mfa.gov.by/ru/bilateral_relations/

James, S. (2010). *Incentives and investments: Evidence and policy implications. World Bank*. Washington, DC: Investment Climate Advisory Services of the Word Bank Group.

Jash, A. (2015). *China's Quest for Food Security: Challenges & Policies*. Retrieved from https://papers.ssrn.com/sol3/papers.cfm?abstract_id=2773903

Kaempfer, W. H., Tower, E., & Willett, T. D. (2004). Trade protectionism. In C. K. Rowley & F. Schneider (Eds.), *The Encyclopedia of Public Choice* (pp. 570–590). Boston: Springer.

Karamursal, Z. (1989). *Osmanlı Mali Tarihi Hakkında Tetkikler*. Ankara: Türk Tarih Kurumu.

Karataşer, B. (2013). Birinci Dünya Savaşı ve Mütareke Döneminde İstanbul'un İaşesi. Kahraman Maraş Sütçü İmam Üniversitesi İİBF Dergisi, 3(2), 97-114.

Karataşer, B. (2016). İkinci Meşrutiyet Dönemi Osmanlı Donanma Politikası: Milli Donanmayı Kurma Çabaları. In *VIII. Türk Deniz Ticareti Tarihi Sempozyumu* (pp. 138-143).

Karataşer, B. (2018). *İslam İktisadi Anlayışının Osmanlı'da Kurumsal Yansımaları*. Bursa: Ekin Basım Yayın Dağıtım.

Kaymak, H. (2005). Yabancı doğrudan yatırımları artırmak için teşvikler gerekli ve/veya yeterli mi?.*Maliye Dergisi, 149*(Mayıs-Aralık), 74-104.

Kazgan, H. (1991). *Galata Bankerleri*. İstanbul: Türkiye Ekonomi Bankası A.Ş Yayınları.

Kee, H., Nicita, A., & Olarreaga, M. (2005). Import Demand Elasticities and Trade Distortions. *The World Bank. The European Trade Study Group (ETSG)*. Retrieved from http://www.etsg.org/ETSG2005/papers/olarr.pdf

Kenanoğlu, M. M. (2005). Miri. Türkiye Diyanet Vakfı İslam Ansiklopedisi. *Ankara:Türkiye Diyanet Vakfı*, 30.

Kheyfets, B.A. (2018). Perspektivi sozdaniya zoni svobodnoy torgovli mezhdu EAES i ASEAN [Prospects of a free trade area between the EAEU and ASEAN]. *Bulletin of Institute of Economics RAS, 5*, 107-120.

Kim, M. H. (2014, January 02). The U.S.–China Trade Deficit. *The International Trade Journal*, *28*(1), 65–83. doi:10.1080/08853908.2013.814555

Kim, S. H., & Kim, S. H. (2006). *Global corporate finance: text and cases*. John Wiley & Sons.

Kinda, T. (2014). *The quest for non-resource-based foreign direct investment: Do taxes matter?* Washington, D.C: IMF.

Kitay – EAES: korrektsiya disbalansov [China – the EAEU: correction of imbalances]. (2017, July 10). Eurasian Development Bank. Retrieved from https://eabr.org/press/comments/kitay-eaes-korrektsiya-disbalansov/

Klemm, A., & Parys, S. V. (2010). *Empirical Evidence on the Effects of Tax Incentives.*

Knobel, A. Yu. (2010). *Zakonomernosti formirovaniya urovnya tarifov v mezhdunarodnoj torgovle* [Regularities of the formation of the tariffs in international trade]. Moscow: Gaidar Institute. (in Russian)

Kodaman, B. (2002). İkinci Meşrutiyet Dönemi(1908-1914). Türkler. *Ankara:Yeni Türkiye Yayınları*, 13.

Koktysh, K. Ye. (2004). *Dinamika mezhdunarodnykh i mezhregional'nykh vzaimodeystviy* [*Dynamics of international and interregional interactions*]. Moscow: ROSSPAN.

Kommerskollegium National Board of Trade. (2016). Protectionism in the 21st Century.

Konukman, A., & Çiftçi, C. (2008). Küreselleşmenin Gelir Dağılımı Üzerindeki Etkileri.*Ekonomik Yaklaşım*, *19*, 59-83.

Kransdorff, M. (2010). Tax incentives and foreign direct investment in South Africa. *Journal of Sustainable Development*, *3*(1), 68–84.

Krieg, A. (2016). Externalizing the burden of war: The Obama Doctrine and US foreign policy in the Middle East. *International Affairs*, *92*(1), 97–113. doi:10.1111/1468-2346.12506

Kütükoğlu, M. S. (1974). Osmanlı-İngiliz İktisadi Münasebetleri (1580-1838). *Ankara. Türk Kültürünü Araştırma Enstitüsü*, 1.

Kuz'mina, Ye. (2018). *Rossiysko-belorusskaya torgovlya: vozmozhen li proryv?* [*Russian-Belarusian trade: is a breakthrough possible?*]. Retrieved from http://eurasia.expert/rossiysko-belorusskaya-torgovlya-vozmozhen-li-proryv/

Kuz'mina, Ye. M. (2017). Ekonomicheskoye razvitiye stran YEAES i perspektivy ekonomicheskoy integratsii do 2025 g. [Economic development of the countries of the EAEU and the prospects for economic integration until 2025]. Analiticheskaya zapiska RSMD. Moscow.

Kwon, G., & Suh, T. (2005). Trust, commitment and relationships in supply chain management: A path analysis. *Supply Chain Management*, *10*(1), 26–33. doi:10.1108/13598540510578351

Lamaj, J. (2015). The Impact of International Trade and Competition Market on Developing Countries. In *Proceedings of the International Conference "Managing Intellectual Capital and Innovation for Sustainable and Inclusive Society*. Bari: Management, Knowledge and Learning; Technology, Innovation and Industrial Management.

Langensiepen, B. (2000). *Osmanlı Donanması 1828-1923. Çev. Renan Mengü.* İstanbul: Denizler Kitabevi.

Lardy, N. R. (1999, April 1). China's WTO Membership. *Brooking Policy Brief Series*. Retrieved from https://www.brookings.edu/research/chinas-wto-membership/

Lardy, N. R. (2002). *Integrating China into the World Economy*. Washington, DC: Brookings Institution Press.

Larson, A. (1992). Network dyads in entrepreneurial settings: A study of the governance of exchange relationships. *Administrative Science Quarterly*, *3*(1), 76–104. doi:10.2307/2393534

Lawrence, G., & McMichael, P. (2012). The Question of Food Security. *International Journal of Sociology of Agriculture and Food*, *2*(19), 135–142.

Leamer, E. E. (1988). Cross-Section Estimation of the Effects of Trade Barriers. In R. Feenstra (Ed.), *Empirical Methods for International Trade*. The MIT Press.

Lechmacher, W., & Mcwaters, J. (2017). How blockchain can restore trust in trade. Weforum. Retrieved from https://www.weforum.org/agenda/2017/02/blockchain-trade-trust-transparency

Lederman, J. (2017, January 30). Trump courts Jordan's king amid embassy, refugee concerns. *Associated Press*. Retrieved from http://www.dailymail.co.uk/wires/ap/article-4173794/Trump-courts-Jordans-king-amid-embassy-refugee-concerns.html

Lee, G. B. (2018). China's Forced Technology Transfer Problem— And What to Do About It. Retrieved from https://piie.com/system/files/documents/pb18-13.pdf

Lee, J. W. (1995). Capital Goods Import and Long-Run Growth. *The Developing Economies*, *48*(1), 91–110. doi:10.1016/0304-3878(95)00015-1

Levchenko, A., & Zhang, J. (2016). The Evolution of Comparative Advantage: Measurement and Welfare Implications. *Journal of Monetary Economics*, *78*, 96–111. doi:10.1016/j.jmoneco.2016.01.005

Lewicki, R. J., & Bunker, B. B. (1996). Developing and maintaining trust in work relationships. In R.M. Kramer & T.R. Tyler (Ed.), Trust in Organizations: Frontiers of Theory and Research (pp. 438-458). Thousand Oaks, CA: Sage Publications. doi:10.4135/9781452243610.n7

Liapis, P. (2011). *Changing Patterns of Trade in Processed Agricultural Products*. Paris: OECD Publishing.

Liberalizatsiya torgovogo rezhima mezhdu EAES i Vietnamom pozvolila za posledniy god narastit tovarooborot mezhdu storonami na 36% [The liberalization of the trade regime between the EAEU and Vietnam allowed to increase the trade turnover between the parties by 36%]. (2018, June 19). Eurasian Economic Commission. Retrieved from http://www.eurasiancommission.org/ru/nae/news/Pages/19-06-2018-2.aspx

Liberthal, K. (2004). *Governing China: From Revolution Through Reform*. New York, NY: W. W. Norton.

Lindsay, J. M. (2011). George W. Bush, Barack Obama and the future of US global leadership. *International Affairs*, *87*(4), 772. doi:10.1111/j.1468-2346.2011.01003.x

Lisovolik, Y. (2017). Evraziyskiy ekonomicheskiy soyuz i ASEAN: otsenka vzaimodopolnyaemosti [The Eurasian Economic Union and ASEAN: assessment of complementarity] *International trends*, 15(3), 46-54. doi:10.17994/IT.2017.15.3.50.4

Lisovolik, Y. (2017, July 2). *Pereosmyslenie BRIKS: BRIKS+ i BRIKS++ [Rethinking of BRICS: BRICS+ and BRICS++]*. National Committee on BRICS research, Russia. Retrieved from http://www.nkibrics.ru/posts/show/589af8e7627269598602000

Lisovolik, Ya. (2016). Geoekonomika i naslediye yevraziytsev. [Geoeconomics and the legacy of Eurasians Russia in global politics]. *Rossiya v global'noy politike,* 6, 61-69.

Liu, J., & Diamond, J. (2005). China's Environment in a Globalizing World. *Nature*, *435*(7046), 1179–1186. doi:10.1038/4351179a PMID:15988514

Liu, T., & Woo, W. T. (2018, October 04). Understanding the U.S.-China Trade War. China. *Economic Journal (London), 11*(3), 319–340. doi:10.1080/17538963.2018.1516256

Llambi, C., Rius, A., Carbajal, F., Carrasco, P., & Cazulo, P. (2017). *Are taxes credits effective ın developing countries? The recent Uruguayan experience.* Development Bank of Latin America Working Paper, No 2017/5.

Lombardo, C. (n.d.). 13 most valid protectionism pros and cons. Retrieved from https://vittana.org/13-most-valid-protectionism-pros-and-cons

Los Angeles Times. (2010, April 12). Obama discusses Mideast peace prospects with Jordan's King Abdullah. Retrieved from http://latimesblogs.latimes.com/dcnow/2010/04/obama-discusses-mideast-peace-prospects-with-jordans-abdullah.html

Lukashenko: sozdaniye EAES ne otmenyayet perspektiv Soyuznogo gosudarstva Rossii i Belorussii [Lukashenko: the creation of the EAEU does not cancel the prospects of the Union State of Russia and Belarus]. (2015, March 3). *Informatsionnoye Agentstvo TASS*. Retrieved from https://tass.ru/mezhdunarodnaya-panorama/1805062

Lu, N. (1997). *The Dynamics of Foreign-Policy Decisionmaking in China*. Boulder, CO: Westview Press.

Lyon, S., Lefton, R., & Daniel Weiss. (2010, April 23). Quenching Our Thirst for Oil: Growing Global Oil Demand Harms U.S. Security and Economy. *American Progress*. Retrieved from https://www.americanprogress.org/issues/green/news/2010/04/23/7657/quenching-our-thirst-for-oil/

Maasho, A. (2017). Ethiopia devalues currency by 15 percent to boost exports. *Reuters*. Retrieved from https://www.reuters.com/article/ethiopia-rates/update-1-ethiopia-devalues-currency-by-15-percent-to-boost-exports-idUSL8N1ML40J

Macrotrends. (2018). *Dollar Yuan Exchange Rate - 35 Year Historical Chart.* Retrieved November 11, 2018, from https://www.macrotrends.net/2575/us-dollar-yuan-exchange-rate-historical-chart

Maitah, M., Kuzmenko, E., & Smutka, L. (2016). Real Effective Exchange Rate of Rouble and Competitiveness of Russian Agrarian Producers. *Economies*, *4*(3), 12. doi:10.3390/economies4030012

Maksakova, M. A. (2018). Problemi vneshney tiorgovli Serbii s ES i EAES [Problems of foreign trade of Serbia with the EU and the EAEU], Russian *Foreign. Economic Bulletin*, (1): 37–45.

Mallampally, P., & Sauvant, K. P. (1999). Foreign direct investment in developing countries. *Finance & Development*, *36*(1), 1–3.

Malpass, D. (2005). Exchange rate protectionism: A harmful diversion for trade and development policy. *The Cato Journal*, *25*(1), 107–110.

Mamedov, S. (2017, August 07). *Soglashenie mejdu EAES i MERKOSUR razvernet globalnie torgovie potoki s Severa na Yug [The agreement between the EEU and MERCOSUR will redirect global trade flows from North to South].* Retrieved from http://mirperemen.net/2017/08/soglashenie-mezhdu-eaes-i-merkosur-razvernet-globalnye-torgovye-potoki-s-severa-na-yug/

Mariani, B. (2013). *China's Role and Interests in Central Asia*. London: Saferworld.

Márquez-Ramos, L. (2007). *Understanding the determinants of international trade in African countries: An empirical analysis for Ghana and South Africa*. Instituto de Economía Internacional.

Martinsen, K. D. (2002, October). The Russian Takeover of Belarus. *Comparative Strategy*, *21*(5), 401–416. doi:10.1080/01495930290043119

Mashko, V. V. (2011). *Dinamika razvitiya rossiysko-belorusskikh torgovykh otnosheniy* [*Dynamics of development of Russian-Belarusian trade relations*]. Retrieved from http://economicarggu.ru/2011_2/mashko.pdf

Mashko, V. V. (2009). Iz istorii Soyuznogo gosudarstva Belarusi i Rossii: Byudzhet i byudzhetnaya politika. [From the history of the Union State of Belarus and Russia: budget and budget policy]. *MGIMO*, *17*, 182–190.

Matziorinis, K. N. (2006). *A Brief History of the International Monetary System*. Montreal, Canada: Economics Centre for Continuing Education McGill University.

Mauri, A. (2010). Monetary developments and decolonization in Ethiopia. *Acta Universitatis Danubius Œconomica, 6*(1).

McClellan, M. (2003). *Collaborative manufacturing: using real time information to support the supply chain*. Florida: St. Lucie Press.

Mcgowan, B. (1981). *Economic Life in Ottoman Europe*. Newyork: Cambridge University.

Mel'nik, V. A. (2004). Gosudarstvennaya ideologiya Respubliki Belarus': kontseptual'nyye osnovy [State ideology of the Republic of Belarus: conceptual framework]. Minsk.

Melitz, M. J. (2003). The impact of trade on intra-industry reallocations and aggregate industry productivity. *Econometrica*, *71*(6), 1695–1725. doi:10.1111/1468-0262.00467

Memorandum of understanding between Eurasian Economic Commission and Association of Southeast Asian Nations in the sphere of economic cooperation. (2018). Eurasian Economic Union. Retrieved from https://docs.eaeunion.org/docs/ru-ru/01319988/ms_22112018

Memorandum on the cooperation on trade and economic issues between the Eurasian Economic Union and Southern Common Market (MERCOSUR). (2018). Eurasian Economic Union. Retrieved from https://docs.eaeunion.org/docs/ru-ru/01320292/ms_21122018

Mezhgosudarstvennyye otnosheniya RF i Belarusi (2018, December 25). [Interstate relations of the Russian Federation and Belarus. *RIA Novosti*. Retrieved from https://ria.ru/20181225/1548544649.html

Mezhgosudarstvennyye otnosheniya Rossii i Belarusi [Interstate relations of Russia and Belarus]. (14 May 2018). *RIA Novosti*. Retrieved from https://ria.ru/20180514/1520366481.html

Ministr torgovli EAES Verinika Nikishina: my idem k polnotsennoy zone svobodnoy torgovli s Iranom [Minister of trade of the EAEU Veronika Nikishina: we are going to a full-fledged free trade area with Iran]. (2018, November 10). BFM.RU. Retrieved from https://news.rambler.ru/other/41249616/?utm_content=rnews&utm_medium=read_more&utm_source=copylink

Mogilevskaya i Novosibirskaya oblasti namereny razvivat' mezhregional'noye sotrudnichestvo [Mogilev and Novosibirsk regions intend to develop interregional cooperation]. (2018). *Informatsionno-analiticheskiy portal Soyuznogo gosudarstva*. Retrieved from http://www.soyuz.by/news/region/43081.html

Mohr, J., & Spekman, R. (1994). Characteristics of partnership success: Partnership in attributes, communication behavior, and conflict resolution techniques. *Strategic Management Journal*, *15*(2), 135–152. doi:10.1002mj.4250150205

Momayezi, N., & Rosenburg, R. B. (2011). Oil, the Middle East and U.S. National Security. *International Journal of Humanities and Social Science*, *1*(10), 1–7.

Monthly Merchandise Trade Value. (2018). WTO. Retrieved from https://www.wto.org/english/res_e/statis_e/daily_update_e/monthly_trade_e.xls

Moore, J. (2017, January 6). Jordan Tells Trump: Moving U.S. Embassy to Jerusalem a 'Red Line.' *Newsweek*.

Moorman, C., Zaltman, G., & Desphande, R. (1992). Relationships between providers and users of market research: The dynamics of trust within and between organizations. *JMR, Journal of Marketing Research*, *29*(3), 314–328. doi:10.1177/002224379202900303

Morisset, J., & Pirnia, N. (2000). *How tax policy and incentives affect foreign direct investment a review*. The World Bank and International Finance Corporation Foreign Investment Advisory Service.

Munongo, S., Akanbi, O. A., & Robinson, Z. (2017). Do tax incentives matter for investment? A literature review. *Business and Economic Horizons*, *13*(2), 152–168. doi:10.15208/beh.2017.12

Nath, R., Luan, Y., Yang, W., Yang, C., Chen, W., Li, Q., & Cui, X. (2015). Changes in Arable Land Demand for Food in India and China: A Potential Threat to Food Security. *Sustainability*, *7*(5), 5371–5397. doi:10.3390u7055371

National Bureau of Statistics China. (2018). *China Labor Costs*. Retrieved from https://tradingeconomics.com/china/labour-costs

Nega, M.K. (2015) Assessment on Real Effective Exchange Rate and External Sector Development of Ethiopia. *Economics*, *4*(4), 64-70. doi:10.11648/j.eco.20150404.12

Nemtsev, Yu. (2017). Rossiya i Vietnam: Razvitie i protsvetanie [Russia and Vietnam: development and prosperity]. *International Affairs*, *4*(June). Retrieved from https://interaffairs.ru/news/show/17673

Nielsen, L. (2011). *Classifications of countries based on their level of development: How it is done and how it could be done*.

Nikulina, Yu. V. (2016). *Regionalizatsiya v globaliziruyushchemsya mire: problemy i perspektivy*. [*Regionalization in a Globalizing World: Problems and Prospects*]. Retrieved from http://elib.bsu.by/bitstream/123456789/156751/1/276-279.pdf

Nkoro, E., & Uko, A. K. (2016). Autoregressive Distributed Lag (ARDL) cointegration technique: Application and interpretation. *Journal of Statistical and Econometric Methods*, *5*(4), 63–91.

Nunnenkamp, P. (2002). *Determinants of FDI in developing countries: Has globalization changed the rules of the game?*

O proekte resheniya Vysshego Evraziyskogo ekonomicheskogo soveta "Ob Osnovnikh napravleniyakh mezhdunarodnoy deyatel'nosti Evraziyskogo ekonomicheskogo soyuza na 2019 god" [On the draft of the decision of the Supreme Eurasian Economic Council "On the main directions of international activities of the Eurasian Economic Union in 2019"]. (2018). Alta Soft. Retrieved from https://www.alta.ru/tamdoc/18r00164/

Ob itogakh vneshney torgovli Respubliki Belarus' s Rossiyskoy Federatsiyey v 2018 godu (2018). [On the results of foreign trade of the Republic of Belarus with the Russian Federation in 2018]. *Posol'stvo Respubliki Belarus' v Rossiyskoy Federatsii*. Retrieved from http://www.embassybel.ru/trade-relations/

Ob itogakh vneshney torgovli tovarami Evraziyskogo ekonomicheskogo soyuza [On the results of foreign trade in goods of the Eurasian Economic Union]. (2018, April 24). *Analytical review*. Retrieved from http://www.eurasiancommission.org/ru/act/integr_i_makroec/dep_stat/tradestat/analytics/Documents/2018/Analytics_E_201802.pdf

Obama, B. (2010a, September 1). Remarks Following a Meeting With Prime Minister Benjamin Netanyahu of Israel. Retrieved from http://www.presidency.ucsb.edu/ws/?pid=88375

Obama, B. (2010b, October 21). Remarks and a Question-and-Answer Session in Seattle, Washington. Retrieved from http://www.presidency.ucsb.edu/ws/index.php?pid=88609&st=Jordan&st1=

Obama, B. (2011, May 17). Remarks Following a Meeting With King Abdullah II of Jordan. Retrieved from http://www.presidency.ucsb.edu/ws/index.php?pid=90389&st=Jordan&st1=

Obama, B. (2012, January 17). Remarks Following a Meeting With King Abdullah II of Jordan. Retrieved from http://www.presidency.ucsb.edu/ws/?pid=98978

Obama, B. (2013, April 26). Remarks Prior to a Meeting With King Abdullah II of Jordan and an Exchange With Reporters. Retrieved from http://www.presidency.ucsb.edu/ws/?pid=103550

Obama, B. (2015a, July 24). Interview with Jon Sopel of BBC. Retrieved from http://www.presidency.ucsb.edu/ws/?pid=128836

Obama, B. (2015b, December 11). Letter to Congressional Leaders on the Global Deployment of United States Combat-Equipped Armed Forces. Retrieved from www.presidency.ucsb.edu/ws/?pid=111236

Obama, B. (2016, April 1). Joint Statement on Sustaining Action To Strengthen Global Nuclear Security. Retrieved from http://www.presidency.ucsb.edu/ws/?pid=117319

Oberman, N. G. (1997). *Transfer of risk from seller to buyer in international commercial contracts: A comparative analysis of risk allocation under the CISG.* UCC and Incoterms.

Obzor itogov vneshney politiki Respubliki Belarus' i deyatel'nosti Ministerstva inostrannykh del v 2018 godu. [Review of the results of the foreign policy of the Republic of Belarus and the activities of the Ministry of Foreign Affairs in 2018]. *Doklady Ministerstva inostrannykh del.* Retrieved from http://mfa.gov.by/publication/reports/b7fe6b330b96c9b7.html

OECD. (1995). *Taxation and foreign direct investment: The experince of the economies in transition.* Paris: OECD.

OECD. (2007). Tax incentives for investment – A global perspective: Experiences in MENA and non-MENA countries. Retrieved from http://www.oecd.org/mena/competitiveness/38758855.pdf

OECD. (2008a). *OECD Benchmark definition of foreign direct investment* (4th ed.).

OECD. (2008b). *Policy brief, tax effects on foreign direct investment.* Retrieved from https://www.oecd.org/investment/investment-policy/40152903.pdf

Office of the United States Representative. *China, Mongolia and Taiwan.* Retrieved from https://ustr.gov/countries-regions/china-mongolia-taiwan

Office of the United States Trade Representative (2018, March 22). *Findings of the Investigation into China's Acts, policies, and Practices related to Technology Transfer, Intellectual Property, and Innovation under Section 301 of the Trade Act of 1974.*

Office of the United States Trade Representative. (2018). *2017 Report to Congress on China's WTO Compliance.*

Office of the United States Trade Representative. (2018). President Trump Approves Relief for U.S. Washing Machine and Solar Cell Manufacturers. Retrieved from https://ustr.gov/about-us/policy-offices/press-office/press-releases/2018/january/president-trump-approves-relief-us

Office of the United States Trade Representative. (2018, June 15). *USTR Issues Tariffs on Chinese Products in Response to Unfair Trade Practices.* Retrieved from https://ustr.gov/about-us/policy-offices/press-office/press-releases/2018/june/ustr-issues-tariffs-chinese-products

Office of the United States Trade Representative. (2018, June 29). *Section 301 Product List Fact Sheet.* Retrieved from https://ustr.gov/about-us/policy-offices/press-office/fact-sheets/2018/june/section-301-product-list-fact-sheet

Office of the United States Trade Representative. (2018, June). *USTR Finalizes Tariffs on $200 Billion of Chinese Imports in Response to China's Unfair Trade Practices.* Retrieved from https://ustr.gov/about-us/policy-offices/press-office/press-releases/2018/june/ustr-issues-tariffs-chinese-products

Office of the United States Trade Representative. (2018, September 18). *USTR Finalizes Tariffs on $200 Billion of Chinese Imports in Response to China's Unfair Trade Practices.* Retrieved from https://ustr.gov/about-us/policy-offices/press-office/press-releases/2018/september/ustr-finalizes-tariffs-200#

Olaleye, M. O., Riro, G. K., & Memba, F. S. (2016). Effect of reduced company income tax incentives on foreign direct investment in listed Nigerian manufacturing companies. European Journal of Business. *Economics and Accountancy*, *4*(1), 39–54.

Omoju, O., & Adesanya, O. (2012). Does Trade Promote Growth in Developing Countries? Empirical Evidence from Nigeria. *International Journal of Development and Sustainability*, *1*(2), 743–753.

Öniş, Z. (2014). Küreselleşme,Gelir Adaletsizliği ve Demokrasinin Geleceği:Kriz Sonrası Eğilimler. *İktisat ve Toplum*, *4*(47), 13-25.

Orlov, A. (2014, April 19). *Dorogoy vietnamskiy drug [The dearest Vietnamese friend].* Gazeta RU. Retrieved from https://www.gazeta.ru/business/2014/04/18/5998025.shtml

Özdemir, B. (2010). *Osmanlı Devleti Dış Borçları*. Ankara: Maliye Bakanlığı strateji Geliştirme Başkanlığı.

Pamuk, Ş. (1985). 19.yy'da Osmanlı Dış Ticareti. Tanzimattan Cumhuriyete Türkiye Ansiklopedisi. *İstanbul:İletişim Yayınları*, 3.

Pamuk, Ş. (1994). *Osmanlı Ekonomisinde Bağımlılık ve Büyüme (1820-1913)*. İstanbul: Tarih Vakfı Yurt Yayınları.

Pamuk, Ş. (2002). Küreselleşme Çağında Osmanlı Ekonomisi (1820-1914). Türkler Ansiklopedisi. *Ankara:Yeni Türkiye Yayınları*, 14.

Pamuk, Ş. (2015). *Türkiye'nin 200 Yıllık İktisadi Tarihi*. İstanbul: İş Bankası Kültür Yayınları.

Pamuk, Ş. (2017). *Osmanlı'dan Cumhuriyete Küreselleşme, İktisat Politikaları ve Büyüme*. Türkiye İş Bankası Kültür Yayınları.

Panagariya, A. (2003). International trade. *Foreign Policy*, *139*(139), 20–28. doi:10.2307/3183727

Panitchpakdi, S., & Clifford, M. L. (2002). *China and the WTO: Changing China, Changing World Trade*. Singapore: J. Wiley & Sons.

Park, A., Jin, H., Rozelle, S., & Huang, J. (2002). Market Emergence and Transition: Arbitrage, Transaction Costs, and Autarky in China's Grain Markets. *American Journal of Agricultural Economics*, *84*(1), 67–82. doi:10.1111/1467-8276.00243

Parlamentskoye Sobraniye prinyalo byudzhet Soyuznogo gosudarstva na 2019 god v razmere 7 mlrd 245 mln rossiyskikh rubley [The Parliamentary Assembly adopted the budget of the Union State for 2019 in the amount of 7 billion 245 million Russian rubles]. (2018, December 22). *Informatsionno-analiticheskiy portal Soyuznogo gosudarstva*. Retrieved from http://www.soyuz.by/news/finance/42747.html

Pena, N. A., & Arroyabe, J. C. F. (2002). *Business Cooperation*. New York: Palgrave Macmillan. doi:10.1057/9780230554696

Perez Motta, E. (2016). *Competition Policy and Trade in the Global Economy: Towards an Integrated Approach*. Geneva: International Center for Trade and Sustainable Development; World Economic Forum.

Peter, M. (September,2010). Does the devaluation of our currency benefit or hurt Ethiopia? "ECAD forum".Retrieved from https://ecadforum.com/blog/does-the-devaluation-of-our-currency-benefit-or-hurt-ethiopia/

Peters, G. T., & Kiabel, B. D. (2015). Tax incentives and foreign direct investment in Nigeria. *IOSR Journal of Economics and Finance*, *6*(5), 10–20.

Petroff, A., Iyengar, R., & Mullen, J. (2018). The odds of a messy trade war between the US and China are rising again. *CNN*. Retrieved from https://money.cnn.com/2018/05/30/news/economy/trump-china-us-tariffs-trade-timeline/index.html

Piketty, T. (2013). *Yirmi birinci yüzyılda kapital.(Çev: Hande Koçak).* İstanbul: Türkiye İş Bankası Kültür Publishing.

Podgotovka predlozheniy po razvitiyu mezhdunarodnogo sotrudnichestva s tret'imi stranami i mezhdunarodnimi organizatsiyami [Preparation of proposals for the development of international cooperation with the third countries and international organizations]. (n.d.). Eurasian Economic Commission. Retrieved from http://www.eurasiancommission.org/ru/act/integr_i_makroec/dep_razv_integr/Pages/Международное%20сотрудничество%20(old).aspx

Podvedeny itogi Foruma prigranichnykh territoriy Rossii i Belarusi [The results of the Forum of the border areas of Russia and Belarus]. (2018, November 30). *Informatsionno-analiticheskiy portal Soyuznogo gosudarstva*. Retrieved from http://www.soyuz.by/news/region/42442.html

Poppo, L., Zhou, K. Z., & Zenger, T. (2003). The economic and social embeddedness of relational governance: An empirical study exploring origins and effectiveness. *Paper presented at the Academy of Management 2003 Annual Meetings*, Seattle, WA. 10.5465/ambpp.2003.13793233

Pototsky, A. (2018, August 8). Asbest protiv trusov. Rossiya postavit 'shlagbaum' dlya nizhnego belay iz Vietnama [Asbestos versus pants. Russia will put a 'barrier' for underwear from Vietnam]. *LIFE#Business*. Retrieved from https://life.ru/t/бизнес/1141663/asbiest_protiv_trusov_rossiia_postavit_shlaghbaum_dlia_nizhniegho_bielia_iz_vietnama

Powell, W. W. (1990). Neither market nor hierarchy: Network forms of organization. In B. M. Staw & L. L. Cummings (Eds.), *Research in Organizational Behavior* (pp. 295–336). Greenwich: JAI Press.

Praktika provedeniya belorussko-rossiyskikh molodezhnykh biznes-inkubatorov budet prodolzhena v 2019 godu [The practice of conducting Belarusian-Russian youth business incubators will be continued in 2019]. (2018, December 5). *Informatsionno-analiticheskiy portal Soyuznogo gosudarstva*. Retrieved from http://www.soyuz.by/news/finance/42512.html

Pravitel'stvo Bryanskoy oblasti [*Government of Bryansk region*]. (2018, December 4). Retrieved from http://www.bryanskobl.ru/news/2018/11/28/9393

Productivity Commission. (2017). Rising protectionism: challenges, threats and opportunities for Australia.

Qing, K. G. (April 14, 2012). Timeline: China's reforms of yuan exchange rate. *Reuters*. Retrieved from https://www.reuters.com/article/us-china-yuan-timeline/timeline-chinas-reforms-of-yuan-exchange-rate-idUSBRE83D03820120414

Quora. (n.d.). *How does the International Monetary Fund judge a country as having a developing or developed economy?* Retrieved from https://www.quora.com/How-does-the-International-Monetary-Fund-judge-a-country-as-having-a-developing-or-developed-economy

Rakhimov, K. (2017). Soyuznoye gosudarstvo seychas nakhoditsya v tupike [The Union State is now at a dead end]. *SONAR 2050*. Retrieved from https://www.sonar2050.org/publications/v-blijayshee-vremya-soyuznoe-gosudarstvo-nujno-rassmatrivat-sugubo-v-kontekste-evraziyskoy-integracii/

Ralph, O. (2014). Trade Wars and Trade Talks with Data. *The American Economic Review*, *104*(12), 4104–4146. doi:10.1257/aer.104.12.4104

Ratnayake, R. (1994). Determinants of international trade: A simultaneous equation model. *New Zealand Economic Papers*, *28*(1), 25–52. doi:10.1080/00779959409544214

Ravid, B. (2017, February 19). Exclusive: Kerry Offered Netanyahu Regional Peace Plan in Secret 2016 Summit with al-Sissi, King Abdullah. *Haaretz*. Retrieved from www.haaretz.com/israel-%0Anews/.premium-1.772531?=&ts=_1487969163123

Reinhart, C. M. (1995). Devaluation, relative prices, and international trade: evidence from developing countries. *Staff papers*, *42*(2), 290-312.

Reis Gomes, F. A., & Senne Paz, L. (2005). Can real exchange rate devaluation improve the trade balance? The 1990–1998 Brazilian case. *Applied Economics Letters*, *12*(9), 525-528.

Republic of Turkey Ministry of Trade, Customs and Trade. (n.d.). Retrieved from https://ggm.ticaret.gov.tr/

Reyes, J. D. (2018). *Effects of FDI on high growth firms in developing countries. Global Investment Competitiveness Report*. Foreign Investor Perspectives and Policy Implications.

RF v 2018 godu uvelichila eksport produktsii APK v Belorussiyu na 20% [*The Russian Federation in 2018 increased exports of agricultural products to Belarus by 20%*]. (2019, February 14). Retrieved from http://www.dairynews.ru/news/rf-v-2018-godu-uvelichila-eksport-produktsii-apk-v.html

Rhomberg, R. R. (1973). Toward a General Trade Models. In R.J. Ball (Ed.), The International Linkage of National Economic Models.

Ricardo, D. (2015). Principles of political economy and taxation. Cambridge: Cambridge University Press. (originally printed in 1819)

Rinehart, L. M. (2007). Negotiating throughout the supply chain. In J. T. Mentzer, B. M. Myers, & T. P. Stank (Eds.), *Handbook of Global Supply Chain Management* (pp. 407–426). Thousand Oaks, CA: Sage Publications. doi:10.4135/9781412976169.n24

Rodríguez, A. N. (2015, March 20). Kak MERKOSUR i Evraziyskiy soyuz brosayut vizov Soedinennim Shtatam i gegemonii dollara [How MERCOSUR and the Eurasian Union challenge to the United States and the dollar hegemony]. *INOSMI*. Retrieved from http://inosmi.ru/world/20150320/226991984.html

Rossiya i Belorussiya budut sotrudnichat' po obshchemu zakonu [Russia and Belarus will cooperate under the general law]. *Parlamentskaya gazeta*. (2018, November 29). Retrieved from https://www.pnp.ru/politics/rossiya-i-belorussiya-budut-sotrudnichat-po-obshhemu-zakonu.html

Rosyadi, S. A., & Widodo, T. (2018). Impact of Donald Trump's tariff increase against Chinese imports on global economy: Global Trade Analysis Project (GTAP) model. *Journal of Chinese Economic and Business Studies*, *16*(2), 125–145. doi:10.1080/14765284.2018.1427930

Roy, D., Munasib, A., & Chen, X. (2014). Social trust and international trade: The interplay between social trust and formal finance. *Review of World Economics*, *150*(4), 693–714. doi:10.100710290-014-0197-2

Ruggie, J. G. (1994). Trade, protectionism and the future of welfare capitalism. *Journal of International Affairs*, *48*(1), 1–11.

Rutko, D.F. (2017). *Razvitiye vneshneekonomicheskogo sotrudnichestva Respubliki Belarus' so stranami BRIKS* [*Development of foreign economic cooperation of the Republic of Belarus with the BRICS countries*]. Retrieved from ukros.ru/wpcontent/uploads/2017/03/Рутко_Радюк.doc

Sagar, A. (2017). Free global trade v/s protectionism- a critical review. *International Journal of Engineering Sciences & Research Technology*, *6*(4), 252–254.

Saini, N., & Singhania, M. (2017). Determinants of FDI in developed and developing countries: A quantitative analysis using GMM. *Journal of Economic Studies (Glasgow, Scotland)*, *4*(2), 348–382. doi:10.1108/JES-07-2016-0138

Sako, M. (1992). *Prices, quality and trust: inter-firm relations in Britain and Japan*. Cambridge: Cambridge University Press. doi:10.1017/CBO9780511520723

Santana, R. (2017). 70th Anniversary of the GATT: Stalin, the Marshall Plan, and the Provisional Application of the GATT 1947. *Journal of Trade Law and Development*, *9*(2).

Savaş, V. (2004). *Dünya Ekonomi Sistemi*. İstanbul: Yeditepe Üniversitesi Yayınları.

Savrul, B. K., Özel, H. A., & Kılıç, C. (2013). Osmanlı'nın Son Döneminden Günümüze Türkiye Dış Ticaretinin Gelişimi. Girişimcilik ve Kalkınma Dergisi, 1(8), 55-78.

Şenses, F. (2004). Neoliberal Küreselleşme Kalkınma İçin Bir Fırsat mı, Engel mi? *ERC*.

Şenses, F. (2001). *Küreselleşmenin Öteki Yüzü: Yoksulluk-Kavramlar, Nedenler,Politikalar ve Temel Eğilimler*. İstanbul: İletişim Yayınları.

Serhan, Y. (2018). How Do You Know When It's Officially a Trade War? *The Atlantic*. Retrieved from https://www.theatlantic.com/international/archive/2018/06/trade-war-us-europe/563504/

Seyidoğlu, H. (2003). Uluslararası İktisat Teori Politika ve Uygulama. İstanbul: Güzem Yayınları.

Seyidoğlu, H. (2013). *Uluslararası iktisat teori politika ve uygulama (19. Baskı)*. İstanbul: Güzem Can Yayınları.

Sharp, J. M. (2012). *US Foreign Aid to Israel*. Washington, D.C.: Congressional Research Service. Retrieved from http://www.fas.org/sgp/crs/mideast/RL33222.pdf%3E

Sharp, J. M. (2015). *U.S. Foreign Aid to Israel*. Washington, D.C.: Congressional Research Service. Retrieved from http://securityassistance.org/sites/default/files/RL33222.pdf

Sharp, J. M. (2018). *Jordan : Background and U.S. Relations*. Washington, D.C.: Congressional Research Service.

Shibutov, M. (2018, July 12). *Sopryazhenie EAES i Kitaya: vozmozhno li? [The Conjugation of the EAEU and China: is it possible?]*. Regnum. Retrieved from https://regnum.ru/news/2446781.html

Skonieczny, A. (2018). Trading with the enemy: Narrative, identity and US trade politics. *Review of International Political Economy*, *25*(4), 441–462. doi:10.1080/09692290.2018.1448879

Skousen, M. (2003). *Modern İktisadın İnşası.Çev.Mustafa Acar, Ekrem Erdem, Metin Toprak*. Ankara: Liberte Yayınları.

Slusarczyk, B. (2018). Tax incentives as a main factor to attract foreign direct investments in Poland. *Administratie si Management Public*, *30*(30), 67–81. doi:10.24818/amp/2018.30-05

Soglashenie o zone svobodnoy torgovli mezhdu EAES i Vyetnamom: pervie rezultati realizatsii. (2018). [Agreement on free trade area between the EAEU and Vietnam: first results of its realization]. October 19. ASEAN Centre in MGIMO-University, the MFA of Russia. Retrieved 7 February, 2019, from http://asean.mgimo.ru/ru/790-soglashenie-o-zone-svobodnoj-torgovli-mezhdu-eaes-i-vetnamom-pervye-rezultaty-realizatsii

Soyuz Belarusi i Rossii yavlyayetsya yadrom YEAES – Al.A. Gromyko. [Union of Belarus and Russia is the core of the EAEU - Al.A. Gromyko]. (2017, November 29). *Analiticheskiy Portal Yevraziya Ekspert*. Retrieved from http://eurasia.expert/soyuz-belarusi-i-rossii-yavlyaetsya-yadrom-eaes-gromyko

Soyuznoye gosudarstvo Belarusi i Rossii. Ot Soobshchestva k Soyuznomu gosudarstvu [*Union State of Belarus and Russia. From the Community to the Union State*]. (2018). Moscow: YUNITI-DANA.

Spring, J. (2018). Brazil Record Soy Exports to China Could Expand Further – Official. *Reuters*. Retrieved from https://www.reuters.com/article/brazil-agriculture-trade/brazil-record-soy-exports-to-china-could-expand-further-official-idUSL4N1XP5YI

Spring, J., & Polansek, T. (2018). Trump Trade War Delivers Farm Boom in Brazil, Gloom in Iowa. *Reuters*. Retrieved from https://www.reuters.com/article/us-usa-trade-china-brazil-insight/trump-trade-war-delivers-farm-boom-in-brazil-gloom-in-iowa-idUSKCN1ML0E7

Steinherr, A. (1980). Devaluation in developing countries. *Recherches Économiques de Louvain/Louvain. Economic Review (Federal Reserve Bank of Atlanta), 46*(3), 207–234.

Stern, R. M. (1973). Tariffs and Other Measures of Trade Control: A Survey of Recent Developments. *Journal of Economic Literature, 3*(11), 857–888.

Sun, P., & Heshmati, A. (2010). *International Trade and Its Effects on Economic Growth in China*. Bonn: Institute for the Study of Labor.

Suzdal'tsev, A.I. (2007). Postsovetskoye prostranstvo: ukhodyashchaya real'nost' [Post-Soviet space: a passing reality]. *Mir vokrug Rossii. Kontury nedalekogo budushchego*. Moscow: Kul'turnaya revolyutsiya, 124-137.

Tabakoğlu, A. (2005). *Türkiye İktisat Tarihi*. İstanbul: Dergah Yayınları.

Tabakoğlu, A. (2013). *İslam İktisadına Giriş*. İstanbul: Dergah Yayınları.

Taheripour, F., & Tyner, W. E. (2018a). Impacts of Possible Chinese 25% Tariff on U.S. Soybeans and Other Agricultural Commodities. *Choices, 33*(2).

Taheripour, F., & Tyner, W. E. (2018b). *Impacts of Possible Chinese Protection on US Soybeans*. West Lafayette, IN: Purdue University.

Tan, H. (2018, August 22). Beijing retaliates as new US tariffs kick in on $16 billion of Chinese goods. *CNBC*. Retrieved from https://www.cnbc.com/2018/08/23/us-china-trade-war-new-round-of-american-tariffs-on-chinese-imports.html

Tan, R. (2018). The U.S.-China trade war has begun. Here's how things got to this point. *Washington Post*. Retrieved from https://www.washingtonpost.com/news/worldviews/wp/2018/07/05/a-timeline-of-how-the-u-s-china-trade-war-led-us-to-this-code-red-situation/?utm_term=.cdb09dbf96f5

Tan, R. (2018, July 6). The U.S.-China trade war has begun. Here's how things got to this point. *The Washington Post*. Retrieved from https://www.washingtonpost.com/news/worldviews/wp/2018/07/05/a-timeline-of-how-the-u-s-china-trade-war-led-us-to-this-code-red-situation/?noredirect=on&utm_term=.70088ed928df

Tan, W. (2018). China's Approach to Reduce Poverty: Taking Targeted Measures to Lift People out of Poverty. *United Nations*. Retrieved from https://www.un.org/development/desa/dspd/wp-content/uploads/sites/22/2018/05/31.pdf

TDK. (n.d.). Retrieved from http://www.tdk.gov.tr

Tekin, A. (2006). Vergi teşvikleri ve ekonomik etkileri. *Dumlupınar Üniversitesi Sosyal Bilimler Dergisi, 16*, 301–316.

The White House. (2015). *National Security Strategy*. Washington, D.C.

Thobie, J. (1985). *Osmanlı Devletinde Yabancı Sermaye Tanzimattan Cumhuriyete Türkiye Ansiklopedisi*. İstanbul: İletişim Yayınları.

Thow, A. M., & Hawkes, C. (2009). The Implications of Trade Liberalization for Diet and Health: A Case Study from Central America. *Globalization and Health, 28*(1), 5. doi:10.1186/1744-8603-5-5 PMID:19638196

Trade war. (n.d.). Investopedia. Retrieved from https://www.investopedia.com/terms/t/trade-war.asp#ixzz5XwqZIP5z

Trade wars, Trump tariffs and protectionism explained. (2018, July 26). BBC. Retrieved from https://www.bbc.com/news/world-43512098

Tsvetov, A. (2017, October 17). *Vmesto povorota: ASEAN i evraziyskiy proekt Rossii [Instead of turn: ASEAN and Eurasian project of Russia]*. Carnegie Moscow Center. Retrieved from https://carnegie.ru/2017/10/17/ru-pub-73368

Tung, S., & Cho, S. (2000). The impact of tax incentives on foreign direct investment in China. *Journal of International Accounting, Auditing & Taxation, 9*(2), 105–135. doi:10.1016/S1061-9518(00)00028-8

Turkish Statistical Institute (TURKSTAT). (n.d.). Retrieved from http://www.turkstat.gov.tr/

Türkiye B.F.O. (n.d.). Turkish Interbank Rate. (n.d.). Retrieved from https://tr.tradingeconomics.com/turkey/interbank-rate

U.S. Department of Commerce. (2018). *U.S. Department of Commerce Announces Steel and Aluminum Tariff Exclusion Process*. Retrieved from https://www.commerce.gov/news/press-releases/2018/03/us-department-commerce-announces-steel-and-aluminum-tariff-exclusion

U.S. International Trade Commission. (2018). Large Residential Washers: Investigation No. TA-201-076. Retrieved from https://www.usitc.gov/publications/safeguards/pub4745.pdf

Ugwu, J. I. (2018). Tax incentives and foreign direct investment (fdı): Implication for export promotion in Nigeria, Ghana and South Africa, post ifrs adoption. *International Journal in Management and Social Science, 6*(9), 31–52.

Umakhanov, I. (2018). Rossiya zainteresovana v podkluchenii evropeyskikh partnerov k proektu Bol'shogo evraziyskogo partnerstva [Russia is interested in joining the European partners to Greater Eurasian partnership]. Federative Council. Retrieved from http://council.gov.ru/events/news/91810/

United Nations Conference on Trade and Development. (2019). *Statistics Database* [Data file]. Retrieved from http://unctad.org/en/Pages/Statistics.aspx

United Nations ESCAP. (2017). *Tax incentives and tax base protection in developing countries*. Retrieved from https://www.unescap.org/sites/default/files/S3_Tax-Incentives-and-Tax-Protection-Base.pdf

United Nations. (2018). *Design and assessment of tax incentives in developing countries*. New York.

United States Census Bureau. (2018). *Trade in Goods with China*. Retrieved from https://www.census.gov/foreign-trade/balance/c5700.html

United States Department of Agriculture. (2018). *Top U.S. Agricultural Exports in 2017*. Retrieved from https://www.fas.usda.gov/data/top-us-agricultural-exports-2017

US Department of State Archive. (2008, September 22). The United States and the Hashemite Kingdom of Jordan Sign Memorandum of Understanding on Assistance.

US Energy Information Administration. (2015). Monthly Energy Review October 2015. Retrieved from 3Cwww.eia.gov/totalenergy/data/monthly/pdf/sec11_5.pdf%3E

US-China trade war: New tariffs come into force. (2018). BBC News. Retrieved from https://www.bbc.com/news/business-45255623

VakıfBank Economic Research Department (2018). Ticaret Savaşları Endişeleri Artırıyor. *VakıfBank Haftalık Rapor*.

Valovaya, T. (2016). Vremya dlya yedinoy valyuty yeshcho ne prishlo [Gross: The time for a single currency has not yet come]. *Mezhdunarodlnaya zhizn'*. Retrieved from https://interaffairs.ru/news/show/16157

Van Parys, S., & James, S. (2010). The effectiveness of tax incentives in attracting investment: Panel data evidence from the CFA Franc zone. *International Tax and Public Finance*, *17*(4), 400–429. doi:10.100710797-010-9140-1

Vardomskiy, L.B. (2011). Ekonomicheskiy rost i regional'naya integratsiya na postsovetskom prostranstve. [Economic growth and regional integration in the post-Soviet space]. *Zhurnal novoy ekonomicheskoy assotsiatsii*, *11*, 142-143.

Vijayasri, G. V. (2013). The importance of International Trade in the World. *International Journal of Marketing Financial Services and Management Research*, *9*(2), 111–119.

Vinokurov, E. (2014, October 14). Evropeyskiy i Evraziyskiy soyuzi: povod dlya integratsii [European and Eurasian Unions: the reason for integration]. TASS. Retrieved from http://tass.ru/opinions/1597482

Vinokurov: soglasheniya EAES s Iranom i Kitaem nosyat kompromissniy kharakter [Vinokurov: the EAEU agreements with Iran and China have a compromise nature]. (2018, May 17). Sputnik Kazakhstan. Retrieved from https://ru.sputniknews.kz/economy/20180517/5654270/eaeu-soglashenie-iran-china.html

Vistuplenie Vladimira Putina na PMEF-2016 [Speech of Vladimir Putin in SPIEF-2016]. (2016, June 17). Vesti FM. Retrieved from https://radiovesti.ru/brand/60963/episode/1374750/

Vitebskoy, P. Pskovskoy i Smolenskoy oblastey podpisali soglasheniye o sotrudnichestve [Trade unions of Vitebsk, Pskov and Smolensk regions signed a cooperation agreement]. (2019, January 18). *Sotrudnichestvo regionov*. Retrieved from http://www.soyuz.by/news/region/43039.html

Vneshnyaya torgovlya Belarusi [Belarus' foreign trade]. (2018, January-July). *Ministerstvo inostrannykh del Respubliki Belarus*. Retrieved from http://mfa.gov.by/export

Vneshnyaya torgovlya Belorussii [Foreign trade of Belarus]. (2018, March 24). *EurAsia Daily*. Retrieved from https://eadaily.com/ru/news/2018/03/24/vneshnyaya-torgovlya-belorussii-ocherednaya-diversifikaciya-ocherednoy-proval

Vneshnyaya torgovlya Respubliki Belarus' (2015). [Foreign Trade of the Republic of Belarus]. S*tatisticheskiy sbornik. Natsional'nyy statisticheskiy komitet Respubliki Belarus*'. Minsk: Nats. statisticheskiy komitet Resp. Belarus.

Von Mises, L. (1996). Human action: A treatise on economics. Retrieved from https://mises.org/library/human-action-0/html/c/245

Wagner, J. (2007). Exports and Productivity: A Survey of the Evidence from Firm Level Data. *World Economy*, *30*(1), 60–82. doi:10.1111/j.1467-9701.2007.00872.x

Wang, H. (1999). The Asian Financial Crisis and Financial Reforms in China. *The Pacific Review*, *12*(4), 537-556. Retrieved from https://www.tandfonline.com/doi/pdf/10.1080/09512749908719305

Wang, Q. (2001). Import-Reducing Effect of Trade Barriers: a Cross-Country Investigation. *IMF*. Retrieved from https://www.imf.org/external/pubs/ft/wp/2001/wp01216.pdf

Warner, D., & Kreinin, M. E. (1983). Determinants of international trade flows. *The Review of Economics and Statistics*, *65*(1), 96–104. doi:10.2307/1924413

Warr, P. (2011). *Food Security vs. Food Self-Sufficiency: The Indonesian Case*. Canberra, Australia: The Australian National University.

Wei, S. J. (2000). How taxing is corruption on international investors? *The Review of Economics and Statistics*, *82*(1), 1–11. doi:10.1162/003465300558533

Welty, B., & Becerra-Fernandez, I. (2001). Managing trust and commitment in collaborative supply chain relationships. *Communications of the ACM*, *44*(6), 67–73. doi:10.1145/376134.376170

Wikipedia. (2018). China–United States trade war. Retrieved from https://en.wikipedia.org/wiki/2018_China–United_States_trade_war#cite_note-:10-15

Wikipedia. (n.d.). 2018 China–United States trade war. Retrieved from https://en.wikipedia.org/wiki/2018_China%E2%80%93United_States_trade_war#cite_note-143

Williamson, O. E. (1979). Transaction cost economics: The governance of contractual relations. *The Journal of Law & Economics*, *22*(2), 233–261. doi:10.1086/466942

Williamson, O. E. (1993). Calculativeness, trust and economic organization. *The Journal of Law & Economics*, *36*(1, Part 2), 453–486. doi:10.1086/467284

Williams, S. (2000). An empirical application of transaction-costs theory to organizational design characteristics. *The Journal of Psychology*, *34*(1), 81–92. doi:10.1080/00223980009600851 PMID:10654849

Wilson, A. (2011). *The last European dictatorship. Yale*. Belarus: Yale University Press.

Wilson, J. (1999). Theories of tax competition. *National Tax Journal*, *5*(2), 269–304.

Winter, N. (2017). Why America would lose a trade war with China. *IMD*. Retrieved from https://www.imd.org/research-knowledge/articles/why-america-would-lose-a-trade-war-with-china/

World Bank. (2018). *China, Exports of goods and services (% of GDP)*. Retrieved from https://wits.worldbank.org/CountryProfile/en/Country/CHN/StartYear/1992/EndYear/2016/Indicator/NE-EXP-GNFS-ZS#

World Trade Organization. (2001, September 17). *WTO successfully concludes negotiations on China's entry*. Retrieved from https://www.wto.org/english/news_e/pres01_e/pr243_e.htm

World Trade Organization. (2018). *China Trade Profile*. Retrieved from from https://www.wto.org/english/res_e/statis_e/daily_update_e/trade_profiles/CN_e.pdf

World Trade Organization. (2018). *World Trade Statistical Review 2018*. Retrieved from https://www.wto.org/english/res_e/statis_e/wts2018_e/wts2018_e.pdf

World Trade Organization. (n.d.). *Disputes by Member States*. Retrieved from https://www.wto.org/english/tratop_e/dispu_e/dispu_by_country_e.htm

WTO. (2012). A Practical Guide to Trade Policy Analysis. Retrieved from https://www.wto.org/english/res_e/publications_e/wto_unctad12_e.pdf

Wu, Y. (2006). *Economic Growth, Transition and Globalization in China*. Cheltenham, UK: Edward Elgar Publishing Limited.

Yan, D., & John, W. (2012). Gains and Losses from potential bilateral US-China Trade Retaliation. *Economic Modelling*. Retrieved from https://ac.els-cdn.com/S0264999312002222/1-s2.0-S0264999312002222-main.pdf?_tid=5dc7258f-bde3-40b3-a0d0-f13d5f5e71c5&acdnat=1543220182_c1b9f972f64c60cd733ecc67f4faaa0a)

Yanikeyeva, I. (2018, November 30). Uglubleniye integratsii v ramkakh Soyuznogo gosudarstva [The deepening of integration within the framework of the Union State]. *Mezhdunarodnaya zhizn'*. Retrieved from https://interaffairs.ru/news/show/21126

Yanikkaya, H. (2003). Trade Openness and Economic Growth: A Cross-Country Empirical Investigation. *Journal of Development Economics*, *72*(1), 57–89. doi:10.1016/S0304-3878(03)00068-3

Yavuz, A., & Çiçek, S. (2010). Doğrudan yabancı yatırımlar-vergi ilişkisi: Bazı Avrupa Birliği ülkeleri ve Türkiye. *Gaziantep Üniversitesi Sosyal Bilimler Dergisi*, *9*(1), 69–85.

Yıldız, A. (Ekim 2007). Osmanlı İmparatorluğu'nun Borçlanmasında Yabancı Sermaye'nin Etkisi. *İstanbul Üniversitesi Siyasal Bilgiler Fakültesi Dergisi*, *37*, 113-125.

Yu, W., Elleby, C., & Zobbe, H. (2015). Food Security Policies in India and China: Implications for National and Global Food Security. *Food Security*, *7*(2), 405–414. doi:10.100712571-015-0432-2

Yu, Y. (2018). *The reform of China's exchange rate regime*. Canberra, Australia: ANU Press, The Australian National University.

Yu, Y., Feng, K., Hubacek, K., & Sun, L. (2016). Global Implications of China's Future Food Consumption. *Journal of Industrial Ecology*, *20*(3), 593–602. doi:10.1111/jiec.12392

Zaheer, A., & Harris, J. (2006). Inter-organizational trust. In O. Shenkar & J. Reuer (Eds.), *Handbook of Strategic Alliances* (pp. 169–197). Thousand Oaks, CA: Sage Publication. doi:10.4135/9781452231075.n10

Zaheer, A., McEvily, B., & Perrone, V. (1998). Does trust matter? Exploring the effects of inter-organizational and interpersonal trust on performance. *Organization Science*, *9*(2), 141–159. doi:10.1287/orsc.9.2.141

Zanotti, J. (2017). *Israel : Background and U.S. Relations in Brief.* Washington, D.C.: Congressional Research Service; Retrieved from https://fas.org/sgp/crs/mideast/R44245.pdf

Zee, H. H., Stotsky, G. J., & Ley, E. (2002). Tax incentives for business investment: A primer for policy makers in developing countries. *World Development*, *30*(9), 1497–1516. doi:10.1016/S0305-750X(02)00050-5

Zhang, H. (2016). Food in Sino-U.S. Relations. From Blessing to Curse? In F. Wu & H. Zhang (Eds.), *China's Global Quest for Resources. Energy, Food and Water* (pp. 100–118). London: Routledge.

Zhang, H., & Chen, G. (2016). China's Food Security Strategy Reform: An Emerging Global Agricultural Policy. In F. Wu & H. Zhang (Eds.), *China's Global Quest for Resources. Energy, Food and Water* (pp. 23–41). London: Routledge.

Zhou, Z. (2010). Achieving Food Security in China: Past Three Decades and Beyond. *China Agricultural Economic Review*, *2*(3), 251–275. doi:10.1108/17561371011078417

Zhu, Y. (2016). International Trade and Food Security: Conceptual Discussion, WTO and the Case of China. *China Agricultural Economic Review*, *8*(3), 399–411. doi:10.1108/CAER-09-2015-0127

Zolt, E.M. (2014). Tax incentives: Protecting the tax base, papers on selected topics in protecting the tax base of developing countries.

ZST EAES-Vietnam – chert kroetsya v melochakh [FTA EAEU-Vietnam: devil is in the details]. (2015, June 4). Russian International Affairs Council. Retrieved from http://russiancouncil.ru/analytics-and-comments/analytics/zst-eaes-vetnam-chert-kroetsya-v-melochakh/

Zucker, L. G. (1986). The production of trust: Institutional sources of economic structure. *Research in Organizational Behavior*, *8*, 53–111.

Related References

To continue our tradition of advancing information science and technology research, we have compiled a list of recommended IGI Global readings. These references will provide additional information and guidance to further enrich your knowledge and assist you with your own research and future publications.

Abtahi, M. S., Behboudi, L., & Hasanabad, H. M. (2017). Factors Affecting Internet Advertising Adoption in Ad Agencies. *International Journal of Innovation in the Digital Economy*, *8*(4), 18–29. doi:10.4018/IJIDE.2017100102

Agrawal, S. (2017). The Impact of Emerging Technologies and Social Media on Different Business(es): Marketing and Management. In O. Rishi & A. Sharma (Eds.), *Maximizing Business Performance and Efficiency Through Intelligent Systems* (pp. 37–49). Hershey, PA: IGI Global. doi:10.4018/978-1-5225-2234-8.ch002

Alnoukari, M., Razouk, R., & Hanano, A. (2016). BSC-SI: A Framework for Integrating Strategic Intelligence in Corporate Strategic Management. *International Journal of Social and Organizational Dynamics in IT*, *5*(2), 1–14. doi:10.4018/IJSODIT.2016070101

Alnoukari, M., Razouk, R., & Hanano, A. (2016). BSC-SI, A Framework for Integrating Strategic Intelligence in Corporate Strategic Management. *International Journal of Strategic Information Technology and Applications*, *7*(1), 32–44. doi:10.4018/IJSITA.2016010103

Altındağ, E. (2016). Current Approaches in Change Management. In A. Goksoy (Ed.), *Organizational Change Management Strategies in Modern Business* (pp. 24–51). Hershey, PA: IGI Global. doi:10.4018/978-1-4666-9533-7.ch002

Alvarez-Dionisi, L. E., Turner, R., & Mittra, M. (2016). Global Project Management Trends. *International Journal of Information Technology Project Management, 7*(3), 54–73. doi:10.4018/IJITPM.2016070104

Anantharaman, R. N., Rajeswari, K. S., Angusamy, A., & Kuppusamy, J. (2017). Role of Self-Efficacy and Collective Efficacy as Moderators of Occupational Stress Among Software Development Professionals. *International Journal of Human Capital and Information Technology Professionals, 8*(2), 45–58. doi:10.4018/IJHCITP.2017040103

Aninze, F., El-Gohary, H., & Hussain, J. (2018). The Role of Microfinance to Empower Women: The Case of Developing Countries. *International Journal of Customer Relationship Marketing and Management, 9*(1), 54–78. doi:10.4018/IJCRMM.2018010104

Arsenijević, O. M., Orčić, D., & Kastratović, E. (2017). Development of an Optimization Tool for Intangibles in SMEs: A Case Study from Serbia with a Pilot Research in the Prestige by Milka Company. In M. Vemić (Ed.), *Optimal Management Strategies in Small and Medium Enterprises* (pp. 320–347). Hershey, PA: IGI Global. doi:10.4018/978-1-5225-1949-2.ch015

Aryanto, V. D., Wismantoro, Y., & Widyatmoko, K. (2018). Implementing Eco-Innovation by Utilizing the Internet to Enhance Firm's Marketing Performance: Study of Green Batik Small and Medium Enterprises in Indonesia. *International Journal of E-Business Research, 14*(1), 21–36. doi:10.4018/IJEBR.2018010102

Atiku, S. O., & Fields, Z. (2017). Multicultural Orientations for 21st Century Global Leadership. In N. Baporikar (Ed.), *Management Education for Global Leadership* (pp. 28–51). Hershey, PA: IGI Global. doi:10.4018/978-1-5225-1013-0.ch002

Atiku, S. O., & Fields, Z. (2018). Organisational Learning Dimensions and Talent Retention Strategies for the Service Industries. In N. Baporikar (Ed.), *Global Practices in Knowledge Management for Societal and Organizational Development* (pp. 358–381). Hershey, PA: IGI Global. doi:10.4018/978-1-5225-3009-1.ch017

Ávila, L., & Teixeira, L. (2018). The Main Concepts Behind the Dematerialization of Business Processes. In M. Khosrow-Pour, D.B.A. (Ed.), Encyclopedia of Information Science and Technology, Fourth Edition (pp. 888-898). Hershey, PA: IGI Global. doi:10.4018/978-1-5225-2255-3.ch076

Bartens, Y., Chunpir, H. I., Schulte, F., & Voß, S. (2017). Business/IT Alignment in Two-Sided Markets: A COBIT 5 Analysis for Media Streaming Business Models. In S. De Haes & W. Van Grembergen (Eds.), *Strategic IT Governance and Alignment in Business Settings* (pp. 82–111). Hershey, PA: IGI Global. doi:10.4018/978-1-5225-0861-8.ch004

Bashayreh, A. M. (2018). Organizational Culture and Organizational Performance. In W. Lee & F. Sabetzadeh (Eds.), *Contemporary Knowledge and Systems Science* (pp. 50–69). Hershey, PA: IGI Global. doi:10.4018/978-1-5225-5655-8.ch003

Bedford, D. A. (2018). Sustainable Knowledge Management Strategies: Aligning Business Capabilities and Knowledge Management Goals. In N. Baporikar (Ed.), *Global Practices in Knowledge Management for Societal and Organizational Development* (pp. 46–73). Hershey, PA: IGI Global. doi:10.4018/978-1-5225-3009-1.ch003

Benmoussa, F., Nakara, W. A., & Jaouen, A. (2016). The Use of Social Media by SMEs in the Tourism Industry. In I. Lee (Ed.), *Encyclopedia of E-Commerce Development, Implementation, and Management* (pp. 2159–2170). Hershey, PA: IGI Global. doi:10.4018/978-1-4666-9787-4.ch155

Berger, R. (2016). Indigenous Management and Bottom of Pyramid Countries: The Role of National Institutions. In U. Aung & P. Ordoñez de Pablos (Eds.), *Managerial Strategies and Practice in the Asian Business Sector* (pp. 107–123). Hershey, PA: IGI Global. doi:10.4018/978-1-4666-9758-4.ch007

Bharwani, S., & Musunuri, D. (2018). Reflection as a Process From Theory to Practice. In M. Khosrow-Pour, D.B.A. (Ed.), Encyclopedia of Information Science and Technology, Fourth Edition (pp. 1529-1539). Hershey, PA: IGI Global. doi:10.4018/978-1-5225-2255-3.ch132

Bhatt, G. D., Wang, Z., & Rodger, J. A. (2017). Information Systems Capabilities and Their Effects on Competitive Advantages: A Study of Chinese Companies. *Information Resources Management Journal*, *30*(3), 41–57. doi:10.4018/IRMJ.2017070103

Bhushan, M., & Yadav, A. (2017). Concept of Cloud Computing in ESB. In R. Bhadoria, N. Chaudhari, G. Tomar, & S. Singh (Eds.), *Exploring Enterprise Service Bus in the Service-Oriented Architecture Paradigm* (pp. 116–127). Hershey, PA: IGI Global. doi:10.4018/978-1-5225-2157-0.ch008

Bhushan, S. (2017). System Dynamics Base-Model of Humanitarian Supply Chain (HSCM) in Disaster Prone Eco-Communities of India: A Discussion on Simulation and Scenario Results. *International Journal of System Dynamics Applications*, *6*(3), 20–37. doi:10.4018/IJSDA.2017070102

Biswas, A., & De, A. K. (2017). On Development of a Fuzzy Stochastic Programming Model with Its Application to Business Management. In S. Trivedi, S. Dey, A. Kumar, & T. Panda (Eds.), *Handbook of Research on Advanced Data Mining Techniques and Applications for Business Intelligence* (pp. 353–378). Hershey, PA: IGI Global. doi:10.4018/978-1-5225-2031-3.ch021

Bücker, J., & Ernste, K. (2018). Use of Brand Heroes in Strategic Reputation Management: The Case of Bacardi, Adidas, and Daimler. In A. Erdemir (Ed.), *Reputation Management Techniques in Public Relations* (pp. 126–150). Hershey, PA: IGI Global. doi:10.4018/978-1-5225-3619-2.ch007

Bureš, V. (2018). Industry 4.0 From the Systems Engineering Perspective: Alternative Holistic Framework Development. In R. Brunet-Thornton & F. Martinez (Eds.), *Analyzing the Impacts of Industry 4.0 in Modern Business Environments* (pp. 199–223). Hershey, PA: IGI Global. doi:10.4018/978-1-5225-3468-6.ch011

Buzady, Z. (2017). Resolving the Magic Cube of Effective Case Teaching: Benchmarking Case Teaching Practices in Emerging Markets – Insights from the Central European University Business School, Hungary. In D. Latusek (Ed.), *Case Studies as a Teaching Tool in Management Education* (pp. 79–103). Hershey, PA: IGI Global. doi:10.4018/978-1-5225-0770-3.ch005

Campatelli, G., Richter, A., & Stocker, A. (2016). Participative Knowledge Management to Empower Manufacturing Workers. *International Journal of Knowledge Management*, *12*(4), 37–50. doi:10.4018/IJKM.2016100103

Căpusneanu, S., & Topor, D. I. (2018). Business Ethics and Cost Management in SMEs: Theories of Business Ethics and Cost Management Ethos. In I. Oncioiu (Ed.), *Ethics and Decision-Making for Sustainable Business Practices* (pp. 109–127). Hershey, PA: IGI Global. doi:10.4018/978-1-5225-3773-1.ch007

Carneiro, A. (2016). Maturity in Health Organization Information Systems: Metrics and Privacy Perspectives. *International Journal of Privacy and Health Information Management*, *4*(2), 1–18. doi:10.4018/IJPHIM.2016070101

Chan, R. L., Mo, P. L., & Moon, K. K. (2018). Strategic and Tactical Measures in Managing Enterprise Risks: A Study of the Textile and Apparel Industry. In K. Strang, M. Korstanje, & N. Vajjhala (Eds.), *Research, Practices, and Innovations in Global Risk and Contingency Management* (pp. 1–19). Hershey, PA: IGI Global. doi:10.4018/978-1-5225-4754-9.ch001

Chandan, H. C. (2016). Motivations and Challenges of Female Entrepreneurship in Developed and Developing Economies. In N. Baporikar (Ed.), *Handbook of Research on Entrepreneurship in the Contemporary Knowledge-Based Global Economy* (pp. 260–286). Hershey, PA: IGI Global. doi:10.4018/978-1-4666-8798-1.ch012

Charlier, S. D., Burke-Smalley, L. A., & Fisher, S. L. (2018). Undergraduate Programs in the U.S: A Contextual and Content-Based Analysis. In J. Mendy (Ed.), *Teaching Human Resources and Organizational Behavior at the College Level* (pp. 26–57). Hershey, PA: IGI Global. doi:10.4018/978-1-5225-2820-3.ch002

Chaudhuri, S. (2016). Application of Web-Based Geographical Information System (GIS) in E-Business. In U. Panwar, R. Kumar, & N. Ray (Eds.), *Handbook of Research on Promotional Strategies and Consumer Influence in the Service Sector* (pp. 389–405). Hershey, PA: IGI Global. doi:10.4018/978-1-5225-0143-5.ch023

Choudhuri, P. S. (2016). An Empirical Study on the Quality of Services Offered by the Private Life Insurers in Burdwan. In U. Panwar, R. Kumar, & N. Ray (Eds.), *Handbook of Research on Promotional Strategies and Consumer Influence in the Service Sector* (pp. 31–55). Hershey, PA: IGI Global. doi:10.4018/978-1-5225-0143-5.ch002

Dahlberg, T., Kivijärvi, H., & Saarinen, T. (2017). IT Investment Consistency and Other Factors Influencing the Success of IT Performance. In S. De Haes & W. Van Grembergen (Eds.), *Strategic IT Governance and Alignment in Business Settings* (pp. 176–208). Hershey, PA: IGI Global. doi:10.4018/978-1-5225-0861-8.ch007

Damnjanović, A. M. (2017). Knowledge Management Optimization through IT and E-Business Utilization: A Qualitative Study on Serbian SMEs. In M. Vemić (Ed.), *Optimal Management Strategies in Small and Medium Enterprises* (pp. 249–267). Hershey, PA: IGI Global. doi:10.4018/978-1-5225-1949-2.ch012

Daneshpour, H. (2017). Integrating Sustainable Development into Project Portfolio Management through Application of Open Innovation. In M. Vemić (Ed.), *Optimal Management Strategies in Small and Medium Enterprises* (pp. 370–387). Hershey, PA: IGI Global. doi:10.4018/978-1-5225-1949-2.ch017

Daniel, A. D., & Reis de Castro, V. (2018). Entrepreneurship Education: How to Measure the Impact on Nascent Entrepreneurs. In A. Carrizo Moreira, J. Guilherme Leitão Dantas, & F. Manuel Valente (Eds.), *Nascent Entrepreneurship and Successful New Venture Creation* (pp. 85–110). Hershey, PA: IGI Global. doi:10.4018/978-1-5225-2936-1.ch004

David, F., van der Sijde, P., & van den Besselaar, P. (2016). Enterpreneurial Incentives, Obstacles, and Management in University-Business Co-Operation: The Case of Indonesia. In J. Saiz-Álvarez (Ed.), *Handbook of Research on Social Entrepreneurship and Solidarity Economics* (pp. 499–518). Hershey, PA: IGI Global. doi:10.4018/978-1-5225-0097-1.ch024

David, R., Swami, B. N., & Tangirala, S. (2018). Ethics Impact on Knowledge Management in Organizational Development: A Case Study. In N. Baporikar (Ed.), *Global Practices in Knowledge Management for Societal and Organizational Development* (pp. 19–45). Hershey, PA: IGI Global. doi:10.4018/978-1-5225-3009-1.ch002

Delias, P., & Lakiotaki, K. (2018). Discovering Process Horizontal Boundaries to Facilitate Process Comprehension. *International Journal of Operations Research and Information Systems*, *9*(2), 1–31. doi:10.4018/IJORIS.2018040101

Denholm, J., & Lee-Davies, L. (2018). Success Factors for Games in Business and Project Management. In *Enhancing Education and Training Initiatives Through Serious Games* (pp. 34–68). Hershey, PA: IGI Global. doi:10.4018/978-1-5225-3689-5.ch002

Deshpande, M. (2017). Best Practices in Management Institutions for Global Leadership: Policy Aspects. In N. Baporikar (Ed.), *Management Education for Global Leadership* (pp. 1–27). Hershey, PA: IGI Global. doi:10.4018/978-1-5225-1013-0.ch001

Deshpande, M. (2018). Policy Perspectives for SMEs Knowledge Management. In N. Baporikar (Ed.), *Knowledge Integration Strategies for Entrepreneurship and Sustainability* (pp. 23–46). Hershey, PA: IGI Global. doi:10.4018/978-1-5225-5115-7.ch002

Dezdar, S. (2017). ERP Implementation Projects in Asian Countries: A Comparative Study on Iran and China. *International Journal of Information Technology Project Management*, *8*(3), 52–68. doi:10.4018/IJITPM.2017070104

Domingos, D., Martinho, R., & Varajão, J. (2016). Controlled Flexibility in Healthcare Processes: A BPMN-Extension Approach. In M. Cruz-Cunha, I. Miranda, R. Martinho, & R. Rijo (Eds.), *Encyclopedia of E-Health and Telemedicine* (pp. 521–535). Hershey, PA: IGI Global. doi:10.4018/978-1-4666-9978-6.ch040

Domingos, D., Respício, A., & Martinho, R. (2017). Reliability of IoT-Aware BPMN Healthcare Processes. In C. Reis & M. Maximiano (Eds.), *Internet of Things and Advanced Application in Healthcare* (pp. 214–248). Hershey, PA: IGI Global. doi:10.4018/978-1-5225-1820-4.ch008

Dosumu, O., Hussain, J., & El-Gohary, H. (2017). An Exploratory Study of the Impact of Government Policies on the Development of Small and Medium Enterprises in Developing Countries: The Case of Nigeria. *International Journal of Customer Relationship Marketing and Management*, *8*(4), 51–62. doi:10.4018/IJCRMM.2017100104

Durst, S., Bruns, G., & Edvardsson, I. R. (2017). Retaining Knowledge in Smaller Building and Construction Firms. *International Journal of Knowledge and Systems Science*, *8*(3), 1–12. doi:10.4018/IJKSS.2017070101

Edvardsson, I. R., & Durst, S. (2017). Outsourcing, Knowledge, and Learning: A Critical Review. *International Journal of Knowledge-Based Organizations*, *7*(2), 13–26. doi:10.4018/IJKBO.2017040102

Edwards, J. S. (2018). Integrating Knowledge Management and Business Processes. In M. Khosrow-Pour, D.B.A. (Ed.), Encyclopedia of Information Science and Technology, Fourth Edition (pp. 5046-5055). Hershey, PA: IGI Global. doi:10.4018/978-1-5225-2255-3.ch437

Ejiogu, A. O. (2018). Economics of Farm Management. In *Agricultural Finance and Opportunities for Investment and Expansion* (pp. 56–72). Hershey, PA: IGI Global. doi:10.4018/978-1-5225-3059-6.ch003

Ekanem, I., & Abiade, G. E. (2018). Factors Influencing the Use of E-Commerce by Small Enterprises in Nigeria. *International Journal of ICT Research in Africa and the Middle East*, *7*(1), 37–53. doi:10.4018/IJICTRAME.2018010103

Ekanem, I., & Alrossais, L. A. (2017). Succession Challenges Facing Family Businesses in Saudi Arabia. In P. Zgheib (Ed.), *Entrepreneurship and Business Innovation in the Middle East* (pp. 122–146). Hershey, PA: IGI Global. doi:10.4018/978-1-5225-2066-5.ch007

El Faquih, L., & Fredj, M. (2017). Ontology-Based Framework for Quality in Configurable Process Models. *Journal of Electronic Commerce in Organizations, 15*(2), 48–60. doi:10.4018/JECO.2017040104

El-Gohary, H., & El-Gohary, Z. (2016). An Attempt to Explore Electronic Marketing Adoption and Implementation Aspects in Developing Countries: The Case of Egypt. *International Journal of Customer Relationship Marketing and Management, 7*(4), 1–26. doi:10.4018/IJCRMM.2016100101

Entico, G. J. (2016). Knowledge Management and the Medical Health Librarians: A Perception Study. In J. Yap, M. Perez, M. Ayson, & G. Entico (Eds.), *Special Library Administration, Standardization and Technological Integration* (pp. 52–77). Hershey, PA: IGI Global. doi:10.4018/978-1-4666-9542-9.ch003

Faisal, M. N., & Talib, F. (2017). Building Ambidextrous Supply Chains in SMEs: How to Tackle the Barriers? *International Journal of Information Systems and Supply Chain Management, 10*(4), 80–100. doi:10.4018/IJISSCM.2017100105

Fernandes, T. M., Gomes, J., & Romão, M. (2017). Investments in E-Government: A Benefit Management Case Study. *International Journal of Electronic Government Research, 13*(3), 1–17. doi:10.4018/IJEGR.2017070101

Fouda, F. A. (2016). A Suggested Curriculum in Career Education to Develop Business Secondary Schools Students' Career Knowledge Management Domains and Professional Thinking. *International Journal of Technology Diffusion, 7*(2), 42–62. doi:10.4018/IJTD.2016040103

Gallardo-Vázquez, D., & Pajuelo-Moreno, M. L. (2016). How Spanish Universities are Promoting Entrepreneurship through Your Own Lines of Teaching and Research? In L. Carvalho (Ed.), *Handbook of Research on Entrepreneurial Success and its Impact on Regional Development* (pp. 431–454). Hershey, PA: IGI Global. doi:10.4018/978-1-4666-9567-2.ch019

Gao, S. S., Oreal, S., & Zhang, J. (2018). Contemporary Financial Risk Management Perceptions and Practices of Small-Sized Chinese Businesses. In I. Management Association (Ed.), Global Business Expansion: Concepts, Methodologies, Tools, and Applications (pp. 917-931). Hershey, PA: IGI Global. doi:10.4018/978-1-5225-5481-3.ch041

Garg, R., & Berning, S. C. (2017). Indigenous Chinese Management Philosophies: Key Concepts and Relevance for Modern Chinese Firms. In B. Christiansen & G. Koc (Eds.), *Transcontinental Strategies for Industrial Development and Economic Growth* (pp. 43–57). Hershey, PA: IGI Global. doi:10.4018/978-1-5225-2160-0.ch003

Gencer, Y. G. (2017). Supply Chain Management in Retailing Business. In U. Akkucuk (Ed.), *Ethics and Sustainability in Global Supply Chain Management* (pp. 197–210). Hershey, PA: IGI Global. doi:10.4018/978-1-5225-2036-8.ch011

Giacosa, E. (2016). Innovation in Luxury Fashion Businesses as a Means for the Regional Development. In L. Carvalho (Ed.), *Handbook of Research on Entrepreneurial Success and its Impact on Regional Development* (pp. 206–222). Hershey, PA: IGI Global. doi:10.4018/978-1-4666-9567-2.ch010

Giacosa, E. (2018). The Increasing of the Regional Development Thanks to the Luxury Business Innovation. In L. Carvalho (Ed.), *Handbook of Research on Entrepreneurial Ecosystems and Social Dynamics in a Globalized World* (pp. 260–273). Hershey, PA: IGI Global. doi:10.4018/978-1-5225-3525-6.ch011

Gianni, M., & Gotzamani, K. (2016). Integrated Management Systems and Information Management Systems: Common Threads. In P. Papajorgji, F. Pinet, A. Guimarães, & J. Papathanasiou (Eds.), *Automated Enterprise Systems for Maximizing Business Performance* (pp. 195–214). Hershey, PA: IGI Global. doi:10.4018/978-1-4666-8841-4.ch011

Gianni, M., Gotzamani, K., & Linden, I. (2016). How a BI-wise Responsible Integrated Management System May Support Food Traceability. *International Journal of Decision Support System Technology*, *8*(2), 1–17. doi:10.4018/IJDSST.2016040101

Glykas, M., & George, J. (2017). Quality and Process Management Systems in the UAE Maritime Industry. *International Journal of Productivity Management and Assessment Technologies*, *5*(1), 20–39. doi:10.4018/IJPMAT.2017010102

Glykas, M., Valiris, G., Kokkinaki, A., & Koutsoukou, Z. (2018). Banking Business Process Management Implementation. *International Journal of Productivity Management and Assessment Technologies*, *6*(1), 50–69. doi:10.4018/IJPMAT.2018010104

Gomes, J., & Romão, M. (2017). The Balanced Scorecard: Keeping Updated and Aligned with Today's Business Trends. *International Journal of Productivity Management and Assessment Technologies*, *5*(2), 1–15. doi:10.4018/IJPMAT.2017070101

Gomes, J., & Romão, M. (2017). Aligning Information Systems and Technology with Benefit Management and Balanced Scorecard. In S. De Haes & W. Van Grembergen (Eds.), *Strategic IT Governance and Alignment in Business Settings* (pp. 112–131). Hershey, PA: IGI Global. doi:10.4018/978-1-5225-0861-8.ch005

Grefen, P., & Turetken, O. (2017). Advanced Business Process Management in Networked E-Business Scenarios. *International Journal of E-Business Research, 13*(4), 70–104. doi:10.4018/IJEBR.2017100105

Haider, A., & Saetang, S. (2017). Strategic IT Alignment in Service Sector. In S. Rozenes & Y. Cohen (Eds.), *Handbook of Research on Strategic Alliances and Value Co-Creation in the Service Industry* (pp. 231–258). Hershey, PA: IGI Global. doi:10.4018/978-1-5225-2084-9.ch012

Haider, A., & Tang, S. S. (2016). Maximising Value Through IT and Business Alignment: A Case of IT Governance Institutionalisation at a Thai Bank. *International Journal of Technology Diffusion, 7*(3), 33–58. doi:10.4018/IJTD.2016070104

Hajilari, A. B., Ghadaksaz, M., & Fasghandis, G. S. (2017). Assessing Organizational Readiness for Implementing ERP System Using Fuzzy Expert System Approach. *International Journal of Enterprise Information Systems, 13*(1), 67–85. doi:10.4018/IJEIS.2017010105

Haldorai, A., Ramu, A., & Murugan, S. (2018). Social Aware Cognitive Radio Networks: Effectiveness of Social Networks as a Strategic Tool for Organizational Business Management. In H. Bansal, G. Shrivastava, G. Nguyen, & L. Stanciu (Eds.), *Social Network Analytics for Contemporary Business Organizations* (pp. 188–202). Hershey, PA: IGI Global. doi:10.4018/978-1-5225-5097-6.ch010

Hall, O. P. Jr. (2017). Social Media Driven Management Education. *International Journal of Knowledge-Based Organizations, 7*(2), 43–59. doi:10.4018/IJKBO.2017040104

Hanifah, H., Halim, H. A., Ahmad, N. H., & Vafaei-Zadeh, A. (2017). Innovation Culture as a Mediator Between Specific Human Capital and Innovation Performance Among Bumiputera SMEs in Malaysia. In N. Ahmad, T. Ramayah, H. Halim, & S. Rahman (Eds.), *Handbook of Research on Small and Medium Enterprises in Developing Countries* (pp. 261–279). Hershey, PA: IGI Global. doi:10.4018/978-1-5225-2165-5.ch012

Hartlieb, S., & Silvius, G. (2017). Handling Uncertainty in Project Management and Business Development: Similarities and Differences. In Y. Raydugin (Ed.), *Handbook of Research on Leveraging Risk and Uncertainties for Effective Project Management* (pp. 337–362). Hershey, PA: IGI Global. doi:10.4018/978-1-5225-1790-0.ch016

Hass, K. B. (2017). Living on the Edge: Managing Project Complexity. In Y. Raydugin (Ed.), *Handbook of Research on Leveraging Risk and Uncertainties for Effective Project Management* (pp. 177–201). Hershey, PA: IGI Global. doi:10.4018/978-1-5225-1790-0.ch009

Hassan, A., & Privitera, D. S. (2016). Google AdSense as a Mobile Technology in Education. In J. Holland (Ed.), *Wearable Technology and Mobile Innovations for Next-Generation Education* (pp. 200–223). Hershey, PA: IGI Global. doi:10.4018/978-1-5225-0069-8.ch011

Hassan, A., & Rahimi, R. (2016). Consuming "Innovation" in Tourism: Augmented Reality as an Innovation Tool in Digital Tourism Marketing. In N. Pappas & I. Bregoli (Eds.), *Global Dynamics in Travel, Tourism, and Hospitality* (pp. 130–147). Hershey, PA: IGI Global. doi:10.4018/978-1-5225-0201-2.ch008

Hawking, P., & Carmine Sellitto, C. (2017). Developing an Effective Strategy for Organizational Business Intelligence. In M. Tavana (Ed.), *Enterprise Information Systems and the Digitalization of Business Functions* (pp. 222–237). Hershey, PA: IGI Global. doi:10.4018/978-1-5225-2382-6.ch010

Hawking, P., & Sellitto, C. (2017). A Fast-Moving Consumer Goods Company and Business Intelligence Strategy Development. *International Journal of Enterprise Information Systems, 13*(2), 22–33. doi:10.4018/IJEIS.2017040102

Hawking, P., & Sellitto, C. (2017). Business Intelligence Strategy: Two Case Studies. *International Journal of Business Intelligence Research, 8*(2), 17–30. doi:10.4018/IJBIR.2017070102

Haynes, J. D., Arockiasamy, S., Al Rashdi, M., & Al Rashdi, S. (2016). Business and E Business Strategies for Coopetition and Thematic Management as a Sustained Basis for Ethics and Social Responsibility in Emerging Markets. In M. Al-Shammari & H. Masri (Eds.), *Ethical and Social Perspectives on Global Business Interaction in Emerging Markets* (pp. 25–39). Hershey, PA: IGI Global. doi:10.4018/978-1-4666-9864-2.ch002

Hee, W. J., Jalleh, G., Lai, H., & Lin, C. (2017). E-Commerce and IT Projects: Evaluation and Management Issues in Australian and Taiwanese Hospitals. *International Journal of Public Health Management and Ethics, 2*(1), 69–90. doi:10.4018/IJPHME.2017010104

Hernandez, A. A. (2018). Exploring the Factors to Green IT Adoption of SMEs in the Philippines. *Journal of Cases on Information Technology*, *20*(2), 49–66. doi:10.4018/JCIT.2018040104

Hernandez, A. A., & Ona, S. E. (2016). Green IT Adoption: Lessons from the Philippines Business Process Outsourcing Industry. *International Journal of Social Ecology and Sustainable Development*, *7*(1), 1–34. doi:10.4018/IJSESD.2016010101

Hollman, A., Bickford, S., & Hollman, T. (2017). Cyber InSecurity: A Post-Mortem Attempt to Assess Cyber Problems from IT and Business Management Perspectives. *Journal of Cases on Information Technology*, *19*(3), 42–70. doi:10.4018/JCIT.2017070104

Igbinakhase, I. (2017). Responsible and Sustainable Management Practices in Developing and Developed Business Environments. In Z. Fields (Ed.), *Collective Creativity for Responsible and Sustainable Business Practice* (pp. 180–207). Hershey, PA: IGI Global. doi:10.4018/978-1-5225-1823-5.ch010

Ilahi, L., Ghannouchi, S. A., & Martinho, R. (2016). A Business Process Management Approach to Home Healthcare Processes: On the Gap between Intention and Reality. In M. Cruz-Cunha, I. Miranda, R. Martinho, & R. Rijo (Eds.), *Encyclopedia of E-Health and Telemedicine* (pp. 439–457). Hershey, PA: IGI Global. doi:10.4018/978-1-4666-9978-6.ch035

Iwata, J. J., & Hoskins, R. G. (2017). Managing Indigenous Knowledge in Tanzania: A Business Perspective. In P. Jain & N. Mnjama (Eds.), *Managing Knowledge Resources and Records in Modern Organizations* (pp. 198–214). Hershey, PA: IGI Global. doi:10.4018/978-1-5225-1965-2.ch012

Jabeen, F., Ahmad, S. Z., & Alkaabi, S. (2016). The Internationalization Decision-Making of United Arab Emirates Family Businesses. In N. Zakaria, A. Abdul-Talib, & N. Osman (Eds.), *Handbook of Research on Impacts of International Business and Political Affairs on the Global Economy* (pp. 1–22). Hershey, PA: IGI Global. doi:10.4018/978-1-4666-9806-2.ch001

Jain, P. (2017). Ethical and Legal Issues in Knowledge Management Life-Cycle in Business. In P. Jain & N. Mnjama (Eds.), *Managing Knowledge Resources and Records in Modern Organizations* (pp. 82–101). Hershey, PA: IGI Global. doi:10.4018/978-1-5225-1965-2.ch006

Jamali, D., Abdallah, H., & Matar, F. (2016). Opportunities and Challenges for CSR Mainstreaming in Business Schools. *International Journal of Technology and Educational Marketing*, *6*(2), 1–29. doi:10.4018/IJTEM.2016070101

James, S., & Hauli, E. (2017). Holistic Management Education at Tanzanian Rural Development Planning Institute. In N. Baporikar (Ed.), *Management Education for Global Leadership* (pp. 112–136). Hershey, PA: IGI Global. doi:10.4018/978-1-5225-1013-0.ch006

Janošková, M., Csikósová, A., & Čulková, K. (2018). Measurement of Company Performance as Part of Its Strategic Management. In R. Leon (Ed.), *Managerial Strategies for Business Sustainability During Turbulent Times* (pp. 309–335). Hershey, PA: IGI Global. doi:10.4018/978-1-5225-2716-9.ch017

Jean-Vasile, A., & Alecu, A. (2017). Theoretical and Practical Approaches in Understanding the Influences of Cost-Productivity-Profit Trinomial in Contemporary Enterprises. In A. Jean Vasile & D. Nicolò (Eds.), *Sustainable Entrepreneurship and Investments in the Green Economy* (pp. 28–62). Hershey, PA: IGI Global. doi:10.4018/978-1-5225-2075-7.ch002

Jha, D. G. (2016). Preparing for Information Technology Driven Changes. In S. Tiwari & L. Nafees (Eds.), *Innovative Management Education Pedagogies for Preparing Next-Generation Leaders* (pp. 258–274). Hershey, PA: IGI Global. doi:10.4018/978-1-4666-9691-4.ch015

Joia, L. A., & Correia, J. C. (2018). CIO Competencies From the IT Professional Perspective: Insights From Brazil. *Journal of Global Information Management*, *26*(2), 74–103. doi:10.4018/JGIM.2018040104

Juma, A., & Mzera, N. (2017). Knowledge Management and Records Management and Competitive Advantage in Business. In P. Jain & N. Mnjama (Eds.), *Managing Knowledge Resources and Records in Modern Organizations* (pp. 15–28). Hershey, PA: IGI Global. doi:10.4018/978-1-5225-1965-2.ch002

K., I., & A, V. (2018). Monitoring and Auditing in the Cloud. In K. Munir (Ed.), *Cloud Computing Technologies for Green Enterprises* (pp. 318-350). Hershey, PA: IGI Global. doi:10.4018/978-1-5225-3038-1.ch013

Kabra, G., Ghosh, V., & Ramesh, A. (2018). Enterprise Integrated Business Process Management and Business Intelligence Framework for Business Process Sustainability. In A. Paul, D. Bhattacharyya, & S. Anand (Eds.), *Green Initiatives for Business Sustainability and Value Creation* (pp. 228–238). Hershey, PA: IGI Global. doi:10.4018/978-1-5225-2662-9.ch010

Kaoud, M. (2017). Investigation of Customer Knowledge Management: A Case Study Research. *International Journal of Service Science, Management, Engineering, and Technology*, *8*(2), 12–22. doi:10.4018/IJSSMET.2017040102

Kara, M. E., & Fırat, S. Ü. (2016). Sustainability, Risk, and Business Intelligence in Supply Chains. In M. Erdoğdu, T. Arun, & I. Ahmad (Eds.), *Handbook of Research on Green Economic Development Initiatives and Strategies* (pp. 501–538). Hershey, PA: IGI Global. doi:10.4018/978-1-5225-0440-5.ch022

Katuu, S. (2018). A Comparative Assessment of Enterprise Content Management Maturity Models. In N. Gwangwava & M. Mutingi (Eds.), *E-Manufacturing and E-Service Strategies in Contemporary Organizations* (pp. 93–118). Hershey, PA: IGI Global. doi:10.4018/978-1-5225-3628-4.ch005

Khan, M. A. (2016). MNEs Management Strategies in Developing Countries: Establishing the Context. In M. Khan (Ed.), *Multinational Enterprise Management Strategies in Developing Countries* (pp. 1–33). Hershey, PA: IGI Global. doi:10.4018/978-1-5225-0276-0.ch001

Khan, M. A. (2016). Operational Approaches in Organizational Structure: A Case for MNEs in Developing Countries. In M. Khan (Ed.), *Multinational Enterprise Management Strategies in Developing Countries* (pp. 129–151). Hershey, PA: IGI Global. doi:10.4018/978-1-5225-0276-0.ch007

Kinnunen, S., Ylä-Kujala, A., Marttonen-Arola, S., Kärri, T., & Baglee, D. (2018). Internet of Things in Asset Management: Insights from Industrial Professionals and Academia. *International Journal of Service Science, Management, Engineering, and Technology*, *9*(2), 104–119. doi:10.4018/IJSSMET.2018040105

Klein, A. Z., Sabino de Freitas, A., Machado, L., Freitas, J. C. Jr, Graziola, P. G. Jr, & Schlemmer, E. (2017). Virtual Worlds Applications for Management Education. In L. Tomei (Ed.), *Exploring the New Era of Technology-Infused Education* (pp. 279–299). Hershey, PA: IGI Global. doi:10.4018/978-1-5225-1709-2.ch017

Kożuch, B., & Jabłoński, A. (2017). Adopting the Concept of Business Models in Public Management. In M. Lewandowski & B. Kożuch (Eds.), *Public Sector Entrepreneurship and the Integration of Innovative Business Models* (pp. 10–46). Hershey, PA: IGI Global. doi:10.4018/978-1-5225-2215-7.ch002

Kumar, J., Adhikary, A., & Jha, A. (2017). Small Active Investors' Perceptions and Preferences Towards Tax Saving Mutual Fund Schemes in Eastern India: An Empirical Note. *International Journal of Asian Business and Information Management*, *8*(2), 35–45. doi:10.4018/IJABIM.2017040103

Lassoued, Y., Bouzguenda, L., & Mahmoud, T. (2016). Context-Aware Business Process Versions Management. *International Journal of e-Collaboration*, *12*(3), 7–33. doi:10.4018/IJeC.2016070102

Lavassani, K. M., & Movahedi, B. (2017). Applications Driven Information Systems: Beyond Networks toward Business Ecosystems. *International Journal of Innovation in the Digital Economy*, *8*(1), 61–75. doi:10.4018/IJIDE.2017010104

Lazzareschi, V. H., & Brito, M. S. (2017). Strategic Information Management: Proposal of Business Project Model. In G. Jamil, A. Soares, & C. Pessoa (Eds.), *Handbook of Research on Information Management for Effective Logistics and Supply Chains* (pp. 59–88). Hershey, PA: IGI Global. doi:10.4018/978-1-5225-0973-8.ch004

Lederer, M., Kurz, M., & Lazarov, P. (2017). Usage and Suitability of Methods for Strategic Business Process Initiatives: A Multi Case Study Research. *International Journal of Productivity Management and Assessment Technologies*, *5*(1), 40–51. doi:10.4018/IJPMAT.2017010103

Lee, I. (2017). A Social Enterprise Business Model and a Case Study of Pacific Community Ventures (PCV). In V. Potocan, M. Üngan, & Z. Nedelko (Eds.), *Handbook of Research on Managerial Solutions in Non-Profit Organizations* (pp. 182–204). Hershey, PA: IGI Global. doi:10.4018/978-1-5225-0731-4.ch009

Lee, L. J., & Leu, J. (2016). Exploring the Effectiveness of IT Application and Value Method in the Innovation Performance of Enterprise. *International Journal of Enterprise Information Systems*, *12*(2), 47–65. doi:10.4018/IJEIS.2016040104

Lee, Y. (2016). Alignment Effect of Entrepreneurial Orientation and Marketing Orientation on Firm Performance. *International Journal of Customer Relationship Marketing and Management*, *7*(4), 58–69. doi:10.4018/IJCRMM.2016100104

Leon, L. A., Seal, K. C., Przasnyski, Z. H., & Wiedenman, I. (2017). Skills and Competencies Required for Jobs in Business Analytics: A Content Analysis of Job Advertisements Using Text Mining. *International Journal of Business Intelligence Research*, *8*(1), 1–25. doi:10.4018/IJBIR.2017010101

Leu, J., Lee, L. J., & Krischke, A. (2016). Value Engineering-Based Method for Implementing the ISO14001 System in the Green Supply Chains. *International Journal of Strategic Decision Sciences*, *7*(4), 1–20. doi:10.4018/IJSDS.2016100101

Levy, C. L., & Elias, N. I. (2017). SOHO Users' Perceptions of Reliability and Continuity of Cloud-Based Services. In M. Moore (Ed.), *Cybersecurity Breaches and Issues Surrounding Online Threat Protection* (pp. 248–287). Hershey, PA: IGI Global. doi:10.4018/978-1-5225-1941-6.ch011

Levy, M. (2018). Change Management Serving Knowledge Management and Organizational Development: Reflections and Review. In N. Baporikar (Ed.), *Global Practices in Knowledge Management for Societal and Organizational Development* (pp. 256–270). Hershey, PA: IGI Global. doi:10.4018/978-1-5225-3009-1.ch012

Lewandowski, M. (2017). Public Organizations and Business Model Innovation: The Role of Public Service Design. In M. Lewandowski & B. Kożuch (Eds.), *Public Sector Entrepreneurship and the Integration of Innovative Business Models* (pp. 47–72). Hershey, PA: IGI Global. doi:10.4018/978-1-5225-2215-7.ch003

Lhannaoui, H., Kabbaj, M. I., & Bakkoury, Z. (2017). A Survey of Risk-Aware Business Process Modelling. *International Journal of Risk and Contingency Management, 6*(3), 14–26. doi:10.4018/IJRCM.2017070102

Li, J., Sun, W., Jiang, W., Yang, H., & Zhang, L. (2017). How the Nature of Exogenous Shocks and Crises Impact Company Performance?: The Effects of Industry Characteristics. *International Journal of Risk and Contingency Management, 6*(4), 40–55. doi:10.4018/IJRCM.2017100103

Lu, C., & Liu, S. (2016). Cultural Tourism O2O Business Model Innovation-A Case Study of CTrip. *Journal of Electronic Commerce in Organizations, 14*(2), 16–31. doi:10.4018/JECO.2016040102

Machen, B., Hosseini, M. R., Wood, A., & Bakhshi, J. (2016). An Investigation into using SAP-PS as a Multidimensional Project Control System (MPCS). *International Journal of Enterprise Information Systems, 12*(2), 66–81. doi:10.4018/IJEIS.2016040105

Malega, P. (2017). Small and Medium Enterprises in the Slovak Republic: Status and Competitiveness of SMEs in the Global Markets and Possibilities of Optimization. In M. Vemić (Ed.), *Optimal Management Strategies in Small and Medium Enterprises* (pp. 102–124). Hershey, PA: IGI Global. doi:10.4018/978-1-5225-1949-2.ch006

Malewska, K. M. (2017). Intuition in Decision-Making on the Example of a Non-Profit Organization. In V. Potocan, M. Üngan, & Z. Nedelko (Eds.), *Handbook of Research on Managerial Solutions in Non-Profit Organizations* (pp. 378–399). Hershey, PA: IGI Global. doi:10.4018/978-1-5225-0731-4.ch018

Maroofi, F. (2017). Entrepreneurial Orientation and Organizational Learning Ability Analysis for Innovation and Firm Performance. In N. Baporikar (Ed.), *Innovation and Shifting Perspectives in Management Education* (pp. 144–165). Hershey, PA: IGI Global. doi:10.4018/978-1-5225-1019-2.ch007

Martins, P. V., & Zacarias, M. (2017). A Web-based Tool for Business Process Improvement. *International Journal of Web Portals*, *9*(2), 68–84. doi:10.4018/IJWP.2017070104

Matthies, B., & Coners, A. (2017). Exploring the Conceptual Nature of e-Business Projects. *Journal of Electronic Commerce in Organizations*, *15*(3), 33–63. doi:10.4018/JECO.2017070103

McKee, J. (2018). Architecture as a Tool to Solve Business Planning Problems. In M. Khosrow-Pour, D.B.A. (Ed.), Encyclopedia of Information Science and Technology, Fourth Edition (pp. 573-586). Hershey, PA: IGI Global. doi:10.4018/978-1-5225-2255-3.ch050

McMurray, A. J., Cross, J., & Caponecchia, C. (2018). The Risk Management Profession in Australia: Business Continuity Plan Practices. In N. Bajgoric (Ed.), *Always-On Enterprise Information Systems for Modern Organizations* (pp. 112–129). Hershey, PA: IGI Global. doi:10.4018/978-1-5225-3704-5.ch006

Meddah, I. H., & Belkadi, K. (2018). Mining Patterns Using Business Process Management. In R. Hamou (Ed.), *Handbook of Research on Biomimicry in Information Retrieval and Knowledge Management* (pp. 78–89). Hershey, PA: IGI Global. doi:10.4018/978-1-5225-3004-6.ch005

Mendes, L. (2017). TQM and Knowledge Management: An Integrated Approach Towards Tacit Knowledge Management. In D. Jaziri-Bouagina & G. Jamil (Eds.), *Handbook of Research on Tacit Knowledge Management for Organizational Success* (pp. 236–263). Hershey, PA: IGI Global. doi:10.4018/978-1-5225-2394-9.ch009

Mnjama, N. M. (2017). Preservation of Recorded Information in Public and Private Sector Organizations. In P. Jain & N. Mnjama (Eds.), *Managing Knowledge Resources and Records in Modern Organizations* (pp. 149–167). Hershey, PA: IGI Global. doi:10.4018/978-1-5225-1965-2.ch009

Mokoqama, M., & Fields, Z. (2017). Principles of Responsible Management Education (PRME): Call for Responsible Management Education. In Z. Fields (Ed.), *Collective Creativity for Responsible and Sustainable Business Practice* (pp. 229–241). Hershey, PA: IGI Global. doi:10.4018/978-1-5225-1823-5.ch012

Muniapan, B. (2017). Philosophy and Management: The Relevance of Vedanta in Management. In P. Ordóñez de Pablos (Ed.), *Managerial Strategies and Solutions for Business Success in Asia* (pp. 124–139). Hershey, PA: IGI Global. doi:10.4018/978-1-5225-1886-0.ch007

Muniapan, B., Gregory, M. L., & Ling, L. A. (2016). Marketing Education in Sarawak: Looking at It from the Employers' Viewpoint. In B. Smith & A. Porath (Eds.), *Global Perspectives on Contemporary Marketing Education* (pp. 112–130). Hershey, PA: IGI Global. doi:10.4018/978-1-4666-9784-3.ch008

Murad, S. E., & Dowaji, S. (2017). Using Value-Based Approach for Managing Cloud-Based Services. In A. Turuk, B. Sahoo, & S. Addya (Eds.), *Resource Management and Efficiency in Cloud Computing Environments* (pp. 33–60). Hershey, PA: IGI Global. doi:10.4018/978-1-5225-1721-4.ch002

Mutahar, A. M., Daud, N. M., Thurasamy, R., Isaac, O., & Abdulsalam, R. (2018). The Mediating of Perceived Usefulness and Perceived Ease of Use: The Case of Mobile Banking in Yemen. *International Journal of Technology Diffusion*, *9*(2), 21–40. doi:10.4018/IJTD.2018040102

Naidoo, V. (2017). E-Learning and Management Education at African Universities. In N. Baporikar (Ed.), *Management Education for Global Leadership* (pp. 181–201). Hershey, PA: IGI Global. doi:10.4018/978-1-5225-1013-0.ch009

Naidoo, V., & Igbinakhase, I. (2018). Opportunities and Challenges of Knowledge Retention in SMEs. In N. Baporikar (Ed.), *Knowledge Integration Strategies for Entrepreneurship and Sustainability* (pp. 70–94). Hershey, PA: IGI Global. doi:10.4018/978-1-5225-5115-7.ch004

Nayak, S., & Prabhu, N. (2017). Paradigm Shift in Management Education: Need for a Cross Functional Perspective. In N. Baporikar (Ed.), *Management Education for Global Leadership* (pp. 241–255). Hershey, PA: IGI Global. doi:10.4018/978-1-5225-1013-0.ch012

Ndede-Amadi, A. A. (2016). Student Interest in the IS Specialization as Predictor of the Success Potential of New Information Systems Programmes within the Schools of Business in Kenyan Public Universities. *International Journal of Information Systems and Social Change*, *7*(2), 63–79. doi:10.4018/IJISSC.2016040104

Nedelko, Z., & Potocan, V. (2016). Management Practices for Processes Optimization: Case of Slovenia. In G. Alor-Hernández, C. Sánchez-Ramírez, & J. García-Alcaraz (Eds.), *Handbook of Research on Managerial Strategies for Achieving Optimal Performance in Industrial Processes* (pp. 545–561). Hershey, PA: IGI Global. doi:10.4018/978-1-5225-0130-5.ch025

Nedelko, Z., & Potocan, V. (2017). Management Solutions in Non-Profit Organizations: Case of Slovenia. In V. Potocan, M. Üngan, & Z. Nedelko (Eds.), *Handbook of Research on Managerial Solutions in Non-Profit Organizations* (pp. 1–22). Hershey, PA: IGI Global. doi:10.4018/978-1-5225-0731-4.ch001

Nedelko, Z., & Potocan, V. (2017). Priority of Management Tools Utilization among Managers: International Comparison. In V. Wang (Ed.), *Encyclopedia of Strategic Leadership and Management* (pp. 1083–1094). Hershey, PA: IGI Global. doi:10.4018/978-1-5225-1049-9.ch075

Nedelko, Z., Raudeliūnienė, J., & Črešnar, R. (2018). Knowledge Dynamics in Supply Chain Management. In N. Baporikar (Ed.), *Knowledge Integration Strategies for Entrepreneurship and Sustainability* (pp. 150–166). Hershey, PA: IGI Global. doi:10.4018/978-1-5225-5115-7.ch008

Nguyen, H. T., & Hipsher, S. A. (2018). Innovation and Creativity Used by Private Sector Firms in a Resources-Constrained Environment. In S. Hipsher (Ed.), *Examining the Private Sector's Role in Wealth Creation and Poverty Reduction* (pp. 219–238). Hershey, PA: IGI Global. doi:10.4018/978-1-5225-3117-3.ch010

Nycz, M., & Pólkowski, Z. (2016). Business Intelligence as a Modern IT Supporting Management of Local Government Units in Poland. *International Journal of Knowledge and Systems Science*, *7*(4), 1–18. doi:10.4018/IJKSS.2016100101

Obaji, N. O., Senin, A. A., & Olugu, M. U. (2016). Supportive Government Policy as a Mechanism for Business Incubation Performance in Nigeria. *International Journal of Information Systems and Social Change*, *7*(4), 52–66. doi:10.4018/IJISSC.2016100103

Obicci, P. A. (2017). Risk Sharing in a Partnership. In *Risk Management Strategies in Public-Private Partnerships* (pp. 115–152). Hershey, PA: IGI Global. doi:10.4018/978-1-5225-2503-5.ch004

Obidallah, W. J., & Raahemi, B. (2017). Managing Changes in Service Oriented Virtual Organizations: A Structural and Procedural Framework to Facilitate the Process of Change. *Journal of Electronic Commerce in Organizations*, *15*(1), 59–83. doi:10.4018/JECO.2017010104

Ojasalo, J., & Ojasalo, K. (2016). Service Logic Business Model Canvas for Lean Development of SMEs and Start-Ups. In N. Baporikar (Ed.), *Handbook of Research on Entrepreneurship in the Contemporary Knowledge-Based Global Economy* (pp. 217–243). Hershey, PA: IGI Global. doi:10.4018/978-1-4666-8798-1.ch010

Ojo, O. (2017). Impact of Innovation on the Entrepreneurial Success in Selected Business Enterprises in South-West Nigeria. *International Journal of Innovation in the Digital Economy, 8*(2), 29–38. doi:10.4018/IJIDE.2017040103

Okdinawati, L., Simatupang, T. M., & Sunitiyoso, Y. (2017). Multi-Agent Reinforcement Learning for Value Co-Creation of Collaborative Transportation Management (CTM). *International Journal of Information Systems and Supply Chain Management, 10*(3), 84–95. doi:10.4018/IJISSCM.2017070105

Ortner, E., Mevius, M., Wiedmann, P., & Kurz, F. (2016). Design of Interactional Decision Support Applications for E-Participation in Smart Cities. *International Journal of Electronic Government Research, 12*(2), 18–38. doi:10.4018/IJEGR.2016040102

Pal, K. (2018). Building High Quality Big Data-Based Applications in Supply Chains. In A. Kumar & S. Saurav (Eds.), *Supply Chain Management Strategies and Risk Assessment in Retail Environments* (pp. 1–24). Hershey, PA: IGI Global. doi:10.4018/978-1-5225-3056-5.ch001

Palos-Sanchez, P. R., & Correia, M. B. (2018). Perspectives of the Adoption of Cloud Computing in the Tourism Sector. In J. Rodrigues, C. Ramos, P. Cardoso, & C. Henriques (Eds.), *Handbook of Research on Technological Developments for Cultural Heritage and eTourism Applications* (pp. 377–400). Hershey, PA: IGI Global. doi:10.4018/978-1-5225-2927-9.ch018

Parry, V. K., & Lind, M. L. (2016). Alignment of Business Strategy and Information Technology Considering Information Technology Governance, Project Portfolio Control, and Risk Management. *International Journal of Information Technology Project Management, 7*(4), 21–37. doi:10.4018/IJITPM.2016100102

Pashkova, N., Trujillo-Barrera, A., Apostolakis, G., Van Dijk, G., Drakos, P. D., & Baourakis, G. (2016). Business Management Models of Microfinance Institutions (MFIs) in Africa: A Study into Their Enabling Environments. *International Journal of Food and Beverage Manufacturing and Business Models, 1*(2), 63–82. doi:10.4018/IJFBMBM.2016070105

Patiño, B. E. (2017). New Generation Management by Convergence and Individual Identity: A Systemic and Human-Oriented Approach. In N. Baporikar (Ed.), *Innovation and Shifting Perspectives in Management Education* (pp. 119–143). Hershey, PA: IGI Global. doi:10.4018/978-1-5225-1019-2.ch006

Pawliczek, A., & Rössler, M. (2017). Knowledge of Management Tools and Systems in SMEs: Knowledge Transfer in Management. In A. Bencsik (Ed.), *Knowledge Management Initiatives and Strategies in Small and Medium Enterprises* (pp. 180–203). Hershey, PA: IGI Global. doi:10.4018/978-1-5225-1642-2.ch009

Pejic-Bach, M., Omazic, M. A., Aleksic, A., & Zoroja, J. (2018). Knowledge-Based Decision Making: A Multi-Case Analysis. In R. Leon (Ed.), *Managerial Strategies for Business Sustainability During Turbulent Times* (pp. 160–184). Hershey, PA: IGI Global. doi:10.4018/978-1-5225-2716-9.ch009

Perano, M., Hysa, X., & Calabrese, M. (2018). Strategic Planning, Cultural Context, and Business Continuity Management: Business Cases in the City of Shkoder. In A. Presenza & L. Sheehan (Eds.), *Geopolitics and Strategic Management in the Global Economy* (pp. 57–77). Hershey, PA: IGI Global. doi:10.4018/978-1-5225-2673-5.ch004

Pereira, R., Mira da Silva, M., & Lapão, L. V. (2017). IT Governance Maturity Patterns in Portuguese Healthcare. In S. De Haes & W. Van Grembergen (Eds.), *Strategic IT Governance and Alignment in Business Settings* (pp. 24–52). Hershey, PA: IGI Global. doi:10.4018/978-1-5225-0861-8.ch002

Perez-Uribe, R., & Ocampo-Guzman, D. (2016). Conflict within Colombian Family Owned SMEs: An Explosive Blend between Feelings and Business. In J. Saiz-Álvarez (Ed.), *Handbook of Research on Social Entrepreneurship and Solidarity Economics* (pp. 329–354). Hershey, PA: IGI Global. doi:10.4018/978-1-5225-0097-1.ch017

Pérez-Uribe, R. I., Torres, D. A., Jurado, S. P., & Prada, D. M. (2018). Cloud Tools for the Development of Project Management in SMEs. In R. Perez-Uribe, C. Salcedo-Perez, & D. Ocampo-Guzman (Eds.), *Handbook of Research on Intrapreneurship and Organizational Sustainability in SMEs* (pp. 95–120). Hershey, PA: IGI Global. doi:10.4018/978-1-5225-3543-0.ch005

Petrisor, I., & Cozmiuc, D. (2017). Global Supply Chain Management Organization at Siemens in the Advent of Industry 4.0. In L. Saglietto & C. Cezanne (Eds.), *Global Intermediation and Logistics Service Providers* (pp. 123–142). Hershey, PA: IGI Global. doi:10.4018/978-1-5225-2133-4.ch007

Pierce, J. M., Velliaris, D. M., & Edwards, J. (2017). A Living Case Study: A Journey Not a Destination. In N. Silton (Ed.), *Exploring the Benefits of Creativity in Education, Media, and the Arts* (pp. 158–178). Hershey, PA: IGI Global. doi:10.4018/978-1-5225-0504-4.ch008

Radosavljevic, M., & Andjelkovic, A. (2017). Multi-Criteria Decision Making Approach for Choosing Business Process for the Improvement: Upgrading of the Six Sigma Methodology. In J. Stanković, P. Delias, S. Marinković, & S. Rochhia (Eds.), *Tools and Techniques for Economic Decision Analysis* (pp. 225–247). Hershey, PA: IGI Global. doi:10.4018/978-1-5225-0959-2.ch011

Radovic, V. M. (2017). Corporate Sustainability and Responsibility and Disaster Risk Reduction: A Serbian Overview. In M. Camilleri (Ed.), *CSR 2.0 and the New Era of Corporate Citizenship* (pp. 147–164). Hershey, PA: IGI Global. doi:10.4018/978-1-5225-1842-6.ch008

Raghunath, K. M., Devi, S. L., & Patro, C. S. (2018). Impact of Risk Assessment Models on Risk Factors: A Holistic Outlook. In K. Strang, M. Korstanje, & N. Vajjhala (Eds.), *Research, Practices, and Innovations in Global Risk and Contingency Management* (pp. 134–153). Hershey, PA: IGI Global. doi:10.4018/978-1-5225-4754-9.ch008

Raman, A., & Goyal, D. P. (2017). Extending IMPLEMENT Framework for Enterprise Information Systems Implementation to Information System Innovation. In M. Tavana (Ed.), *Enterprise Information Systems and the Digitalization of Business Functions* (pp. 137–177). Hershey, PA: IGI Global. doi:10.4018/978-1-5225-2382-6.ch007

Rao, Y., & Zhang, Y. (2017). The Construction and Development of Academic Library Digital Special Subject Databases. In L. Ruan, Q. Zhu, & Y. Ye (Eds.), *Academic Library Development and Administration in China* (pp. 163–183). Hershey, PA: IGI Global. doi:10.4018/978-1-5225-0550-1.ch010

Ravasan, A. Z., Mohammadi, M. M., & Hamidi, H. (2018). An Investigation Into the Critical Success Factors of Implementing Information Technology Service Management Frameworks. In K. Jakobs (Ed.), *Corporate and Global Standardization Initiatives in Contemporary Society* (pp. 200–218). Hershey, PA: IGI Global. doi:10.4018/978-1-5225-5320-5.ch009

Renna, P., Izzo, C., & Romaniello, T. (2016). The Business Process Management Systems to Support Continuous Improvements. In W. Nuninger & J. Châtelet (Eds.), *Handbook of Research on Quality Assurance and Value Management in Higher Education* (pp. 237–256). Hershey, PA: IGI Global. doi:10.4018/978-1-5225-0024-7.ch009

Rezaie, S., Mirabedini, S. J., & Abtahi, A. (2018). Designing a Model for Implementation of Business Intelligence in the Banking Industry. *International Journal of Enterprise Information Systems*, *14*(1), 77–103. doi:10.4018/IJEIS.2018010105

Riccò, R. (2016). Diversity Management: Bringing Equality, Equity, and Inclusion in the Workplace. In J. Prescott (Ed.), *Handbook of Research on Race, Gender, and the Fight for Equality* (pp. 335–359). Hershey, PA: IGI Global. doi:10.4018/978-1-5225-0047-6.ch015

Romano, L., Grimaldi, R., & Colasuonno, F. S. (2017). Demand Management as a Success Factor in Project Portfolio Management. In L. Romano (Ed.), *Project Portfolio Management Strategies for Effective Organizational Operations* (pp. 202–219). Hershey, PA: IGI Global. doi:10.4018/978-1-5225-2151-8.ch008

Rostek, K. B. (2016). Risk Management: Role and Importance in Business Organization. In D. Jakóbczak (Ed.), *Analyzing Risk through Probabilistic Modeling in Operations Research* (pp. 149–178). Hershey, PA: IGI Global. doi:10.4018/978-1-4666-9458-3.ch007

Rouhani, S., & Savoji, S. R. (2016). A Success Assessment Model for BI Tools Implementation: An Empirical Study of Banking Industry. *International Journal of Business Intelligence Research*, *7*(1), 25–44. doi:10.4018/IJBIR.2016010103

Ruan, Z. (2016). A Corpus-Based Functional Analysis of Complex Nominal Groups in Written Business Discourse: The Case of "Business". *International Journal of Computer-Assisted Language Learning and Teaching*, *6*(2), 74–90. doi:10.4018/IJCALLT.2016040105

Ruhi, U. (2018). Towards an Interdisciplinary Socio-Technical Definition of Virtual Communities. In M. Khosrow-Pour, D.B.A. (Ed.), Encyclopedia of Information Science and Technology, Fourth Edition (pp. 4278-4295). Hershey, PA: IGI Global. doi:10.4018/978-1-5225-2255-3.ch371

Ryan, J., Doster, B., Daily, S., & Lewis, C. (2016). A Case Study Perspective for Balanced Perioperative Workflow Achievement through Data-Driven Process Improvement. *International Journal of Healthcare Information Systems and Informatics*, *11*(3), 19–41. doi:10.4018/IJHISI.2016070102

Safari, M. R., & Jiang, Q. (2018). The Theory and Practice of IT Governance Maturity and Strategies Alignment: Evidence From Banking Industry. *Journal of Global Information Management*, *26*(2), 127–146. doi:10.4018/JGIM.2018040106

Sahoo, J., Pati, B., & Mohanty, B. (2017). Knowledge Management as an Academic Discipline: An Assessment. In B. Gunjal (Ed.), *Managing Knowledge and Scholarly Assets in Academic Libraries* (pp. 99–126). Hershey, PA: IGI Global. doi:10.4018/978-1-5225-1741-2.ch005

Saini, D. (2017). Relevance of Teaching Values and Ethics in Management Education. In N. Baporikar (Ed.), *Management Education for Global Leadership* (pp. 90–111). Hershey, PA: IGI Global. doi:10.4018/978-1-5225-1013-0.ch005

Sambhanthan, A. (2017). Assessing and Benchmarking Sustainability in Organisations: An Integrated Conceptual Model. *International Journal of Systems and Service-Oriented Engineering*, *7*(4), 22–43. doi:10.4018/IJSSOE.2017100102

Sambhanthan, A., & Potdar, V. (2017). A Study of the Parameters Impacting Sustainability in Information Technology Organizations. *International Journal of Knowledge-Based Organizations*, *7*(3), 27–39. doi:10.4018/IJKBO.2017070103

Sánchez-Fernández, M. D., & Manríquez, M. R. (2018). The Entrepreneurial Spirit Based on Social Values: The Digital Generation. In P. Isaias & L. Carvalho (Eds.), *User Innovation and the Entrepreneurship Phenomenon in the Digital Economy* (pp. 173–193). Hershey, PA: IGI Global. doi:10.4018/978-1-5225-2826-5.ch009

Sanchez-Ruiz, L., & Blanco, B. (2017). Process Management for SMEs: Barriers, Enablers, and Benefits. In M. Vemić (Ed.), *Optimal Management Strategies in Small and Medium Enterprises* (pp. 293–319). Hershey, PA: IGI Global. doi:10.4018/978-1-5225-1949-2.ch014

Sanz, L. F., Gómez-Pérez, J., & Castillo-Martinez, A. (2018). Analysis of the European ICT Competence Frameworks. In V. Ahuja & S. Rathore (Eds.), *Multidisciplinary Perspectives on Human Capital and Information Technology Professionals* (pp. 225–245). Hershey, PA: IGI Global. doi:10.4018/978-1-5225-5297-0.ch012

Sarvepalli, A., & Godin, J. (2017). Business Process Management in the Classroom. *Journal of Cases on Information Technology, 19*(2), 17–28. doi:10.4018/JCIT.2017040102

Satpathy, B., & Muniapan, B. (2016). Ancient Wisdom for Transformational Leadership and Its Insights from the Bhagavad-Gita. In U. Aung & P. Ordoñez de Pablos (Eds.), *Managerial Strategies and Practice in the Asian Business Sector* (pp. 1–10). Hershey, PA: IGI Global. doi:10.4018/978-1-4666-9758-4.ch001

Saygili, E. E., Ozturkoglu, Y., & Kocakulah, M. C. (2017). End Users' Perceptions of Critical Success Factors in ERP Applications. *International Journal of Enterprise Information Systems, 13*(4), 58–75. doi:10.4018/IJEIS.2017100104

Saygili, E. E., & Saygili, A. T. (2017). Contemporary Issues in Enterprise Information Systems: A Critical Review of CSFs in ERP Implementations. In M. Tavana (Ed.), *Enterprise Information Systems and the Digitalization of Business Functions* (pp. 120–136). Hershey, PA: IGI Global. doi:10.4018/978-1-5225-2382-6.ch006

Seidenstricker, S., & Antonino, A. (2018). Business Model Innovation-Oriented Technology Management for Emergent Technologies. In M. Khosrow-Pour, D.B.A. (Ed.), Encyclopedia of Information Science and Technology, Fourth Edition (pp. 4560-4569). Hershey, PA: IGI Global. doi:10.4018/978-1-5225-2255-3.ch396

Senaratne, S., & Gunarathne, A. D. (2017). Excellence Perspective for Management Education from a Global Accountants' Hub in Asia. In N. Baporikar (Ed.), *Management Education for Global Leadership* (pp. 158–180). Hershey, PA: IGI Global. doi:10.4018/978-1-5225-1013-0.ch008

Sensuse, D. I., & Cahyaningsih, E. (2018). Knowledge Management Models: A Summative Review. *International Journal of Information Systems in the Service Sector, 10*(1), 71–100. doi:10.4018/IJISSS.2018010105

Sensuse, D. I., Wibowo, W. C., & Cahyaningsih, E. (2016). Indonesian Government Knowledge Management Model: A Theoretical Model. *Information Resources Management Journal, 29*(1), 91–108. doi:10.4018/irmj.2016010106

Seth, M., Goyal, D., & Kiran, R. (2017). Diminution of Impediments in Implementation of Supply Chain Management Information System for Enhancing its Effectiveness in Indian Automobile Industry. *Journal of Global Information Management, 25*(3), 1–20. doi:10.4018/JGIM.2017070101

Seyal, A. H., & Rahman, M. N. (2017). Investigating Impact of Inter-Organizational Factors in Measuring ERP Systems Success: Bruneian Perspectives. In M. Tavana (Ed.), *Enterprise Information Systems and the Digitalization of Business Functions* (pp. 178–204). Hershey, PA: IGI Global. doi:10.4018/978-1-5225-2382-6.ch008

Shaikh, A. A., & Karjaluoto, H. (2016). On Some Misconceptions Concerning Digital Banking and Alternative Delivery Channels. *International Journal of E-Business Research, 12*(3), 1–16. doi:10.4018/IJEBR.2016070101

Shams, S. M. (2016). Stakeholder Relationship Management in Online Business and Competitive Value Propositions: Evidence from the Sports Industry. *International Journal of Online Marketing, 6*(2), 1–17. doi:10.4018/IJOM.2016040101

Shamsuzzoha, A. (2016). Management of Risk and Resilience within Collaborative Business Network. In R. Addo-Tenkorang, J. Kantola, P. Helo, & A. Shamsuzzoha (Eds.), *Supply Chain Strategies and the Engineer-to-Order Approach* (pp. 143–159). Hershey, PA: IGI Global. doi:10.4018/978-1-5225-0021-6.ch008

Shaqrah, A. A. (2018). Analyzing Business Intelligence Systems Based on 7s Model of McKinsey. *International Journal of Business Intelligence Research, 9*(1), 53–63. doi:10.4018/IJBIR.2018010104

Sharma, A. J. (2017). Enhancing Sustainability through Experiential Learning in Management Education. In N. Baporikar (Ed.), *Management Education for Global Leadership* (pp. 256–274). Hershey, PA: IGI Global. doi:10.4018/978-1-5225-1013-0.ch013

Shetty, K. P. (2017). Responsible Global Leadership: Ethical Challenges in Management Education. In N. Baporikar (Ed.), *Innovation and Shifting Perspectives in Management Education* (pp. 194–223). Hershey, PA: IGI Global. doi:10.4018/978-1-5225-1019-2.ch009

Sinthupundaja, J., & Kohda, Y. (2017). Effects of Corporate Social Responsibility and Creating Shared Value on Sustainability. *International Journal of Sustainable Entrepreneurship and Corporate Social Responsibility, 2*(1), 27–38. doi:10.4018/IJSECSR.2017010103

Škarica, I., & Hrgović, A. V. (2018). Implementation of Total Quality Management Principles in Public Health Institutes in the Republic of Croatia. *International Journal of Productivity Management and Assessment Technologies, 6*(1), 1–16. doi:10.4018/IJPMAT.2018010101

Smuts, H., Kotzé, P., Van der Merwe, A., & Loock, M. (2017). Framework for Managing Shared Knowledge in an Information Systems Outsourcing Context. *International Journal of Knowledge Management*, *13*(4), 1–30. doi:10.4018/IJKM.2017100101

Soares, E. R., & Zaidan, F. H. (2016). Information Architecture and Business Modeling in Modern Organizations of Information Technology: Professional Career Plan in Organizations IT. In G. Jamil, J. Poças Rascão, F. Ribeiro, & A. Malheiro da Silva (Eds.), *Handbook of Research on Information Architecture and Management in Modern Organizations* (pp. 439–457). Hershey, PA: IGI Global. doi:10.4018/978-1-4666-8637-3.ch020

Sousa, M. J., Cruz, R., Dias, I., & Caracol, C. (2017). Information Management Systems in the Supply Chain. In G. Jamil, A. Soares, & C. Pessoa (Eds.), *Handbook of Research on Information Management for Effective Logistics and Supply Chains* (pp. 469–485). Hershey, PA: IGI Global. doi:10.4018/978-1-5225-0973-8.ch025

Spremic, M., Turulja, L., & Bajgoric, N. (2018). Two Approaches in Assessing Business Continuity Management Attitudes in the Organizational Context. In N. Bajgoric (Ed.), *Always-On Enterprise Information Systems for Modern Organizations* (pp. 159–183). Hershey, PA: IGI Global. doi:10.4018/978-1-5225-3704-5.ch008

Steenkamp, A. L. (2018). Some Insights in Computer Science and Information Technology. In *Examining the Changing Role of Supervision in Doctoral Research Projects: Emerging Research and Opportunities* (pp. 113–133). Hershey, PA: IGI Global. doi:10.4018/978-1-5225-2610-0.ch005

Studdard, N., Dawson, M., Burton, S. L., Jackson, N., Leonard, B., Quisenberry, W., & Rahim, E. (2016). Nurturing Social Entrepreneurship and Building Social Entrepreneurial Self-Efficacy: Focusing on Primary and Secondary Schooling to Develop Future Social Entrepreneurs. In Z. Fields (Ed.), *Incorporating Business Models and Strategies into Social Entrepreneurship* (pp. 154–175). Hershey, PA: IGI Global. doi:10.4018/978-1-4666-8748-6.ch010

Sun, Z. (2016). A Framework for Developing Management Intelligent Systems. *International Journal of Systems and Service-Oriented Engineering*, *6*(1), 37–53. doi:10.4018/IJSSOE.2016010103

Swami, B., & Mphele, G. T. (2016). Problems Preventing Growth of Small Entrepreneurs: A Case Study of a Few Small Entrepreneurs in Botswana Sub-Urban Areas. In N. Baporikar (Ed.), *Handbook of Research on Entrepreneurship in the Contemporary Knowledge-Based Global Economy* (pp. 479–508). Hershey, PA: IGI Global. doi:10.4018/978-1-4666-8798-1.ch020

Tabach, A., & Croteau, A. (2017). Configurations of Information Technology Governance Practices and Business Unit Performance. *International Journal of IT/Business Alignment and Governance*, *8*(2), 1–27. doi:10.4018/IJITBAG.2017070101

Talaue, G. M., & Iqbal, T. (2017). Assessment of e-Business Mode of Selected Private Universities in the Philippines and Pakistan. *International Journal of Online Marketing*, *7*(4), 63–77. doi:10.4018/IJOM.2017100105

Tam, G. C. (2017). Project Manager Sustainability Competence. In *Managerial Strategies and Green Solutions for Project Sustainability* (pp. 178–207). Hershey, PA: IGI Global. doi:10.4018/978-1-5225-2371-0.ch008

Tambo, T. (2018). Fashion Retail Innovation: About Context, Antecedents, and Outcome in Technological Change Projects. In I. Management Association (Ed.), Fashion and Textiles: Breakthroughs in Research and Practice (pp. 233-260). Hershey, PA: IGI Global. doi:10.4018/978-1-5225-3432-7.ch010

Tambo, T., & Mikkelsen, O. E. (2016). Fashion Supply Chain Optimization: Linking Make-to-Order Purchasing and B2B E-Commerce. In S. Joshi & R. Joshi (Eds.), *Designing and Implementing Global Supply Chain Management* (pp. 1–21). Hershey, PA: IGI Global. doi:10.4018/978-1-4666-9720-1.ch001

Tandon, K. (2016). Innovative Andragogy: The Paradigm Shift to Heutagogy. In S. Tiwari & L. Nafees (Eds.), *Innovative Management Education Pedagogies for Preparing Next-Generation Leaders* (pp. 238–257). Hershey, PA: IGI Global. doi:10.4018/978-1-4666-9691-4.ch014

Tantau, A. D., & Frăţilă, L. C. (2018). Information and Management System for Renewable Energy Business. In *Entrepreneurship and Business Development in the Renewable Energy Sector* (pp. 200–244). Hershey, PA: IGI Global. doi:10.4018/978-1-5225-3625-3.ch006

Teixeira, N., Pardal, P. N., & Rafael, B. G. (2018). Internationalization, Financial Performance, and Organizational Challenges: A Success Case in Portugal. In L. Carvalho (Ed.), *Handbook of Research on Entrepreneurial Ecosystems and Social Dynamics in a Globalized World* (pp. 379–423). Hershey, PA: IGI Global. doi:10.4018/978-1-5225-3525-6.ch017

Trad, A., & Kalpić, D. (2016). The E-Business Transformation Framework for E-Commerce Architecture-Modeling Projects. In I. Lee (Ed.), *Encyclopedia of E-Commerce Development, Implementation, and Management* (pp. 733–753). Hershey, PA: IGI Global. doi:10.4018/978-1-4666-9787-4.ch052

Trad, A., & Kalpić, D. (2016). The E-Business Transformation Framework for E-Commerce Control and Monitoring Pattern. In I. Lee (Ed.), *Encyclopedia of E-Commerce Development, Implementation, and Management* (pp. 754–777). Hershey, PA: IGI Global. doi:10.4018/978-1-4666-9787-4.ch053

Trad, A., & Kalpić, D. (2018). The Business Transformation Framework, Agile Project and Change Management. In M. Khosrow-Pour, D.B.A. (Ed.), Encyclopedia of Information Science and Technology, Fourth Edition (pp. 620-635). Hershey, PA: IGI Global. doi:10.4018/978-1-5225-2255-3.ch054

Trad, A., & Kalpić, D. (2018). The Business Transformation and Enterprise Architecture Framework: The Financial Engineering E-Risk Management and E-Law Integration. In B. Sergi, F. Fidanoski, M. Ziolo, & V. Naumovski (Eds.), *Regaining Global Stability After the Financial Crisis* (pp. 46–65). Hershey, PA: IGI Global. doi:10.4018/978-1-5225-4026-7.ch003

Turulja, L., & Bajgoric, N. (2018). Business Continuity and Information Systems: A Systematic Literature Review. In N. Bajgoric (Ed.), *Always-On Enterprise Information Systems for Modern Organizations* (pp. 60–87). Hershey, PA: IGI Global. doi:10.4018/978-1-5225-3704-5.ch004

van Wessel, R. M., de Vries, H. J., & Ribbers, P. M. (2016). Business Benefits through Company IT Standardization. In K. Jakobs (Ed.), *Effective Standardization Management in Corporate Settings* (pp. 34–53). Hershey, PA: IGI Global. doi:10.4018/978-1-4666-9737-9.ch003

Vargas-Hernández, J. G. (2017). Professional Integrity in Business Management Education. In N. Baporikar (Ed.), *Management Education for Global Leadership* (pp. 70–89). Hershey, PA: IGI Global. doi:10.4018/978-1-5225-1013-0.ch004

Vasista, T. G., & AlAbdullatif, A. M. (2017). Role of Electronic Customer Relationship Management in Demand Chain Management: A Predictive Analytic Approach. *International Journal of Information Systems and Supply Chain Management, 10*(1), 53–67. doi:10.4018/IJISSCM.2017010104

Vergidis, K. (2016). Rediscovering Business Processes: Definitions, Patterns, and Modelling Approaches. In P. Papajorgji, F. Pinet, A. Guimarães, & J. Papathanasiou (Eds.), *Automated Enterprise Systems for Maximizing Business Performance* (pp. 97–122). Hershey, PA: IGI Global. doi:10.4018/978-1-4666-8841-4.ch007

Vieru, D., & Bourdeau, S. (2017). Survival in the Digital Era: A Digital Competence-Based Multi-Case Study in the Canadian SME Clothing Industry. *International Journal of Social and Organizational Dynamics in IT, 6*(1), 17–34. doi:10.4018/IJSODIT.2017010102

Vijayan, G., & Kamarulzaman, N. H. (2017). An Introduction to Sustainable Supply Chain Management and Business Implications. In M. Khan, M. Hussain, & M. Ajmal (Eds.), *Green Supply Chain Management for Sustainable Business Practice* (pp. 27–50). Hershey, PA: IGI Global. doi:10.4018/978-1-5225-0635-5.ch002

Vlachvei, A., & Notta, O. (2017). Firm Competitiveness: Theories, Evidence, and Measurement. In A. Vlachvei, O. Notta, K. Karantininis, & N. Tsounis (Eds.), *Factors Affecting Firm Competitiveness and Performance in the Modern Business World* (pp. 1–42). Hershey, PA: IGI Global. doi:10.4018/978-1-5225-0843-4.ch001

von Rosing, M., Fullington, N., & Walker, J. (2016). Using the Business Ontology and Enterprise Standards to Transform Three Leading Organizations. *International Journal of Conceptual Structures and Smart Applications, 4*(1), 71–99. doi:10.4018/IJCSSA.2016010104

von Rosing, M., & von Scheel, H. (2016). Using the Business Ontology to Develop Enterprise Standards. *International Journal of Conceptual Structures and Smart Applications, 4*(1), 48–70. doi:10.4018/IJCSSA.2016010103

Walczak, S. (2016). Artificial Neural Networks and other AI Applications for Business Management Decision Support. *International Journal of Sociotechnology and Knowledge Development, 8*(4), 1–20. doi:10.4018/IJSKD.2016100101

Wamba, S. F., Akter, S., Kang, H., Bhattacharya, M., & Upal, M. (2016). The Primer of Social Media Analytics. *Journal of Organizational and End User Computing*, *28*(2), 1–12. doi:10.4018/JOEUC.2016040101

Wang, C., Schofield, M., Li, X., & Ou, X. (2017). Do Chinese Students in Public and Private Higher Education Institutes Perform at Different Level in One of the Leadership Skills: Critical Thinking?: An Exploratory Comparison. In V. Wang (Ed.), *Encyclopedia of Strategic Leadership and Management* (pp. 160–181). Hershey, PA: IGI Global. doi:10.4018/978-1-5225-1049-9.ch013

Wang, F., Raisinghani, M. S., Mora, M., & Wang, X. (2016). Strategic E-Business Management through a Balanced Scored Card Approach. In I. Lee (Ed.), *Encyclopedia of E-Commerce Development, Implementation, and Management* (pp. 361–386). Hershey, PA: IGI Global. doi:10.4018/978-1-4666-9787-4.ch027

Wang, J. (2017). Multi-Agent based Production Management Decision System Modelling for the Textile Enterprise. *Journal of Global Information Management*, *25*(4), 1–15. doi:10.4018/JGIM.2017100101

Wiedemann, A., & Gewald, H. (2017). Examining Cross-Domain Alignment: The Correlation of Business Strategy, IT Management, and IT Business Value. *International Journal of IT/Business Alignment and Governance*, *8*(1), 17–31. doi:10.4018/IJITBAG.2017010102

Wolf, R., & Thiel, M. (2018). Advancing Global Business Ethics in China: Reducing Poverty Through Human and Social Welfare. In S. Hipsher (Ed.), *Examining the Private Sector's Role in Wealth Creation and Poverty Reduction* (pp. 67–84). Hershey, PA: IGI Global. doi:10.4018/978-1-5225-3117-3.ch004

Wu, J., Ding, F., Xu, M., Mo, Z., & Jin, A. (2016). Investigating the Determinants of Decision-Making on Adoption of Public Cloud Computing in E-government. *Journal of Global Information Management*, *24*(3), 71–89. doi:10.4018/JGIM.2016070104

Xu, L., & de Vrieze, P. (2016). Building Situational Applications for Virtual Enterprises. In I. Lee (Ed.), *Encyclopedia of E-Commerce Development, Implementation, and Management* (pp. 715–724). Hershey, PA: IGI Global. doi:10.4018/978-1-4666-9787-4.ch050

Yablonsky, S. (2018). Innovation Platforms: Data and Analytics Platforms. In *Multi-Sided Platforms (MSPs) and Sharing Strategies in the Digital Economy: Emerging Research and Opportunities* (pp. 72–95). Hershey, PA: IGI Global. doi:10.4018/978-1-5225-5457-8.ch003

Yusoff, A., Ahmad, N. H., & Halim, H. A. (2017). Agropreneurship among Gen Y in Malaysia: The Role of Academic Institutions. In N. Ahmad, T. Ramayah, H. Halim, & S. Rahman (Eds.), *Handbook of Research on Small and Medium Enterprises in Developing Countries* (pp. 23–47). Hershey, PA: IGI Global. doi:10.4018/978-1-5225-2165-5.ch002

Zanin, F., Comuzzi, E., & Costantini, A. (2018). The Effect of Business Strategy and Stock Market Listing on the Use of Risk Assessment Tools. In *Management Control Systems in Complex Settings: Emerging Research and Opportunities* (pp. 145–168). Hershey, PA: IGI Global. doi:10.4018/978-1-5225-3987-2.ch007

Zgheib, P. W. (2017). Corporate Innovation and Intrapreneurship in the Middle East. In P. Zgheib (Ed.), *Entrepreneurship and Business Innovation in the Middle East* (pp. 37–56). Hershey, PA: IGI Global. doi:10.4018/978-1-5225-2066-5.ch003

About the Contributors

Ahu Coşkun Özer was born in Istanbul in 1981, graduated from Marmara University with a bachelor's degree in 2004, graduated from Marmara University with a master's degree in theory of economics in 2007. In 2012, Dr. Özer graduated from Ph.D. in Istanbul University, started to work as a research assistant in 2011, has been working as an assistant professor for 5 years at the Marmara University Vocational School of Social Sciences in Foreign Trade Program. Her research areas are international economics, foreign trade, economics, business, and entrepreneurship.

* * *

Ayman Al Sharafat is a third year Ph.D. student in American studies program at Eötvös Loránd University, Budapest, Hungary. His MA and BS was also in American studies from the University of Jordan. His current research focuses on the president of the US' history and American foreign policy. His MA thesis was about American strategy in the Middle East after the 11/9 attacks. His current dissertation project will analysis language management efforts in the communication of the US presidents from Georg Washington to Donald Trump. Before coming to Hungary, Ayman was a lecturer at the University of Jordan, where he taught courses in American history and foreign policy. Currently, he is teaching in the American studies department of Eötvös Loránd University.

Ekaterina Y. Arapova, PhD in Economics (MGIMO University, 2012), currently the Head of the Department of Assessment of Master's Programs, Senior Research Fellow of the BRICS Center of the Institute of International Studies, MGIMO (University) of the Ministry of Foreign Affairs of the Russian Federation . She is a member of New Economic Association, an expert of the Russian Council of International Affairs, an author of more than 50 academic works, including three monographs and a series of scientific articles in international journals. Research interests: regional economic integration in East Asia and the Asia-Pacific region, Russia's economic interests in East Asia, international trade regulation, cooperation and prospects for economic integration in the BRICS format, economic sanctions and sanction policy.

Birgül Cambazoğlu is an assistant professor of economics, at Soke Faculty of Management, Aydın Adnan Menderes University. Mrs. Cambazoglu holds doctorates in economics from Aydın Adnan Menderes University. Mrs. Cambazoglu also earned a MS degree in international Economics from Marmara University and a BS in international relations from Uludag University. Furthermore, she won a postdoc project scholarship from The Scientific and Technological Research Council of Turkey (TUBITAK) and completed this project in Maryland University, Robert H. Smith School of Business in USA. She previously taught at Gedik University and Halic University. She teaches microeconomics, macroeconomics, monetary theory and policy, international economics courses. Her current research focuses on macro economy, monetary policies and international economy. Her researches have been published in several international and national journals. She is also the reviewer of the several journals, as follows: International Review of Applied Economics, International Journal of Business, Economics and Management, Adnan Menderes University Journal of Social Sciences Institute, Journal of the Banks Association of Turkey.

Natalia Eremina, Doctor of Political Sciences, PhD in History (Candidate of Historical Sciences). Since 2004 till the present time Natalia Eremina is an Associate Professor, School of International Relations, St. Petersburg State University, Saint-Petersburg, Russia. Research interests: comparative politics, political radicalism, ethnopolitical conflicts, nationalism, extreme right parties and movements, para-diplomacy, Eurasian and European integration processes. Publications: author of more than 80 publications in Russian, English, Italian; among them - 13 monographs (7 - collective monographs); 4 educational and teaching aids. Natalia Eremina is a member of the editorial board and deputy editor in two scientific journals: "Azimuth of scientific research: economics and management"; "Vector of science TSU. Series: Economics and Management".

Vasilii Erokhin Associate Professor, School of Economics and Management, Harbin Engineering University, China and brings over 15 years of experience from academia. Previously, he worked as a Head of International Projects and Associate Professor at Moscow University of Finance and Law, Russia and Stavropol

State Agrarian University, Russia. Dr. Erokhin is an author of over 170 scientific works in the areas of international trade, globalization, sustainable development, food security issues with a focus on emerging markets, developing countries, and economies in transition. With IGI Global, Dr. Erokhin has edited Global Perspectives on Trade Integration and Economies in Transition (2016), Establishing Food Security and Alternatives to International Trade in Emerging Economies (2017), Handbook of Research on International Collaboration, Economic Development and Sustainability in the Arctic (2018), as well as published several chapters. Dr. Erokhin is a Guest Editor at MDPI Sustainability and MDPI Economies; an Associate Editor at Springer's Journal of Knowledge Economy; a member of the Editorial Review Board at IGI International Journal of Sustainable Economies Management (IJSEM); an Academic Editor at SCIENCEDOMAIN Asian Journal of Economics, Business and Accounting; an editorial board member at a number of international peer-reviewed journals and publications. Dr. Erokhin is a holder of the honorary awards from the Ministry of Agriculture of the Russian Federation and the Ministry of Education and Science of the Russian Federation. Since 2016, Dr. Erokhin is a researcher at the Polar Development and Northeast Asian Economic Research Center (PAERC) and Center for Russian and Ukrainian Studies (CRUS) at Harbin Engineering University, China. In 2018, Dr. Erokhin joined Key West University (Florida, USA) as an Adjunct Professor in Macroeconomics, Microeconomics, and History of Economic Thought.

Simla Güzel was born in 1983, she is from Bandırma, Turkey. She is assistant professor Dr at Namık Kemal University, Faculty of Economics and Administrative Sciences, Public Finance Department Tekirdag-Turkey. She received undergraduate degree from Uludag University, Faculty of Economics and Administrative Sciences, Department of Public Finance (2005). She holds master's degree (MA) in Public Economics from Uludag University (2008) and Ph.D in Public Finance from Uludag University (2015). Her doctorate thesis is on tax incentives to SMEs R&D expenditures. Her main research fields focus on public finance, tax incentives, public expenditures.

Suadiq Mehammed Hailu is a Ph.D. candidate in Finance at Cukurova University in Turkey. He received a Bachelor`s Degree in Banking and Finance from Jimma University, Ethiopia and Master`s Degree in Banking and Finance from Ankara Yildirim Beyazit University, Turkey. He received Turkish Government Scholarships for both his Master and Ph.D. education programs. His research and publication interests include conventional and Islamic finance.

Büşra Karataşer completed her undergraduate education in the faculty of Economics at Selçuk University, and did her master`s degree in the field of Economic History at Marmara University, between 2007-2009. She completed her doctorate degree in the faculty of Economic History at Marmara University between 2009-2013.Her area of expertise is Ottoman Economic History, the history of Istanbul and the period of II Abdulhamıd. She is currently working as a Dr. academic member inthe faculty of Economics at Tekırdag Namık Kemal University.

Maria L. Lagutina is Associate Professor, World Politics Department at St.Petersburg State University. She holds a Ph.D. in Political Science (2006, St. Petersburg State University, the Russian Federation) and Doctoral Degree (2017, St. Petersburg State University, the Russian Federation). Her current research interests are oriented towards Eurasian integration and its regional and global dimensions, BRICS, Global Governance, Regional Integration, Comparative Regionalism, international cooperation in the Arctic. She's an author of more then 70 publications in Russian and English.She is a member of the International Studies Association (ISA). In 2016 she was invited as a Visiting Professor at Carleton University (Ottawa, Canada).

Elena A. Maslova, PhD in Political Science (MGIMO-University, 2012), is Research Policy Manager of MGIMO-University. She is also Associate Professor at the Department of Integration Studies where she teaches courses on integration (theory and practice) to students at all university levels. Since 2013, she has worked as a senior research fellow at the Institute of Europe (Centre for Black Sea and Mediterranean Studies) of the Russian Academy of Sciences. Elena Maslova graduated from Moscow State University with a Specialist's degree in International Relations. In 2012, she completed a postgraduate doctoral course at MGIMO and presented a PhD thesis on Italy's foreign policy during the Second Republic. She has completed a number of traineeship programmes in Italy. "Valdai" discussion club expert, Russian International Affairs Council expert.

Abdela Yasin Saliya is a Ph.D. candidate in Finance at Cukurova University in Turkey. He received a Bachelor`s Degree in Cooperative accounting and auditing from Haramaya University, Ethiopia and a Master`s Degree in Finance and Investment from Mekelle University, Ethiopia. He received Turkish Government Scholarships for his Ph.D. program. His research and publication interests include microfinance, behavioral finance, and corporate finance in general.

Yeşim Pınar Sarıca is an Associate Professor at Işık University, Management Department. Her research areas are labour relations and social politics. She conducted funded scientific research projects on fields like employee and industrial relations in Turkey and microcredits for women. She has also worked as a short-term consultant with FSWW (the Foundation for the Support of Women's Work). She has several articles in national and international journals and is the author of books and book chapters in the field.

Aslı Taşbaşı is an Associate Professor of Economics at Işık University. Her research focuses on international economics, particularly on international trade and its environmental extensions. Her undergraduate, master's and Ph.D. degrees are from Istanbul University, Yildiz Technical University, and Marmara University, respectively. Awarded with a Tubitak scholarship, she conducted research at the Department of Economics, Lund University, Sweden during her PhD studies. Dr. Taşbaşı also received a UNESCO grant for her research on international trade policy.

Özlem Yılmaz was born on January 13th, 1977. He completed the business program in German at Marmara University in 2001 and received his MBA and Ph.D. degrees from Marmara University on European Union Economics in 2005 and 2012 consecutively. He has been contributing to the academic life as an Assistant Professor since 2014. Currently, He is an Economics and Finance Program coordinator and double major coordinator in Istanbul Yeni Yuzyil University. He teaches courses on Introduction to Economics, International Economics, Money and banking etc. He is married with two children.

Ahmet Hakan Yüksel is an academic at Işık University, Istanbul/Turkey, where he received his Ph.D. degree in contemporary management. He has received his M.A. degree in Organizational Behavior and B.Sc. in Economics from Istanbul University. He has worked as a corporate finance executive in Turkish capital markets for five years during when he was in charge of many initial public offering projects, debt restructuring projects, due diligence and private placement projects as well as providing portfolio management consultancy to foreign investors. He teaches 'Leadership', 'Principles of Management', 'Organizational Behavior' and 'Knowledge Management' at undergraduate and graduate levels. His academic areas of concentration include theories of leadership, organizational behavior, management theory and complexity thinking in management.

Index

F

G

I

J

L

M

N

O

P

Q

R

S

T

U

W

www.ingramcontent.com/pod-product-compliance
Lightning Source LLC
LaVergne TN
LVHW080602300926
849162LV00005B/1025